Everyday Streets

To Brian and Una,

For many more collaboration opportunities!

Thanks for coming to the launch!

Best wishes,
Agustina

Everyday Streets

Inclusive approaches to understanding and designing streets

Edited by Agustina Martire, Birgit Hausleitner and Jane Clossick

 UCLPRESS

First published in 2023 by
UCL Press
University College London
Gower Street
London WC1E 6BT

Available to download free: www.uclpress.co.uk

A CIP catalogue record for this book is available from The British Library.

ISBN: 978-1-80008-442-1 (Hbk.)
ISBN: 978-1-80008-441-4 (Pbk.)
ISBN: 978-1-80008-440-7 (PDF)
ISBN: 978-1-80008-443-8 (epub)
DOI: https:// doi.org/10.14324/111.9781800084407

Contents

List of figures and tables

Figures

Tables

Notes on contributors

Deepti Adlakha is Lecturer in Planning at Queen's University Belfast. She is an interdisciplinary scientist with a varied educational background including degrees in architecture, urban design and public health.

Gene Bawden is Associate Professor and Head of Design at Monash University, Faculty of Art Design and Architecture, and co-director of XYX Lab. As a team of researchers, the XYX Lab unites bespoke co-design processes with scholarly research with the aim of mitigating gender inequality in urban spaces.

Jess Berry is Senior Lecturer and Researcher at Monash University XYX Lab. Her research explores how gender identities are articulated and mediated through, and by, spatial practices. She is co-editor of *Contentious Cities: Design and the gendered production of space* (Routledge 2021) and author of *Cinematic Style: Fashion, architecture and interior design on film* (Bloomsbury 2022).

Bedour Braker is an Egyptian researcher based in Germany. She embraces a political approach in her research, questioning the societal means of reclaiming public spaces as a necessity to reactivate democracy. In addition to her research, Braker has also been part of the Jan Braker Architekt team in Hamburg since 2013.

Kate Buckley lectures in visual culture at the National College of Art and Design (NCAD) and in history & theory of architecture at Cork Centre for Architectural Education (UCC/CCAE) at undergraduate and postgraduate levels. With a BSc (Hons) in Architecture and an MA in Design History and Material Culture, her research and teaching intersect the two, currently focusing on streets, design activism and urban dissent.

Matthew Carmona is Professor of Planning and Urban Design at The Bartlett, UCL. He is an architect/planner with research focused on urban design governance, the design and management of public space, and the value of urban design. He chairs the Place Alliance, which campaigns for place quality in England. https://matthew-carmona.com.

Jane Clossick is an urbanist, Senior Lecturer in Architecture, course leader for MA Architecture, Cities and Urbanism and studio leader for the Cities Unit in MArch Architecture at the School of Art, Architecture and Design at London Metropolitan University.

James Davis is Reader in Medieval History at Queen's University Belfast, and he specialises in the urban, economic and cultural history of late medieval England. His publications include the monograph *Medieval Market Morality* (Cambridge University Press 2012) and his current project, funded by the British Academy, examines medieval street life.

Miriam Delaney is an architect, lecturer and PhD candidate at the Dublin School of Architecture, TUDublin. She was part of the *Free Market* team which represented Ireland at the 2018 Venice Architecture Biennale and works as a consultant for community-led rural town regeneration projects.

Christopher Falliers is partner/founder of ideal x design (2015–), u l a design (1999–), and Associate Professor of Architecture at California College of the Arts, San Francisco (2004–). His practice engages in architecture, public art design, urban research, temporary urban/community engagements, and environmental awareness and advocacy through creative practices.

Orfina Fatigato is Associate Professor of Architecture at DiARC University Federico II of Naples and Laboratoire ACS, ENSA Paris Malaquais. She studies the urban regeneration project as an adaptive process system, and social housing and intermediary spaces in contemporary cities. She is a member of the Research team 'Short-term City' (www.stcity.it), which looks at the effects of tourism on Italian cities.

Elen Flügge is a sonic researcher, writer and performer focusing on personal and urban sonic experience. With a background in philosophy and sound studies, she has published about sound art and listening scores. Her practice includes violin and vocal performance, site-specific installation and soundwalking. She completed her PhD 'Listening Practices for Urban Sound Space in Belfast' at SARC.

Birgit Hausleitner is an architect and urbanist, lecturer and researcher in the Urban Design section in the Department of Urbanism, Faculty of Architecture and the Built Environment, Delft University of Technology. Her research comprises work on urban diversity and mixed-use cities, focusing on the multi-scalar and configurational aspects of urban conditions that facilitate, introduce or improve combinations of living and working.

Nicole Kalms is Associate Professor in the Department of Design and founding director of the Monash University XYX Lab, which leads national and international research in Gender and Place. Dr Kalms is author of *Hypersexual City: The provocation of soft-core urbanism* (Routledge 2017).

Thomas-Bernard Kenniff is Professor at the École de Design, Université du Québec à Montréal (UQAM), where he teaches design studio, theory and criticism, and research by design. His work addresses the relationship between the built environment, design processes and society with a specific interest in public space and municipal architecture. He is the cofounder of the Bureau d'étude de pratiques indisciplinées (BéPI).

Sigrid Kroismayr is Senior Researcher at the Institute for Multilevel Governance and Development at the Vienna University of Economics and Business Administration, and Lecturer at the University of Innsbruck and the University of Applied Sciences Vienna. She is editor of the journal *Sozialwissenschaftliche Rundschau*. Her main fields of work are urban district research, rural development and qualitative methods.

Carole Lévesque's work explores the representation and practices of urban space and architecture. Through drawing and various modes of representation, her research investigates the processes of abandonment and renewal. Co-founder of the Bureau d'étude de pratiques indisciplinées (BéPI), she is a full-professor and director of the École de design, UQAM, where she teaches studio, theory and criticism as well as research by design methods.

David Littlefield is Senior Lecturer at the University of Westminster, London, where he leads the Masters programme in Interior Architecture. David's research focuses on place, architectural 'voice' and the representation of historic surfaces through time. He has written widely on subjects ranging from transgression to urban regeneration.

Aisling Madden gained her Masters of Architecture from Queen's University Belfast in 2020. During her two years of study, Aisling was in the StreetSpace studio with Dr Agustina Martire and Pat Wheeler, developing ethnographic methods to analyse the historical urban fabric of Belfast. Aisling now works in Studio idir.

Agustina Martire is Senior Lecturer in Architecture at Queen's University Belfast. She specialises in the study of everyday streets and their fabric, histories and experiences. She is especially interested in the way people experience the built environment, and how design can enable a more inclusive and just urban space. She has worked in schools of architecture in Buenos Aires, Delft, Dublin and Belfast and collaborates with a range of government and non-government organisations.

Gill Matthewson's research focus is on connecting research with making a real difference in the daily lives of women: for those using public space with her XYX Lab work and in the lives and careers of women in the built environment professions with the activist collective, Parlour.

Orla Murphy is an architect and Lecturer at University College Dublin. Her research focuses on towns, and engaged practice that considers their resilience and future(s). She is co-director of the UCD Centre for Irish Towns and a member of the High Level Round Table of the New European Bauhaus.

Maria Luna Nobile is Associate Professor in Architectural and Urban Design at Umeå University, Sweden. A PhD architect in the same field, her research focuses on the design of the contemporary city, with special attention to local urban regeneration policies, interdisciplinary and innovative practices between art and architecture, and the urban commons.

Andreas Novy is a socioeconomist, Associate Professor and Head of the Institute for Multi-Level Governance and Development at Vienna University of Economics and Business. He is president of the International Karl Polanyi Society and a member of the Foundational Economy Collective.

Manuel João Ramos is Associate Professor of Anthropology and researcher at the Centre of International Studies of the University Institute of Lisbon (ISCTE-IUL), Portugal. He conducts fieldwork research in Northern Ethiopia and in Portugal, and investigates urban touristification, street life, and migratory flows.

Anna Skoura is an urban heritage researcher, holding an MEng in Civil Engineering, an MSc in Conservation of Monuments and Sites, and a PhD in Architecture. Her research combines methods from architecture, heritage and the social sciences. She has worked in conservation and architecture in Belgium and Northern Ireland.

Rebecca Smink graduated with a Masters in Urbanism from Delft University of Technology in 2020. During her years of study, designing for people was her key motivator, aiming to develop a deeper understanding of the impact of urban planning and design on socio-spatial processes. Rebecca now works at BURA urbanism Amsterdam.

Antje Steinmuller is Associate Professor at California College of the Arts, where she co-directs the Urban Works Agency research lab. Her research is focused on new typologies of urban commons, new forms of collective living, and the agency of design at the intersection of citizen-led and city-regulated processes.

Mae-Ling Stuyt graduated with a Masters in Urbanism from Delft University of Technology in 2020. She aims to create places that enable and balance the diverse lives of people in cities, while leaving room for flexibility in the future. Since graduating she has been working on several inner-city transformation projects at Urhahn Urban Design and Strategy.

Timothy Waddell is a PhD candidate at Queen's University Belfast, investigating improvisation in architectural practice. Adjacent to this research is an interest in the social relations that particular streetscapes enable or restrict.

Acknowledgements

The development of this book has been a complex and challenging venture, but an exciting one. The book would not have been possible without the support of its publisher, the team at UCL Press, who have been understanding, flexible and helpful throughout the process of writing. The anonymous reviewers were also very generous and helpful with their comments and helped shape the final approach of the book. We would also like to thank all the contributors, who have been fundamental to the development of the book, for their engagement, enthusiasm and participation in shaping their chapters.

This book builds on the work of StreetSpace (www.streetspaceresearch.com), a decade-long collaborative project led by Agustina. The project encompasses design studios, international and interdisciplinary workshops, conference sessions and a series of collaborative projects with government and non-government organisations. The project brought Agustina, Birgit and Jane together, which led to the production of this book. Most of the authors in this book come from the wide network of people who have been part of StreetSpace. The funders include the Department for Communities of Northern Ireland and Belfast City Council, the Culture and Society Research Cluster and Public Engagement at Queen's University Belfast, the Oak Foundation, and Participation and the Practice of Rights.

We would also like to thank the universities that participated in StreetSpace through local student workshops, and supported us to undertake research: Queen's University Belfast, Delft University of Technology, London Metropolitan University, Universidad de Buenos Aires, Università degli Studi di Napoli Federico II, University of Ljubljana and Instituto Universitario de Lisboa. Our friends and colleagues at our respective institutions are always helpful, supportive and interested in new research.

Most of all, we would like to thank our families for supporting us while we produced this book; there have been babies born, toddlers growing into children, children growing into teenagers, and our patient partners always beside us. And finally, writing this book has cemented the relationship between the three of us. We have had great laughs and fascinating conversations, and have always been mutually supportive, so we would like to thank one another for being part of the team that made this book happen. We are very proud of what we have done together.

Introduction

Agustina Martire, Birgit Hausleitner and
Jane Clossick

Everyday streets are both the most used and the most undervalued
of cities' public spaces. They constitute the inclusive backbone of
urban life – the chief civic amenity – though they are challenged by
optimisation processes. Everyday streets are as profuse, rich and
complex as the people who use them; they are places of social
aggregation, bringing together those belonging to different classes,
genders, ages, ethnicities and nationalities. They comprise not just
the familiar outdoor spaces that we use to move and interact and the
facades that are commonly viewed as their primary component but
also urban blocks, interiors, depths and hinterlands, which are integral
to their nature and contribute to their vitality. Everyday streets are
physically and socially shaped by the lives of the people and things that
inhabit them through a reciprocal dance with multiple overlapping
temporalities. This book offers an analysis of many aspects of everyday
streets. It examines examples from all over the globe using a range of
methodological approaches. It is a palimpsest of overlapping examples,
methods and perspectives that provides a solid understanding of
everyday streets and their degree of inclusiveness. This book comes
at a critical moment, as the Covid-19 pandemic has highlighted the
importance of streets as the linear centre of urban life, pushing people
out of enclosed spaces and into the public realm.

    The primary focus of this book is an inclusive approach to under-
standing and designing everyday streets. 'Inclusive' means accessible
to everybody, with 'accessibility' covering social and economic factors
in addition to physical factors. Inclusiveness is not always prioritised
in street design. In fact, everyday streets have often been the focus of
vehicle-focused 'optimisation' processes. Of course, optimisation for

cars reduces inclusiveness for pedestrians. Julienne Hanson (2004) describes inclusive design as 'creating environments and products that are usable by all, without the need for specialist adaptation or design'. Tihomir Viderman and Sabine Knierbein (2019) go a step further, suggesting an 'inclusive design praxis' that includes a 'collective capacity to negotiate belonging, to appropriate space and to contest structural constraints through practices of improvising and inventing that are part of everyday life'. The central question framing this book's descriptions of everyday streets is as follows: *What qualities and processes make everyday streets inclusive places?*

The everyday streets covered in this book were all planned to some degree, whether by engineers, urban planners or the military. We do not discuss informal development processes – that would be far beyond the scope of this book – though it is important to note that everydayness also emerges in informal and peri-urban areas. From the regular rectilinear urban blocks of Montreal to the military-regulated narrow alleyways of Naples; from the resilient market streets of London to the crammed commercial streets of Chennai, the streets in this book were all conceived with a certain level of control. This universal fact enables us to, at the end of the book, make recommendations on the planning and design of everyday streets aimed at increasing their inclusiveness.

What is an everyday street?

Everyday streets constitute the backbone of all urban settlements. They are not merely routes from one place to another; they are linear centres of civic activity where much of everyday life takes place. As expressed by Allan B. Jacobs, 'Streets are more than public utilities, more than the equivalent of water lines and sewers and electrical cables; more than linear physical spaces that permit people and goods to get from here to there' (1995, 3). The kinds of streets that we explore in this book are never purely residential or monofunctional; they bring together most of the activities carried out in people's everyday life. They have precise technical functions for the movement of people and traffic. They host services, sewers and a wide mix of both commercial and civic uses. They have depth and hinterlands, which themselves serve a wide range of functions – including residential functions – contributing to their 'everydayness'. However, they also have a diverse set of forms and meanings that extend beyond physical functionality into the economic, social, historical and political realms. Our interpretation of these streets' significance is based on the idea of the everyday (Lefebvre 1991; Lefebvre 1947; De Certeau 1984; De Certeau 1980; Highmore 2012), as a palimpsest of the ordinary and extraordinary in constant flux.

The phenomenon that we term an 'everyday street' has many names. It is also referred to as 'mixed-use street', 'high street' (Carmona 2015; Jones et al. 2007) and, more recently in the UK, 'ordinary street' (Hall 2012). It is also called 'hoogstraat' (street on top of a dijk) (Dings 2017) and 'voorstraat' (front street) in the Netherlands (Meyer 2005), 'main street' in the US (Jacobs 1993; Mehta 2010) and 'Hauptstrasse' (main street) in German-speaking countries. In other languages, cultural, historical and typological contexts determine how these streets are named. Swahili, for example, uses 'mtaa Mkuu' (general street), while Vietnamese uses 'đường lớn' (big street). Generic words such as 'calle' (Spanish), 'rue' (French) and 'Ōdōri' (Japanese) indicate that most streets in these places have 'everyday' qualities. We employ Anna Skoura's term 'everyday streets' (this volume) because it captures the vast range of forms that these streets can take.

Each everyday street has a life of its own, shaped by the histories and cultures of the people who have resided on or passed through it. The term 'everyday' effectively captures the variety inherent in these streets; it is inclusive of all types of civic and social life. As Jan Gehl said, 'The street is the largest stage in the city, and the most used'. Spiro Kostof called the street 'a complex civic institution, culture specific and capable of dazzling formal variation and calculated nuance' (1992, 220). Joseph Rykwert defined streets as 'human movement institutionalised' (1978, 15). Everyday streets act as a space that hosts the performance of everyday life – whatever form it takes. They are rich, layered and multifaceted; they contain more intriguing elements than a single book, or even a whole library, could ever hope to capture.

Despite long being the backbone of urban settlements, everyday streets have only recently come to be considered a significant element of a city's heritage. Introduced in the 1960s, the concept of urban heritage long favoured the aesthetic qualities of buildings and monuments rather than their everyday uses. However, since the advent of the Historic Urban Landscape (HUL) approach (Rodwell 2010, 100), the culture of giving value to urban areas has become embedded in heritage scholarship. This approach goes beyond considering the beauty and age of streets' built fabric; it values the continuity of use types within buildings, the local roots of shops, communal senses of ownership, their function as a cultural route linking different parts of the city, and the small everyday practices adopted by users. For our authors, the cultural heritage of spatial and material practices is equally as significant as the physical heritage of monuments and museums.

Everyday streets, in both their heritage and contemporary uses, are the product of their local neighbourhood; they are never generic, and they are most significant for those who do not have the financial means to go elsewhere. Streets have been described as 'rooms' by Louis Kahn (1973) – significant urban spaces that are highly local and domestic in nature. However, they are simultaneously a manifestation of global forces, linking people and economic activity to a locality (Hall 2012). The capacity of everyday streets to host social and demographic diversity is boundless; they tend to host various classes, genders, races and religions, which often results in negotiation and conflict between groups. Sam Griffiths and Phil Hubbard have commented on local culture and class on streets, concluding that everyday streets appear as key sites for the 'realisation and perpetuation of locality' (Griffiths 2015, 32), playing 'an important economic and social role in the lives of working class populations' (Hubbard 2017, 8). Sharon Zukin and colleagues also highlighted the ordinary nature of streets and links between the local and global (2015). Therefore, everyday streets also play an important role in the creation of sustainable neighbourhoods (UN Habitat 2014) by serving as places of mutual support and social integration. From Melbourne to Montreal, from village to metropolis, everyday streets are everywhere; understanding their variations and nuances is crucial to grasping the role that they play in society.

A brief history of everyday streets: inclusion, optimisation and value

In the design of everyday streets, there is constant conflict between inclusion and optimisation. We propose that everyday streets have value beyond profit optimisation. They are capable of fostering the inclusion of different age groups, cultures, ethnicities and genders, yet optimisation generally prioritises aspects that result in the exclusion of certain groups by neglecting particular aspects of streets' value. The everyday street is a multi-layered and complex system that operates at many scales, so it is impossible to predict what may be lost through optimisation. Optimisation at one scale, such as increasing traffic speeds, can hinder important elements at other scales, such as people's ability to have a quiet conversation.

Everyday streets have always been places where multiple uses and users jostle for space. The first-century streets of Rome featured traffic regulations (van Tilburg 2011). Seventeenth-century urbanisation resulted in everyday streets having copious sanitation problems (Rudofsky 1968). Eighteenth-century streets were cluttered with traffic jams and excessive trade (Corfield 1990). In the nineteenth century, rapid urban growth and industrialisation resulted in streets being noisy, loaded with traffic and highly polluted (Cartwright 1973). The urban plans devised to deal with this problem (Burnham and Bennett 1908; Cerda 1859; Hausmann 1850s; Sitte 1889; Stübben 1907) carefully managed the relationship between different modes of transport. However, the growth of motor vehicle dependence in the twentieth century resulted globally in highly regulated systems of urban segregation that optimised streets and roads for car use.

The conflict between inclusion and optimisation aligned with twentieth-century modernist movements in architecture and urban planning. The demise of the traditional everyday street was made clear by plans for new and existing cities in the 1960s. Le Corbusier, Josep Lluis Sert and Lucio Costa, among others, denied the importance of the street by advocating for the separation of its functions, the prioritisation of motorised traffic and the disruption of the way streets had traditionally been used. In fact Le Corbusier defined the street as 'a traffic machine' (1929, 131), stating: 'Streets are an obsolete notion. There ought not to be such things as streets; we have to create something that will replace them' (1933, 121). Transport policy, such as Buchanan's (1963) Traffic in Towns in the UK, slum clearance and urban renewal in the US and other similar approaches around the world, instituted the domination of car-centric planning. Post-war reconstruction in Europe and rapid population growth in the US and the Global South meant that, by the 1960s, most cities across the world were undertaking a systematic and unprecedented investment in car-focused infrastructure (Kingsley and Urry 2009).

Despite the predominance of cars in cities across the world, many streets have survived as inclusive and resilient public spaces that are central to their local civic and economic life. Car-focused modernist urbanism has faced a wave of criticism since it was introduced, with critics denouncing modern land-use and zoning policies in the US and Europe as detached from the lives and experiences of local people (e.g. Alexander 1977; Appleyard 1980; Cullen 1961; Jacobs 1961; Lynch

1960; Rudofsky 1968; Whyte 1980). These critical writers, journalists and architects recognised the flaws of urban schemes that obliterated traditional street systems. Jane Jacobs gave sidewalks a leading role in *The Death and Life of Great American Cities* (1961), which discussed the importance of ground-floor uses and 'eyes on the street'. Lewis Mumford (1958) argued early on that motorways were not the proper solution for the future growth of cities, while Richard Rogers (1984) highlighted the role of the car in 'undermining the cohesive social structure of the city'. Donald Appleyard (1973) used drawings to highlight the damage done by traffic to neighbourhood streets, and William H. Whyte (1980) emphasised the importance of streets as central to the placemaking process. The late twentieth century saw a return to the town centre as the focus of human life; in fact, Tim Marshall described this return to traditional urban streets as 'one of the most significant reversals in urban design history' (2005, 9).

The 2020s are witnessing another street transformation. The push to minimise the dominance of cars led by Northern European cities since the 1970s has finally begun to influence the rest of the world (Agervig Carstensen and Ebert 2012; Gehl 1989; Gehl 2015; Pucher and Buehler 2008). Latin American cities, such as Bogotá, Medellín and Curitiba, have since the 1970s introduced temporary and permanent 'ciclovias', while also prioritising public transport over private cars. The Covid-19 pandemic served as a catalyst for this change, with cities around the world opening more outdoor public spaces to encourage and facilitate social distancing. Groups in the UK, the US and Europe have been a part of this push to make streets more inclusive and replace cars with multi-modal transport systems. The Project for Public Spaces (Whyte 1975), Create Streets (Boys Smith 2013), Manual for Streets (Hamilton-Bailie 2007), The City at Eye Level (Glaser 2012) and Human Cities (2006) have all advocated for more inclusive streets. Cities like Pontevedra in Spain have completely pedestrianised their main centres, boosting local foot traffic, while the recent removal of urban motorways in Paris, Seoul, San Francisco and Madrid has transformed swathes of land in city centres (Nieuwenuijzen 2021). While the editors and authors of this book consider these efforts to be largely positive, we must remain vigilant to ensure that they do not merely benefit the affluent to the detriment of less privileged groups. This harmful type of optimisation is common, and often subtle and overlooked.

The ordinary is extraordinary: understanding and designing everyday streets

Everyday life, epitomised by the street's ubiquity, is sometimes understood as a scene of 'relentless boredom' – ordinary and mundane. Here, we aim to emphasise the opposite view – to show that streets are, in Highmore's words, 'a problem, a contradiction, a paradox: both ordinary and extraordinary, self-evident and opaque, known and unknown, obvious and enigmatic' (Highmore 2002). Rita Felski uses feminist theory to critique the way in which modern literature depicts everyday life and its 'congealed patterns', suggesting that the 'work of theory is to break the spell of the habitual and the everyday' (2000, 90). This is the precise challenge that we have set for ourselves in this book. Its chapters are as revolutionary as Lefebvre (1974) would expect, showing that streets are saturated by the dominance of powerful interests in how they are transformed (De Certeau 1984) while maintaining the humour and serendipity that Walter Benjamin (1935, 1999) often discussed in his accounts of the everyday. We dispel the idea that the everyday is either mundane or extraordinary; instead, the everyday is in a state of constant flux between mundane and extraordinary.

Understanding what a street really is – in all its layering and richness – is complicated. In addition to assessing everyday streets' inclusiveness, our objective is to highlight the importance of learning about streets and never taking them for granted. Everyday streets may be 'ordinary' spaces (Hall 2012), but they are nonetheless multifaceted, layered and rich. They undoubtedly warrant academic attention. Shedding light on what Highmore (2002) calls the 'ordinary and the extraordinary of the everyday' and Solnit (2000) calls the 'errand and the epiphany', the chapters in this book seek to expose the everyday street in all its glory. Framed by the overarching question of what qualities and processes make everyday streets inclusive places, we aim to answer the following three questions: *How do people's social lives interact with everyday streets? What is the relationship between the urban form of everyday streets and the activities that occur there? What methodologies are best suited to capturing the multiplicity and complexity of everyday streets?* This book is divided into three sections, each of which explores one of these three questions.

Part I: The social life of everyday streets. This section examines the social processes taking place on streets across the world. It explores the social and historical institution of streets, evaluates cases of touristification, ritual and displacement, and looks at the role of women, ethnic minorities and working-class people.

Part II: The form and use of everyday streets. This section focuses on the relationship between urban form and everyday street activities. It explores diverse geographies, topographies, morphologies, uses and users, and examines how these factors are interdependent and mutually influential.

Part III: Localography. This section explores the range of methods and approaches that may be employed to assess the nuances of streets. It uses walks, recordings, drawings, occupations, installations and more traditional social science methods to analyse the subtle nuances of everyday streets across a wide variety of locations.

This book, like the StreetSpace project from which it grew, transcends the disciplinary boundaries of architecture and aims to revolutionise the methodological approach to the study of everyday streets. The copious diverse qualities that make up streets must be explored further in a way that avoids institutional and regional silos. This book aims to kickstart that process. StreetSpace has encouraged a new kind of interdisciplinary and democratic understanding of everyday streets. In this book we enrich the existing discussion by presenting perspectives from various authors, places and fields, enabling readers to compare and contrast different ideas while opening up new lines of inquiry for understanding and designing everyday streets. The book's stylistic and methodological diversity offers new perspectives on everyday streets, effectively delineating their urgencies. The knowledge presented in this book can inform the practices of urban planners, architects and designers.

Finally, this book has a political objective: to reclaim street spaces for people. We do not claim to write from a neutral position. This book is a manifesto for streets. It aims to help them resist car-focused and commercial optimisation, which sucks away the socio-spatial characteristics that make streets useful to unprivileged groups. In the spirit of Dennis Crow's philosophical streets, we believe that combining theoretical concepts with empirical research can 'remove barriers to citizen participation on policy making, break down ... stereotypes and examine the long-term global consequences of uneven development' (1990, 5). This book aims to '[fight] against the pro-gentrification agendas implicit in British retail policy' (Hubbard 2017, 8). It is valuable to support and maintain everyday streets as diverse, significant and slowly evolving public places. We must study streets to ensure that their redevelopment and redesign are inclusive and accessible. Everyday streets must be highlighted – they must be protected.

Bibliography

Agervig Carstensen, Trine and Anne Katrin Ebert. 2012. 'Cycling Cultures in Northern Europe: From "Golden Age" to "Renaissance"'. In *Cycling and Sustainability* (vol. 1), edited by J. Parkin, 23–58. Bingley: Emerald Group. https://doi.org/10.1108/S2044-9941(2012)0000001004.

Alexander, Christopher. 1977. *A Pattern Language: Towns, buildings, construction*. New York: Oxford University Press.

Appleyard, Donald. 1987. *Public Streets for Public Use*. New York: Columbia University Press, Van Nostrand Reinhold.

Burnham, Daniel and Edward Bennett. 1993. *The Plan of Chicago*. Princeton, NJ: Princeton Architectural Press.

Cartwright, William and Richard Watson. 1973. *The Reinterpretation of American History and Culture*. Washington, DC: National Council for the Social Studies.

Corfield, Penelope. 1990. 'Walking the City Streets: The urbanist odyssey in eighteenth-century England', *Journal of Urban History* 16: 132–74.

Crow, Dennis.1990. *Philosophical Streets, New Approaches to Urbanism*. Washington: Maisonneuve Press.

Cullen, Gordon. 1961. *The Concise Townscape*. Oxford: Architectural Press, Elsevier.

Dings, Rene. 2017. *Over straatnamen met name*. Amsterdam: Nijgh & vanDitmar.

Felski, Rita. 2000. *Doing Time: Feminist theory and postmodern culture*. New York: NYU Press.

Gehl, Jan. 1989. 'A Changing Street Life in a Changing Society', *Places Journal* 6(1): 8–17.

Griffiths, Sam. 2015. 'The High Street as a Morphological Event'. In *Suburban Urbanities: Suburbs and the life of the high street*, edited by Laura Vaughan. London: UCL Press.

Hanson, Julienne. 2004. 'The Inclusive City: Delivering a more accessible urban environment through inclusive design'. In *RICS Cobra 2004 International Construction Conference: Responding to change. Proceedings*, edited by R. Ellis and M. Bell. Accessed 1 November 2022. https://discovery.ucl.ac.uk/id/eprint/3351/.

Hubbard, Phil. 2017. *The Battle for the High Street: Retail gentrification, class and disgust*. London: Palgrave Macmillan.

Jacobs, Allan B. 1995. *Great Streets*. Cambridge, MA: MIT Press.

Jacobs, Jane. 1961. *The Death and Life of Great American Cities*. New York: Modern Library.

Jones, P., M. Roberts and L. Morris. 2007. *Rediscovering Mixed-Use Streets: The contribution of local high streets to sustainable communities*. Bristol: Policy Press in association with the Joseph Rowntree Foundation.

Kahn, Louis. 1973. *Silence and Light*. Tokyo: A+U.

Kostof, Spiro. 1992. City Assembled: The elements of urban form through history. London: Thames & Hudson.

Laitinen, Riitta and Thomas V. Cohen (eds). 2009. *Cultural History of Early Modern European Streets*. Leiden: Brill.

Le Corbusier. 1929. *The City of To-morrow and its Planning*. London: Dover.

Lefebvre, Henri. 1992. *The Production of Space*. Oxford: Wiley-Blackwell.

Lynch, Kevin. 1960. *The Image of the City*. Cambridge, MA: MIT Press.

Meyer, H. 2005. 'The Urban Block as Microcosm of the City'. In *Atlas of the Dutch Urban Block*, edited by S. Komossa, H. Meyer, M. Risselada, S. Thomaes and N. Jutten, 251–58. Bussum: Thoth Publishers.

Pucher, John and Ralph Buehler. 2008. 'Making Cycling Irresistible: Lessons from the Netherlands, Denmark and Germany', *Transport Reviews* 28(4): 495–528. https://doi.org/10.1080/01441640701806612.

Rodwell, Dennis. 2010. 'Historic Urban Landscapes: Concept and management', *Managing Historic Cities: World heritage papers* 27: 100.

Rudofsky, Bernard. 1968. *Streets for People*. New York: Doubleday.

Rykwert, Joseph. 1978. 'The Street: The use of its history'. In *On Streets: Streets as elements of urban structure*, edited by Stanford Anderson. Cambridge, MA: MIT Press.

Stubben, Joseph. 1907. *City Building*. Translated by Julia Koschinsky and Emily Talen. Accessed 1 November 2022. https://urbanism.uchicago.edu/content/joseph-st%C3%BCbbens-city-building.

Viderman, Tihomir and Sabine Knierbein. 2019. 'Affective Urbanism: Towards inclusive design praxis', *URBAN DESIGN International* 25(1): 53–62. https://doi.org/10.1057/S41289-019-00105-6.

Whyte, William. 1980. *The Social Life of Small Urban Spaces*. Project for public spaces.

Zukin, Sharon, Philip Kasinitz and Xianming Chen. 2015. *Global Cities, Local Streets: Everyday diversity from New York to Shanghai*. New York: Routledge.

Part I
The social life of everyday streets
Agustina Martire, Birgit Hausleitner and
Jane Clossick

The first section of this book looks at the social life of everyday streets, aiming to answer the following question: *How do people's social lives interact with everyday streets?* The authors of these chapters discuss the ways in which social processes are linked to the evolving physical fabric of everyday streets, the memories and histories embedded in everyday streets, and everyday streets as sites of conflict where various identity groups negotiate shared spaces. They consider streets in the United Kingdom, Ireland, Germany, Portugal and Australia, making connections between various disciplinary approaches to provide a comprehensive understanding of streets and the ways in which they are experienced across different settings.

The chapters in this section all address, in one way or another, the interdependence between built space and social processes across several scales. On a small scale, David Littlefield addresses the lack of attention paid to built details on streets, particularly those that are not designed by architects (e.g. signage). Analysing one area in Liverpool and another in Belfast, he highlights how the agency of developers and the government is imposed on the inhabitants of everyday streets through small physical details, such as bollards, signs and railings, dictating people's behaviours. On a larger scale, Buckley discusses the relevance of regulation to O'Connell Street in Dublin, detailing how the street creates opportunities for public display but noting that these opportunities are currently being threatened by new public regulations.

In terms of the histories and memories contained within everyday streets, this section's chapters discuss the ways in which streets are inhabited, imagined and memorialised. History contributes to our feelings about places, with ideas and images about particular places passed down through generations. However, streets have not featured prominently in our collective history. Rudofsky (1969) highlighted the general lack of interest in streets as independent units. Kostof (1992) agreed, arguing that 'the history of the street is yet to be written'. Since the early 1990s, however, many attempts have been made to address the absence of streets in our history (e.g. Andersson 2013; Çelik 1994; Jerram 2011; Laitiinen and Cohen 2009) through accounts of street histories focused on themes of community, working-class dynamics, gender, surveillance, crime, commerce, consumption, culture, performance and rituals. In this book, Kate Buckley and James Davis add to these attempts with histories of two streets from different angles. Davis discusses the ordinary and mundane qualities of class and gender in late medieval Cheapside. He identifies behaviours, images and notions of identity in archival documents and discusses the resilience and permanence of socio-cultural behaviours through space and time. Buckley discusses extraordinary practices on O'Connell Street, which both the state and the public use as a site of celebration and protest. Buckley and Davis remind us of how streets are understood as places through history and discuss how ideas of place are enshrined in collective memories and traditions.

Everyday streets engage with inhabitants' social lives through their physical structure: the configuration of buildings, the thresholds separating the interior and exterior, and public-private dynamics. Urban morphologists (e.g. Caniggia and Maffei 2017; Conzen 1960; Larkham 2006; Vaughan 2018; Vernez Moudon 1987) have found that the evolution of everyday streets boasts continuity but note that the disruption of their fabric often stems from the social processes that they accommodate. The physical, social and historical conditions of everyday streets are intimately linked to the lives of the people who inhabit them. These streets are sites of everyday practices, habits and rituals. O'Connell Street in Dublin hosts funerals, processions and protests; Kate Buckley notes the significance of its location in the city, its spatial layout and design in its ritual functions. Similarly, James Davis' Cheapside exemplifies the persistence of urban form on a late medieval street, where traditional trade practices still occur despite centuries of social and technological change. The relationship between street fabric and everyday practices is particularly poignant in Agustina Martire and Aisling Madden's chapter, which covers the demolition of the built fabric of Sailortown in Belfast and how it led to the loss of a working-class neighbourhood's population, memories and unique local nuances.

With regard to everyday streets being sites of conflict, such conflicts impact people's memories, experiences and senses of place and belonging. The social space of the street has always been contested. Appleyard (1987) described these conflicts as typically benefiting those in power to the detriment of marginal, silenced and disenfranchised groups. Considering the social critique in Hubbard's 'Battle for the High Street' (2008), Manuel Ramos' chapter discusses the gentrification and touristification of Lisbon's Rua das Portas de Santo Antão. Building on David Harvey's idea of the 'right to the city' (2010) and Manuel Delgado's concept of '*urbs*' (1999), Ramos analyses the development of this 'secondary' street from an abandoned side street to a completely touristified main thoroughfare – one that excludes its local residents. Groups and individuals occupy different streets, spaces and thresholds depending on their class, gender, age, race, culture and many other factors.

Also writing on how cultural differences interact with everyday streets, Braker details the organic transformation of Lange Reihe and Steindamm in Hamburg. She discusses the social prejudices exhibited toward one street populated by LGBTQ+ residents and another that houses a Muslim community. The chapter by Gill Matthewson, Nicole Kalms, Jess Berry and Gene Bawden builds on recent international research (Colomina 1992; Davidson 2016; Kern 2020; Pain 1997) on women's experiences of walking city streets at night – the constant feeling of vulnerability – and how they can be influenced by elements of street design. Martire and Madden point out how power structures in places of institutionalised conflict like Belfast can completely transform the infrastructure of streets through a process of control and optimisation, resulting in their complete destruction.

Everyday streets epitomise their locality; they are imbued with the meaning and essence of their local area. Edward Relph (1972) pointed out the need for a more nuanced understanding of place. However, Relph's attempt at a complete definition of 'authenticity' and 'identity' did not leave room for the dynamic and evolving nature of streets. Holloway and Hubbard (2001) drew a connection between the changing nature of the everyday street and its relationship with places, while Tim Cresswell reminded us that place is not just a location but a 'way of understanding the world' (2015, 18). Acknowledging that everyday streets are places can help us to understand the work of Davis, Buckley and Martire/Madden, shedding light on how Cheapside, O'Connell Street and Sailortown respectively are receptacles of meaning and memory. By looking at the fabrics, memories and conflicts of everyday streets, the chapters that follow expose the nuance, complexity and value of such places.

These chapters touch on the main theme of this book: inclusiveness. They highlight how the physical and regulatory contexts of these streets can lead to the inclusion or exclusion of certain groups or individuals. In Littlefield, for example, the metal studs on the boundary of Liverpool ONE sets a boundary, exerting power over certain members of the population, such as street vendors and those suffering from homelessness. Buckley argues that the regulation of protest could affect the balance between ritual, opposition and dissent, hampering political inclusion. Davis discusses inclusion in the fabric of Cheapside, showing how the street is more egalitarian, mixed and inclusive than its side streets. Braker, through her Hamburg case studies, clearly defines the groups in each street and details how they appropriate space, excluding others in some locations but offering inclusion for all in other locations. The Australian cases boast an explicitly inclusive agenda by exposing the ways in which urban streets exclude women, especially at night. Ramos finds that local people are generally excluded, as RPSA mainly welcomes tourists. The strongest case of spatial exclusion can be found in the chapter by Martire and Madden, which features the demolition of Sailortown and the displacement of its entire community. To achieve inclusiveness, we must consider the needs and social lives of all groups that use and reside on everyday streets.

Bibliography

Andersson, Peter. 2013. *Streetlife in Late Victorian London*. Basingstoke: Palgrave Macmillan.
Appleyard, Donald. 1987. Foreword. In *Public Streets for Public Use*, edited by Anne Vernez Moudon. New York: Columbia University Press, Van Nostrand Reinhold.
Caniggia, Gianfranco and Gian Luigi Maffei. 2017. *Interpreting Basic Buildings*. Florence: Altralinea Edizioni.
Çelik, Zeynep, Diane Favro and Richard Ingersoll. 1994. *Streets: Critical perspectives on public space*. Los Angeles, CA: University of California Press.
Colomina, Beatriz (ed.). 1992. *Sexuality and Space*. New York: Princeton Architectural Press.
Conzen, Michael R.G. 1960. *Alnwick, Northumberland: A study in town-plan analysis*. London: Institute of British Geographers.
Cresswell. 2015. *Place: An introduction*. Chichester and Malden: Wiley-Blackwell.
Davidson, Meghan, Michael S. Butchko, Krista Robbins, Lindsey W. Sherd and Sarah J. Gervais. 2016. 'The Mediating Role of Perceived Safety on Street Harassment and Anxiety', *Psychology of Violence* 6(4): 553–61.
Delgado, Manuel. 1999. *Ciudad líquida, ciudad interrumpida: La urbs contra la polis*. Colombia: Universidad de Almeria.
Harvey, David. 2010. *Rebel Cities: From the right to the city to the urban revolution*. London and New York: Verso.
Holloway, L. and Phil Hubbard. 2001. *People and Place: The extraordinary geographies of everyday life*. Harlow: Prentice Hall.

Leif, Jerram. 2011. 'Streetlife: The untold history of Europe's twentieth century', *Journal of Urban History* 39(1): 195–6.

Kern, Leslie. 2020. *Feminist City Claiming: Space in a man-made world*. London: Verso.

Kostof, Spiro. 1992. *City Assembled: The elements of urban form through history*. London: Thames & Hudson.

Laitinen, Riitta and Thomas V. Cohen (eds). 2009. *Cultural History of Early Modern European Streets*. Leiden: Brill.

Larkham, Peter. 2006. 'The Study of Urban Form in Great Britain', *Urban Morphology* 10(2): 117–41.

Pain, Rachel. 1997. 'Whither Women's Fear? Perceptions of sexual violence in public and private space', *International Review of Victimology* 4: 297–312.

Relph, Edward. 1972. *Place and Placelessness*. London: Sage.

Rudofsky, Bernard. 1969. *Streets for People: A primer for Americans*. New York: Doubleday.

Vaughan, Laura. 2018. *Mapping Society*. London: UCL Press.

Vernez Moudon, Anne. 1987. *Public Streets for Public Use*. New York: Van Nostrand Reinhold.

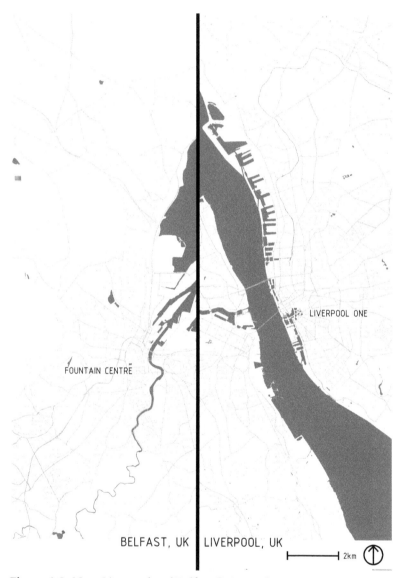

FOUNTAIN CENTRE

LIVERPOOL ONE

BELFAST, UK | LIVERPOOL, UK

2km

Figure 1.0: Maps Liverpool and Belfast © Anna Skoura

1
The agency of small things: indicators of ownership on the streets of Liverpool and Belfast

David Littlefield

Streets are undesigned as much as they are designed. Markers and traces of occupation, ownership and belonging can shape streetscapes beyond the designed intention of architect, planner or urbanist. These signs and visual clues can have a transformative effect, and thus can be considered as having agency – they are 'things' of the street just as level changes and building surfaces are things. It is important that all stakeholders concerned with the life of the street consider the agency of small, post hoc and undesigned details – their power is far in excess of their physical presence.

Undesigned streets

Nathaniel Hawthorne knew that streets were places of experience rather than raw dimensions. Describing the principal 'roughly hewn street' of seventeenth-century Boston in his 1850 novel *The Scarlet Letter*, Hawthorne observed: 'It was no great distance, in those days, from the prison-door to the market-place. Measured by the prisoner's experience, however, it might be reckoned a journey of some length' (1850, 345). For Hester Prynne (the novel's central character, on her way to the pillory) a simple walk along the length of the street is transformed into an ordeal by the 'thousand unrelenting eyes' of the crowd, the gossip, and the Puritan hoods, hats and beards.

The transformative effect of what is *not designed* by architects or urban designers is familiar to all of us. In parallel to the deliberate, mappable realm of building plot, form, facade, level change etc., there is another realm – this is the realm of temporality, erosion, change, occupation and day-to-day management that shifts the elegance and simplicity of the architectural intention into a complex and nuanced place that demands a high degree of spatial literacy and sensitivity from those using it. Occasionally this sensitivity flourishes as the poetic imagination: 'I have always preferred the winter to the summer in Istanbul ... I love the overwhelming melancholy when I look at the walls of old apartment buildings and the dark surfaces of neglected, unpainted, fallen-down wooden mansions: only in Istanbul have I seen this texture, this shading,' writes Orhan Pamuk (2006, 31). For others, of a more practical sensibility, the subtle coding of the street has a far more direct agency, indicating degrees of welcome or defining behaviours.

Agency

Agency is key. For the purposes of this paper, I use the term 'agency' in the sense of anything that can 'modify a state of affairs by making a difference' (Latour 2005, 71). Jane Bennett uses the useful phrase 'thing power' (2010, 6) to describe the phenomenon of artefacts (or the *non-human*) performing an active role in the human world. For Bennett, things are not 'passive' but have an 'ability to make things happen' (5), to provoke a response and 'produce effects dramatic and subtle' (6). Things can indeed 'provoke' and 'produce', in the same way as (drawing on Latour's Actor-Network Theory) kettles 'boil' and knives 'cut'. However, I suggest that some care is required when investing things with what you might call verb-power; knives do indeed cut, though any agency surely resides in the human operator of the knife? What the knife does is make a difference to a situation.

Frederic Vandenberghe argued that when agency appears to be a property of an object, it is merely illusory – instead, agency or social power is an emergent property of a 'larger social system in which the nonhumans are embedded' (2002, 60). Agency, in this chapter, is considered within these terms, whereby objects appear to perform a role *as if* their transformative role is an inherent, dynamic, active property of the object itself. 'The root of the trail leads eventually back to humans. However humans are interconnected with nonhumans, at the end of the day, it is humans who encounter nonhumans and endow them with meaning, use or value' (55).

Things can, therefore, exercise power (as we shall see) – though we must remind ourselves that power is negotiated through the relationships that people negotiate with those things. Once humans have endowed the object with meaning, things far more subtle than knives can make a difference to a situation. What is essential is for both human and object to be present in order for that meaning to manifest itself. 'Simply put, nonhumans do not have agency by themselves, if only because they are never by themselves' (Sayes 2014, 144). In locating agency (that power to make a difference) within the relationships between people and things, the role of the material realm is acknowledged, while recognising too what Coole and Frost call its 'complex, contingent modes of appearing' (2010, 27). It is also important to consider quite what is meant by a 'thing' – a material artefact, yes, but other human constructions such as the rule of law, property ownership and what Jane Clossick calls 'decorum' also have the force of things. And these things (the institutions and protocols which direct behaviour) are often mediated by material artefacts such as signs, lines, symbols and other surface phenomena. The social world and symbolic systems become folded into material objects which perform agentic roles when people are brought into relationship with them. However, these are reflexive relationships – by establishing relationships with things, we ourselves are changed.

Here, I consider two places in terms of quotidian or trace characteristics which have agentic properties. In spite of large differences in scale, these places have similarities; both are privately operated, publicly accessible, retail-led schemes at the centre of UK maritime cities. And both can be re-seen through paying very close attention to details which might well go unnoticed by most users of these places: the junction of Paradise Street and *School Lane* in Liverpool, and the Fountain Centre extension to *College Street* in Belfast. Both are representative of the increasing privatisation of public space – certainly in the UK and North America, but also more widely. Such privately owned, publicly accessible places often 'hide in plain sight', and are revealed only through the detail, or shifts in regulation, as considered below (much has been written on the subject of privatised space. See especially Layard 2010; Layard 2019, also: Carmona 2010; Carmona 2015; Carmona 2017; De Magalhães 2010; Kohn 2001).

Liverpool ONE and Paradise Street

Liverpool ONE is a 42 acre (17 ha) mixed-use estate developed and owned by Grosvenor in the centre of Liverpool. Constructed in 2004–8, this zone borders a series of conservation and heritage sites such as the Albert Dock and Ropewalks, as well as what was (until this development expanded and redefined it) the main retail district of Lord and Church streets. In many ways, Liverpool ONE has many of the characteristics of the conventional mall. Flanked by department stores, hotels, multi-storey car parks and service yards, this zone comprises largely pedestrian streets giving access to retail and leisure outlets, as well as some residential and office units, clustered around the open space of Chavasse Park (under which is a further car park). However, unlike a conventional mall, Liverpool One is not encompassed by a unifying roof, and the street spaces within the development are, in fact, rather diverse in terms of scale and response to historic context. Further, one of the defining characteristics of the site is the attempt to integrate these privately owned streets into the urban pattern of Liverpool itself:

> Underlying all ideas for regeneration was the following principle: that any development should become an integral part of Liverpool and link almost seamlessly into the city as found. This was not to be a self-contained, inward-facing and self-absorbed scheme which would sit, shiny and in splendid isolation, as a distinct and separate part of Liverpool. (Littlefield 2009, 31)

This is a theme that is reinforced in Liverpool ONE's *Occupier Handbook*, which states: 'Liverpool ONE is not a self-contained shopping centre; we integrate seamlessly with the wider city centre'. However, as a privately owned estate there is, inevitably, a boundary marking the separation between the City of Liverpool and Liverpool One. It is a boundary of some complexity and ambiguity, however, and is better described as zone rather than line. Local maps and visitor guides, which simplify boundaries and omit inconvenient details, indicate the facilities available within the estate but do not address the line of legal property ownership. Physical branding (such as banners and bollards) is often sited deep inside that line of legal ownership, thus visitors may be within the private estate but unaware of it; at other points visitors may feel they are within the Liverpool One estate when, in fact, they are not. 'At one scale, the Liverpool One land registry title shows an almost uniform, uncomplicated block of land with a clear boundary … but on the ground at a detailed scale, the reality of Liverpool One is a complicated, intricate set of thresholds butting up against the wider city' (Littlefield and Devereux 2018, 19).

The boundary conditions of Liverpool ONE are, in places, very deep. This is especially the case in Paradise Street, a now pedestrianised

Figure 1.1: Paradise Street / School Lane intersection, Liverpool
ONE. The deep threshold is characterised by three elements (closest to
furthest: security, branding, legal). © David Littlefield

thoroughfare dating back (at least in name) to the 1730s. Characterised by premier retail brands, Paradise Street is something of a
destination, although the street also performs what Kevin Lynch
would call the connector role, linking the civic buildings close to the
principal rail station with the historic docks and 'Ropewalks' zone.
Approximately one quarter of this street remains under the ownership
and administration of Liverpool City Council; the remainder falls under
the ownership of Grosvenor Estates as part of the property settlement
which underpinned the comprehensive regeneration programme of
2004–8. One of the characteristics, then, of Paradise Street is the
boundary condition (if one cares to look for it) marking the transition
from public to private ownership.

Figure 1.1 shows this well. Taken from inside Liverpool One
looking 'outwards', the photograph of Paradise Street at the junction
with School Lane captures a zone where three boundary conditions
are evident. Closest is the security boundary comprised of bollards
which carry the '1' estate logo; approximately seven metres beyond
the security boundary is a more visible branding boundary comprising
large red banners containing the same '1' logo; approximately

Figure 1.2: Paradise Street, Liverpool ONE; from the outside, looking in. The metal stud reveals the location of the legal ownership boundary. © David Littlefield

14m deeper into the picture is the third boundary – a series of metal studs set into the paving which indicates the line of legal ownership (Figure 1.2).

Any visitor will therefore traverse approximately 21m from crossing the line representing a shift in property ownership before they encounter the security bollards. These metal studs are located on the

Figure 1.3: Liverpool ONE: metal studs reveal the legal boundary, and are not always situated at the branding boundary. © David Littlefield

legal boundary line around the entire Liverpool One estate, and the example of Paradise Street is not the only occurrence of their spatial separation from the branding line (Figure 1.3). In some respects this is unimportant; the urban integration of Liverpool One into the wider city does imply more of a fuzzy transition from one place to the other rather than the particularity of a measurable edge.

Anecdotally, during a series of 'walking lectures' as part of the Being Human Festival, which was sponsored by the UK's Arts and Humanities Research Council in November 2017, it became clear that participants had little or no sense of where the legal boundary of Liverpool One was situated, even when standing on it.[1] From a general user perspective, the metal studs are either unnoticed or (if noticed) inconsequential; in other words, they have no 'thing power' or agency. For others, such as homeless people or informal street vendors, these studs are highly consequential. Representing the shift in ownership from public to private, these innocuous studs signify a dramatic shift in rights and sense of belonging, as well as the powers of security personnel to enforce the regulations of a private estate. Sleeping rough within Liverpool One is forbidden; licensed busking and selling are permitted, meaning that unlicensed vendors must remain on the outside. The locations of a homeless person's tent (Figure 1.4) and street vendor (Figure 1.5) are not, then, accidental; in these cases, those subtle metal studs have a significance which is out of scale to their physical presence. In terms of *modifying a state of affairs* and *making a difference*, these studs unarguably have agency for particular social groups.

This agency manifests itself in terms of verbs – in that, in relation to particular social groups, these studs operate *as if* they 'have' power, 'prevent' access and 'exert' influence. These studs, arguably, 'become' gates and therefore take on a symbolic meaning in a rather extraordinary way. They don't just *signify* gates; under certain circumstances, or perceived by certain groups, they actually *are* gates.

Rom Harré describes this transformative phenomenon as the creation of 'social substance' – the combination of 'material stuff' and the 'properties of some social world' (2002, 24). He provides the following example: alcohol is mere material stuff; add a narrative, such as transubstantiation, and the result is communion wine – social substance. The socially constructed narrative, then, is key to the agentic power of the object. For those who don't know the story, the material object loses some or all of its agentic power; but to those privy to the narrative, the physical properties of the object become animated and elevated to a whole new order of expression. 'An object is transformed from a piece of stuff definable independently of any story-line into a social object by its embedment in a narrative' (Harré 2002, 25). The metal studs of Liverpool One have no efficacy of their own – there are examples where studs have come loose and disappeared, so the remaining holes perform the agentic role; similarly, you cannot remove a stud and place it elsewhere, thereby shifting the legal boundary;

Figures 1.4 and 1.5: Liverpool ONE: homeless people observing the legal boundary. The tent and the vendor are located outside the boundary that defines the legal limit of the privately owned zone. © David Littlefield

equally, you cannot visit the factory where the studs are made and witness the production of thresholds. The social and agentic performance of the studs in Liverpool is tied into the story they tell – a story of mapping and imaginary lines which make tangible the idea of property ownership. The studs provide a translation service, giving the marks on title deeds a tangible presence in the 'real world'. For most visitors it is a story that does not need to be read and therefore goes unseen; for disenfranchised groups, however, the text is very legible and it makes a material difference to the manner in which they negotiate the city's streets.

Belfast's Fountain Centre

What, then, of texts that are seen and legible to all – the literal sign which *instructs* caution, *forbids* smoking and *warns* of danger? Such signs, which have become ubiquitous, are complex in spite of their apparent simplicity. Webmoor and Witmore, drawing on Latour, describe the 'gathering' (2008, 64) of human ideas and invention which have enabled the production of everyday artefacts. 'Achievements, which involved transactions between various entities and which occurred at a distance in space and linear time, are folded into things as utterly familiar as a map or as seemingly mundane as eyeglasses' (65). Further, once gathered together, such artefacts function as prostheses and mediators in the performance of advanced practices such as (in the case of maps and eyeglasses) navigation or the correction of failing eyesight. Signs warning 'mind the step' are similarly mundane yet enfolded with achievements and transactions: writing, printing, literacy, legal codes, processes of ownership and authority, regulations and insurance – all are invoked by such notices. What, though, might be the story through which such street signs become social substance? The story is, as Coole and Frost argue in relation to the material realm, 'contingent'.

The Fountain Centre is a relatively small, two-storey retail development located in central Belfast. Completed in 1978, it is architecturally unremarkable, notable only for its elevated open space (which the centre refers to as its 'piazza') and 'Alice Clock' (a large-scale piece of public art, completed in 2000, which marks the passing of each hour with the chiming of 24 bells). The Fountain Centre is not a street in and of itself but forms part of the retail 'surface' and an elevated extension to College Street, a linear element of the grid system defining the centre of the city. Norberg-Schulz described the nature of the street as generally 'longitudinal', but added, 'this does not imply that it ought to be straight' (1971, 83). I would add that neither does it imply that the street ought to be flat. College Street, then, can be considered as having those *connecting* and *organising* principles described by Lynch and Leslie Martin in the 1960s and 1970s (Blowers et al. 1974); it is also extended horizontally and vertically by the privately owned Fountain Centre, which does not interrupt the street as a square or crossing would, but quietly supplements it. Importantly, just as Liverpool's Paradise Street embodies a shift in 'publicness' due to a shift in legal ownership, Belfast's College Street makes the same shift available through a vertical detour. Apart from the retail function of the centre, this development as a *place* can be understood within two narratives. One is the story recounted on glass in the centre's 'piazza':

> Fountain Street was previously known as Water Street. In the 18th century women and children paid a penny for two pails of water from one of the three fountains in the street ... 1978 saw the opening of Fountain Centre and the celebration was marked by the unveiling of a new fountain by Irish sculptor Marjorie Fitzgibbon, depicting children happily playing in the water.

The second narrative emerges from an abundance of formal notices, cautioning, warning and instructing (Figure 1.6).

These notices might be categorised as:

Warnings:
- *Danger*
- *Warning: CCTV cameras in operation*
- *Caution: wet floor*
- *Caution: mind the step*

Prohibitions:
- *Keep Out*
- *No unauthorised persons allowed beyond this point*

And behavioural codes:
- *No Smoking: smoking is not permitted in the piazza area of the Fountain Centre*
- *No drinking alcohol in this area*
- *Please place litter in bins provided*

Figure 1.6: The Fountain Centre, College Street, Belfast. Notices undercut the designed intention of conviviality. © David Littlefield

- *Children in this area must be supervised at all times*
- *Escalator safety:*
    1. The escalator is not suitable for use by wheelchairs, pushchairs or trolleys
    2. No prams or buggies
    3. No deliveries
    4. Please stand on the left
    5. Stand facing the direction of travel
    6. Hold the handrail
    7. Keep feet and loose clothing away from sides
    8. Small children must be held firmly

The profligacy and visual intrusiveness of these notices becomes ironic. The agency of the metal studs in Liverpool, in spite of their subtlety, lies in their legibility and capacity to modify the situation of particular social groups; property law and ownership rights materialise as a barrier when, in fact, no such physical barrier exists. In the Fountain Centre, however, the opposite is true: the presence of litter bins appears insufficient, requiring written notification of their function; and the purpose of a steel and glass balustrade is similarly reinforced with the written instruction 'No unauthorised persons allowed beyond this point'. Agency, in this context, appears to be looser; thing-power appears diminished. But as a 'gathering' of conditions, these notices are revealing.

It is not within the scope of this chapter to make a judgement about the efficacy of these signs; I suggest, rather, an interpretation. The Fountain Centre embodies a tension, seeking to be at once a place of leisure and joy, and one of control and limitation. This is the same contradiction, albeit on a much smaller scale, that others have observed at work in larger and better-known environments. Certain types of behaviour and 'crowd practice' are acceptable on the public pavement, wrote Shields of Canada's gigantic West Edmonton Mall, but expectations and controls can shift within the mall environment. *'No loitering*, as the signs in the mall say. Certain types of comportment are expected. The emotions linked with boisterous behaviour are smothered under a flood of continuous, calming, psychologically tested "music"' (Shields 1989, 149). Allen, writing of Berlin's Potsdamer Platz, describes this push-and-pull approach to the management of place as being '*both* to encourage *and* to inhibit' how people move and behave within privately owned yet publicly accessible spaces (2006, 445).

The tension between architecture and detail

The abundance of notices within Belfast's Fountain Centre, which serve as a prosthetic for an over-zealous management regime, undercuts the designed intention of conviviality. It reveals an under-appreciation of the power of agency, and the profound effect that even the most subtle of visual clues can have on people who know to look for them. It also reveals an under-appreciation of the 'thing-ness' of a social institution. Although the notices of the Fountain Centre may not make quite as visceral a difference to a situation as the peripheral markers in Liverpool, they do combine to conjure an image of a joyless bureau-cracy – in exactly the same way as the repeated symbols of the Puritan crowd transformed Hester Prynne's short walk into a 'journey of some length'. Layard describes it thus: 'It is the developer-led, articulated sense of place that is able to rely on legal mechanisms to subdue other multiple, heterogenous, and diverse senses of place into submission' (2010, 415).

The smallness of these urban artefacts (studs, cautionary notices) ought not be mistaken, then, for only a marginal effect on the street. The difference they make is, in fact, inversely proportional to their physical size. The investigation of the urban detail can be compared to the method Catherine Gallagher and Stephen Greenblatt (2001) take within New Historicism – an approach to culture which privileges the detail, or the anecdote, as opposed to 'Big Stories' history practice. Through the close examination of the detail, Gallagher and Greenblatt hope to 'puncture' or 'interrupt' conventional histories and cultural interpretations by teasing out the insight offered by irregular, outlandish, eccentric anecdotes – those informal and unnoticed artefacts deemed too innocuous or informal to properly inform a 'grand narrative'. Drawing on Erich Auerbach, the authors aim to 'concentrate on an anecdote and pressure it to reveal a whole system' (Gallagher and Greenblatt 2001, 46). It is a revealing approach when applied to the street, especially when such innocuous or quotidian moments have such representational richness that they reorder a conventional reading, or even reveal what is otherwise repressed. In College Street's Fountain Centre, the charm advertised by the colourful figurines of the Alice Clock and the sculpture of playful children is undone by the sharp whispers of the coercive parent. Enjoy yourselves, says the architecture (but not too much, says the sign).

Scrutiny of the overlooked detail offers a reordering or revelatory process (a retelling of the story) towards which the architect, urban designer and planner would do well to develop a greater sympathy. Urban fragments, such as the details discussed here, have as profound an effect on the street as the grand gestures of architectural form and mass. Both, at either end of the scale, are part of what Coole and Frost call 'intricate interlocking systems' and a 'manifestation of the powerful interests invested therein' (2021, 29). The street, then, is not just a matter of architecture – it is a social phenomenon which is curated, managed and appropriated by all manner of participants over time, revealed through all manner of scales and detail. Importantly, the intangible characteristics of the street (belonging, ambience, ownership) can, through association with things, be considered 'things' also; and as such, ought to be considered within the scope of what it means to create and understand a street.

Notes

1   Paradise (Street) *Lost & Found*, walking tours of Liverpool by David Littlefield and Mike Devereux, part of the AHRC festival of ideas Being Human, 18 November 2017.

Bibliography

Allen, John. 2006. 'Ambient Power: Berlin's Potsdamer Platz and the seductive logic of public spaces', *Urban Studies* 43(2): 441–55.

Bennett, Jane. 2010. *Vibrant Matter: A political ecology of things*. Durham, NC: Duke University Press.

Blowers, Andrew, Chris Hamnett and Philip Sarre (eds). 1974. *The Future of Cities*. London: Hutchinson Educational and the Open University Press.

Carmona, M. 2010. 'Contemporary Public Space: Critique and classification, part one: critique', *Journal of Urban Design* 15(1): 123–48.

Carmona, M. 2015. 'Re-Theorising Contemporary Public Space: A new narrative and a new normative', *Journal of Urbanism: International Research on Placemaking and Urban Sustainability* 8(4): 373–405.

Carmona, M. 2017. 'The Formal and Informal Tools of Design Governance', *Journal of Urban Design* 22(1): 1–36.

Coole, Diana and Samantha Frost. 2010. *New Materialisms*. Durham, NC: Duke University Press.

De Magalhães, C. 2010. 'Public Space and the Contracting-out of Publicness: A framework for analysis', *Journal of Urban Design* 15(4): 559–74.

Gallagher, Catherine and Stephen Greenblatt. 2001. *Practising New Historicism*. Chicago, IL: University of Chicago Press.

Harré, Rom. 2002. 'Material Objects in Social Worlds', *Theory, Culture & Society* 19(5/6): 23–33.

Hawthorne, Nathaniel. 1850. *The Scarlet Letter*. Within *The Portable Hawthorne* (ed. Malcolm Cowley). Harmondsworth: Penguin (1985).

Kohn, M. 2001. 'The Mauling of Public Space', *Dissent*, Spring: 48, 2.

Latour, Bruno. 2005. *Reassembling the Social: An introduction to Actor-Network-Theory*. Oxford: Oxford University Press.

Layard, A. 2010. 'Shopping in the Public Realm: A law of place', *Journal of Law and Society* 37(3): 412–41.

Layard, A. 2019. 'Privatising Land in England', *Journal of Property, Planning and Environmental Law* 11(2): 151–68.

Littlefield, David. 2009. *Liverpool One: Remaking a city centre*. London: John Wiley & Sons.

Littlefield, David and Michael Devereux. 2019. *Urban Design, Place and Integration: A study of Liverpool One*. Commissioned report for Grosvenor Estates. Accessed 1 November 2022. https://uwe-repository.worktribe.com/output/851404/urban-design-place-and-integration-a-study-of-liverpool-one.

Norberg-Schulz, Christian. 1971. *Existence, Space & Architecture*. New York: Praeger.

Pamuk, Oran. 2006. *Istanbul: Memories and the city*. London: Faber & Faber.

Sayes, Edwin. 2014. 'Actor-Network Theory and Methodology: Just what does it mean to say that nonhumans have agency?', *Social Studies of Science* 44(1): 134–49.

Shields, R. 1989. 'Social Spatialization and the Built Environment: The West Edmonton Mall', *Environment and Planning D* 7: 147–64.

Vandenberghe, Frederic. 2002. 'Reconstructing Humans: A humanist critique of Actant-Network Theory', *Theory, Culture & Society* 19(5/6): 51–67.

Webmoor, Timothy and Christopher Witmore. 2008. 'Things Are Us! A Commentary on Human/Things Relations under the Banner of a "Social" Archaeology', *Norwegian Archaeological Review* 41(1): 53–70.

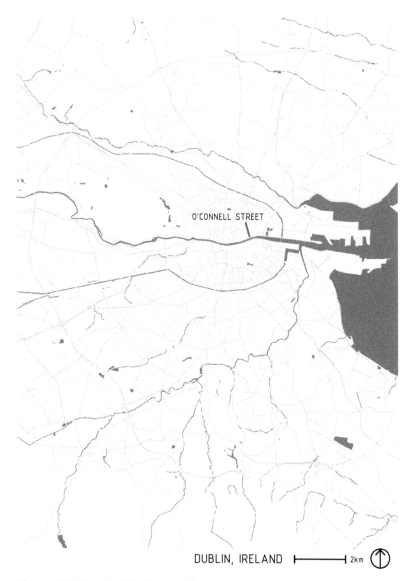

O'CONNELL STREET

DUBLIN, IRELAND ├────┤ 2km

Figure 2.0: Map Dublin © Anna Skoura

2

Rituals of O'Connell Street: commemoration, display and dissent

Kate Buckley

O'Connell Street is Dublin's pre-eminent street; 'there is no other street in the Republic which has such an equivocal role as Ireland's main street' (McDonald 1998). It is a fundamental component of the urban tissue of Dublin and of Ireland. The urban landscape of O'Connell Street has made it a ritual space. It has been appropriated by both the public and the state for commemorations, protests, parades, demonstrations and funerals. It is a platform for communicating with the whole of Irish society.

O'Connell Street

O'Connell Street is the pre-eminent street in Dublin, Ireland, one that has been appropriated by both the public and the state for commemorations, protests, parades, demonstrations and funerals. The 2007 heritage submission report produced for the proposed redevelopment of the area around O'Connell Street affirms that 'O'Connell Street has acted as the Metropolitan Civic Plaza, and has been a centre of civic and national ritual and commemoration' (O'Connell-Mahon Architects 2007). Several studies have looked at other ceremonial and ritual avenues, including the Champs-Elysées in Paris (Deroy and Clegg 2012) and Berlin's Unter den Linden (Stangl 2006), but O'Connell Street has yet to be the focus of similar research. O'Connell Street played a key role in and was the focal point of the Easter Rising and the War of Independence. As a result, it holds a central position in Ireland's political and state history. Beyond this narrative historical context, however, O'Connell Street has not been considered a ritual space. When writing about Washington, DC in the US, Green et al. say that 'something about articulating a grievance or making a demand while standing on the Capitol lawn or in front of the White House seems to resonate with Americans' (2014, 77). The same dynamic could be argued for O'Connell Street in Ireland, as a democratic urban environment. This chapter draws on ideas about O'Connell Street as the main ceremonial and ritual street of the nation and assesses the reasons behind its significance.

Ritual

Ritual is difficult to define. While some definitions have religious connotations, others are so broad that anything could be considered a ritual (Grimes et al. 2011). Repetition is not a requirement for a ritual, as 'sometimes rituals derive their force not from repetition but from their singularity, their rarity' (Grimes et al. 2011, 12). This study understands public rituals as 'social practices that generate common knowledge' (Chwe 2013, 13). Public rituals have been divided into 'ritual demonstrations', or expected celebratory processions and commemorations, and 'reactive protests', which are less structured and sometimes adversarial (Inclán and Almeida 2017). However, in assessing the public rituals that occur on O'Connell Street, three categories emerge: commemoration, display and dissent. As a public space, the street is a place for rituals. The idea of O'Connell Street as a public ritual space entails the morphology of the street and its associated ideas and perceptions.

History and design of O'Connell Street

O'Connell Street is often viewed as the centre of Dublin. 'Its scale, symmetry, history, architectural grandeur and central location endow it with a powerful sense of place which has embedded itself deeply in the psyche of the city's people' (Dublin Corporation 1993, 3). Often referred to as 'Main Street Ireland' (Dublin Corporation 2000, 112), it has played an important role in the country's history and holds a strong presence in the minds of the Irish people.

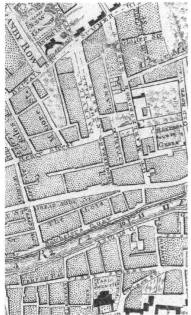

Figure 2.1: A survey of the city harbour bay and environs of Dublin on the same scale as those of London, Paris & Rome / with improvements & additions to the year 1773 by Mr. Bernard Scalé. 1773. A scale of an Irish mile, 320 Perches (= 168 mm). © John Rocque. UCD Digital Library, https://digital.ucd.ie/view/ivrla:452 (accessed 1 November 2022)
Figure 2.2: Ordnance Survey. Map of the city of Dublin and its environs, constructed for Thom's almanac and official directory. 1874. Six inches to one statute mile. © Ordnance Survey. UCD Digital Library, https://digital. ucd.ie/view/ucdlib:33001 (accessed 1 November 2022)

Origins

O'Connell Street is first shown as a formal entity on Charles Brookings' 1728 map as the narrow Drogheda Street. It was later widened by Luke Gardiner around 1750 to create Sackville Street, featuring two roadways and a central mall (see Figure 2.1). Gardiner's street was 'one of the three or four most prestigious places of aristocratic residence in the city' (Walsh 1987, 37). In 1784, the Wide Streets Commission began to extend Sackville Street to the river, imposing geometric spatial harmony in the medieval plan of the wider area. Carlisle Bridge (now O'Connell Bridge) opened in 1795, linking Sackville Street on the north side of the River Liffey to Westmoreland Street and D'Olier Street on the south side. This link opened up the street, which had previously been an enclosed area, making it a long, straight thoroughfare and public space (see Figure 2.2).

O'Connell Street has hosted many protests and public gatherings because Sackville Street was arguably conceived as a ritual space, featuring a mall at the centre of the street with plenty of space for people to see and be seen (Boyd 2006). On Faden's 1797 map, it appears as though the mall had fallen into decline, no longer being formally listed. However, in the nineteenth century, O'Connell Street assumed the form of a memorial space, with a monument erected to commemorate British admiral Horatio Nelson and his success in battle. Erected in 1808, Nelson's Pillar was a four-metre statue atop a fluted Doric column; 'the lofty position of the statue made it widely visible' (Murphy 2010, 18).

Conflict and protest

O'Connell Street suffered substantial damage between 1916 and 1922, when it became a battleground in the Irish War of Independence. As the main location of the 'mythic and symbolic event' (Wills 2010, 14) that was the Easter Rising in 1916, O'Connell Street and the General Post Office (GPO) came to constitute a focal point in its commemoration. The prominence of the street reinforces its status as a ritual space – the chosen space for any event that wishes to be heard by many.

In 1916, the British demolished much of the lower section of the street, from the GPO to Bachelors Walk; again, in 1922, the northeast side was destroyed from Cathedral Street to Parnell Street. Its reconstruction after both events was seen as a matter of national importance (McDonald 1991). In 1924 it was renamed O'Connell Street. At 1:32 am on 8 March 1966, Nelson's Pillar, which had stood at the centre of O'Connell Street for over 150 years, was blown to pieces by Republican militants two weeks before the official state commemoration of the Easter Rising. The 37-metre Doric column was reduced to a stump, and Nelson's stone head was all that was distinguishable amid the rubble. Nelson's Pillar was intentionally destroyed as an act of 'urban iconoclasm' (Boetcher 2020, 596), and this act firmly established O'Connell Street as a public ritual site for Dublin and Ireland. This demonstration of 'urban fallism' (Frank and Ristic 2020, 557) replicated the rubble on O'Connell Street in 1916; the main street of the nation was the centrepiece of what can be described as a ritual act.

Built form and morphology of O'Connell Street as a ritual space

Ellis, in an analysis of streets' spatial structure, suggested that 'there are three categories of physical properties, any or all of which can obtain to give a street a special connotation relative to its context: special size, special configuration, and special position' (1986, 123). An investigation of these features in the context of O'Connell Street allows for an understanding of how the street became the chosen space for rituals and the 'performance of democracy' (Azlan 2018, 24) in Dublin.

Scale

At approximately 50 metres in width and 500 metres in length, the dimensions of O'Connell Street provide a long vista of the entire street. Kostof says that 'the primary purpose of a vista is the framing of a distant view' (1991, 263). The perspective from O'Connell Bridge, the entrance to the street from the south side of the city, offers a complete view of the street. The rotunda at the north end of the street closes the vista – albeit in a slightly off-centre manner – while the Spire, a stainless-steel needle-like monument designed by Ian Ritchie, takes the historical place of Nelson's Pillar (Lynch 1972) (see Figure 2.3). It fixes the gaze of onlookers without blocking that which lies behind it, accentuating the long vista, achieving a grand sense of perspective, and cementing O'Connell Street as a ritual space. For rituals to be noticed, they must feature visibility and exposure (Azlan 2018) – and the sheer scale of O'Connell Street fulfils these requirements.

Configuration

Spatial arrangements determine the types of activities that can occur within a space (Azlan 2018). Haussmann's nineteenth-century Parisian boulevards may allow for mass gatherings, but the straight 'anti-riot streets' (Kostof 1991, 230) impede rebellion and suppress dissent through a long vista for surveillance (Parkinson 2012). Straight streets quickly connect two points, encouraging people to move through them (Kostof 1991, 231). This has led to the idea of O'Connell Street as a thoroughfare for moving rituals, such as parades and processions. The plaza developed outside the GPO as part of the 1998 'Integrated Area Plan' (Dublin Corporation 1998) acts as an enclave and a civic

Figure 2.3: O'Connell Street, Dublin. © Kate Buckley 2014

space (see Figure 2.4). It is a pedestrianised space enclosed by trees on three sides; it seeks to draw people in and encourage them to rest there for some time 'out of the main directional stream' (Cullen 1971, 25). The rectangular space juxtaposes the long linear street on which it is located and facilitates difficult-to-ignore physical occupations (Parkinson 2012).

Figure 2.4: O'Connell Street Plaza. © Kate Buckley 2014

O'Connell Street is experienced as a whole, with a definitive beginning at O'Connell Bridge and a clear end at the Rotunda. When Nelson's Pillar was still located on the street prior to 1966, the space was divided into upper and lower O'Connell Street. Even though the Spire is now located where Nelson once stood, the street can be considered in its entirety. It is a designed space, in that the street was considered before anything else. Smaller streets (e.g. Henry Street, Earl Street, Cathal Brugha Street, Abbey Street, Sackville Place, Cathedral Street, Princes Street) intersect with O'Connell Street, allowing for several access and circulation points without distracting from the notion of the street as a single entity. These smaller streets allow participants to both access and disperse from the ritual space with ease.

Dublin City Council has noted that 'the considerable width and spatial coherence of O'Connell Street has promoted its use for over two hundred years as a place of public assembly and civic ritual' (Dublin City Council 2001a, 18). As Clair Wills mentioned in her account of the 1916 Rising, the street has become a 'locus for nationalist protest' (2010, 8). The morphology of O'Connell Street has allowed it to become a ritual space. 'O'Connell Street has certainly the scale of a grand urban room, ideal for organised pageantry and formal display' (Ryan 1998, 64). Rituals depend on visibility to be successful, and the scale of the street facilitates mass gatherings while allowing tremendous visibility. A large audience is essential to rituals on O'Connell Street, as 'the crowd legitimates the ritual' (Parkinson 2012, 146). Ritual spectators and participants are all actively aware of their location on O'Connell Street, having chosen the site due to its ability to command physical exposure.

Perceptions of O'Connell Street as a ritual space

O'Connell Street hosts countless everyday rituals – meeting somebody at Clerys clock or at the Spire, waiting for a bus or getting on the Luas – but its extraordinary rituals are those that arouse public interest. In these spectacles, 'ritual actors elevate actions to make them noticeable, different from the ordinary' (Grimes et al. 2011, 12). In the case of O'Connell Street, the rituals are tied to their specific location. 'Place is important to ritual' (Grimes 2006, 108), and the spatial arrangements – driven by the history of O'Connell Street – have made it the chosen space for extraordinary ritual in Dublin. 'Rituals have a particular way of adapting to existing spaces and subsequently determining the character of those spaces' (Çelik 1996, 4). Participants strategically situate their rituals in symbolic spaces (Azlan 2018), which explains why O'Connell Street is perceived as the ideal space for ritual in Dublin. Three main types of extraordinary public rituals occur on O'Connell Street, namely commemoration, display and dissent.

Distinct pathways or routes through cities have prompted streets to become ritual spaces. The spatial experience of moving through streets sequentially itself constitutes a ritual (Kostof 1991). Just as it was agreed that official parades would occur on Unter den Linden in Berlin (Stangl 2006) or how the Champs-Elysées is located along the *axe historique*, O'Connell Street is located on a prominent route. The 'Civic Spine' is 'the route connecting the network of the city's most historic civic places' (Dublin City Council, OPW and Kennedy Wilson 2013, 9). The spine runs from Parnell Square to Christchurch, linking medieval Dublin to its main street and connecting the north and south sides of the city. The connected streets become a processional thoroughfare of historic, civic and ceremonial significance. O'Connell Street is the key point on the 'Civic Spine', confirming its status as a ritual space.

Commemoration

Commemorations tend to be state-organised. This includes the annual commemoration of the Easter Rising on Easter Sunday, which is a formal and highly organised repetitive ritual to remember past contentions. The plaza opposite the GPO is appropriate for such 'ritual demonstrations' (Inclán and Almeida 2017), as the backdrop immediately associates the commemoration with the Irish struggle for freedom and provokes memories among viewers. The collective public memory of the space has allowed O'Connell Street to become a 'memory palace'. The memories have been socially constructed and repeatedly confirmed by others, allowing them 'to be properly stabilised' (McBride 2001, 6). Halbwachs and Coser (1992) suggest that actions such as protests, ceremonies and commemorations transmit personal memories into the collective sphere; they are interpretations of the past that attempt to shape collective memory. O'Connell Street and its use as a ritual space have formed a collective social consciousness. Pierre Nora argues that history is a representation of the past – a reconstruction of what is no longer – while memory 'takes root in the concrete, in spaces, gestures, images, and objects' (1989, 9). In this sense, memory is embedded in rituals performed on O'Connell Street; it has attached itself to the space: a *lieu de mémoire*. Considering the ideas of both Nora and Halbwachs, O'Connell Street constitutes a key site of memory in Ireland. Both official and non-official rituals take place there. Military parades, fly-overs, the laying of a wreath at the GPO – all are associated with the commemoration of 1916 and all take place on O'Connell Street. Without the use of this space, the rituals would not evoke a collective memory among the public. The use of O'Connell Street as a *lieu de mémoire* is what ensures its continued association with memories of the Easter Rising.

Display

O'Connell Street – a wide, straight street – has long been chosen as the street to march through by the public, institutions, collectives and the government. It is almost never excluded from parade spectacles, no matter the specific route through the city. Display rituals, also 'ritual demonstrations' (Inclán and Almeida 2017), use O'Connell Street as a space in which to be seen, in which ideas and identities can be presented to the public (Parkinson 2012). The rituals that take place vary from repetitive to singular actions, from demonstrations such as the St Patrick's Day parade, the final stage of the Irish cycling race *Rás*, a festival announcement or the switching on of the Christmas lights. They can be celebrations about social solidarity or jovial and festive affairs. They can move through the street or be static. But the most important aspect of these rituals is that they adopt O'Connell Street as a stage for public visibility.

Dissent

O'Connell Street is 'the favourite site not only of official commemorations but also of unofficial public protest. The first choice for demonstrations on a whole raft of national and international issues' (Wills 2010, 19). Dissent rituals encompass demonstrations, protests and displays of resistance. These democratic performances can take the form of a rally – a static occupation of the plaza outside the GPO (see Figure 2.5) – or a march through O'Connell Street on a specific route (see Figure 2.6). These can be responses to potential or actual actions, often against the government or state-associated institutions. O'Connell Street has hosted numerous events, including housing protests, student and taxi protests, abortion rights rallies and even a protest against the cancellation of Garth Brooks concerts. Rallies and marches against the government held on O'Connell Street are potentially 'crucial in political and social change' (Chwe 2013, 13). However, in contrast to the displays and commemorations discussed earlier, they can be confrontational and lead to a riot-like atmosphere (Edwards 2006) due to their often unstructured and antagonistic nature. Protest serves to communicate displeasure, and while 'space structures protest' (Azlan 2018, 50) one cannot ignore the antisocial and unpublic nature of many of these 'reactive protests' (Inclán and Almeida 2017) such as the 2006 riots on O'Connell Street that resulted in numerous hospitalisations and arrests.

Figure 2.5: Static protest on O'Connell Street. © Kate Buckley 2014

Figure 2.6: Protest march on O'Connell Street. © Kate Buckley 2014

The threat of the performance of democracy disappearing from O'Connell Street

O'Connell Street is a contentious ritual space. In fact, there have been several threats to the right to protest on the street. Protests are permitted in Ireland as long as they do not 'promote violence' or 'incite hatred'; nor must they be 'unlawful' (Irish Council for Civil Liberties 2020). However, in 1969, 2001 and 2006 there were calls for legislation to limit the right to parade or assemble on O'Connell Street. The 2001 proposal suggested the need to 'balance the right of access and egress to O'Connell Street with the rights of public assembly on O'Connell Street' (Dublin Corporation 2011). The potential limiting of access to O'Connell Street for rituals met with varied responses, with some calling it 'unconstitutional' and 'unacceptable' (Dublin City Council 2001b), claiming that it would violate Article 40 of the Irish Constitution:

> 6 1° The State guarantees liberty for the exercise of the following rights, subject to public order and morality: ...
> ii The right of the citizens to assemble peaceably and without arms.

Removing the right to gather on O'Connell Street would remove its ritual aspect and remove the potential spontaneity of meetings, demonstrations and protests. It would limit both 'ritual demonstrations' and 'reactive protests (Inclán and Almeida 2017). O'Connell Street was arguably designed to support the 'performance of democracy', and having public space for rituals – including dissent – is a key condition for democracy (Parkinson 2012). Cities and streets are the 'privileged sites for understanding the social and historical nature of dissent expressed by struggles and protests' (Allegra et al. 2013, 1667). By removing rituals from O'Connell Street, they would become invisible to the passing public and lose their purpose, which is to make people aware of their cause or motivation. Kostof, in a dialogue on streets and public places, says that 'the fundamental aim of the public place is to ensconce community and to arbitrate social conflict ... We are meant to come and go as we please, without the consent of authorities and without any declaration of a justifying purpose' (1992, 124). Should extraordinary public rituals be banished from O'Connell Street, it would no longer be a 'theatre of protest' (Allegra et al. 2013, 1676). In an increasingly online world, one might think that traditional sites of ritual are becoming less relevant, but public debate and democracy still depend on physical public space (Parkinson 2012). If spaces such as O'Connell Street were to become over-regulated, it would risk the loss of their ritual associations, 'undermining some important conditions of democracy in the modern world' (Parkinson 2012, 2).

Conclusion

The public rituals that occur on O'Connell Street – including those of commemoration, display and dissent – are key to the transmission of information and ideas to a wide audience (Chwe 2013). Deroy and Clegg assert that the Champs-Elysées 'brings together individuals and the community in a bond that causes a feeling of collective and individual enjoyment that reception of the spectacle makes visible' (2012, 369). This notion also applies to O'Connell Street. It is a key site of spectacle – a loaded democratic urban space that is well known to the people of Dublin and Ireland.

Grimes (2011) has suggested that rituals are dynamic and can become obsolete, so it is worth wondering whether O'Connell Street and its function as a ritual space could fall into disuse. Covid-19 put a pause on the use of O'Connell Street as a ritual space, with one Irish journalist referring to the street as being 'unpatriotically silent and empty' (Ingle 2021) when discussing the lack of the St Patrick's Day parades in 2020 and 2021. However, the street remains a symbolic space for 'speaking to the nation' (Wills 2010, 19). In fact, it was the focal point of a Black Lives Matter protest held during an early Covid-19 lockdown, protests against gender-based violence in May 2021, and anti-lockdown protests throughout 2020 and 2021. The Proclamation was read to an empty O'Connell Street from the steps of the GPO for the state-organised commemoration of the Easter Rising in 2021, further solidifying the ritual aspect of the street: when no crowds were there to witness it, the street was still utilised as a ritual space. The city street is a suitable space for such rituals, as it is a public space in which 'large numbers of individuals and communities cohabit and coexist, encounter and interact but also confront their ideologies, values, desires and needs' (Boetcher 2020, 558). All over the world, public space is becoming increasingly commercialised and controlled, with space for ritual, opposition and dissent shrinking. O'Connell Street needs to maintain its perception as a public ritual space to facilitate the performance of democracy. If we disregard the need for ritual space in our cities we arguably lose 'a part of public life' (Azlan 2018). Extraordinary rituals on O'Connell Street are not about the individual. They are experienced as a collective, with others, and as a result they are spontaneous, with unpredictable outcomes. Without a doubt antisocial and violent 'reactive protests' such as those in 2006 are not welcomed, but how can we define or limit what rituals can occur on O'Connell Street when public space should remain public?

> 'The public's image of O'Connell Street as a place for spontaneous assembly, meetings or protests, confers a hallmark of civic character of which any town should be proud.' (Meagher 2001)

Bibliography

Allegra, Marco, Irene Bono, Jonathan Rokem, Anna Casaglia, Roberta Marzorati and Haim Yacobi. 2013. 'Rethinking Cities in Contentious Times: The mobilisation of urban dissent in the "Arab Spring"', *Urban Studies* 50(9): 1,675–88. https://doi.org/10.1177/0042098013482841.

Azlan, Nurul Azreen. 2018. 'Seditious Spaces', *Architecture and the Built Environment* (October): 1–240. https://doi.org/10.7480/ABE.2018.26.2661.

Boetcher, Derek N. 2020. 'Iconoclasm and Response on Dublin's Sackville/O'Connell Street, 1759–2003', *City* 24(3–4): 594–604. https://doi.org/10.1080/13604813.2020.1784582.

Boyd, Gary A. 2006. *Dublin, 1745–1922: Hospitals, spectacle and vice. The making of Dublin City.* Dublin: Four Courts.

Çelik, Zeynep (ed.). 1996. *Streets: Critical perspectives on public space.* Berkeley, CA: University of California Press.

Chwe, Michael Suk-Young. 2013. *Rational Ritual: Culture, coordination, and common knowledge.* Princeton, NJ: Princeton University Press.

Cullen, Gordon. 1971. *The Concise Townscape.* London: Architectural Press.

Deroy, Xavier and Stewart Clegg. 2012. 'Contesting the Champs-Elysées', *Journal of Change Management* 12(3): 355–73. https://doi.org/10.1080/14697017.2012.673075.

Dublin City Council. 2001a. 'O'Connell Street Architectural Conservation Area: Executive summary'.

Dublin City Council. 2001b. 'Minutes of the Monthly Meeting'.

Dublin City Council, OPW and Kennedy Wilson. 2013. 'Parnell Square Cultural Quarter: A catalyst for renewal and growth along the civic spine'.

Dublin Corporation. 1993. 'O'Connell Street Dublin: A street to represent our capital city'.

Dublin Corporation. 1998. 'O'Connell Street: Integrated area plan'.

Dublin Corporation. 2000. 'New monument & improvement works scheme at O'Connell Street Dublin'.

Dublin Corporation. 2011. 'Draft / O'Connell Street integrated area plan, (event management) bye-laws'.

Edwards, Elaine. 2006. 'Ugly Scenes at Site of 1916 Rising', *Irish Times*, 25 February.

Ellis, William C. 1986. 'The Spatial Structure of Streets'. In *On Streets: Streets as elements of urban structure*, edited by Stanford Anderson. Cambridge, MA: MIT Press.

Frank, S. and Mirjana Ristic. 2020. 'Urban Fallism: Monuments, iconoclasm and activism', *City* 24(3–4): 552–64. https://doi.org/10.1080/13604813.2020.1784578.

Green, Matthew N., Julie Yarwood, Laura Daughtery and Maria Mazzenga. 2014. 'A Center of American Protest'. In *Washington 101*, edited by Matthew N. Green, Julie Yarwood, Laura Daughtery and Maria Mazzenga, 77–87. New York: Palgrave Macmillan. https://doi.org/10.1057/9781137426246_6.

Grimes, Ronald L. 2006. *Rite Out of Place: Ritual, media, and the arts.* Oxford: Oxford University Press. https://doi.org/10.1093/acprof:oso/9780195301441.001.0001.

Grimes, Ronald L., Ute Husken, Udo Simon and Eric Venbrux. 2011. *Ritual, Media, and Conflict.* Oxford: Oxford University Press.

Halbwachs, Maurice and Lewis A. Coser. 1992. *On Collective Memory* (Heritage of Sociology series). Chicago, IL: University of Chicago Press.

Inclán, María and Paul D. Almeida. 2017. 'Ritual Demonstrations Versus Reactive Protests: Participation across mobilizing contexts in Mexico City', *Latin American Politics and Society* 59(4): 47–74. https://doi.org/10.1111/laps.12033.

Ingle, Roisin. 2021. 'How Long, How Long Must We Sing This Song?', *Irish Times*, 17 March.

Irish Council for Civil Liberties. 2020. 'Know Your Rights: The right to protest'. Accessed 1 November 2022. https://www.iccl.ie/wp-content/uploads/2020/01/Know-Your-Rights-Protest.pdf.

Kostof, Spiro. 1991. *The City Shaped: Urban patterns and meanings through history*. London: Thames and Hudson.

Kostof, Spiro. 1992. *The City Assembled: The elements of urban form through history*. London: Thames and Hudson.

Lynch, Kevin. 1972. *The Image of the City*. Cambridge, MA: MIT Press [1960].

McBride, Ian. 2001. 'Memory and National Identity in Ireland'. In *History and Memory in Modern Ireland*, edited by Ian McBride, 1–42. Cambridge: Cambridge University Press.

McDonald, Frank. 1991. 'From the Rubble of the Rising', *Irish Times*, 27 April.

McDonald, Frank. 1998. 'Plans for O'Connell Street "Renaissance" Unveiled', *Irish Times*.

Meagher, Niall. 2001. 'O'Connell Street', *Irish Times*, 17 April.

Murphy, Paula. 2010. *Nineteenth-Century Irish Sculpture: Native genius reaffirmed*. New Haven, CT: Yale University Press.

Nora, Pierre. 1989. 'Between Memory and History: Les lieux de mémoire', *Representations* 26 (April): 7–24. https://doi.org/10.2307/2928520.

O'Connell-Mahon Architects. 2007. 'The Evolution of O'Connell Street'. Accessed 1 November 2022. http://www.oconnellmahon.ie/wp-content/uploads/2013/02/Evolution_of_OConnell_Street.pdf.

Parkinson, John. 2012. *Democracy and Public Space: The physical sites of democratic performance*. Oxford: Oxford University Press.

Ryan, R. 1998. 'The Monument in the City'. In *A Monument in the City: Nelson's Pillar and its aftermath*, edited by John O'Regan, 63–71. Oysterhaven, Kinsale and Cork: Gandon Editions.

Stangl, Paul. 2006. 'Restoring Berlin's Unter den Linden: Ideology, world view, place and space', *Journal of Historical Geography* 32(2): 352–76.

Walsh, E. 1987. 'Sackville Mall: The first one hundred years'. In *The Gorgeous Mask: Dublin 1700–1850*, edited by David Dickson. Dublin: Trinity History Workshop.

Wills, Clair. 2010. *Dublin 1916: The siege of the GPO*. London: Profile Books.

CHEAPSIDE

LONDON, UK ├─────────┤ 5km

Figure 3.0: Map London © Anna Skoura

3

Street life in medieval London

James Davis

This chapter provides an analysis of how we might reconstitute the everyday life and space of a pre-modern street, namely Cheapside in late medieval London. Street life in the past can be difficult to recapture in all its complexity and inter-relations. Written documents, such as deeds, purveyances, regulations and court cases, can tell us much, but it is only through a broader range of evidence – archaeological, architectural, literary and visual – that we achieve a better understanding. Such an approach also reminds us how both the built environment and culture of urban space shapes its use, and that the form of the street can be resilient over time despite radical changes.

Cheapside

Cheapside has been referred to as medieval London's greatest street and shopping space (Keene 1985a). On a normal day in the fourteenth century, it thronged with shops, stalls, street traders, officials, clerics and beggars; a congested space, but also undoubtedly one that was vibrant and lively. Henri Lefebvre (1974) understood that the use of public space is shaped by the surrounding private spaces and material environment. To what extent can we recapture the built environment of such a medieval street, and how this shaped the movement of people? How do we develop this analysis further by understanding how medieval people navigated and perceived this particular street? This chapter presents the evidence of historical geographers and archaeologists, alongside cultural insights from visual and literary sources (Harding 2002), in order to see how far we can recapture a medieval streetscape.

As Jeremy Whitehand noted, 'Each society leaves its mark on the landscape, creating forms that reflect the aspirations and problems of its day. These forms are part of the inheritance of future societies, which they in their turn variously alter, add to, preserve or erase' (1992, 6). A cumulative process is at work in which the streetscape might be regarded as a canvas upon which urban societies inscribe their experiences and values. Michael Conzen (1960; Whitehand 1981) pioneered our approach to understanding urban space across time, focusing primarily on morphological development and 'historical layering in the townscape'. The current urban fabric is a culmination of changes in buildings, plots and use, as well as the surviving plan and edifices, and this reminds us that the life of modern streets is made more complex by characteristics of their past (Whitehand 1987, 2). Ultimately, a historical perspective can inform modern understanding of streets, their use and design, while there is evidence within streets today that can help us better understand the societies that created them.

The street

Cheapside was the main commercial thoroughfare of late medieval London, some 50–60 feet broad and running west–east from St Paul's Cathedral precinct to the narrower Poultry and then Cornhill. It remained one of the busiest English streets until the end of the nineteenth century, and is still the main shopping area for the financial 'City' of London. More specifically, Cheapside was often known as 'Westchepe', with 'Estchepe' lying further south and to the east of London Bridge. 'Cheap' derives from the Old English 'ceap', meaning 'market' or 'to buy'.

London was by far the largest city in late medieval England, by area and population, and as such it generated a significant amount of legal and administrative documentation. Derek Keene and Vanessa Harding (1987) have produced the most detailed work around medieval and early modern Cheapside, particularly in reconstructing from conveyances and deeds the property patterns, physical layout, rental values and occupants (see also Keene 1985a; Harding 1985; Harding 2012). There has also been considerable effort in mapping the streets of medieval London, particularly by the Historic Towns Trust (Lobel 1989), which led to recent mapping of London for c.1300 and

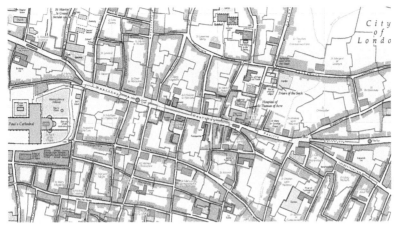

Figure 3.1: Map of Cheapside c.1300. Source: *A Map of Medieval London: The City, Westminster & Southwark, 1270 to 1300*, edited by Caroline Barron and Vanessa Harding. © Historic Towns Trust

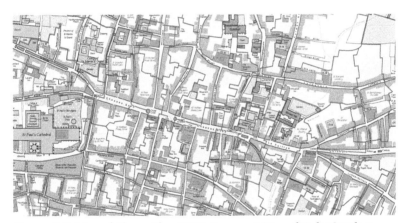

Figure 3.2: Map of Cheapside c.1520. Source: *A Map of Tudor London: The City in 1520*, edited by Caroline Barron and Vanessa Harding, rev edn 2021. © Historic Towns Trust

c.1520, including the street layout, landmark buildings and prominent structures. Figures 3.1 and 3.2 are sections that cover the Cheapside area, the hatching in the former indicating that the street itself was a market space.

The material fabric and built environment have thus been reconstructed to a considerable degree. What, however, can this tell us about the lived experience in Cheapside from the late thirteenth to fifteenth centuries? As Ron Johnston (1991, 97) stated, the three components that make up a place are the physical environment, the built environment and the people that occupy it. The physical constitutes the natural topography, such as the gradient, landscape and water courses, which in turn influences settlement and human-created aspects. However, the people might be considered the crucial element, through their sense of place and their daily interactions. This chapter provides a brief survey of late medieval Cheapside, its main structures and activity, and the types of evidence that historians can use to reveal its streetscape.

A commercial space

Primarily, Cheapside was a commercial thoroughfare. The streets and lanes that run off Cheapside provide a reminder of the types of commodity sold there. For example, on the north side, there was 'Wodestrate' (Wood Street), 'Melkstrete' (Milk Street), 'Ismongerelane' (Ironmonger Lane); and to the south, 'Bredstrete' (Bread Street), 'Corveyserestrate' (Cordwainer Street), 'Goselane' (Goose Lane), and the more generic 'Soper Lane' (Shopper's Lane). Although these are not precise indicators – use was flexible and trades relocated – there was a certain clustering of occupations in particular periods (Colson 2016). In addition, the Shambles – the main meat market – was just beyond the west end by St Nicholas church, while corn was sold nearby at the 'Pavement', near the church of St Michael le Querne.

By 1300, the street's shops were dominated by better-off retail and distributive traders, particularly in metals, textiles and spices (Burch et al. 2011, 95). Other manufacturers were relegated to the side lanes, while foodstuffs were sold by poorer, wandering hawkers, often women. There is therefore a sense of a division by social and gender status in the built environment and its access, though the open space of the street itself was more mixed and egalitarian. There were four main types of commercial venues in Cheapside: the shop, the seld (a type of bazaar, discussed below), the market stall, and the street itself. In general, this was a densely occupied street with hundreds of shops by 1300, so frontage was at a premium. Many shop frontages were narrow, some only six feet wide and many less than 10 feet (Burch et al. 2011, 192). In 1314, John le Botonner's shop on the corner of Soper Lane was only five feet square and six feet high (LAN 43). This pressure for space dissipated somewhat after the population decrease caused by the Black Death (1348–9), shown in the evidence for declining average rental values and the amalgamation of some properties (Keene 1985a, 20).

However, the pressures of the thirteenth and fourteenth centuries meant that one option was to build upwards. The rental and archaeological evidence suggest that the height of many buildings along Cheapside stretched to three or four storeys, unusual for domestic or commercial sites at this time. Derek Keene (2008, 206–9) estimates that a three-storey house was about 36–44 feet to the roof ridge. However, he notes that there was a limit to vertical extension, and the value of upper rooms diminished according to distance from the street. It is likely that servants and lodgers lived in the upper floors (Burch et al. 2011, 192). Commonly, the cellars were used for storage, the ground floor for commercial activity, and the floors above for living and sleeping. Multiple use was the standard in medieval urban communities, with many premises used for both retail and manufacture, as well as for the household. Indeed, women were often at the front of the shop, with their husband occupied in the adjoining workshop (Keene 1990, 41). However, it should be noted that there were numerous smaller shops and stalls that could only function for display and retail (Keene 2008, 207-9).

Selds were covered warehouses that ran off narrow passages from Cheapside. There were examples in other towns, such as Bristol and Winchester (Antrobus 2018, 319; Keene 1985b, 517–19), but London had by far the largest concentration. They often contained a range of petty retailers clustered around benches, small stalls and chests (Keene 1985, 12–14; Keene 1990, 32–40), selling leather and textile goods (Mem, 22). Selds thus resembled a quasi-public bazaar and were popular in the thirteenth century, with perhaps a thousand traders in total operating within them. Each developed a distinct identity to promote their trade, such as the Painted Seld, Girdlers' Seld and Broad Seld; 'in 1385–6 the owner of one seld spent 8s 4d on making and painting a sign and hanging it from a pole with an iron hook on the Cheapside frontage' (Keene 1985, 14). However, trading patterns changed as the population fell in the late fourteenth century and these tiny retail units significantly declined in number compared to shops with their more elaborate street-facing displays.

Beyond fixed shops and selds, there were semi-permanent stalls and chests in the street from which itinerant traders sold goods during the morning. Specific sites were designated for many of the commodities brought into Cheapside, such that fish was to be sold near the Great Conduit (Mem, 436, 508; CLB H, 190; CLB I, 67) and meat at the

Shambles (CLB I, 67, 122). Those who travelled in from the countryside were restricted in where they could sell and even how they could move about whilst carrying goods; the privileges of London citizenship influenced the use of space. There was a tendency for some temporary stalls to take on an air of permanency, in both form and occupation, and this led to an order in 1274 to clear away such structures from Cheap. In 1310 it was declared that market stalls and benches were to be cleared away from Cheap's highway after the hour of 'None' (the canonical hour of mid-afternoon; Mem, 75; CLB D, 218). Such regulation was undoubtedly initiated by wealthier shopkeepers, who disliked the hindrance caused by traders in front of their premises, again emphasising the differing rights between citizens of the city and others.

In 1347, the civic authorities launched an inquiry into how to manage the nuisance caused by mobile vendors of victuals in the public highways of Cheap and Cornhill, but reached no conclusion (CLB F, 179). Numerous incoming retailers remained a fact of commercial life and contributed to the crowded bustle of Cheapside. Some traders were nevertheless expected to remain mobile, such as the 'birlisters' – female fish-sellers who were to keep moving along the streets and lanes, only standing to make a specific deal (CLB G, 123; CLB H, 243–4; CPMR, III, 74). They were also not to buy any fish before 10 am, reminding us that the temporal trading patterns in London's streets were strictly regulated.

A medieval perambulation

So far, the environment of Cheapside has been reconstructed through legal and civic records, such as deeds and regulations, which provide a valuable insight into occupational patterns and governing anxieties. Recapturing the sensory and everyday experience is more difficult given the lack of diaries and writings from urban residents. However, a fifteenth-century poem provides an unusual insight into the sights and sounds of Cheapside, as seemingly evoked by a Kentish peasant visiting the city to seek justice in Westminster's law courts. *London Lyckpeny* (Gray 1985) purports to describe this humble visitor's journey back from Westminster, and the following verses (translated from Middle English) relate to the central streets specifically:

> Then I drew towards Cheapside, where I saw many people standing. One offered me velvet, silk and linen, and another took me by the hand and said, "Here is Parisian thread, the finest in

the land." I was never used to such things and, wanting money, I might not succeed.

I then went forth to London Stone, throughout all Candlewick Street, where drapers offered me much cloth. Then one came crying "Hot sheep's feet!" Another cried "Mackerel, green rushes," while a third bade me to buy a hood to cover my head. But for want of money, I might not succeed.

Next I hurried to Eastcheap and heard a cry, "Beef ribs and many pies!" Pewter pots clattered in a heap, and there were harps, pipes, and minstrelsy. Some began to cry "Yea, by cock!" and "Nay, by cock!" Some sang of "Jenkin and Julian" for their reward. But for lack of money, I might not succeed.

Cornhill was my next stop, where there was much stolen gear. I saw where my hood hung, that had been lost among the crowd. I thought it wrong to buy my own hood – I knew it as well as I did my Creed. But for lack of money, I could not succeed.

The vibrancy of Cheapside and surrounding streets is clearly expressed, with the visitor assailed by the cries of market traders who are competing for his attention. The public streets are depicted as colourful, sensuous and intense, but real access was only obtained through money. Food and drink sellers were especially ubiquitous and civic documents reveal a constant concern over the price and condition of such commodities.

Alongside this, there is an undercurrent of deception and theft. Legal records certainly suggest that Cheap could be a place of petty crime and assaults (CPMR, I, 37, 106, 205, 216; CLB F, 249, 288; Mem, 50, 204). There were also major disputes, such as when the fishmongers and goldsmiths were involved in a major affray at the corner of Cheap and Friday Street in 1339 – several were wounded (Hanawalt 2017, 56–57; CPMR, I, 103–7, 128, 189). One major affray in 1373 even appears to have been the consequence of a football match in the area around Cheap, Soper Lane and Cordwainer Street (CPMR, II, 152).

The poem perhaps reinforces Michel De Certeau's (1984, 115–17) approach to urban space as a quotidian journey, traversing and negotiating spatial interactions. The space of streets can only be understood fully through experiencing them as places, and through the individual choices that are made when interacting with authority, symbols and the built environment. Indeed, Cheapside was a street in which the urban rich, middling and poor lived and worked cheek-by-jowl.

The street also had a temporal rhythm. It was recognised that night-time could turn a reasonably respectable street into a more problematic and criminal setting, dominated more by the lower classes. In 1369 and again in 1392–3, the mayor issued ordinances to regulate 'Evynchepynges' – evening markets selling secondhand goods to the poor – which had long been held in Cheapside and Cornhill despite attempts to disband them (Mem, 339, 380, 532–3; CPMR, I, 1; CLB B, 236; CLB D, 229; CLB E, 156–9, 161–2; CLB G, 248). There were concerns that they encouraged criminal activity, so now nothing was to be sold after the bell ('which hangs upon the Tun at Cornhill') had sounded at sunset.

A general curfew was in place in the city, signalled by church bells. Individuals might be prosecuted for being 'common nightwalkers' against the peace (Mem, 81). Females caught wandering at night were particularly frowned upon because of potential associations with illicit sexual activity. Their activities might have been routine: in 1320 Emma le Wirdrawere was caught after curfew, just off Cheap near St Martin's, carrying a fardel of cloth (perhaps a delivery). She was nevertheless sentenced to a time in the Tun – a small prison in the centre of the street intended to shame the culprit (Mem, 133). This was all partly linked to concerns about street prostitution, and the names of narrow lanes off Cheapside – 'Pupekertilane', 'Groppecountelane', 'Coneyhope Lane', 'Bordhawe' – point towards immoral activities that possibly took place in these areas, particularly after dusk.

Such moral anxieties were embedded in a patriarchal culture verging on misogyny and remind us of the social restrictions that women faced daily (Rose 1993, 17–40). As we have seen, retail was a space in which medieval women could play a distinctive role despite the pervading patriarchal constraints. Derek Keene (1990, 41) noted a high number of female shopkeepers (over 50 per cent) at the Cheapside end of Soper Lane in the late fourteenth century, while many of the perambulating hawkers were women. Women were also active as shoppers, including young female servants, and the streets would have been crowded with both genders. However, such quotidian activity was laced with underlying concerns about sexual mores and harassment. One piece of fifteenth-century advice for young urban women stated: 'Acquaint you not with each man that travels the street, / If any man speak to you, swiftly greet him' (Amt 2001, 410–17). Men could loiter around marketplaces and alehouses, but women's reputation might be harmed for doing the same. Although urban space was not strictly gender-segregated, negotiating the streets could be problematic for medieval women.

Picturing the street

Another view of Cheapside is provided by near-contemporary images, often produced for either ceremonial or civic purposes. Unfortunately, no image survives for the late medieval period itself, but those from the early modern period, before the Great Fire of 1666, allow us to glimpse aspects of the street that remained prominent (Figure 3.3).

The 1547 coronation of Edward VI was encapsulated in a mural of the time (Figure 3.4), which survives in a painting made by Samuel Hieronymous Grimm in 1785. Looking southwards towards the river Thames, we can see the south frontage of Cheapside. The image is a reminder of the prominence of ecclesiastical structures, particularly given their size and height relative to the domestic and commercial

Figure 3.3: Cheapside in 1547. Source: Coronation procession of King Edward VI, 1547. Copy by Samual Hieronymous Grimm (1785) from a mural at Cowdray House. Society of Antiquaries of London. © Bridgeman Images, SOA2916

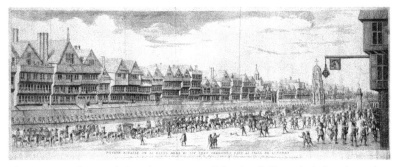

Figure 3.4: Cheapside in 1638. Source: *Histoire de l'entrée de la reine mère dans La Grande Bretagne* (1638) by P. de la Serre. Reprinted by W. Bowyer and J. Nichols, London, 1775. © Alamy, Image ID G38F61

buildings, which would have lent a devotional hue to the city's profile. To the left of the image is St Mary le Bow, which for a time was the city headquarters for the archbishop of Canterbury, while to the right is St Paul's. The verticality of Cheapside is clear in the three-storey timber-framed shops (with garrets in the roof-space), adorned in the 1547 painting with pageantry and hangings to celebrate the king. Also visible are the archways and open windows that would normally have served customers. Medieval shops varied in terms of accessibility, but many bargains were enacted through the hatches, under awnings and across shutters that hung down to form counters, while customers stood outside in the public street.

Although from a later period, Figure 3.5 provides another useful pre-Great Fire image of Cheapside, looking eastwards and showing the north side of the street. It depicts the 1638 visit of Mary de Medici, mother of Henriette Maria (wife of Charles I). By the early seventeenth century, the height of the jettied frontage is notable, with numerous four- and five-storey houses, perhaps indicating a further upward extension of many buildings. The breadth of the street also stands out, facilitating stalls and traders in the open space as well as through-traffic. As these images show, Cheapside was ideal for ceremonial, leading people from the royal hub at the Tower at one end to the ecclesiastical authority embodied in the cathedral. Such political and liturgical processions commonly traversed this street, intended to bind together the various constituents of the city through ritual, but perhaps incidentally emphasising their social separation.

The just-visible awnings would have covered the front projection of shops, encroaching into the street; a temporary façade has been erected specifically for the procession. The image also reveals a signpost in the

Figure 3.5: Civitas Londinum, 1561. Source: *Civitas Londinum: The Map of Early Modern London*, edited by Janelle Jenstad, Greg Newton and Kim McLean-Fiander, edition 6.6 (2021). Accessed 1 November 2022. https://mapoflondon.uvic.ca/agas.htm. © CC BY-NC-SA 4.0 license

foreground, possibly a garland of vine leaves indicating a tavern, with glimpses of many more on the shops behind. Similarly, the medieval streetscape was adorned liberally with signs, projecting outwards by six feet or more (e.g. CLB H, 86). They often figuratively illustrated the products being sold, but sometimes displayed a cultural symbol or folkloric tale, such as the sign of the Elephant (*signum olifantis*) held by Simon Sewale, a saddler (CLB I, 99). There were complaints in 1375 that many signs, particularly alestakes in front of Cheapside's taverns and alehouses, were too long and impeded riders, as well as causing damage to the houses because of their weight. Seven feet was thus stipulated as the upper limit (Mem, 381).

Street furniture

In both Figures 3.4 and 3.5, the most prominent piece of street furniture is the Eleanor Cross, originally built in the reign of Edward I as one of a number erected in memory of his queen. It was rebuilt and elaborated between 1441 and 1486, eventually standing about 12 metres high with gilded ornamentation and religious statues. There was another cross located in Cheapside, at the spot where the wards of Bread Street, Cheap, Cordwainer and Cripplegate met, known originally as the 'Stone Cross' or 'Broken Cross'. It was later synonymous with the rebuilt Standard (adorned with angelic statues according to John Stow), which contained a new conduit by 1443 (CLB H, 422).

Such street furniture played a role beyond aesthetics and cultural memory. Mobile vendors were expected to congregate at the crosses when conducting trade. (Mem, 347; CLB G, 263). 'Stations' around both crosses were annually leased by the city for between 6s 8d and 13s 4d each (1379), mostly to female retailers (Mem, 428; CLB H, 127). The crosses also acted as sites for public proclamations (CPMR, I, 41, 122) and punishments. There are numerous instances of fraudulent manufactures and commodities, such as caps, pouches, gloves, fishing nets and unlawful measures, being publicly burnt in the street, usually near the Stone Cross (Mem, 55, 90–91, 116, 247, 341, 523; CLB A, 186; CLB D, 129, 263; CLB E, 223; CLB F, 201; CLB H, 396; CPMR, I, 33, 99). Indeed, medieval Cheapside was replete with expressions of public authority, whether in punishments of deceitful bakers who might be dragged on a hurdle attached to a horse (LA, 232), or in displays of penance, where the penitent walked barefoot, head uncovered and carrying a lighted wax candle (Mem, 202–3, 490, 500, 660). The humiliation of corporal punishment worked because social credit was important among medieval neighbours, even in towns; similarly, public slander was not tolerated, especially towards officials (CPMR, I, 190–1, II, 4).

The other notable structure, again just visible in both Figures 3.4 and 3.5, was the Great Conduit, a monumental structure (some 45 feet long and 20 feet wide) for supplying water, which was positioned at the entry to the Poultry. The first pipes were laid from 1245, taking water from the Tyburn springs into Charing Cross and then up the Strand, Fleet Street and into Cheapside (Mem, 503–4). The non-central siting of the conduit was not logical in terms of supply, but it was possibly related to the charitable provision of water, for the house of St Thomas the Martyr stood next to the conduit (Burch et al. 2011, 180–1; Barron 2004, 256). In 1345, it was stated that the conduit was originally built so that the better-off might have water for preparing food and the poor for drinking (CLB F, 128; Mem, 225). Like the crosses, it was a gathering point; traders such as the fruiterers congregated there, seeking a ready clientele (Barron 2004, 253; CPMR, VI, 118–19). There were also disputes throughout the period over use of the conduit,

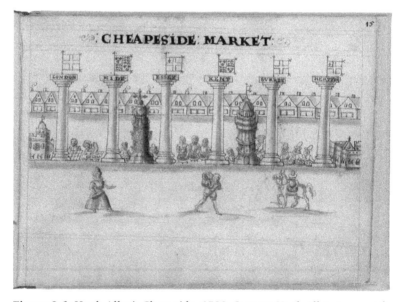

Figure 3.6: Hugh Alley's Cheapside, 1598. Source: *Hugh Alley, A caveat for the city of London* (1598), fol.15r. LUNA: Folger Digital Image Collection, 67931. © CCO 1.0 Universal Public Domain Dedication License. Folger Shakespeare Library, CC BY-SA 4.0

particularly by traders such as brewers, cooks and fishmongers (CLB D, 236–7; CLB I, 139; Mem, 77–78), which eventually led to charges being levied from 1312 for maintenance of the water supply (CLB D, 299; CLB F, 28–29, 303–4; Mem, 107, 201–2).

All these structures added to the sense of a principal public space, acting as meeting places, focal points in pageantry and royal processions, and imbued with symbolic meaning. Indeed, the continuing prominence of these structures are notable in other early modern images, whether the woodblock *Civitas Londinum* from 1561 (often known as the 'Agas map') or Hugh Alley's stylistic illustration of Cheapside in 1598 (Archer et al. 1988). The latter shows mobile vendors, male and female, amidst (from left to right) the church of St Michael le Querne, the Eleanor Cross, the Standard and the Great Conduit (Figure 3.6).

Conclusion

Modern Cheapside remains a notable commercial thoroughfare, but has perhaps lost its central place in city life. There are also only remnants of the medieval fabric, with significant rebuilding after both the Great Fire of 1666 and the Blitz of 1940, as well as the loss of landmarks such as the Standard and Conduits. The open market was relocated to off-street sites, new streets have been laid through it (e.g. King Street), and some side roads widened (Harding 2008, 78, 95; See Figure 3.1). Yet, the broad layout of the street and narrower side lanes largely remains, with their resonant street-names. Although Cheapside lacks its previous public resonance and centrality, with more priority given to traffic, the City Corporation is keen that it should remain a busy shopping space for pedestrians. It is a street replete with twentieth-century buildings, yet its layout and intended use remains medieval in inception.

This case study has provided a historical perspective on the social character of a public street, and discussed what we can uncover about the impact of the built environment and regulation, along with the effect of ideas about private and public space, user appropriation, identity, performance and cultural exclusion. This case study reminds us of the link between the historical context and our modern perception of our streets. Understanding the streets we live in today, and the quality of street life, is contingent not merely on the architectural fabric and design, but also on our understanding of these streets as long-lived places of socio-economic negotiation. Medieval Cheapside encapsulated the vibrancy, intensity and contradictions of a busy commercial street.

Bibliography

Abbreviations:
CLB: Sharpe 1899–1912.
CPMR: Thomas and Jones 1926–61.
LA: Riley 1861.
LAN: Chew and Kellaway 1973.
Mem: Riley 1868.

Amt, Emilie (ed.). 2001. *Medieval England, 1000–1500: A reader.* Toronto: University of Toronto Press.

Antrobus, Abby. 2018. 'Medieval Shops'. In *The Oxford Handbook of Later Medieval Archaeology in Britain*, edited by Christopher Gerrard and Alejandra Gutiérrez, 312–25. Oxford: Oxford University Press.

Archer, Ian, Caroline Barron and Vanessa Harding (eds). 1988. *Hugh Alley's Caveat: The markets of London in 1598.* London: London Topographical Society.

Barron, Caroline. 2004. *London in the Middle Ages: Government and people, 1200–1500.* Oxford: Oxford University Press.

Burch, Mark, Phil Treveil and Derek Keene. 2011. *The Development of Early Medieval and Later Poultry and Cheapside: Excavations at 1 Poultry and vicinity, City of London.* London: Museum of London Archaeology.

Chew, Helena A. and William Kellaway (eds). 1973. *London Assize of Nuisance, 1301–1431: A calendar.* London: London Record Society. **[LAN]**

Colson, Justin. 2016. 'Commerce, Clusters, and Community: A re-evaluation of the occupational geography of London, c.1400–c.1550', *Economic History Review* 69(1): 104–30.

Conzen, Michael R.G. 1960. *Alnwick, Northumberland: A study in town-plan analysis.* London: Institute of British Geographers.

De Certeau, Michel. 1984. *The Practice of Everyday Life.* Berkeley, CA: University of California Press.

Gray, Douglas (ed.). 1985. 'London Lykpeny'. In *The Oxford Book of Late Medieval Verse and Prose*, 16–19. Oxford: Oxford University Press.

Hanawalt, Barbara. 2017. *Ceremony and Civility: Civic culture in late medieval London.* Oxford: Oxford University Press.

Harding, Vanessa. 1985. 'Reconstructing London before the Great Fire', *London Topographical Record* 25: 1–12.

Harding, Vanessa. 2002. 'Space, Property and Propriety in Urban England', *Journal of Interdisciplinary History* 32(4): 549–69.

Harding, Vanessa. 2008. 'Cheapside: Commerce and commemoration', *Huntingdon Library Quarterly* 71(1): 77–96.

Harding, Vanessa. 2012. 'Houses and Households in Cheapside c.1500–1550'. In *London and Beyond: Essays in Honour of Derek Keene*, edited by Matthew Davies and James A. Galloway, 135–54. London: University of London.

Johnston, Ron. 1991. *A Question of Place: Exploring the practice of human geography.* Oxford: Blackwell.

Keene, Derek. 1985a. *Cheapside before the Great Fire.* London: Economic and Social Research Council.

Keene, Derek. 1985b. *Survey of Medieval Winchester.* Oxford: Oxford University Press.

Keene, Derek and Vanessa Harding. 1987. *Historical Gazetteer of London Before the Great Fire, Part 1: Cheapside.* Cambridge: Chadwyck-Healey.

Keene, Derek. 1990. 'Shops and Shopping in Medieval London'. In *Medieval Art, Architecture and Archaeology in London*, edited by Lindy Grant, 29–46. London: Maney.

Keene, Derek. 2008. 'Tall Buildings in Medieval London: Precipitation, aspiration and thrills', *London Journal* 33(3): 201–15.

Lefebvre, Henri. 1974. *The Production of Space*. New York: Horizon Press.

Lobel, Mary D. 1989. *The City of London from Prehistoric Times to c.1520, Historic Town Atlas, Volume III*. Oxford: Oxford University Press.

Riley, Henry T. (ed.). 1861. *Liber Albus: The White Book of the City of London*. London: Corporation of the City of London. **[LA]**

Riley, Henry T. (ed.). 1868. *Memorials of London and London Life in the XIIIth, XIVth and XVth Centuries, AD1276–1419*. London: Longmans. **[Mem]**

Rose, Gillian. 1993. *Feminism and Geography: The limits of geographical knowledge*. Cambridge: Polity Press.

Sharpe, Reginald R. (ed.). 1899–1912. *Calendar of Letter-Books Preserved among the Archives of the Corporation of the City of London at the Guildhall*, 11 vols (A–L). London: Corporation of the City of London. **[CLB]**

Thomas, Arthur H. and Philip E. Jones (eds). 1926–61. *Calendar of Plea and Memoranda Rolls Preserved Among the Archives of the Corporation of the City of London at the Guildhall, A.D. 1323–1482*, 6 vols. Cambridge: Cambridge University Press. **[CPMR]**

Whitehand, Jeremy W.R. (ed.). 1981. *The Urban Landscape: Historical development and management. Papers by M.R.G. Conzen*. London: Institute of British Geographers.

Whitehand, Jeremy W.R. 1987. *The Changing Face of Cities: A study of development cycles and urban form*. Oxford: Blackwell.

Whitehand, Jeremy W.R. 1992. *The Making of the Urban Landscape*. Oxford: Blackwell.

LANGE REIHE

HAMBURG, GERMANY ⊢————⊣ 2km ⊕

Figure 4.0: Map of Hamburg © Anna Skoura

4

Who owns the street? The cases of Lange Reihe and Steindamm in Hamburg

Bedour Braker

The nuances of everyday urban life are exposed on city streets. In Hamburg, two main arteries in the neighbourhood of St Georg – Lange Reihe and Steindamm – reveal profound social tension. The former is a popular destination for the LGBTQ+ community, while the latter is a space for conservative Muslim immigrants. This chapter discusses both streets as public spaces dominated by social prejudice. By tracing their histories, cultural backgrounds, and reasons why they are at odds with each other, this chapter discusses who 'owns' the street, questioning why all streets do not simply belong to everyone.

Signs and signals of minority streets

Amid contemporary global social mobility, some streets have become social enclaves for specific minority groups, signalled by matrices of semiotics and visual signals that give these streets a special identity. It can be difficult for outsiders to decipher street signals moulded by locals. The street is a receptacle for the layering of urban changes over time. It constitutes a living artery, an extension of the home and a domain in which users practise their daily habits and rituals, express their viewpoints, and exchange conversation and laughter. Such streets serve to distinguish each neighbourhood, being perceived and conceived through cultural meanings of lived daily experiences (Lefebvre 1974, 85). In some cases, they become stigmatised due to the presence of the 'other' alongside locals harbouring prejudice.

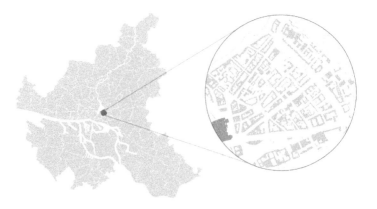

Figure 4.1: A blown-up map of St Georg neighbourhood in relation to the city of Hamburg. Illustration: Rachael Milliner. © Jan Braker Architekt

This chapter discusses two streets in the vicinity of the main train station in Hamburg, Germany, both with unique histories and historical developments (Figure 4.1). East of the station toward Alster Lake is Lange Reihe Street: a vibrant gentrified street and a key destination for the LGBTQ+ community. Lange Reihe underwent many socio-political changes throughout the twentieth century, from property confiscation for nonconforming minorities in the 1930s to constant police raids on gay bars in the 1940s. Nowadays, people using the street feel safer, surrounded by art studios, galleries, trendy bars and outdoor cafes.

A few hundred metres south of Lange Reihe is Steindamm Street, a wide thoroughfare filled with loud vehicles, oriental eateries, sex and betting shops and small grocery shops. The population of Steindamm has become increasingly religious and conservative since the 1970s, with its predominantly Muslim population living in an ethnic enclave. However, as demonstrated by the presence of sex and betting shops, the users of the street are not exclusively religious and conservative. Like Lange Reihe, Steindamm is a social enclave that facilitates a feeling of communal safety among its users. These two streets typify the diversity of the twenty-first-century city and the way in which modern multiplicity is expressed in urban terms.

Participant interviews and observation

In order to explore the social juxtaposition between the trendy, liberal atmosphere of Lange Reihe and the religious, conservative atmosphere of Steindamm, we conducted in-depth interviews and field studies. The interviews were with residents, visitors and shop owners, including 25 Middle Eastern, European and Asian participants between 20 and 50 years of age of different genders and sexual orientations. During field surveys, we also observed street users, focusing on the lived experiences of both LGBTQ+ individuals and conservative immigrants and the ways in which they interact with the existing physical settings of both streets. In this way, we investigated social conflict and urban transformation. The findings shed light on social segregation, the streets' identities, and the ways in which both streets are shaped by globalisation and gentrification.

Street spaces as minority enclaves

> The deepest problems of modern life derive from the claim of the individual to preserve the autonomy and individuality of his existence in the face of overwhelming social forces, of historical heritage, of external culture, and of the technique of life. (Simmel 1950, 409)

Streets as public spaces are potential domains for democracy and acceptance, but they can also serve as enclaves for minorities, especially in cosmopolitan cities. People are often territorial about space, noticing and disliking the presence of strangers who look, act or talk differently. The 'stranger' was discussed by Georg Simmel, who argued that interaction with strangers can sometimes escalate into hatred. This can be avoided through the creation of 'plate-armour': the rational, emotionless perception of others (Simmel 1908). Similarly, Sharon Zukin et al. point out that, despite social interactions being catalysts for generating the unique identities of certain streets, they sometimes facilitate social conflict; people self-defined by ethnicity, religion or sexual orientation mobilise to acquire collective resources and communal territories. They search for an urban refuge in which their lived practices can be maintained despite being in environments that are sometimes unjust or discriminatory (2016, 6–10). Manuel Castells defined emerging minority areas in cities as responsive, democratic and meaningful: responsive because such areas developed based on users' needs; democratic because they are accessible to anyone; and meaningful because they allow their users to create connections between their personal lives and the populated spaces of the wider city (1985, 160–260).

Spaces as socially constructed constitute a foundational assumption of this study. The seminal voice here is Henri Lefebvre, who claimed that every society produces its own space; this space is critical for transforming abstract ideologies into vibrant physical realities, which change in relation to the political, economic and cultural milieu (1974, 48). The formulation of social space, according to Michael Frisch, has always been a socio-political instrument charac-terised by dichotomous ideological structures: order and disorder, public and private, production and reproduction. These juxtapositions sometimes lead to oppressive relationships based on assumptions of heteronormativity and binary gender (2002, 263).

LGBTQ+ enclaves resemble other kinds of minority enclaves. Ann Forsyth explains how scholars have used the quasi-ethnic community model to analyse LGBTQ+ enclaves in terms of residential and commercial structures. There are copious historical similar-ities between both types of enclaves: shared norms, the presence of primary social groups within the population, and isolation from wider society (2001, 38–62). Similarly, Suzanne Hall notes that global economic forces have not only propelled immigrants into cities but have also resulted in polarised urban landscapes between residents and newcomers (2012, 4). The work of Forsyth and Hall supports the ideas in this chapter with regard to the 'push-and-pull' forces between the minority enclaves of Lange Reihe and Steindamm, which are both growing in size and gaining greater recognition across Hamburg.

St Georg: from ghetto to cherished neighbourhood

> It seems as if the people of Hamburg have banished to St. Georg everything that they were unwilling or unable to place in the city. (Heß 1811)

Both Lange Reihe and Steindamm are located in the neighbourhood of St Georg, which has undergone many changes since the twelfth century. The now-famous district, spanning 1.8 km2, is inhabited by

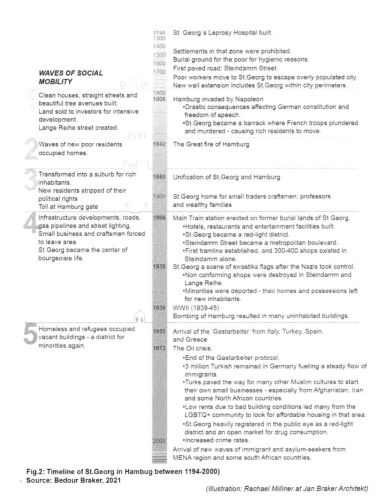

WAVES OF SOCIAL
MOBILITY

1194	St. Georg's Leprosy Hospital built.
1300	
1400	
1500	Settlements in that zone were prohibited.
1600	Burial ground for the poor for hygienic reasons.
1700	First paved road; Steindamm Street.
	Poor workers move to St.Georg to escape overly populated city.
	New wall extension includes St.Georg within city perimeters.
1800	
1806	Hamburg invaded by Napoleon
	•Drastic consequences affecting German constitution and freedom of speech.
	•St.Georg became a barrack where French troops plundered and murdered - causing rich residents to move.
1842	The Great fire of Hamburg
1860	Unification of St.Georg and Hamburg
1900	St.Georg home for small traders craftsmen, professors and wealthy families
1906	Main Train station erected on former burial lands of St Georg.
	•Hotels, restaurants and entertainment facilities built.
	•St Georg became a red-light district.
	•Steindamm Street became a metropolitan boulevard.
	•First tramline established, and 300-400 shops existed in Steindamm alone.
1938	St.Georg a scene of swastika flags after the Nazis took control.
	•Non conforming shops were destroyed in Steindamm and Lange Reihe.
	•Minorities were deported - their homes and possessions left for new inhabitants.
1939	WWII (1939-45)
	Bombing of Hamburg resulted in many uninhabited buildings.
1955	Arrival of the 'Gastarbeiter' from Italy, Turkey, Spain, and Greece
1973	The Oil crisis.
	•End of the Gastarbeiter protocol.
	•3 million Turkish remained in Germany fuelling a steady flow of immigrants.
	•Turks paved the way for many other Muslim cultures to start their own small businesses - especially from Afghanistan, Iran and some North African countries.
	•Low rents due to bad building conditions led many from the LGBTQ+ community to look for affordable housing in that area.
	•St.Georg heavily registered in the public eye as a red-light district and an open market for drug consumption.
	•Increased crime rates.
2000	Arrival of new waves of immigrant and asylum-seekers from MENA region and some south African countries.

1 Clean houses, straight streets and beautiful tree avenues built. Land sold to investors for intensive development. Lange Reihe street created.

2 Waves of new poor residents occupied homes.

3 Transformed into a suburb for rich inhabitants. New residents stripped of their political rights Toll at Hamburg gate

4 Infrastructure developments; roads, gas pipelines and street lighting. Small business and craftsmen forced to leave area. St Georg became the center of bourgeoisie life.

5 Homeless and refugees occupied vacant buildings - a district for minorities again.

Fig.2: Timeline of St.Georg in Hambug between 1194-2000)
Source: Bedour Braker, 2021

(Illustration: Rachael Milliner at Jan Braker Architekt)

Figure 4.2: Timeline of the historical development of St Georg between 1194 and 2000. Illustration: Rachael Milliner. © Jan Braker Architekt

11,358 inhabitants of various nationalities and cultural backgrounds.[1] St Georg has been a refuge for outcast minorities since its establishment, witnessing several waves of demographic change in its social fabric. Figure 4.2 summarises the main historical and social milestones that have shaped the district as we know it today.

The religious diversity of St Georg was always appealing to ethnic minorities, represented in the Evangelical Lutheran Trinity Church, the Catholic St Mary's Cathedral, the Cathedral Church of the Archdiocese, the Centrum Mosque, and the Metropolitan Community Church (the first church in Germany explicitly aimed at gays and lesbians) (Möhring 1995).

In addition to its religious side, St Georg is also an attractive cultural hub in the middle of Hamburg. As you walk onto Steindamm from the direction of the train station, you see the Savoy, an international cinema, the Hansa, a theatre that dates back to 1878, and the famous Politt theatre, a political cabaret built in the 1940s (Streb 2018). St Georg was heavily bombed during WWII, meaning it hosted many urban experiments in the 1960s. This reconstruction is why St Georg is now home to such varied architectural styles.

Another feature contributing to the character of St Georg is its proximity to Hamburg's main train station. As in many other European cities, Hamburg's red-light district is close to the main train station, with sex workers serving visitors to the city (Brown 2008, 131–2; Independent 2006). St Georg became a famous red-light district in the 1980s, known for its relatively open drug market. During this era, drugs were easy to get hold of. Consequently, many sex workers opted to work in St Georg to finance their drug use, contributing to increased crime rates (Ulrich 2001; Welt 2012). The ensuing chaos prompted the majority of St Georg residents to demand the eviction of sex workers from the street, prompting the district to become one of the most heavily policed neighbourhoods in Europe (Friederichs 2014). Rents were low due to the poor condition of local buildings, and members of the LGBTQ+ community began to move in, especially to Lange Reihe (Kalisch 2018).

One of the major milestones in forming the social character of St Georg was the 'Gastarbeiter' protocol initiated by Germany in 1955 to rebuild its economy. This protocol led to the hiring of immigrants from Italy, Turkey, Spain and Greece, most of whom settled in St Georg due to the low rents and local labour-intensive industries. Following the oil crisis in 1973, Germany terminated the programme – but three million people remained, fuelling a steady flow of immigrants mostly from Turkey (Knight 2017). Newcomers slowly established their own food retail and gastronomy trades in places like St Georg, where rents remained affordable. This demographic shift was observed by the German majority, described in the media as a process of replacing German companies with Turkish immigrants (Möhring 1995). The integration of immigrants was also perceived as a failure due to their retention of the Turkish language and the religious solidarity of Islam

(Hall 2012, 3). In time, the Turks paved the way for other Muslim groups – in the 1970s, mainly Afghans, Iranians and some Arabs – to migrate to Germany and start their own small businesses (Spiegel 2008).

The demographic profile of St Georg shifted again during the wave of wars in the MENA region during the 2010s, with a large number of asylum seekers arriving in Germany. Almost 1.6 million refugees were registered in Germany between 2015 and 2018, including approximately 60,000 LGBTQ+ individuals from the MENA region (Woldin 2016). As in the 1960s, this wave of newcomers increased fear and suspicion throughout German society of the growing number of immigrants from Muslim countries and their relatively conservative beliefs (Friederichs 2014; Woldin 2016).

Steindamm: a patriarchal enclave

> Steindamm is grey and dull. It doesn't feel welcoming, and I always try to get out of there really fast. It feels strange to me, because I always like travelling to places and getting lost in streets of other exotic places, but Steindamm feels weird to me. (Interview 2021; German resident, straight female)

The space of Steindamm

Steindamm is a city street with a chaotic four-lane layout, packed pavement, and litter scattered about. It is characterised by copious Middle Eastern eateries and convenience shops, offering a colourful range of commodities. The destruction of the north-eastern part of Steindamm during WWII led to its reconstruction as a mixed residential and commercial street. It was later widened into a four-lane 'office mile', marked by car traffic and dominated by modern high-rise buildings with 12 listed houses dating back to the nineteenth century (Hamburg Authority for Culture 2013). Since the 1950s, immigrants have convened in Steindamm to enhance their economic, social, political and cultural prospects. This tendency for newcomers to form localised communities and open ethnically specific businesses demonstrates their urgent need for a psychological and spatial buffer from the pressure of discrimination within the dominant German culture (Jiang 2018). St Georg's central mosque serves as a cushion from cultural clash, providing Muslim newcomers with a sense of security by strengthening their local religious ties (of the 43 registered mosques in Hamburg, 17 are in St Georg) (Streb 2018, 9). However, since the 1970s, the street's religious profile has not negated its reputation as a sex hub (Spiegel 2008).

The signage of Steindamm's shops constitutes an important element of its streetscape. Its walls offer canvases in various non-German languages. Its shopping windows are full of traditional MENA garments, and its sidewalks feature colourful displays of fruits and vegetables (Figures 4.3 and 4.4). As you approach the main station, the scenery begins to change, with sex shops and sex workers standing discreetly on street corners. This vibrancy belies some of the interviewees' description of Steindamm as 'grey and dull', suggesting that Steindamm's reputation as a conservative enclave colours people's perceptions of it.

The disorderliness of Steindamm – with its packed sidewalks, lack of delivery areas and unstructured footpaths – led the State Authority for Roads, Bridges and Water to develop public-realm plans in 2019. Steindamm was reconfigured in 2020 with two lanes in each direction, separated by 47 trees (Figure 4.5). Parking spaces were rearranged and cycle paths were expanded to boost traffic safety (Streb 2020, 2) and encourage people to walk and cycle rather than drive, hoping, in turn, to reduce social segregation. It is worth mentioning, however, that cyclists are still uncommon in Steindamm.

Figure 4.3: The urban character of Steindamm Street. © Bedour Braker 2020

Figure 4.4: Signage canvas overrules in Steindamm street. © Bedour Braker, 2020

Figure 4.5: State's visualisation of the renewal plan for Steindamm in 2019. Source: © BBS Landscape Engineering GmbH, commissioned by Der Landesbetrieb Straßen, Brücken und Gewässer. Accessed 1 November 2022. https://www.argus-hh.de/aktuelles/der-steindamm-wird-zur-allee/

The people of Steindamm

> You don't feel welcomed as a European with certain features. You get this wave of aggressive visual contact from the Steindamm people. (Interview 2021; German resident, straight male)

Steindamm is a space that reveals the socio-cultural diversification of Hamburg. It provides a palpable presence of several waves of social mobility through intersections of class, race and ethnicity. One German man expressed his changing perception of Steindamm as follows:

> To me, Steindamm feels a bit like a little Istanbul in the middle of Hamburg. There are a lot of immigrant faces, lots of oriental restaurants, and halal meat butchers. In the past, it was actually more [of a mix] of Germans and Turks right after the waves of the Gastarbeiter. Now, it is slowly becoming more concentrated with immigrants than with Germans. (Interview 2021; German resident, straight male)

> In the past, Steindamm used to feel different. It was a street with a Turkish flair like many other streets in Hamburg – nothing so special about it. After the 2015 waves of Arab and African refugees, the street changed dramatically. Now it doesn't feel as safe as before, with all the African drug addicts and the Arab attitudes in the streets that are totally different to the nature of German manners. Also, in the past, drugs and prostitution were a little bit discreet; now, it feels more in your face. (Interview 2021; Egyptian immigrant, straight female)

Many of the interviewed immigrants also expressed a fear of discrimination from Germans – an emotion that may serve as a catalyst behind the creation of ethno-religious enclaves. One gay Arab man expressed discomfort at being associated with other Arabs, which leads to him being treated differently. His Arab identity makes him feel less safe than he would feel if he were a white German, in large part due to right-wing Germans who oppose the country's immigration policies. Most families living in these enclaves are reluctant to shed their traditional values. They stick strictly to their religious roots to preserve their distinct ethnic identities and inherited patriarchy. One woman described only going out with her male partner:

I only go there with my husband, but the people are friendly, and I can hear a lot of Arabic around me, so it feels like home. (Interview 2021; Egyptian immigrant, straight female)

Another woman expressed discomfort at living in Germany when asked if she feels integrated within German society:

No, I feel I need to go back home to Egypt. Here is never going to be home to me. (Interview 2021; Egyptian immigrant, straight female)

Thus, Steindamm may be perceived as a male-dominated space – one not well-suited for women – with facilities targeting male clientele. One interviewee had been verbally harassed by a group of young Arab men while sitting in a restaurant on Steindamm. She asserted that the men felt that they were protected from consequences in their environment:

The men behaved as if the space gave them some form of power. (Interview 2021; Egyptian immigrant in St Georg, straight female)

Such behaviour turns spaces into spaces of power, where some people exert their strength over other, more vulnerable people, and the rest remain silent. Acceptance of LGBTQ+ people in Steindamm is seemingly hindered by conservatives who actively ignore their existence within the local community. When asked if it is possible to create spaces that promote social integration between the LGBTQ+ community and Muslim immigrants, one interviewee responded:

I don't have any gay friends and I don't think I am keen on having any. I have my own reservations regarding them, but I also consider myself a moderate Muslim. (Interview 2021; Egyptian immigrant, straight female)

Another interviewee explained how his conservative circle perceives the LGBTQ+ in Hamburg:

There is a lot of rejection for the gay community within the Muslim community here in Hamburg. They can even become aggressive while talking about other gay members. (Interview 2021; Egyptian immigrant, straight male)

When immigrants reveal their LGBTQ+ sexuality, they are beaten, forced into traditional marriages or indefinitely expelled from the community. One of the Arab interviewees said:

> You need to act and walk in a specific way not to attract unnecessary attention. I heard of an Iraqi trans who got beaten by other Iraqis once they could recognise his origins and sexual transition. (Interview 2021; Yemeni immigrant, gay male)

However, Steindamm is also a place of belonging for some of those who use it. It is the main space where (mostly male) Muslims come every Friday with their children after weekly prayers to get together, exchange news, have a drink or do their weekly shopping. On Eid, after the month of Ramadan, families gather in Steindamm to greet each other while children wear new clothes and are rewarded with candies. For the majority of Muslim immigrants, it is a space that reminds them of home – a space where they can still practise their social traditions.

> Everyone comes wearing new festive outfits. The children as well are proud and happy to show themselves to their friends in their new clothes. They are also happy to get a lot of sweets that day. (Interview 2021; Egyptian immigrant, straight male)

On the other hand, Steindamm is also a restricting space for women and those in the LGBTQ+ community, as they feel that they always need to act, dress and talk in certain ways to avoid offending anybody or provoking conservative men. Walking down the street, one can observe two main elements that signify its conservative, unwelcoming character. The first is the fact that all women's garments on offer are very modest, aiming to cover women from head to toe – veils and burqas dominate store displays. The second consists of the clusters of young men standing at every corner, staring at people in the street while catcalling women who are not properly covered or men who they assume are gay or trans.

Lange Reihe: the 'be free' zone

On Lange Reihe (Figure 4.6), the phrase *frei sein* – be free – is everywhere. You can see it tagged as graffiti or posted on storefront signs. This one-kilometre-long street is considered to be a catwalk for

Figure 4.6: A general view of Lange Reihe Street. © Bedour Braker, 2020

the people of the LGBTQ+ community in St Georg, especially during the 'Christopher Street Day' parade, an annual celebration of LGBTQ+ rights. Galleries, small independent shops, cafes, bars, restaurants and gay sex shops line this pulsing street. Rainbow flags are predominant, and traffic lights feature pictograms of same-sex couples (Figures 4.7 and 4.8). Lange Reihe is a public space shaped by the identities of its inhabitants into a social enclave, constituting a space for protection and freedom – just like Steindamm for conservative Muslims.

The face of Lange Reihe has shifted across several waves of gentrification over the past 30 years. Being a distinct place, it has gradually become a tourist destination with economic opportunities for property developers and investors (ARUP 2021, 7). Over the past two decades, some of its listed buildings have been redeveloped and upgraded, and rents have increased. As a result, some longstanding tenants, despite being protected by law, were forced to move out. In fact, some investors intentionally sabotaged buildings to expedite this process. Old residents who could not afford the new rates were evicted, small businesses were terminated, and buildings with new modifications were automatically unlisted. Some of the commercial spaces on Lange Reihe did not survive these challenges of time and disappeared soon after their launch, mainly due to a combination of high rent and low demand for their products or services. Others succeeded and became street landmarks (Pfadt 2018, 6). Through constant urban renewal, layers of memory have been erased and many properties have become unaffordable to those in the LGBTQ+ community who originally shaped the nature and identity of Lange Reihe. Here is striking evidence of how gentrification succeeds, in many cases, in demolishing identities of old urban fabric, crushing small local businesses in the process (Tieg 2015). As noted by one Lange Reihe user, the aforementioned gentrification stopped the street from being the core location of gay identity that it once was:

> I don't really have the feeling it's a gay street anymore; I can see a mixture of visitors. But you can also see that gay couples feel relaxed to express their passion in the street and no one pays attention to them. (Interview 2021; Spanish immigrant, straight male)

Figure 4.7: Traffic light in Lange Reihe with same-sex pictograms. Photo Pharnyada Pakdeepatthapee. © Jan Braker Architekt

Figure 4.8: Annual Christopher Street parade in Lange Reihe Street.
© Bedour Braker, 2017

German authorities consider Lange Reihe to be one of the most influential streets in Hamburg (Müller 2010). Various plans and strategies have been proposed to retain it as a successful tourist attraction, including the listing of 34 of its buildings as monuments in the Department of Monument Protection Act (Building Cultural Heritage 2020). Lange Reihe was one of five main streets in Hamburg to undergo urban development plans in 2009 following residents' demands for traffic reduction (12,000 cars were using the street daily). The Authority of Urban Development and Environment proposed a 'communal-road' concept: a road space merged with sidewalks with almost all traffic signs removed (Müller 2010). Many residents rejected the idea, claiming that this would further increase rents. Some traders worried about what the removal of parking spaces would do to their businesses. In the end, the plan was called off (Mlo 2010).

While the redevelopment of Steindamm to counteract its chaos has been partially successful in improving social integration, Lange Reihe remains an enclave that excludes conservative groups. This may stem from the fact that state plans, instead of pursuing the social integration of both minority groups, focused on improving the public realm to make it more appealing to investors and international businesses.

> Lange Reihe is mainly visited by Europeans. You rarely see any Arabs there. My Arab friends even feel angry at Lange Reihe due to its reputation as a gay street. Also, they completely refuse to watch the annual Christopher Street parade. (Interview 2021; Egyptian immigrant in St Georg, straight female)

> My neighbour and friend is Lesbian. I think we need to learn how to understand, respect, and accept the other if we ever want to create safer spaces for all of us. (Interview 2021; Egyptian immigrant, straight female)

Lange Reihe is a place where queer people can publicly express their identities without fear of reprisal. Since the 1990s, German society has witnessed a positive social trend toward acceptance of the LGBTQ+ community, and homophobia is no longer accepted in public discourse (Shashkevich 2018). In 1949, 39 per cent of the German population considered homosexuality a disease; by 2019, 88 per cent believed that LGBTQ+ people should enjoy the same rights as heterosexual people (Könne 2018). However, according to the German magazine *Siegessäule* in 2018, many LGBTQ+ people still try to avoid public displays of their identity. Bastian Finke from MANEO, a gay anti-violence project, says: 'They adapt their behaviour to heteronormative expectations: no flashy clothes or nail polish, they control their body movement' (Donath 2018).

On Lange Reihe, however, one can see couples walking freely – hand in hand with same-sex partners – without being judged. Most of the LGBTQ+ interviewees perceive the street as a great space where they can relax and have a good meal, even those who avoid exposing their sexuality elsewhere in Hamburg (especially on Steindamm). When asked about his experience in Steindamm, one interviewee said:

> In Steindamm, I don't feel safe. Everyone looks, and you don't feel welcomed. (Interview 2021; Jordanian immigrant, gay male)

Signs and semiotics play an important role in shaping the public perception of Lange Reihe, like the Pride flag (Figure 4.9). One street user explained that they see Pride flags as a sign of safety:

The bars are the most attractive spaces in Lange Reihe. Once I see the pride flags hanging, I immediately let down my guard; it is when I feel safe to step in. (Interview 2021; Chinese immigrant, gay male)

To approach the Pride flag through semiotics is to recognise it as a signifier of connoted meanings that are deliberately produced, reproduced and applied in acts of communication between users. This interpretation of the Pride flag allows for an understanding of the arbitrary relationship between the sign and its meaning (Tchertov 2019, 10). Lange Reihe, in that sense, demonstrates how human experience and spatial orientation are reflected in the semiotic systems of its spatial configuration. As in Steindamm, where signs in a variety of languages welcome those whose mother tongue is not German, the Pride flag encodes factors that are both semantic and cultural, creating a sense of safety for users (Thiering 2015, 3–41).

Figure 4.9: Gnosa, the first cafe to welcome LGBTQ+ in Lange Reihe Street. Photo Pharnyada Pakdeepatthapee. © Jan Braker Architekt

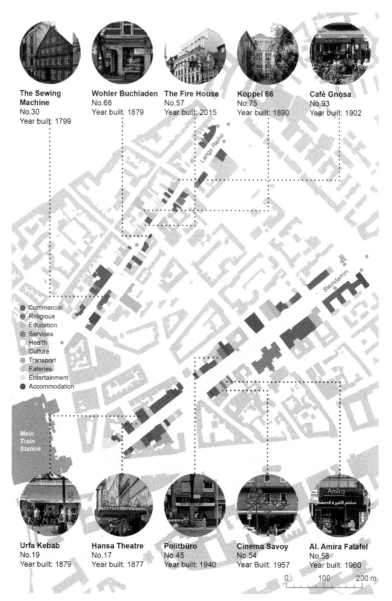

Figure 4.10: The usage of ground floor spaces in both streets.
Illustrations: Rachael Milliner; photos: Pharnyada Pakdeepatthapee.
© Jan Braker Architekt

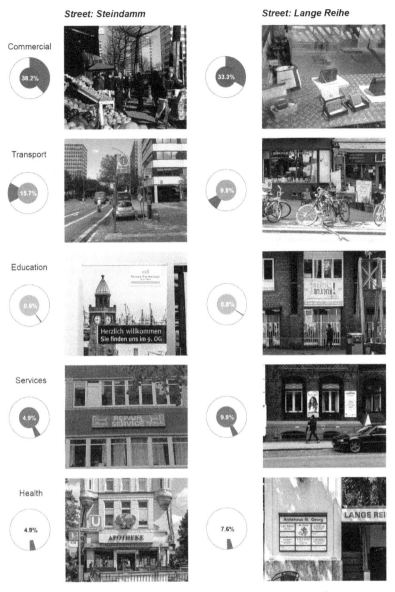

Figure 4.11: Usage diversity: left Steindamm, right Lange Reihe.
Illustrations: Rachael Milliner; photos: Pharnyada Pakdeepatthapee.
© Jan Braker Architekt

Figure 4.12: Distribution of uses on Staindham and Lange Reihe.
© Jan Braker Architekt

Two streets, two cultures

Lange Reihe is generally perceived as a good space that fulfils most human needs in a public place. In contrast, Steindamm is experienced as uncomfortable, unpleasant and unsafe. Figure 4.13 presents the survey results regarding the opinions and perceptions of people on both streets. The interviewees were asked to rate their impressions of both streets regarding accessibility, comfort, safety, pedestrian-friendliness, and atmosphere.

The surveys revealed a huge gap between policymakers and ordinary people who live or work on Lange Reihe or Steindamm. This is problematic, as decisions are frequently made on a top-down basis. Underprivileged users of both streets have been excluded from decision-making processes, making it hard for them to really call the streets their own. Evidently, it is important to consider how minorities can connect to systems of power and have their voices heard. When

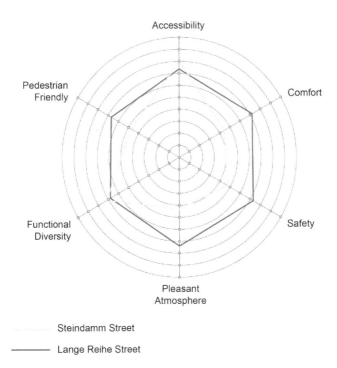

Survey Impressions, 2021

Steindamm Street

Lange Reihe Street

Figure 4.13: Survey Impressions 2021 Staindham and Lange Reihe. © Jan Braker Architekt

asked about what, in their opinion, would be the best way to initiate interactions without prejudice on both streets, most interviewees expressed doubts over the feasibility of such a pursuit due to cultural prejudice and conservative thinking. However, some suggested the creation of events that span different public spaces. It is only when people can acknowledge each other's experiences and perspectives that they can learn how to accept one another, regardless of religion or sexual orientation.

Conclusion

It is difficult for the minority communities of Lange Reihe and Steidamm to participate fully in the cultures of their streets. To understand the nuances of this topic, one must consider a multitude of aspects related to history, culture, religion and sexual orientation, which this chapter has attempted to do. St Georg has historically been a destination for the outcast, with multiple evolving dimensions to its mutable social mobility. The discussions that this research facilitated revealed some of the reasons why different minority groups do not feel welcomed in each other's enclaves. It was important to understand how users perceived both streets, as the everyday life of individual practices is what shapes their nature. Their enclaves may function well for them but may be misperceived by other groups and overlooked by those in power.

Both streets have experienced several socio-demographic shifts and urban gentrification, through which residents' needs have often been overlooked. Cultural and economic diversity on both streets led to crossovers between different identities under threat of dissipation due to rapid increases in land value. Rising land value inevitably attracts investors and urban planners to intervene without necessarily considering the street's identity, cultural heritage or underprivileged users.

To achieve a more inclusive future for streets like Lange Reihe and Steindamm – and to properly understand how the semiotics, social lives and patterns of urban movement occur across different minority enclaves – we must start tracing the social and urban developments of different minorities in cities like Hamburg. This chapter demonstrates, on a small scale, how these objectives could be achieved. We must also reinforce planning practices to generate street spaces that facilitate freedom of expression while respecting the life choices of all inhabitants.

Notes

1   Information taken from German Statistics, 2019.

Bibliography

ARUP. 2021. 'Queering Public Space: Exploring the relationship between queer communities and the public spaces'. University of Westminster. Accessed 1 November 2022. https://www.arup.com/perspectives/publications/research/section/queering-public-space.

Brown, Ron. 2008. *The Train Doesn't Stop Here Anymore: An illustrated history of railway stations in Canada*. Toronto: The Dundurn Group.

Castells, Manuel. 1985. *The City and the Grassroots*. Berkeley, CA: University of California Press.

Donath, Naomi. 2018. 'Stirn Bieten: Wie LGBTI+ mit gewalt im öffentlichen raum umgehen'. *Siegessaüle*.

Forsyth, Anne. 2001. 'Sexuality and Space: Nonconformist population and planning practice', *Journal of Planning Literature*: 38–62. Accessed 1 November 2022. https://www.researchgate.net/publication/245381173_Sexuality_and_Space_Nonconformist_Populations_and_Planning_Practice.

Friederichs, Hauke. 2014. 'Der traum vom schmuddelfreien bahnhofsviertel'. *Die Zeit*. Accessed 1 November 2022. https://www.zeit.de/hamburg/2014-04/hamburg-st-georg-drogen-prostitution-szeneviertel.

Frisch, Michael. 2002. 'Planning as a Heterosexual Project'. *Journal of Planning Education and Research* 21(254). Accessed 1 November 2022. https://www.researchgate.net/publication/238430139_Planning_as_a_Heterosexist_Project.

Hall, Suzanne. 2012. *City, Street and Citizen: The measures of the ordinary*. New York: Routledge.

Hamburg Behörde für Kultur und Medien. 2013. *Denkmalliste*. Accessed 1 November 2022. https://www.hamburg.de/contentblob/3947934/2a9ac6ab018818fc933c760e1ba24975/data/denkmalliste-hamburg-mitte.pdf.

Heß, Jonas Ludwig. 1811. *Hamburg topographisch, politisch und historisch*. Hamburg: Auf Kosten des Verfassers. Accessed 1 November 2022. https://www.zvab.com/buch-suchen/titel/hamburg-topographisch-politisch/autor/he%DF/.

Independent. 2006. 'A Brief History of Brothels'. Accessed 1 November 2022. https://www.independent.co.uk/news/uk/this-britain/a-brief-history-of-brothels-5336946.html#comments-area.

Jiang, Yi. 2018. *Signs in Urban Spaces in Ethnic Enclaves: A case study of Manhattan Chinatown*. Masters thesis, Columbia University. Accessed 1 November 2022. https://academiccommons.columbia.edu/doi/10.7916/D8MD0GH8.

Kalisch, Muriel. 2018. 'St Georg: Faszinierendes chaos'. *Szene Hamburg*. Accessed 1 November 2022. https://szene-hamburg.com/schlagwort/steindamm/.

Knight, Ben. 2017. 'Muslims "Integrate" Well into Germany but Aren't Accepted'. *DW*. Accessed 1 November 2022. https://www.infomigrants.net/en/post/4768/muslims-integrate-well-into-germany--but-arent-accepted#:~:text=Almost%20all%20of%20Germany's%20 4.7,t%20want%20Muslims%20as%20neighbors.&text=The%20study%20did%20not%20 cover%20Muslims%20who%20arrived%20after%202010.

Lefebvre, Henri. 1974. *The Production of Space*. Hoboken, NJ: Wiley-Blackwell.

Mlo. 2010. 'Geminschaftsstraße:Senat will straße für alle verkehrsteilnehmer'. *Shz.de*. Accessed 1 November 2022. https://www.shz.de/regionales/hamburg/meldungen/senat-will-strasse-fuer-alle-verkehrsteilnehmer-id2047686.html.

Möhring, Maren. 1995. 'Die türkische gastronomie in der bundesrepublik, Eine migrations- und konsumgeschichte'. *Heinrich Böll Stiftung*. Accessed 1 November 2022. https://heimatkunde.boell.de/de/2013/11/18/die-türkische-gastronomie-der-bundesrepublik-eine-migrations-und-konsumgeschichte.

Müller, Farid. 2010. 'Langereihe: Bürgerwollenverkehrsberuhigung'. Accessed 1 November 2022. https://www.farid-mueller.de/2010/10/lange-reihe-burger-wollen-verkehrsberuhigung/.

Pfadt, Andreas. 2018. 'Zur entwicklung der langen reihe'. *Blätter aus St. Georg.* Accessed 1 November 2022. https://buergerverein-stgeorg.de/wp-content/uploads/bsk-pdf-manager/2019/04/BV-2018-01.pdf.

Shashkevich, Alex. 2018. 'Stanford Scholar Explores the History of Gay Rights in Germany'. *Stanford.* Accessed 1 November 2022. https://news.stanford.edu/2018/12/29/east-germanys-lenient-laws-helped-unified-germany-become-gay-friendly/.

Simmel, Georg. 1908. 'The Stranger'. Accessed 1 November 2022. https://www.infoamerica.org/documentos_pdf/simmel01.pdf.

Spiegel. 2008. 'The High Price of Freedom: Honor killing victims wanted to live like other German girls'. *Der Spiegel.* Accessed 1 November 2022. https://www.spiegel.de/international/germany/the-high-price-of-freedom-honor-killing-victim-wanted-to-live-like-other-german-girls-a-555667.html.

Streb, Martin. 2018. 'Bürgerverein St. Georg'. *Blätter aus St.Georg.* Accessed 1 November 2022. http://buergerverein-stgeorg.de/wp-content/uploads/bsk-pdf-manager/2019/04/BV-2018-07.pdf.

Tchertov, Leonid. 2019. *Signs, Codes, Spaces, and Arts: Papers on general and spatial semiotics.* Cambridge: Cambridge Scholars Publishing.

Thiering. Martin. 2015. 'Spatial Semiotics and Spatial Mental Models: Figure-ground asymmetries in language'. *De Gryter Mouton.* Accessed 1 November 2022. https://www.researchgate.net/publication/308033761_Spatial_Semiotics_and_Spatial_Mental_Models_Figure-Ground_Asymmetries_in_Language.

Tieg, Alexander. 2015. 'Heisse spuren: Vor zehn jahren wurde in St. Georg ein haus angesteckt-heute gibt es dort luxuwohnungen'. *Die Zeit.* Accessed 1 November 2022. https://www.zeit.de/2015/09/brandstiftung-st-georg-luxuswohnungen-prozess.

Woldin, Philipp. 2016. 'Hier leben Muslime und stricher nebeneinander'. *Welt.* Accessed 1 November 2022. https://www.welt.de/regionales/hamburg/article157868743/Hier-leben-Muslime-und-Stricher-nebeneinander.html.

Zukin, Sharon, Philip Kasinitz and Xianming Chen. 2016. *Global Cities, Local Streets: Everyday diversity from New York to Shanghai.* New York: Routledge.

5

Streets after dark: the experiences of women, girls and gender-diverse people

Gill Matthewson, Nicole Kalms, Jess Berry and Gene Bawden

This chapter examines streets as an often-problematic space for women and gender-diverse people because of gendered percep-tions of safety. These perceptions profoundly impact the use of streets – especially at night – by women and gender-diverse people. The chapter uses the results of innovative crowd-sourced mapping surveys in Melbourne and Sydney to develop nuanced under-standings of safety perceptions and appropriate responses, such as gender-sensitive lighting and awareness campaigns.

Perceptions of street safety

This underpass is the most efficient way to get from the tram stop to the street. However, it's dark, has lots of menacing graffiti and is long and invisible to the street. If someone follows you in there, there's nothing you can do but keep running. (Transport hub St Kilda, Melbourne, female, age 40–44, Anytime, YourGround Victoria)

Never felt safe walking in this area, even if I am not alone. The lighting is terrible and the design of the walkways leaves a lot of spots hidden from view. (Central Station Sydney, female, age 19, Anytime, Free to Be Sydney)

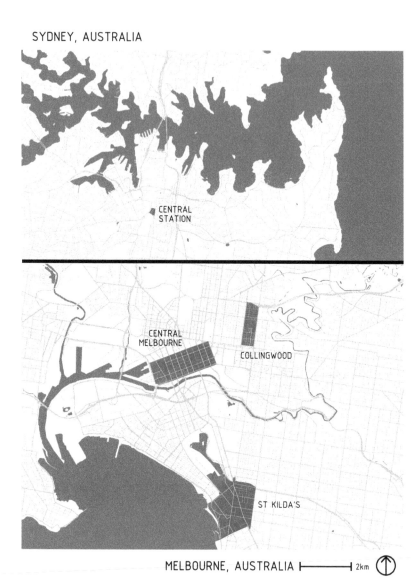

SYDNEY, AUSTRALIA

CENTRAL
STATION

CENTRAL
MELBOURNE

COLLINGWOOD

ST KILDA'S

MELBOURNE, AUSTRALIA |————————| 2km

Figure 5.0: Maps of Sydney and Melbourne © Anna Skoura

The degree to which people feel safe while traversing a city dictates their personal confidence, mobility decisions and engagement with the economic and social life of the city. Perceptions of safety are closely tied to sex and gender identity, with women and gender-diverse people feeling far less safe, especially at night (Lennox 2022, 643; Whitzman et al. 2013). The assertion that the *feeling* of safety is significant – beyond the mere objective safety of a space – is vital to understanding women's perception of safety in their communities (Pain 1991, 417). While 'objective' safety assessments make sense in terms of traffic and other public hazards, it is insufficient when it comes to perceptions of safety, as these arise from complex sociocultural factors.

Emphasising the role of gendered safety perceptions in spatial inequity, feminist academics and activists in recent decades have sought to both qualify and quantify women's perceptions of safety in the urban environment (Davidson et al. 2016; Pain 1991; Pain 1997; Valentine 1990). This chapter introduces crowd-sourced mapping surveys and aligned communication campaigns as a means of developing nuanced understandings of safety perceptions and appropriate responses. Using interactive mapping as a form of digital community engagement, the methods employed in this chapter give insight into women and gender-diverse people's after-dark experiences that are fairly new relative to traditional survey methods. While these surveys (Free to Be and YourGround) were mainly conducted in Australia, the insights that this study provides are relevant to cities across the world. The results can be used in numerous ways, such as improving lighting and informing community awareness campaigns.

The gendered urban environment

Gender bias and gender inequity produce a gendered world. There are two key consequences of this gendering that impact the access and inclusion of women in public spaces: gender bias in the production of the built environment, and gender-based violence. These consequences work together to reinforce social and economic inequities, leading to a lack of agency among women and gender-diverse people in influencing public space.

The urban environment has, for the most part, been designed by men to advance their own interests (Colomina 1992; Kern 2020). Despite the increasing number of women involved in professions pertaining to the built environment, city design and policy are largely dominated by male perspectives. One way this manifests can be found in how policies and designers imagine a 'default user'. As a result of unacknowledged gender bias, streets and public spaces in the West are geared toward a dominant user – often White, heterosexual, male, able-bodied and English-speaking. This professional bias intersects with many other forms of systemic inequality, including gender-based violence, which has profound implications for perceptions of safety.

Gender-based violence includes intimate partner violence, family violence and sexual violence, and it is responsible for more ill-health among Australian women aged 18–44 than any other public health issue (VicHealth 2017). The main type of gender-based violence that affects the presence of women and gender-diverse people in public spaces is sexual violence, which ranges from harassment to assault. While the impact of actual assaults may be clear, the ongoing threat of street-based sexual harassment is less acknowledged but nonetheless 'related to decreased levels of perceived safety in busy and isolated public spaces as well as increased levels of general anxiety' (Davidson et al. 2016, 558). This is partially due to the fact that women have no way of knowing what interactions could suddenly escalate into a serious situation. Overall, sexual harassment reminds women of their vulnerability to sexual assault and negatively influences how they perceive their own safety (Pain 1997, 300; Viswanath 2013, 81; Walklate 2018, 288). This fear of violence has social, physical, psychological and economic impacts on women and gender-diverse people (Lenton et al. 1999).

As Fatma El Nahry states, 'despite claims made by many men, harassment is not a harmless, direct reaction by men to women and gender-diverse people but an institutionalized system of violence that functions to police participation, freedom of movement and behaviour in public spaces' (cited in Levy 2019, 56). Importantly, the degree of this impact is shaped by various intersecting factors, including age, ethnicity, race, sexuality, ability, indigeneity, religion and socioeconomic status.

The level of vulnerability felt by individuals on the street is also dependent on numerous other factors, including whether they are alone or in a group, whether there are other people nearby and, crucially, the time of day (Plan International 2018a). An unwanted comment from an unknown man in a crowded place during the day is quite different from a similar comment made in a deserted street at night. Thus, even areas deemed 'safe' during the day become off-limits when darkness falls, suggesting a need to consider different strategies for improving public safety after dark.

I always correlate darkness with bad stuff happening. Even the places that I like, I probably wouldn't go there late at night. (Comment, Free to Be Sydney Reflection Workshop)

Among women and gender-diverse people, late-night employment and leisurely nights out can be seriously curtailed by the perception that going out at night is riskier. In Australia, 50 per cent of women do not feel safe walking alone at night, a figure far higher than that of 20 per cent among men (Community Council for Australia 2019, 32). Another study found that a third of the young female respondents believed that they should never be in public spaces at night *at all* (Plan International Australia 2016, 3).

The sociocultural mythology that 'bad things happen at night' looms large and cannot be underestimated (Mason et al. 2013; Viswanath 2013, 81). Women and girls learn about cities and are groomed into trepidation by shows, movies and news stories that highlight their vulnerability in cities at night. While there is a dearth of research on the experiences of gender-diverse people, we can predict, based on the limited research that does exist, that their experiences are at least equally as pervasive (Hubbard 2005; Williams 2008).

After dark, I don't want to leave [the] train station to catch [the] bus. I will catch [a] taxi from rank. I don't go [out] at night if I don't have to. (Suburban street in Frankston, Melbourne, gender-diverse, age 40–44, Night, YourGround)

This situation is further exacerbated by current and historical cultural norms that place the responsibility for their own safety on women and gender-diverse people, shifting culpability away from perpetrators (Lennox 2022, 643; Plan International 2018a; Viswanath 2013, 83). Women and gender-diverse people engage in a wide range of self-protective behaviours and hypervigilant practices, especially at night. Such practices include dressing in ways that avoid attracting attention, talking on a mobile phone with friends or family members, having their keys in hand, and avoiding certain locations, such as car parks, underpasses and parks (Valentine 1992; Vera-Grey and Kelly 2020). Women are advised to routinely undertake 'safety work' to mitigate risk: walk confidently, stay in well-lit areas, keep your hands free, don't take shortcuts and remain 'situationally aware' (Boomsma and Steg 2014; Vera-Gray and Kelly 2020). Women and gender-diverse people employ all these strategies (and more) to keep themselves safe from male sexual violence and harassment in cities after dark. This daily burden has an ongoing debilitating impact on their ability to engage in public spaces and enjoy public amenities and employment.

The strategies contribute to the complex gendering of responsibility, which fosters a culture of fear and alienation that radically limits women's ability to participate actively and freely in urban nightlife (Preez and Wadds 2016). For those who do not have the economic and social capital to undertake avoidance strategies – such as taking taxis to avoid public transportation – there are extra risks (Lennox 2022).

These types of safety measures show how women restrict their movement and adopt bodily strategies as mechanisms to negotiate public space. On the streets, women and gender-diverse people implicitly understand that they must strike a balance between freedom and safety (Vera-Gray 2021). Part of that negotiation entails continuously reading the environment and calculating risk, and what results are places where specific, minoritised groups may be reluctant to walk, exercise, play and connect.

Mapping the impact: crowd-sourced mapping of safety perceptions

Because of the complexities associated with perceptions of safety, each woman or gender-diverse person has their own personal geography of their city: places they will and won't go. Crowd-sourced mapping is able to delve into this complexity. The management of complex personal urban geographies at night is a recurring theme of a series of projects undertaken by Monash University's XYX Lab and CrowdSpot (a social engagement and tech platform) in collaboration with local and state government authorities and organisations. Free to Be and YourGround (Figure 5.1) are collaborative online mapping surveys that ask women, girls and gender-diverse people to identify and share information about what makes them feel uneasy and at ease – unsafe and safe – in their city.

Crowd-sourced mapping actively encourages participatory ways of thinking about public space. It aims to reduce the barriers to engagement for women and gender-diverse people through interactive, visual and intuitive means. This technique is particularly useful for illuminating stories and issues from people whose voices are not always heard in traditional fora. Sharing experiences on digital platforms connects, empowers and supports women and gender-diverse people; it wields enormous potential to affect positive change, especially for

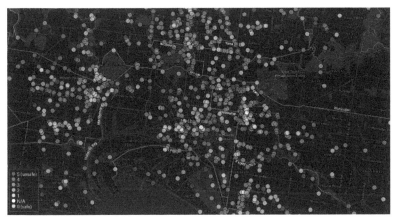

Figure 5.1: 'Stress' map of Melbourne (green spots are safe; pink are unsafe. The darker the pink spot, the more stressful it is). © CrowdSpot 2021; Monash University XYX Lab

minoritised communities increasingly using digital technology to expedite change (Kalms 2017). The #MeToo movement is a strong example of this potential, as is Safetipin, an ongoing project to collect data on women's safety (Viswanath and Basu 2015). It uses geolocation mapping like Free to Be and YourGround, but it is ongoing rather than a time-limited survey.

The mapping survey approach can democratise the research process by providing autonomy and power to a wide range of participants, as well as drawing upon a wider range of participants – therefore breaking down structural barriers, such as class and race. Women and gender-diverse people participating and sharing their experiences online effectively serves to challenge dominant narratives. Importantly, crowd-sourced mapping provides anonymity and safety to women and gender-diverse people who wish to disclose instances of gender-based violence but fear reprisals from other methods of disclosure and who avoid the traditional justice system in terms of reporting.

The impact: insights from Sydney and Melbourne

The suite of projects drawn on in this chapter stems from significant collaboration. The collaborative partnership model has benefits for strategic communication, and the insights derived from site-specific surveys can be used to inform community awareness campaigns and dialogue by focusing attention on narratives of gender that influence how public spaces are accessed and occupied. Free to Be Melbourne in 2016 and Free to Be Sydney in 2018 (alongside four other cities) in collaboration with Plan International explicitly sought to capture street-based sexual harassment of young women (Plan International 2018a; Plan International 2018b). The findings were supplemented by reflection and co-design workshops held in each city with young women, stakeholders and advocates. In 2021, YourGround – in collaboration with local and state governments in Victoria, Australia – aimed to elicit information on aspects of the built environment that influence perceptions of safety among women and gender-diverse people.

> I pass through here twice a day to get to work and am routinely verbally abused by men. I feel unsafe and would never go through here at night. I wish the police or government would listen to women's stories and do something about this place. (Park near Central Station, female, age 25, Anytime, Free to Be Sydney)

In Sydney, sexual harassment and violence constituted the primary reason why the young women surveyed felt unsafe in public spaces (Plan International 2018b). This result is very similar to those in the four other cities surveyed in the 2018 Free to Be project – Delhi, Kampala, Lima and Madrid (Plan International 2018a). In Sydney, following an incident, nearly half of the respondents avoided going back to a location alone; 12 per cent never returned, and 1 per cent even moved house, left a job or changed school. Even after just a single unsafe experience, women's behaviour can change for their lifetime, including avoiding the particular location.

Incidents in Sydney were so ubiquitous that young women were resigned to their occurrence. Thirty-six per cent of the 2,700 participants said that they were 'used to' incidents, viewing them as a normal part of navigating streets in their community. This tolerance of sexual harassment and violence – due to recurrence – is part of the gendered world that movements like #MeToo and these surveys aim to change.

Further analysis of the Free to Be Sydney data revealed an increased incidence of sexual harassment during the hours of darkness, particularly among those who were in the city for recreational purposes but also for those who were travelling to and from work during these hours (Committee for Sydney 2019, 6). Moreover, most women participating in the survey expected it to occur at night and were even used to it.

While sexual harassment committed by men was the dominant driving force behind the negative perceptions of safety on the streets of Melbourne and Sydney among women and gender-diverse people, environmental qualities also played a strong role. Participants described being wary of areas that are dark, poorly maintained and deserted, especially those that provide opportunities for perpetrators to hide or entrap. Such spaces are described by other research showing that stairs, tunnels, underpasses, poorly lit streets and alleyways contain physical properties of urban space that increase the potential of attackers to go unseen (Koskela and Pain 2000).

> This area feels so dodgy. The level light means you can't see who is approaching you. (Street near Flinders Street Station, female, age 39, Night, Free to Be Melbourne)

As a consequence, women and gender-diverse people learn to 'read' both the physical and social aspects of a public space for risk, believing that certain environmental elements indicate the potential for threatening behaviour. Adding to the complexity, individual risk perceptions are shaped by both personal experiences and identity factors, such as age, ethnicity, religion and socioeconomic status. Thus, women and gender-diverse people have varied and sometimes divergent experiences of public spaces.

One of the aims of the YourGround Victoria research project in 2021 was to elicit more detail about the environmental elements that influence safety perceptions. The survey received 6,043 submissions from women and gender-diverse people of all ages, though nearly half of the participants were between 30 and 44. Just 18 per cent of the locations pinned on the map were identified as 'safe', though nearly a fifth of these designations were qualified, often with a note about how they are only safe during daylight hours. Streets were the most commonly pinned location type – and just 8 per cent of street pins were identified as safe places. Eighty-five per cent of these streets were identified as unsafe at any time of day, night or dawn/dusk. Parks and green spaces attracted markedly more 'safe' designations – 32 per cent – than streets. While 15 per cent of respondents stated that they would not return to a place after having an unsafe experience, 7 per cent indicated that they had no choice but to continue using that particular street or location. The survey allowed respondents to record their stress level in the location; among all of the location types, underpasses recorded the highest levels of stress.

The alleys around this area have people drinking and being loud and obnoxious. They are usually minding their own business, but do stare a lot. I feel at any time 'the pack' could turn against me and I'll need to run. (Urban street Collingwood, Melbourne, female, age 30–34, Dawn/dusk, YourGround)

One of the key findings of the survey was that activity type and location type (street, park, public transport, and the like) made a difference in perceptions of safety (XYX Lab and CrowdSpot 2021). For example, dog walkers felt safer than leisure walkers in parks at night. Runners and dog walkers both had concerns about lighting at the beginning and end of a standard 9–5 workday during winter (when these hours are dark). Those who need or want to exercise on a daily basis often need to do so in the dark, so the lack of lighting is strongly felt. Fifty-seven per cent of respondents said that poor lighting was a concern when moving through their communities; this was fairly consistent across all groups (XYX Lab and CrowdSpot 2021).

YourGround participants were asked what might be done to improve the safety of an area; unsurprisingly, better lighting was the overwhelming answer (XYX Lab and CrowdSpot 2021, 16). This was often phrased as 'more' lighting; however, many participants also commented that over-lighting a space was not always the right solution, in terms of both their own safety and the natural amenity of an area. This observation that 'good' lighting does not necessarily mean 'more' lighting has also arisen from other XYX Lab research.

A 2018 collaboration between Plan International, Monash University's XYX Lab and Arup saw lighting researchers analyse 80 of the most safe and unsafe 'hotspots' identified by young women in the Free to Be Melbourne project (Arup 2019; Kalms 2019). The analysis suggested that high illuminance in urban lighting did not create positive perceptions of safety among women and gender-diverse people navigating city streets after dark. In fact, the places deemed 'unsafe' by women in the Melbourne study were, on average, four times more luminous than those designed as 'safe'. Thus, the solution is not necessarily more or brighter light, but careful lighting design that enhances the area rather than floodlighting it. This research provides a foundation for planners and urban designers who often invest in extra lighting due to a belief that bright lighting will automatically increase feelings of safety. In reality, lighting streets to create positive and inclusive urban experiences for women requires a more nuanced approach. This finding has shaped recommendations regarding lighting to enhance urban safety and crime prevention in Melbourne (Community Crime Prevention 2020).

> There is lighting all the way along the whole path but, on a regular basis, only half of the lighting is activated. It leaves the area feeling very unsafe and scary. (Beachfront Geelong, female, age 50–54, Dawn/dusk, YourGround Victoria)

In addition, YourGround emphasised that safety is not just about feeling safe from potential violence; it is also about feeling welcome in an area due to amenities designed for and with local women and gender-diverse people. Well-designed environmental elements targeted to women help to attract people to an area and so activate the area, increasing the sense of safety through positive passive surveillance. Positive amenities noted by participants include public toilets (especially family-friendly ones), play equipment, seats and resting places. Additionally, all infrastructure – including lighting infrastructure – must be well maintained to ensure positive perceptions of safety.

> This is a good size recreation ground with paths around. It is well maintained and just about always has people around it, so it feels safe. The street lights help keep the whole area lit at night. The sports building looks good and has a good car parking area as well. (Sporting park, Tarneit, female, age 45–49, Anytime, YourGround)

It is clear from the surveys that enhancing safety perceptions among women and gender-diverse people requires a fundamental shift in approach. One way to achieve this shift is to listen to women and gender-diverse people, incorporating their views, experiences and expertise into urban strategies and policies. In addition to providing designers with insights regarding the spatial conditions that can impact feelings of safety in particular urban environments, crowd-sourced mapping surveys can be used to amplify the voices and experiences of those left out of formal consultation processes, allowing their perspectives to be recognised in the broader community through awareness campaigns.

An example of this type of awareness campaign was drawn from the compelling narratives and data brought to light by YourGround. Through a series of poster and billboard interventions throughout greater Melbourne, women and gender-diverse people's experiences

Figure 5.2: Gene Bawden, Monash University XYX Lab, 2021–2, 'Keep Running'. Photo: Brett Brown. © Monash University XYX Lab

of navigating urban spaces were made visible to the public. 'Keep Running' (XYX Lab 2021; Figures 5.2–5.5) used dynamic graphics to re-insert YourGround research into public spaces. In highlighting the types of spatial conditions that can cultivate fear as well as those that can facilitate feelings of safety, the project prompted dialogue about women and gender diverse people's right to access public space.

Figure 5.3: Gene Bawden, Monash University XYX Lab, 2021–2, 'Keep Running'. Photo: Brett Brown. © Monash University XYX Lab

Figure 5.4: Gene Bawden, Monash University XYX Lab, 2021–22, 'Keep Running'. Photo: Brett Brown. © Monash University XYX Lab

Figure 5.5: Gene Bawden, Monash University XYX Lab, 2021–22, 'Keep Running'. Photo: Brett Brown. © Monash University XYX Lab

Conclusion

Whether someone steps out onto the streets and takes advantage of their city's potential largely depends on how safe they feel on those streets. Concerns over personal safety in public space are pervasive among women and gender-diverse people, especially at night. Individual perceptions of safety alter behaviour; for many, navigating their local community is complex, requiring the avoidance of certain places and at certain times. This forced strategic navigation restricts the access of women and gender-diverse people to employment, services and entertainment, significantly impacting their long-term health and well-being.

While the behaviour of unpredictable people is unquestionably a key factor in places feeling unsafe, the environmental and physical factors of streets and public spaces strongly contribute to perceptions of safety among women and gender-diverse people. In particular, poor lighting and spaces that feel entrapping are problematic. Surfacing the realities of women and gender-diverse people's experiences in streets and public spaces through crowd-sourced mapping surveys provides fine-grained information that can inform better design policy decisions. While changing design processes to include gender-sensitive approaches would undoubtedly lead to better experiences for women, evidence suggests that cities that address the needs of women end up benefiting universally. In addition, the awareness campaigns drawn from the finding of these surveys provide a call to action for communities to develop an understanding of safety and risk in public spaces that moves beyond simplistic advice to women to avoid these spaces at night.

Bibliography

Arup. 2019. 'Lighting the Way for Women and Girls: A new narrative for lighting design in cities'. Accessed 1 November 2022. https://www.arup.com/perspectives/lighting-the-way-for-women-and-girls-a-new-narrative-for-lighting-design-in-cities.

Boomsma, Christine and Linda Steg. 2014. 'Feeling Safe in the Dark: Examining the effect of entrapment, lighting levels, and gender on feelings of safety and lighting policy acceptability', *Environment and Behavior* 46(2): 193–212.

Colomina, Beatriz (ed.). 1992. *Sexuality and Space*. New York: Princeton Architectural Press.

Committee for Sydney. 2019. *Safety after Dark: Creating a city for women living and working in Sydney*.

Community Council for Australia. 2019. *The Australia We Want: Second report*. Accessed 1 November 2022. https://www.communitycouncil.com.au/sites/default/files/Australia-we-want-Second-Report_ONLINE.pdf.

Community Crime Prevention. 2020. *Designing Better Lighting: Fact sheet*. Victorian State Government. Accessed 1 November 2022. https://files.crimeprevention.vic.gov.au/2021-05/Fact%20sheet%20Designing%20better%20lighting.pdf.

Davidson, M. Meghan, Michael S. Butchko, Krista Robbins, Lindsey W. Sherd and Sarah J. Gervais. 2016. 'The Mediating Role of Perceived Safety on Street Harassment and Anxiety', *Psychology of Violence* 6(4): 553–61.

Hubbard, Phil. 2005. 'The Geographies of "Going Out": Emotion and embodiment in the evening economy'. In *Emotional Geographies*, edited by Joyce Davidson, Liz Bondi and Mick Smith, 117–34. Farnham: Ashgate.

Kalms, Nicole. 2017. 'Digital Technology and the Safety of Women and Girls in Urban Space: Personal safety apps or crowd-sourced activism tools?'. In *Architecture and Feminisms: Ecologies, economies, technologies*, edited by Hélène Frichot, Catharina Gabrielsson and Helen Runting, 112–21. Abingdon: Routledge.

Kalms, Nicole. 2019. 'More Lighting Alone Does Not Create Safer Cities. Look at what research with young women tells us'. *The Conversation,* 28 May. Accessed 1 November 2022. https://theconversation.com/more-lighting-alone-does-not-create-safer-cities-look-at-what-research-with-young-women-tells-us-113359.

Kern, Leslie. 2020. *Feminist City Claiming: Space in a man-made world*. London: Verso.

Koskela, Hille and Rachel Pain. 2000. 'Revisiting Fear and Place: Women's fear of attack in the built environment', *Geoforum* 31(2): 269–80.

Lennox, Rebecca A. 2022. 'There's Girls Who Can Fight and there's Girls Who Are Innocent: Gendered safekeeping as virtue maintenance work', *Violence Against Women* 28(2): 641–63.

Lenton, Rhonda, Michael D. Smith, John Fox and Norman Morra. 1999. 'Sexual Harassment in Public Places: Experiences of Canadian women', *Canadian Journal of Anthropology* 36(4): 517–40.

Levy, Caren. 2019. 'Travel Choice Reframed: "Deep distribution" and gender in urban transport'. In *Integrating Gender into Transport Planning: From one to many tracks*, edited by Christina Lindkvist Scholten and Tanja Joelsson, 43–65. London: Palgrave Macmillan.

Mason, Phil, Ade Kearns and Mark Livingston. 2013. '"Safe Going": The influence of crime rates and perceived crime and safety on walking in deprived neighbourhoods', *Social Science & Medicine* 91: 15–24.

Pain, Rachel. 1991. 'Space, Sexual Violence and Social Control: Integrating geographical and feminist analyses of women's fear of crime', *Progress in Human Geography* 15(4): 415–31.

Pain, Rachel. 1997. 'Whither Women's Fear? Perceptions of sexual violence in public and private space', *International Review of Victimology* 4: 297–312.

Plan International. 2018a. *Unsafe in the City: The everyday experiences of girls and young women*. Woking: Plan International. Accessed 1 November 2022. https://plan-international.org/unsafe-city.

Plan International. 2018b. *Free to be Sydney*. Woking: Plan International. Accessed 1 November 2022. https://plan-international.org/publications/free-to-be-country-reports#download-options.

Plan International Australia. 2016. *A Right to the Night. Australian girls on their safety in public places*. Woking: Plan International.

Preez, Leisha and Phillip Wadds. 2016. 'Gendered Responsibilisation in the Night Time Economy'. In *Cities and Successful Societies: Refereed proceedings of the Australian Sociological Association Conference*, pp. 62–68, Melbourne, 28 November – 1 December.

Valentine, Gill. 1990. 'Women's Fear and the Design of Public Spaces', *Built Environment* 16(4): 288–303.

Valentine, Gill. 1992. 'Images of Danger: Women's sources of information about the spatial distribution of male violence', *Arena* 24(1): 22–29.

Vera-Gray, Fiona. 2021. 'From Porn to True Crime Stories, We Must End the Portrayal of Violence Against Women', *The Guardian*, 16 March. Accessed 1 November 2022. https://www.theguardian.com/commentisfree/2021/mar/16/porn-true-crime-violence-against-women.

Vera-Gray, Fiona and Liz Kelly. 2020. 'Contested Gendered Space: Public sexual harassment and women's safety work', *International Journal of Comparative and applied Criminal Justice* 44(4): 265–75.

VicHealth. 2017. *Violence Against Women in Australia. An overview of research and approaches to primary prevention*. Melbourne: Victorian Health Promotion Foundation.

Viswanath, Kalpana. 2013. 'Gender Inclusive Cities Programme: Implementing change for women's safety'. In *Building Inclusive Cities: Women's safety and the right to the city*, edited by Carolyn Whitzman, Crystal Legacy, Caroline Andrew, Fran Klodawsky and Kalpana Viswanath, 75–89. London: Earthscan.

Viswanath, Kalpana and Ashish Basu. 2015. 'Safetipin: An innovative mobile app to collect data on women's safety in Indian cities', *Gender and development* 23(1): 45–60.

Walklate, Sandra. 2018. 'Reflections on Community Safety: The ongoing precarity of women's lives', *Crime Prevention and Community Safety* 20(4): 284–95.

Whitzman, Carolyn, Crystal Legacy, Caroline Andrew, Fran Klodawsky and Kalpana Viswanath. 2013. *Building Inclusive Cities: Women's safety and the right to the city*. London: Earthscan.

Williams, Robert. 2008. 'Night Spaces: Darkness, deterritorialization, and social control', *Space and Culture* 11(4): 514–32.

XYX Lab and CrowdSpot. 2021. *YourGround Victoria*. Melbourne: Monash University XYX Lab.

6

A tourist catwalk: the pedestrianisation of Rua das Portas de Santo Antão, Lisbon

Manuel João Ramos

The unassuming Rua das Portas de Santo Antão, in downtown Lisbon, was once the unlikely epicentre of the city. During the authoritarian regime of Estado Novo, it fell into progressive decline. Its partial pedestrianisation in 1994 didn't revive it but rather helped sanitise it and empty it to make way for an influx of international tourists. This chapter details the steps by which a central street ended up being touristified, and how the rehabilitation of its heritage, enabling walkability and liveability, failed to connect with its local dwellers. Its rich history is not the object of intense praise, official or otherwise, but rather is lived by its heteroclite users, thanks to recurring acts of ritual appropriation.

The transformation of Lisbon's centre

Universal motorisation arrived late to Portugal, and hence to its capital city, Lisbon. It was only when the country became a member of the then European Economic Community that car ownership became accessible for the majority of the population (Branco and Ramos 2003, 6–8). The city's street redesign shows clear marks of a traffic planning mindset that leans heavily toward favouring private car usage. Given the craggy, meandering character of Lisbon's older neighbourhoods, this policy resulted, during the 1980s and 1990s, in chaotic overlaps of driving and walking needs that greatly diminished its streets' liveability. The city is famed for its picturesque sandstone cobbled sidewalks – both the decorated type in the historic centre and the plain type in every artery of the city (Cabrera and Nunes 1998) – but walkability has

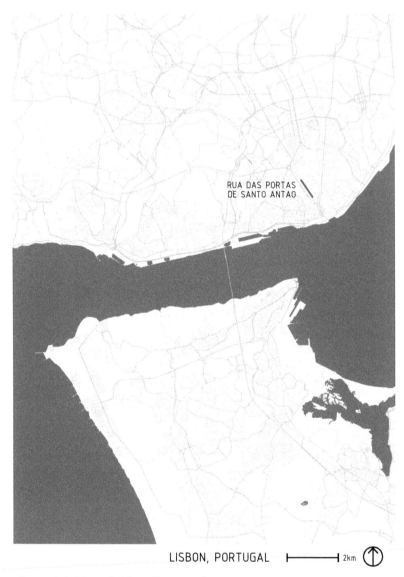

RUA DAS PORTAS
DE SANTO ANTAO

LISBON, PORTUGAL ├──────┤ 2km

Figure 6.0: Map of Lisbon © Anna Skoura

hardly been the prime goal of this infrastructure. This kind of paving, particularly in the hilly areas, although advantageous as it retains the soil's permeability, has always been contentious for being challenging to walk on and very slippery when it rains. The idea that Lisbon could be a walkable city was for many decades a very marginal one. Now, in the midst of an unprecedented tourist boom, the city council has embraced pedestrianisation, albeit for the most part targeting areas assigned for tourist development (Balsas Mendes 2021; Delgado 2007; Gehl 2010; Malet Calvo and Ramos 2018).

In 1984, Rua Augusta was the first street in Lisbon to be pedestrianised. This street in Baixa (the eighteenth-century grid near the river) was the main artery connecting Terreiro do Paço, the monumental square facing the Tagus, and Praça da Figueira, a square next to Rossio. As is frequently the case, this drew universal criticism from businesses and drivers, and for a long time failed to attract pedestrians. The next attempt was made on Rua Garrett, a steep street leading to Chiado. The consequence of its poor design was tragic: in 1988 a fire spread uncontrollably when fire trucks found it impossible to navigate the maze of concrete stools the council had installed there (Sá Fernandes and Fidalgo 2020, 146). The third instance, though initially resisted, proved immensely successful: only 450 metres of cobblestone pavement were laid in Rua das Portas de Santo Antão (RPSA), in 1994. This was part of the cultural programme for Lisbon as European Capital of Culture, but was enough to completely change its use, ambiance and attractiveness (Costa, Gutierrez and Kother 2015, 752–4). Interestingly, the councillor who proposed the change at the time offered in argument the idea that this limited pedestrianisation would be the starting point for the eventual creation of a 'green corridor' to connect the city centre to the forested mountain of Monsanto, 'the city's lung', as per the urbanists' lingo (Ribeiro Telles 1997; Matos 2018). After decades of resistance, this project finally came to fruition 26 years later, when Lisbon was awarded European Green Capital 2020.

The gentry and the tourist in the old city

The topic of touristification is gaining ground in both sociology and political economy studies, as the forces unleashed by expanding international mobility and neoliberal land policies have begun to impact communities around the world, changing landscapes, cultures and identities. Touristification – a process whereby urban and non-urban areas are transformed to attract and accommodate large influxes of tourists – is a concept frequently associated with gentrification – the transformation of areas through the influx of affluent residents and businesses (Cocola-Gant 2018). Both processes imply changes in composition, morphology, usage of specific territories and forms of up-marketing, but they also lead to symbolic and imaginary alterations that very frequently result in the eviction of poorer dwellers, voluntarily or otherwise. While there is no necessary causal relationship between the two, they seem deeply intertwined – they can occur simultaneously, and one can generate or piggyback on the other. In urban settings, changes in residential typology can be brought about by changes in commercial usage, and vice versa. In any case, the actions and decisions of authorities tend to be instrumental to them. When authorities cater for 'outsiders' as a means of attracting capital to an area to be 'developed', they tend to alienate poorer inhabitants by failing to provide for them. They create new infrastructures, promote new usages, and offer new opportunities to investors, promoters and affluent residents alike (Delgado 2007, 53; Minton 2006; Minton 2017; Harvey 1989).

The touristification and gentrification of old central quarters are processes that one would not, at least until very recently, easily have associated with Lisbon. Nonetheless, they have featured in the city's urban and economic plans, at least as aspirational elements, ever since Portugal's accession to the then European Economic Community in 1985. Before then, a more socialist narrative inherited from the 1974 revolution had prevailed at both national and local levels, making any suggestion of musealisation – or rather Disneyfication (Sorkin 1992) – of old central Lisbon virtually unthinkable. Considering its particular setting, its challenging mountainous location and the historical effects of the exodus to the peripheries, central Lisbon arrived in the twenty-first century in a curious position, showing the visible effects of many years of disinvestment, a lack of coherent territorial planning programmes, and intense signs of a rent-gap structure. In other words, at the dawn of the new century the inner city was ready for the take and primed for the processes of touristi-fication and gentrification. When they set in, the two processes were deeply intertwined with the ambiguously defined and used trope of 'heritage' (Mendes 2018; Malet Calvo and Ramos 2018; Sjöholm 2017; Casagrande et al. 2017).

Brief history of the city's fate

Lisbon's centrality as the capital of a world trading empire suffered an irrecoverable blow during the Napoleonic wars, as the country's royal court moved to Brazil and Portugal's relevance in world affairs was all but extinguished. The long, narrow, meandering way of which Rua das Portas de Santo Antão (RPSA) is the first track was once peppered with the kinds of local small commerce that reigned in Lisbon, complementing the long-established shopping streets of Baixa and Chiado, two adjoining areas that were the locus of the most intense and vigorously planned reconstruction efforts after the devastating earthquake of 1755, and later of heritagisation discourses and practices (Balsas 2005; Cunha Leal 2009). This panorama began to change with both the opening of commercial centres in the city's more affluent quarters and then in its outer rings, and the arrival of international shops to the Avenida da Liberdade, the haussmanesque axis that connects lower and upper Lisbon.

Portugal's inland expansion in the twentieth century, resulting from internal migration caused by the economic unsustainability of traditional agriculture, coincided with a long freeze in the country's house-rental market. By the dawn of the twentieth century, RPSA had become the unlikely centre of the city – the place where all sorts of attractions could be found: political and civic meetings, popular education programmes, scientific conferences, drama and musical shows and, and gambling clubs offering food and wine, drugs and high-end prostitution. Although class segregation was the norm in the interior spaces, the street itself was a showcase of the growing city's mix (Magalhães 2021; Villaverde 2006, 164–5). The extravaganza ground to a halt when the deeply conservative and moralistic Estado Novo regime managed to consolidate itself from 1933, and the street fell into decadence and irrelevance.

The 1974 revolution and ensuing period marked by galloping inflation contributed to the growth of the city's periphery. This led to the historic centre becoming a ghost town, with hundreds of buildings left empty as their owners had neither the means nor the incentive to maintain them. The fire that devastated a number of blocks in Chiado in 1988 was the low-point in a long period of urban neglect that seemed to serve as a wake-up call for the national government and the municipality to launch a number of revival programs in the city highlighting the heritage value of its decadent centre and branding it as a tourist attraction (Malet Calvo and Ramos 2018, 54).

The setting: Rua das Portas de Santo Antão

RPSA is a quaint, pedestrianised, heavily touristified street. It runs parallel to central Lisbon's main road axis, Avenida da Liberdade – an epitome of the celebrated French export, the boulevard. RPSA is one of the city's oldest thoroughfares, linking the squeezed riverain valley that is Baixa to the northern road system. Its name derives from its being the exit lane of one of the medieval city gates (Porta de Santo Antão, previously Porta de São Domingos). Despite its narrow and cramped character, oddly it became the nerve centre of the city in the late nineteenth century: the capital's political and business elite, and the growing petty bourgeoisie, would gather there. The hilly Chiado area, not far to the west, was its intellectual and artistic pole (Villaverde 2006, 153). Further away from Rossio, the old city's main square, the street becomes more tortuous and shoddier, appropriately changing its name a few times. After a mere 400 metres, RPSA morphs into Rua de São José for a stretch of 450 metres, and then to Rua de Santa Marta; after the Largo de Andaluz it becomes Rua de São Sebastião da Pedreira, which now dissolves in the Praça de Espanha hub. The line of the ancient way connecting to the also faded Estrada de Sintra can still be guessed in maps, but urban spread has in practice obliterated it. Over the course of the last century, Avenida da Liberdade, which had previously been a public garden split in two by a creek, evolved in (relative) monumentality, hosting new large new cinemas, theatres and cafes (Silva 2016, 71–2; Cunha Leal 2005). Concurrently, the old, narrow street's previous centrality shrank into irrelevance and the space became a shabby, polluted, inhospitable one. The restaurants, beer houses, clubs and societies that had boomed during the last years of the monarchy and in the early Republic became progressively frozen in time during the rule of the authoritarian Estado Novo.

After the 1974 revolution, as the city and the country moved on, RSPSA became a weird no man's land where gipsy drug dealers and cheap prostitutes rubbed alongside small shops and poor inhabitants. But, crucially, given the street's proximity to Rossio, the few remaining restaurants and bars managed to retain their ability to attract the odd international tourist who ventured into Lisbon – especially the Spanish visitors who would arrive every Easter for a quick holiday dash. Its partial pedestrianisation greatly helped to establish it as a magnet for a growing number of visitors. The street was diligently sanitised by the city council in the 2010s, monitored by the police, and transformed into a place to go – for Lisboners and tourists alike – thanks to the overhauling of the old Coliseum and the theatre just opposite. When tourism was soaring by the mid-2010s, RPSA was already well charted in every paper and online tourist guide. Unlike the Bairro Alto and the recently overhauled Rua de São Paulo, to the West, which have become major rallying points for international millennials in search of the city's nightlife, RPSA offers a slow strolling space and numerous spots to enjoy the city's mild climate and the country's offer of cheap beer and wine, along with the promise of 'typical Portuguese cuisine' to attract respectable tourists.

The council's decision to pedestrianise RPSA in 1994, rather than choose one of the myriad other alternatives, was driven by the low political price of closing it to road traffic, since it was (and is) almost void of residents. Besides, businesses were failing and voiceless, and as RPSA runs parallel to Avenida da Liberdade, it was basically cost-free to divert the few cars that used that stretch. But there was another, deeper reason, as Villaverde stresses in his exhaustive study of the history of the street from the mid-nineteenth century to the end of the first Republic in the 1920s: RPSA is the epitome of the contradictions of the abortive modernisation of the country in that period (Villaverde 2006, 175–6). The unlikely choice, by the bourgeoisie, to implant visible signs of their empowerment (the gigantic coliseum, above all) along that narrow and unassuming street, rather than in the monumental new Avenida da Liberdade, demonstrates the smallness of the city and the half-hearted will to bring modern European forms of leisure (operettas, variety shows, circuses) to a city that had little wish, or capital, to reject its medieval character. Another factor in this empowerment was the *nouveau riche*'s impetus to occupy palaces belonging to the old order and change their function by opening them up to the public (Villaverde 2006, 146). The 1994 pedestrianisation was the first of a number of successive steps taken by the council to erase – under the cloak of urban regeneration – the memories of its past exuberance and package the city up for tourist consumption.

The reconstruction that was carried out in Chiado after the fire of 1988, facilitated by generous council tax benefits for major landmarks, further fostered this rapid internationalisation of commerce. The demolition of old derelict buildings, either empty or populated by vulnerable sitting tenants, had already started in the late 1970s in parts of the upper city to make way for office buildings, which also led to 'upmarket' changes in the types of shops in the area, now providing goods for an expanding middle class. Informal street markets were extinguished in an effort to sanitise street life – concurrent with a city-wide program financed by the European Union to eradicate the numerous shantytowns that dotted the city and its outskirts. By the early 2000s the transformation was complete (Allegra et al. 2017, 4). This was a low period for RPSA: its centrality long gone, it was emptied of its people, commerce, memories, life; now sanitised and hollow, it lay still, waiting for the sought-after tourist boom but still offering a few food and drink places, local versions of international musicals in a renovated theatre, and infrequent attractions at the Coliseum (rock concerts, circus at Christmas and Carnival).

Meanwhile, a tumbling process of planned regeneration of the Baixa-Chiado axis was taking place. This included a failed attempt at classifying it as a world heritage site and a sequence of aborted real estate swaps. Major banks owned large tracts of the downtown area and attempted to develop them, but most development deals were affected by the subprime crisis of 2008–9 and the ensuing sovereign debt collapse of 2011–15 (Lestegás 2019). The post-2015 boom in the Portuguese economy was driven by radical liberalising changes in the rent and job markets, and a very aggressive opening up to international real estate investors, in the form of hyper-generous tax exemptions and the sale of residency permits (so-called gold visas). Low-cost flights and the lightning-fast spread of hostels and short-term rented rooms and flats (mostly via Airbnb), aided by the after-effects of the Arab Spring on international tourism, fuelled the exponential growth of tourism in the city and country (Mendes 2018; Mendes 2019). Starting in the northern section of Baixa, RPSA immediately felt the effects of this prodigious transformation. Overnight, it became lively, busy, crowded and attractive. Tourists flooded in, filling the restaurants and bars, and wandering the street until cobblestone gave way to asphalt and suddenly there was nothing to see. Taking the words of Manuel Delgado, referring to the same process in central Barcelona, RPSA became the epitome of a caricature of a city – a popular catwalk for modelling tourists (Delgado 2007).

Tourists in, tourists out, and then in again

Elsewhere I have discussed how the 20-odd years of branding Lisbon a welcoming tourist destination by the national government and the city's municipality ran parallel to aborting efforts towards gentrifying its deserted historical centre (Malet Calvo and Ramos 2018). Later,

Figure 6.1: Enticing clients, enticed clients, West side. © Manuel Ramos
Figure 6.2: Tourist facing tourist shop window. © Manuel Ramos

both internal factors (the abovementioned structural transformations in the housing market) and external factors (the redirection of tourist flows due to fears of Islamic terrorism in the Maghreb, after-effects of the Arab Spring) suddenly brought about the necessary conditions for transforming Lisbon into both one of the world's top tourist destinations in the second half of the 2010s and a hotspot for real-estate specu-lation that resulted in the effective gentrification of the half-deserted historic centre. This process was coupled with a series of transform-ative adaptations of public areas to make the city more appealing to strolling multitudes of tourists (particularly on the riverfront). In tandem, private initiatives, both local and international, renewed and rebranded old shops or bought out failing commercial and residential spaces to transform them into charming hotels, jazzy hostels, local lodging, trendy bars, and fusion restaurants (Figures 6.1 and 6.2).

All of a sudden, following in the footsteps of the successful pedestrianisation of RPSA, large sections of the old city centre became walkable, liveable and attractive, but most Lisboners – those not directly involved in the new tourist industry – became strangers in their own city. Public and private efforts to make the city's public spaces liveable and welcoming resulted in the partial privatisation of those same spaces, as public balconies, verandas, terraces, gardens and squares

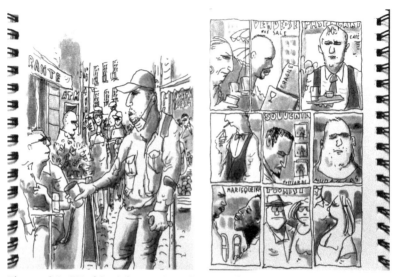

Figure 6.3: 'Working' the tourists. © Manuel Ramos
Figure 6.4: Snapshots of passers-by. © Manuel Ramos

were leased to cafes, bars, and restaurants, aggressively cornering and expelling the locals. Silently witnessing the roving hosts of tourists, new international residents and workers catering for the new set-up (Figures 6.3 and 6.4), they now faced being expelled to the suburbs: victims of the ever-expanding Airbnb-isation of the city (Mendes 2019).

During the Covid-19 pandemic years (2020–2), when harsh travel restrictions were imposed and the long periods of lockdown stopped most tourist activity, life in RPSA was deeply impacted (Almeida, Silva 2020). Its restaurants and bars followed the general trend: they resorted to catering for take-aways, reoriented their activities to provide for the local population, suspended their activities, or closed for good. Social and cultural venues – a major source of temporary occupation of the street – were suspended, and of course tourist strollers almost disappeared completely. Those who remained faithful users of the street space were the impoverished locals and the occasional workers from nearby offices and businesses. Between mid-2020 and early 2022, the Lisbon Council offered provisional tax exemptions for restaurants and bars willing to occupy the now empty sidewalks, but that did not really impact RPSA, as it was one of the few streets where that kind of occupation was already the norm (Minton 2006).

The pandemic provided an invaluable opportunity to visually assess how disproportionately high the ratio of tourists and

Figure 6.5: North-south view towards the National Theatre and Rossio Square. © Manuel Ramos

Figure 6.6: Looking North, Rua das Portas do Santo Antao
© Manuel Ramos

tourist-related activities is in RPSA. For a brief moment in its long history, the street returned to what it had been before the 1994 pedestrianisation, except that now the long-gone car traffic was replaced by bicycle and scooter traffic – producing new, milder forms of conflict and appropriation of public walking space. Made invisible under the flood of tourists, and of theatre- or concert-goers, the usual clients of the few surviving untouristified cafes and taverns, the remnants of traditional businesses, and all those who tend to use the street not as a place in itself but as a means, again became conspicuous. During the lull caused by the pandemic, RPSA became a *liveable* street – its pavement already pedestrianised, its buildings already rehabilitated, its stillness was now reinstated. But, since it is so much part of the touristified nucleus of the city, and because council social housing policies are not directed at repopulating the historic quarter, once the tourist flow reignited it reverted to being a caricature of its former self (Figures 6.5–6.7).

The progressive lifting of Covid-19 restrictions has led to a 'return to normality' and the tourism sector has been revived. However, while the expected pouring of public money into large infrastructure was destined to feed the city's tourism industry (including a new airport,

Figures 6.7: People on Rua das Portas do Santo Antao © Manuel Ramos

a new bridge, new urbanisation programmes, new railways, the revamping of squares, streets and avenues, and further musealisation projects), it may be hampered by the spectre of inflation and economic downturn that followed the Russian military intervention in Ukraine in February 2022. Forecasts suggest an expected fall of more than 11 per cent in GDP over the next few years.

Final note: speak about commoning

It is fitting to interpret the life of a historic street such as RPSA as an instance of the right of the commons, taken not in a strict but rather in an extensive sense (Borch and Kornberger 2015, 7; Dellenbaugh et al. 2015; Ostrom 1990). The ritualised appropriation of its spaces and flow lines, intersected by recurring segmentation – both temporal (daily, weekly, seasonally) and spatial (southern vs northern sections, sunny vs shady sides) – is founded on a dialogic play between remembrance and oblivion. The memories it harbours are rendered not so much by verbalised narratives, for there are no collectively recognised stories or storytellers beyond the blurbs produced in travel guides and official tourist literature, and the occasional research paper or dissertation, but by the re-enacting of the rituals of being there, and of passing through there. Those who sit in its cafes, stroll over its cobblestones, and gather in its corners and niches, looking unobservantly at its buildings, signs and colours, do so incognisant of the weight of history and of the spiralling webs that capture unquantifiable layers of individual and collective anecdotal episodes the street has witnessed through time. Invisibly stuck somewhere between private and public rights, it is the common right to the liveability of the street that gives it its ultimate sense, for it is through this right that past memories, present acts and expected futures are summoned together. It is also fitting that such common rights are not consciously recognised by the heterogenous and ever-changing multitude of its users, for that is the way it is meant to be. Every conscious intention of reclaiming them negates their essence and paves the way to asserting hegemonising private, or public, rights: the right to speak about the street, the right to decide upon its usages and its forms, the right to own its history, the right to categorise it. Importantly, accepting this evidence entails what Douglas Hofstadter (1999) would call a 'strange loop': the mere mention of it, in these pages, is an act of private – written as well as sketched – unwarranted appropriation.

Bibliography

Allegra, Marco, Simone Tulumello, Roberto Falanga, Rita Cachado, A. Ferreira, A. Colombo and S. Alves. 2017. *Um novo PER? Realojamento e políticas de habitação em Portugal*. Observa Policy Brief. Lisbon: UL-ICS.

Borch, C. and M. Kornberger (eds). 2015. *Urban Commons: Rethinking the city*. Abingdon: Routledge.

Branco, Jorge Freitas and Manuel João Ramos (eds). 2003 *Estrada Viva? Aspectos da motorização da sociedade portuguesa*. Lisbon: Assírio & Alvim.

Cabrera, Ana and Marília Nunes. 1998. *Olhar o Chão. A glance at Portuguese mosaic pavement. Regarder le Sol. Ein Blick auf den Portuguiesische Steinpflaster* [1990]. Lisbon: INCM.

Cocola-Gant, Agustín. 2018. 'Tourism Gentrification'. In *Handbook of Gentrification Studies*, edited by Loretta Lees and Martin Phillips, 281–93. Cheltenham: Edward Elgar.

Cunha Leal, Joana. 2005. *Arquitectura Privada, Política e Factos Urbanos em Lisboa: da cidade pombalina à cidade liberal*, PhD thesis, Lisbon: UNL-FCSH.

Cunha Leal, Joana. 2009. 'Baixa Pombalina: Estratégias de Legitimação Patrimonial (Parte 1 e 1/2)'. In *Memória e Artifício: A matéria do património II*, edited by M.J. Ramos and A. Medeiros, 201–18. Lisbon: Sociedade de Geografia de Lisboa.

Delgado, Manuel. 2007. *La Ciudad Mentirosa. Fraude y miseria del modelo Barcelona*. Barcelona: Catarata.

Dellenbaugh, M., M. Kip, M. Bieniok, A. Müller and M. Schwegmann (eds). 2015. *Urban Commons: Moving beyond state and market*. Berlin; Bauverlag Gütersloh; Basel: Birkhäuser.

Gehl, Jan. 2010. *Cities for People*. Washington, DC: Island Press.

Harvey, D. 1989. 'From Managerialism to Entrepreneurialism: The transformation in urban governance in late capitalism', *Geografiska Annaler* 71: 3–17.

Hofstadter, Douglas R. 1999. *Gödel, Escher, Bach: An eternal golden braid* [1979]. New York: Basic Books.

Lestegás, Iago. 2019. 'Lisbon After the Crisis: From credit-fuelled suburbanization to tourist-driven gentrification', *International Journal of Urban and Regional Research* 43(4): 705–23.

Magalhães, Paula. 2021. *Os Loucos Anos 20. Diário da Lisboa Boémia*. Lisbon: Planeta.

Malet Calvo, Daniel and Manuel João Ramos. 2018. 'Suddenly Last Summer: How the tourist tsunami hit Lisbon', *Revista Andaluza de Antropología* 15: 47–73.

Matos, Maria João. 2018. 'The Green Corridor: A vision for Lisbon'. In *Changing Representations of Nature and the City: The 1960s–1970s and their legacies*, edited by N. Gabriel and Alison Vogelaar, 165–79. Abingdon: Routledge.

Mendes, Luís. 2018. 'Tourism Gentrification in Lisbon: The panacea of touristification as a scenario of a post-capitalist crisis'. In *Crisis, Austerity and Transformation: How disciplinary neoliberalism is changing Portugal*, edited by Isabel David, 25–46. London: Lexington.

Mendes, Luís. 2019. 'Airbnb, Gentrificação Turística e Injustiça Espacial'. In *Lisboa e a Airbnb*, edited by J. Rio Fernandes, L. Carvalho, P. Chamusca, A. Gago and T. Mendes, 65–67. Lisbon, Book Cover.

Minton, Anna. 2006. *The Privatisation of Public Space: What kind of world are we building?* London: Royal Institution of Chartered Surveyors.

Ostrom, Elinor. 1990. *Governing the Commons. The evolution of institutions for collective action*. Cambridge: Cambridge University Press.

Ribeiro Telles, Gonçalo. 1997. *Plano Verde de Lisboa, Componente do Plano Director Municipal de Lisboa*. Lisbon: Edições Colibri.

Sá Fernandes, Ana and António Fidalgo. 2020. 'Relembrar o grande incêndio de Lisboa 30 anos depois', *Territorium* 27(II): 143–58.

Silva, João. 2016. *Entertaining Lisbon: Music, Theater, and modern life in the late 19th century*. Oxford: Oxford University Press.

Sjöholm, Jennie. 2017. 'Authenticity and Relocation of Built Heritage: The urban transformation of Kiruna, Sweden', *Journal of Cultural Heritage Management and Sustainable Development* 7(2): 110–28.

Sorkin, Maichel. 1992. *Variations on a Theme Park: The New America City and the End of Public Space*. New York: Hill and Wang.

Villaverde, Manuel. 2006. 'Rua das Portas de Santo Antão e a singular modernidade lisboeta (1890–1925): arquitectura e práticas urbanas', *Revista de História da Arte* 2: 142–76.

7

The streets that were there are gone ... but Sailortown's stories remain

Agustina Martire and Aisling Madden

The demolition of Sailortown in the 1970s erased the neighbour-hood's everyday streets – displacing over 1,000 families and 300 businesses – to make way for the Belfast Urban Motorway. Despite this displacement, the scattered Sailortown community remains resilient, with a sustained sense of belonging to the place. Aware of the class-driven segregation of Belfast, this chapter contrasts the view of this motorway as 'progress' with the loss of the complex everyday experiences of Sailortown. By making people's stories visible, this chapter presents a methodology that enables a nuanced, thorough and people-focused understanding of the complexity of everyday streets. It shows the degree to which people's stories are connected to the past urban grain and street fabric. We argue that a proper understanding of the complexity of these stories could prevent such large-scale planning mistakes from occurring in the future.

Sailortown and the Belfast Urban Motorway

Just as the tramways did in the nineteenth century, motorways promised in the twentieth century to transform people's everyday lives by moving them out of congested and polluted city streets and into healthier, greener, new towns and suburbs. However, not everyone benefited from large-scale investment in urban infrastructure and housing. Urban motorways cut through inner-city neighbourhoods, replacing streets with roads and segregating or displacing commu-nities. They created derelict, abandoned, dystopian urban spaces out of previously thriving, rich, functional streets. These transformations

BELFAST, UK ├──────┤ 2kɪɪɪ

Figure 7.0: Map of Belfast © Anna Skoura

of the urban fabric have been well documented and discussed since the 1960s (Jacobs 1963; Gunn 2013; Mumford 1963; Urry 2009), but there is still great dissonance between the academic literature and planning policy, which continues to disproportionately harm working-class groups (Thomsen et al. 2016; Urban 2018; Zukin et al. 2015).

The streets of Sailortown in Belfast suffered the demolition of its fabric and the displacement of its people. Since the early nineteenth century, this dense working-class neighbourhood had housed workers of the docks, linen and tobacco factories, smaller industries and all services needed at the time. Between 1969 and 1973, local homes and businesses in Sailortown were demolished to make space for the Belfast Urban Motorway, displacing at least 1,000 families and 300 businesses from one of the city's most lively and diverse neighbourhoods (BBC, 1973).

Prior to the construction of the Belfast Urban Motorway, Sailortown was a thriving and lively neighbourhood despite its relatively high poverty level. As with many other 'Sailortowns' (Milne 2016) and other so-called 'slums' (Wilson 1987), the urban form of Sailortown was a network of terraced houses, small workshops and large factories framed by streets, alleys and courtyards (Figure 7.1a). This urban form enabled a complex sense of community shared by people of various backgrounds and ethnicities (Appleyard in Vernez Moudon 1989; Jacobs 1961; Moran 2016; Smithson 1957; Vaughan 2015).

The contested nature of Belfast over the last 60 years has been well explored by historians and anthropologists, but the need for a more detailed oral history of Belfast's neighbourhoods has been highlighted by Purdue (2020), O'Connell (2018) and Pierse (2020). The planning and spatial transformations aligned with this social context have been investigated by Sterrett et al. (2012), Ellis et al. (2015) and Gaffikin et al. (2016), among others. Sterrett et al. state that 'inner-city working-class communities … continue to suffer from the impact of 1970s major road infrastructure and defectively designed social housing' (2012, 49). Research has largely focused on ethnonational divides, neglecting the transformations of everyday life among working-class people and the streets on which they work. These transformations are crucial, as they are comparable to global cases of displacement, which erode public street life and exacerbate social polarisation in cities. By 'everyday life', we refer to what Highmore (2002) called the 'ordinary and extraordinary' and how Solnit (2000) framed streets by calling them the mingling of the 'errand and the epiphany'.

Figure 7.1a: Sailortown in 1963 (left). © StreetSpace (Agustina Martire)

The rational, permeable and connected street network of 1960s Sailortown facilitated the transportation of goods from the docks. The many front doors opening onto the streets, which served countless functions, encouraged social interactions. The street was a collective zone where conversations, play and conflict were in constant flux:

Figure 7.1b: Sailortown 2020 (right). © StreetSpace (Agustina Martire)

'working-class street life had all the compromises and demands of intimacy; it was not the undiscriminating flow of public discourse' (Moran 2012, 168) but 'a constantly shifting pattern of exposure and suppression, as the participants sought both to repair and defend the limitations of their private lives' (Vincent 1998, 145). The activities,

Figure 7.2: Sailortown stories from social media on a 1963 map.
© Aisling Madden, Juliette Moore, Aisha Holmes and Nathan Cilona

interactions and relationships that we discuss in this study are tightly linked to the qualities of the spaces in which they took place; they are a vivid part of the histories and memories of Sailortown, and a testament to the value of mixed uses in the area (Hausleitner 2019). By illustrating them, we make them visible and permanent – we give them the value that they deserve (Figure 7.2).

'Progress' and a 'way of life'

Following the trend set by Traffic in Towns (1963), the Belfast Urban Motorway was introduced as a solution to Belfast's traffic problems – as a symbol of 'progress' (Belfast Telegraph 1962–4; Johnston 2014; Kingsley and Urry 2009). However, its impact was detrimental to the working-class communities of Belfast's inner city. A series of policy documents resulted in the demise of Sailortown: the Housing and Rent Restriction Law (1956), the Matthew Plan (1963), the Wilson Economic Plan (1964) and the Building Design Partnership Plan (1969). These all aimed to 'demagnetise' the city by relocating entire communities to satellite towns and suburbs. The demolition of Sailortown began in

Figure 7.3: Newspaper articles '60s, '70s, '80s. © StreetSpace
(Agustina Martire)

the mid-1960s, and people were rehoused with little objection from the local communities and local government (Figure 7.3).

Criticism of slum clearance was widespread in the 1950s but did not reach Belfast until the late 1960s. Peter Smithson pointed out as early as 1953 that 'the short narrow street of the slum succeeds where spacious redevelopment frequently fails'. Roger Mayne wrote, 'This I think is a positive way of life, at the moment the planners are not sufficiently awake to the qualities of these streets which ultimately will have to go' (quoted in Hardcastle 2008). Jack Lynn (1961) believed that in tearing down whole streets which 'despite their sanitary short-comings, harboured a social structure of friendliness and mutual aid', we had 'thrown the baby out with the bathwater' (Dickens et al. 1985, 176).

As it progressed, the Belfast Urban Motorway was increas-ingly questioned locally, but ideas of 'progress' overrode the value of people's everyday lives, with councillors highlighting its inevitability despite calling it 'soulless' (BT 22-9-1964) (BT 20-8-1966). Urbanists George Huxley and Cliff Moughtin led the critique, arguing against the motorway (BT 28-10-1968). Inquiries into the Belfast Urban Motorway (1972, 1976) showed that it would be particularly detrimental to working-class areas (BBC 1973; BT 18-1-1971). By the end of 1973, 27 Belfast city councillors had voted against the motorway, while only 8 voted for it (BT 2-10-1973). However, the damage had already been done. Despite protests backed by John Tyme (1978) and Ron Weiner (1978), the urban motorway had destroyed places, streets and communities. In 1983, the link between the M1 and M2 was built, creating a gap between the city centre and the north and west ends of the inner city.

The demolition and displacement of Sailortown's streets led to the loss of many sites: houses, pubs, churches and, most importantly, the ordinary and extraordinary everyday stories of its people.

The stories of Sailortown: methodology

> We would all be failing in our duty to let the history of Sailortown be forgotten and to die along with its many personalities and characters. A book should be written of all her times and of the great people and their warmth and humour which that district by the docks produced or adopted. (Eddie McIlwaine; BT 17-11-82)

Responding to demolition and displacement in city streets, which disproportionately affect working-class areas, the StreetSpace project[1] (Martire 2019; Martire 2020) investigates the value, urban form and histories of those everyday streets. Between 2019 and 2020, the project focused on Sailortown, using interdisciplinary methods to make its stories visible. This methodological overlap between anthropology and architecture shed light on the nuances and qualities of a place that are sometimes overlooked by historians and frequently ignored by urban planners.

The powerful stories of Sailortown have been brought to life by both scholars and community activists. Similar to Fyfe's (1996) understanding of Glasgow's working-class neighbourhoods through poetry, Fagan and Anderson (2016) discussed a project that used song, installation and performance to preserve the memories of Sailortown residents in the shape of an exhibition in the MAC Belfast (2012). Sean O'Connell has spent decades investigating oral histories and the power that they have to depict the complexity of working-class experiences, with a particular focus on Sailortown (2018) in recent years. Following short-lived campaigns in the 1990s and 2000s, local activist Terry McKeown of Sailortown Regeneration has played a pivotal role in revealing many of Sailortown's stories, bringing it back to life, while SHIP (Shared History Interpretive Project) has been collecting and publishing the stories of the docks and its workers since 2016.

Our approach highlights the value of Sailortown's stories by detailing the relationship between stories and streets through drawing – an exercise of graphic anthropology (Azevedo and Ramos 2016; Clossick 2017; Ingold 2013; Kuschnir 2016; Lucas 2008; Pink 2013). Ethnographic approaches aim to 'provide a depth of understanding that is not achievable with other research approaches' (Schembri and Boyle 2013, 1,252). They entail researchers using their 'embodied experience, to … comprehend the places [they seek] to analyse' (Pink 2008, 175). Ray Lucas writes extensively about the important contributions that anthropological and ethnographic methods can make in architectural research and practice, noting that they can provide 'the scaffolding for thinking about complex, real-world situations' (2020, 5).

Through this unique architectural and ethnographic approach, we discovered the value of the everyday street fabric in unveiling Sailortown's stories while exposing how the power of a few erased the very fabric in which these stories were formed. The StreetSpace project involved collaboration between architectural academics and students, anthropologists, artists and Sailortown community groups. Informal conversations with both former and current local residents built up a rich and diverse collection of stories from Sailortown's past and present (Martire and Madden 2022). Over time, relationships between the students and the participants grew, and memories, thoughts and opinions were shared. The students attended the weekly prayer service held by former residents outside the now deconsecrated St Joseph's Church amid preparations for a Halloween party organised for local children. They also attended a charity event at the Mission for Seafarers. Others visited former residents at their businesses, attended local history lectures and spent time getting to know the members of the Dockers Club. This wide range of experiences alongside the diversity of the participants in terms of age, class, gender and occupation resulted in a complex and multi-layered bank of information that covered both the historical character of Sailortown and the modern everyday struggles that the area contends with as it continues to strive to exist, retain relevance and adapt to evolving circumstances.

The collected information was processed by the students through traditional architectural drawings (e.g. plans, sections, axonometrics, perspectives, collages) as they combined their architectural training with their research into graphic anthropology. This enabled the students to gain rich insights into the urban morphology and character of Sailortown. Combining urban morphology and graphic anthropology exposed nuances, details and characteristics of everyday life that other methods generally fail to identify. The aim of this research was not to develop a nostalgic, rose-tinted memory of Sailortown. Still, the diversity of the stories gathered – and the humour and wit with which they were told – conveyed the grit and camaraderie of this industrial area, demonstrating how the area is viewed and remembered by its current and former residents and users.

The stories of Sailortown: findings

The selection of stories below offers insight into the ordinary and extraordinary experiences of people in the streets of 1960s Sailortown, before much of it was demolished. These stories of community, conflict, work, leisure, age and gender reflect the built fabric of Sailortown as a specific place in a specific time – one whose memory must be maintained and whose qualities should be valued. As John Campbell wrote, 'The characters have vanished but the memories linger on' (2009).

Community

> Nearly everybody talked to each other. Their doors were always open, and there was no break-ins, burglaries – there was nothing like that. (Billy)

The stories indicated that community strength was deeply embedded in the street fabric. Billy's stories were some of the most revealing. The students developed a friendly rapport with Billy, a retired Merchant Seaman who grew up in the area in the 1950s and 1960s. In 1969, just as the Troubles were brewing in Belfast, Billy's family encouraged the then 16-year-old to follow in the footsteps of his older male relatives and join the Merchant Navy. Soon after, his family was relocated to a nearby housing estate, and their home on Nelson Street was demolished to make room for the new motorway. Permanently settled back on land following his retirement, Billy spent much of his time aiding in community efforts to bring housing back to Sailortown and volunteering at the local Mission for Seafarers.

A natural storyteller, Billy vividly described the many adventures he had around Sailortown in his youth. The students brought a historical

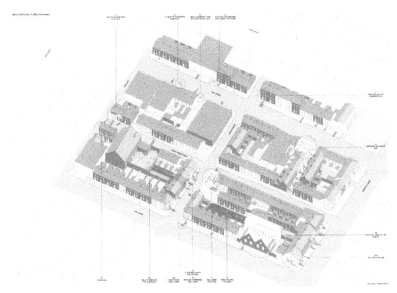

Figure 7.4: Sailortown blocks in the 1960s (based on Billy's stories).
© Aisling Madden

map of 1960s Sailortown and asked Billy to point out his family home, homes of his friends and nearby businesses. Based on maps, photographs and Billy's stories, the students drew an axonometric of the four urban blocks around Billy's home on Nelson Street. This axonometric (Figure 7.4) enabled us to develop a thorough understanding of the morphology and spatial organisation of the area. Through his stories, Billy described and identified many shortcuts, courtyards and outbuildings that were not legible in the old maps. Furthermore, his anecdotes enabled us to develop an understanding of how the urban fabric shaped Sailortown's social and economic dynamics and sense of community.

Describing Sailortown as 'Aladdin's cave', Billy believed that exploring his neighbourhood was his true education in life, providing him with more worth than school. Based on Billy's encounters with sailors from around the world – witnessing the arrival of exotic new produce and being the first to hear global news and current affairs off the boats – it is clear that Sailortown was like nowhere else in the city of Belfast. Billy recounted stories of the many unusual goings-on that he witnessed within the four urban blocks surrounding his home. The everyday use of the streets featured heavily in his stories, including one anecdote about Billy's next-door neighbour Peter, who stole a series of ornaments from a grave and gave them to his wife, prompting her to say to a friend, 'Ohhh, what am I going to do Bridget? I'm going to end up in hell!' (Billy).

The humour in Billy's tales makes them vivid yet relevant, helping us to understand cultural elements as well as the built environment, which served as the backdrop of these stories. The density of the area is evident, with the front doors of the narrow terrace houses opening onto the streets of Sailortown. The rhythm and proximity of these doors encouraged a sociable and close-knit community, with neighbours helping one another in times of need.

Ethnonational and class integration

> Here, it was all mixed: Protestants and Catholics. (Billy)

Unlike many neighbourhoods in Belfast, Sailortown was a mixed community, where both ethnonational groups – Protestants and Catholics – lived in relative camaraderie. Despite street-by-street divisions, there were many shared spaces and moments. Nelson Street created a boundary that divided Sailortown: Catholic to the east and Protestant to the west. The west side was described by Seánie as 'the other side' (Deeney 2018) and was not considered to constitute 'Sailortown' by some in the local community. However, according to residents Seánie and Pam, there were a series of businesses, such as pubs, bookmakers and 'The Earl Chipper', where residents from the 'other side' were welcome. Paul and Gerry, other former residents (Molloy 2014), also pointed out that there were many crossovers between the two communities. The conflict was solved through everyday experiences. However, integration in Sailortown was not only related to ethnonationality. Sailortown is generally thought of as an exclusively working-class area, but this idea neglects the middle-class residents, whose experiences in larger houses and wider streets were far removed from the poverty seen in other parts of the neighbourhood. Both Great George's Street and Pilot Street were considered to be outside the working-class area, reflecting the diversity of Sailortown's inhabitants.

> There were very few houses on the lower end of Great George's Street where we were. Great George's Street was a very wide street, which was unusual; most of these little streets were like guts – blink and you miss them. (Pam)

You had to be a pilot to live in Pilot Street; they were nice houses, so they were. (Seánie)

This wealth difference often resulted in neighbours supporting one another, encouraging social mobility in the area. Marianne, for example, 'had money lying all over the f***ing house. It was in jars, tins … But she was very, very good to the community down in Sailortown' (Billy). Seánie described certain living and washing arrangements: 'If you were lucky enough to have a bath in your house, you would be sure as hell there would be a bed beside it.' However, these differences also led to conflict. One of the many pubs in Sailortown was The Bunch of Grapes, 'run by Liam McMahon, and his clientele were all the businessmen from around here, and that's where they all congregated on a Friday … if someone went into the bar that he didn't like, he said, "Get you out of here!"' (Billy).

The variety of uses and possible occupations within Sailortown led to an economically diverse population. The urban grid was varied, with the wealthier living on wider, airy and healthy streets in three-storey houses, while multiple families lived on narrow streets with two-storey terraces. This grain facilitated and encouraged everyday interaction between diverse groups. The demolition of this fabric, in contrast, deepened the segregation of local communities into areas divided by ethnicity and class.

Men's work: Dockers Club

The dockers lined up every morning, and they called it schooling. They would pick out you, you, you and you. Then they all had to be at the gate. If the boss was picking them, it would be on a whim. He decided, "yes, I like your face", "no, I don't like yours – I don't like red hair, so you're not getting a job". (Pam)

The dockers were an integral part of the community, seen every morning looking for work and filling the numerous pubs in the evenings. To further understand the experience of Sailortown's residents, one of the students became a member of the Dockers Club and, through conversations with retired dockers, documented the solidarity present in this group.

If the men walking to work in the morning stood on the "half-moon", they were going to get it! (Seánie)

Figure 7.5: The Dockers Club. © Jonny Yau

The male-dominated industries of Sailortown were a tough and competitive backdrop to this part of the city, with the daily sight of dockers looking for work remembered by many. The resultant camaraderie is still evident in modern Sailortown. The dockers built their club (Figure 7.5) in the 1970s, and it remains a popular community building, hosting events and witnessing reunions between former Sailortown residents who are now living around the world:

> A few of them went to Australia … the word went out, and the smoke signals went out, and everyone converged on the dockers who knew them ones, you know. (Billy)

The material culture of Sailortown is demonstrated by the antiques and objects in the club's collection. These histories could be framed as the 'trash aesthetics' of Walter Benjamin (1940), which helps us to understand their importance as unique experiences of those struggling to get by and finding value in what has been devalued or outmoded (Highmore 2002, 63).

Women's experiences

> A man never works. Okay, they go out in the morning – eight o'clock, seven o'clock – they go to work, and they enjoy their day. Women work. They have the children, they carry all the shopping,

they do all the housework, the cooking, they have to manage whatever their husband gave them. They had no control over their own money, so they were dependent on whatever the man put on the mantelpiece as their wages. (Pam)

The women of Sailortown constituted the backbone of the community, either looking after their families or working in nearby factories. Narratives of everyday experiences have long neglected the experiences of women (Silva 2002; Woodley-Baker 2009). Feminist geographer Gillian Rose points out that many women do not share the 'rosy' view of home and place that humanist geographers (Relph et al. 2008; Tuan 1977) place at the centre of the discipline (Rose 1993, 53). This resonates with the stories surrounding Gallagher's tobacco factory, where female workers would be recognised in the dances by their 'stink'; 'the first thing a bloke would say was "I KNOW WHERE YOU WORK!"' (Gallaher's Belfast Forum). Sailortown was a tough place to be a woman, either having to work long shifts in the factories or looking after large extended families. Once married or a mother, women had limited options for employment (Multimedia Heritage) and were often forced to stay at home while their husbands went to sea or spent long hours at work and at the pub. Pubs were also segregated by gender:

Women were forced to be hidden away – not to annoy the men. A little anteroom, as big as a very small toilet, [with] a bench, anything but comfort. They didn't offer you comfort. (Pam)

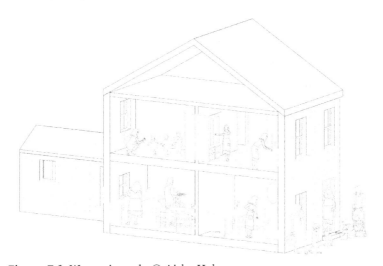

Figure 7.6: Woman's work. © Aisha Holmes

This division was a manifestation of social relationships and part of everyday life across classes and geographies (Figure 7.6). In fact, it is still seen in many contexts today. Given the high number of pubs in the area, the fact that women were rarely allowed to enter clearly demonstrates that Sailortown was an environment designed for and controlled by men. However, it is evident from the many collected stories that the women of Sailortown were responsible for supporting their families and local community.

Children

> a spool of thread on someone's door knocker, and then away up the street we'd go … [and then we would knock on the door by pulling the string] and we'd get chased around the whole area! (Billy)

Kids in Sailortown often played traditional games, such as hopscotch and pavement chalking. The small, terraced houses were often inhabited by large families that struggled to make ends meet. The eldest children often had to think of imaginative ways to support their parents. The close proximity of different households helped children like Billy to support their family by climbing into their neighbour's yard, lifting lead and selling it back to them: 'And that was how I helped sustain the family because we did, as I said, come from a large family' (Billy). Pam, describing children's everyday experiences, explained how Frank, a local grocer, used to ride a bike with a basket in one hand and a rattle in the other to get children out of the way.

The changing practices and reduced presence of street play among children in modern Western cities is well documented (Karsten and van Vliet 2006; Tranter and Doyle 1996) – and Sailortown suffered the same demise with the demolition of its everyday streets.

The overlap of all these diverse and unique stories shows the nuances that are mostly neglected and forgotten in the planning of urban areas – the palimpsest of images, sounds, ideas and memories that help us to understand a place in all its colours (Figure 7.7).

Conclusion

The pursuit of progress – and the belief that all forms of progress are inevitable – contributed to the development of the Belfast Urban Motorway and led to the demise of Sailortown. The few who questioned

Figure 7.7: Sailortown palimpsest. © Juliette Moore

or protested the development did not have a loud enough voice to stop the displacement. This contrasts with other parts of the UK, where resistance by local residents, politicians and scholars prevailed. Appleyard once stated, 'Streets have always been scenes of conflict. The most powerful or well established groups win but they do not by any means represent the public interest' (in Vernez Moudon 1989, 5). The streets of Sailortown were scenes of both mundane everyday routines and extraordinary conflict. In this case, the well-established and powerful actors won. Sailortown disappeared from the map, its community displaced across the city and around the world – but its stories will remain so long as we are able to safeguard them.

Today, the few people left in Sailortown see new threats to their community and the potential growth of the local neighbourhood and its local streets: an enhanced York Road interchange and a high-rise commercial development, once again threatening the remaining community, and denying the potential of a growing local neighbourhood and its everyday streets. The loss of Sailortown's terraced streets had a significant impact on its social and urban fabric. A more thorough and people-focused understanding of the complexity of everyday streets could prevent such large-scale planning mistakes from occurring in the future.

Alternative approaches to urban design and street design are currently emerging all over the world, prioritising pedestrians and cyclists and paying greater attention to street life and its links to people and programmes. Focusing on streets to start conversations with local current and former residents facilitated the unravelling of Sailortown's stories, enabling them to take a spatial form and giving value to the fabric of Sailortown's streets. This method could enable a more people-focused and participatory process in the development of future streets and urban spaces.

'It's born in you, it's in your blood.' (Seánie)

Notes

1 The StreetSpace project is a teaching and research project that explores the significance of everyday streets through workshops, design studios and partnerships between academia, governments, NGOs and practices. See www.streetspaceresearch.com (accessed 1 November 2022).

Bibliography

Azevedo, Aina and Manuel João Ramos. 2016. 'Drawing Close: On visual engagements in fieldwork, drawing workshops and the anthropological imagination', *Visual Ethnography* 5(1). 135–60.
Belfast Telegraph. 1968. 'Motorway Plan is Criticised', 28 October.
Belfast Telegraph. 1971. 'Belfast in Grip of Big Business', 18 January.
Belfast Telegraph. 1973. 'Scrap the Ring Road Plan, Please', 14 November.
Building Design Partnership. 1969. *Report on Belfast Corporation on Planning Policy in the City Centre*. Belfast: Building Design Partnership in association with N. Lichfield and Associates, D. Lovejoy and Associates and John Madge.

Campbell, J. John. 2009. *Once there was a Community Here: A Sailortown miscellany*. Belfast: Lagan Press.

Clossick, Jane. 2021. 'Uncovering Urban Depth: Urban depth and autonomy'. PhD thesis, London Metropolitan University. Accessed 1 November 2022. https://urbandepth. research.londonmet.ac.uk/uncovering-urban-depth/.

Ellis, Geraint, Brendan Murtagh and Andrew Grounds. 2015. 'City of Dreams? Belfast, planning and the "myth" of development'. Paper presented at the 47th Conference of Irish Geographers. United Kingdom.

Fyfe, Nicholas R. 1996. 'Contested Visions of a Modern City: Planning and poetry in postwar Glasgow', *Environment and Planning A* 28(3): 387–403.

Gaffikin, Frank, Chris Karelse, Mike Morrissey, Clare Mulholland and Ken Sterrett. 2016. 'Making Space for Each Other: Civic place-making in a divided society'. Queen's University Belfast.

Gunn, Simon. 2013. 'People and the Car: The expansion of automobility in urban Britain, c.1955–70', *Social History* 38(2): 220–37.

Hausleitner, Birgit. 2019. 'Mixed-Use City: Configurations from Street Network to Building Plot'. In DASH, *Home Work City*. Delft: Nai010 publishers.

Ingold, T. 2013. *Making: Anthropology, archaeology, art and architecture*. Abingdon: Routledge.

Johnston, Wesley. 2014. *The Belfast Urban Motorway*. Belfast: Colourprint Books.

Karsten, Lia and Willem van Vliet. 2006. 'Children in the City: Reclaiming the street', *Children, Youth and Environments* 16(1): 151–67.

Kingsley, Dennis and John Urry. 2009. *After the Car*. Cambridge: Wiley.

Lucas, Ray. 2020. *Anthropology for Architects*. London: Bloomsbury Visual Arts.

Martire, Agustina. 2019. 'Exploring the Significance of Local Mixed Streets', *Urban Design Journal* 150: 10–11.

Martire, Agustina. 2020. 'StreetSpace Studio: Architecture learns', *Irish Journal of Anthropology*. Accessed 1 November 2022. http://anthropologyireland.org/ija-2019-martire/.

Martire, Agustina and Aisling Madden. 2022. 'Billy's Sailortown Stories: Unpacking the dense and compact city through graphic anthropology'. Paper presented at Urban Form and the Sustainable Prosperous City, Glasgow, United Kingdom.

Matthew, Robert Hogg. 1963. *Belfast Regional Survey and Plan: Recommendations and conclusions. Presented to Parliament by command of His Excellency, the Governor of Northern Ireland*. Belfast: HMSO.

Milne, Graeme J. 2016. *People, Place and Power on the Nineteenth-Century Waterfront*. London: Palgrave Macmillan.

Moran, J. 2012. 'Imagining the Street in Post-War Britain', *Urban History* 39(1): 166–86.

Multimedia Heritage. *Gallaher's Booklet*. Accessed 1 November 2022. https://mmhireland. com/stories/gallahers/.

O'Connell, Sean. 2018. 'The Troubles with a Lower Case t: Undergraduates and Belfast's difficult history', *Transactions of the Royal Historical Society* 28: 219–39.

Pierse, Michael 2020. 'Ireland's Working-Class Literature: Neglected themes, amphibian academics and the challenges ahead', *Irish University Review* 50(1): 67–81.

Pink, Sarah. 2013. *Doing Visual Ethnography*. London: Sage.

Purdue, Olwen. 2020. 'Dealing with Difficult Pasts: The role of public history in post-conflict Northern Ireland', *Studia Hibernica* 46(1): 91–97.

Silva, Elizabeth Bortolaia. 2002. 'Routine Matters: Narratives of everyday life in families'. In *Social Conceptions of Time: Explorations in sociology*, edited by Graham Crow and Sue Heath. London: Palgrave Macmillan.

Smithson, Peter. 1953. Congrès Internationaux d'Architecture Moderne, Aix-en-Provence, France.

Sterrett, K., M. Hackett and D. Hill. 2012. 'The Social Consequences of Broken Urban Structures: A case study of Belfast', *Journal of Transport Geography* 21: 49–61.

Tranter, P. and J. Doyle. 1996. 'Reclaiming the Residential Street as Play Space', *International Play Journal* 4: 81–97.

Travers Morgan. 1972. 'Belfast Transportation Plan Public Inquiry. General dossier no. 5: Implications of doing nothing'. February.

Tyme, John. 1978. *Motorways versus Democracy. Public inquiries into road proposals and their political significance*. London: Springer.

Vernez Moudon, Anne. 1987. *Public Streets for Public Use*. New York: Columbia University Press.

Wilson, William J. 1987. *The Truly Disadvantaged: The inner city, the underclass, and public policy*. Chicago, IL: University of Chicago Press.

Woodley-Baker, Rochelle. 2009. Private and Public Experience Captured: Young women capture their everyday lives and dreams through photo-narratives', *Visual Studies* 24(1): 19–35.

Part II
The form and use of everyday streets
Birgit Hausleitner, Jane Clossick and
Agustina Martire

Everyday streets facilitate various activities and movements, both indoors and outdoors. The second section of this book addresses the following question: *What is the relationship between the urban form of everyday streets and the activities that occur on them?* Each chapter describes this relationship as well as the spatial forms, features and uses that make up everyday streets. In all of the considered cases, ongoing urban transformations underpin the visualised processes, adding a temporal layer. Andre Corboz (1983) calls this a 'palimpsest' – a reflection of the understanding of urban form as a process shaped by its site and social processes and the understanding that, in turn, spatial form builds the conditions for social processes. This section explores the spatial qualities of everyday streets in Italy, the Netherlands, Sweden, Austria, India and the UK. This introduction begins with an outline of the key morphological mechanisms that underpin everyday streets. It then outlines the themes addressed by the chapters in this section: walkability and pedestrian prioritisation, the accommodation of social and economic change, urban depth, and site significance.

Research on urban morphology considers there to be three key spatial components in urban form: buildings (and their associated open spaces), plots and streets (Scheer 2016). The street network offers choice of way, differentiates the centrality of a place and constitutes the base from which to understand the relationship between places (Hillier and Hanson 1984), while its centres have a particular kind of spatial configuration (Chiaradia et al. 2009). The plot structure represents the 'distribution of landowners … which act according to different strategies … that, in effect, can lead to a higher diversity' (Marcus 2005). Building types influence the available size and proximity of occupiable units as well as the availability of and access to open spaces (Berghauser Pont and Haupt 2010). Similarly, building density serves as a proxy for potential access to people and activities.

Meaningful places, such as everyday streets, comprise specific combinations of building types, plots and streets. The relationship between building types, plots and streets and their differentiation into urban types has recently become central in quantitative studies (Berghauser Pont et al. 2017; Fleischmann et al. 2021; Gil et al. 2012) that investigate the extent of whole urban systems with the resolution of the buildings, plots or street segments. Some studies have tied urban form types to specific objectives, such as walkability and pedestrian movement (Berghauser Pont et al. 2019), or micro-business activities (Hausleitner and Berghauser Pont 2017). The results of these typological studies indicate that main streets constitute the most central streets in their neighbourhoods and the primary links between different districts; they generally feature fine-grain parcellation and medium-rise buildings with related open spaces, mostly on the plots' 'back' sides.

A lack of spatial complexity – a lack of rich variety of spaces – may offer fewer opportunities for different types of uses. To understand the relationship between physical characteristics and activities, Anne Moudon Vernez (2019) suggests an 'operational approach, which recognises the nestedness of urban form elements ... multi-levelness of urban form parallels that of societal structures'. Thus, we can conclude that spatial design likely needs to produce nested spaces to achieve 'environmental and social complexity' (Habraken 2016). Everyday streets generally feature these nested spaces. The typical form of main streets generates 'the presence of people in public space' (Berghauser Pont et al. 2019) and micro-businesses in ground-floor spaces (Hausleitner and Berghauser Pont 2017). Although main streets are planned in different ways, relatively similar configurations tend to emerge. While such quantitative methods are useful for identifying general trends, more local, fine-grain spatial descriptions are necessary to achieve a full understanding of the relationship between the form and use of everyday streets. The chapters in this section feature such descriptions.

The buildings and public spaces of everyday spaces accommodate necessary, optional and social activities (Gehl 2006). Matthew Carmona refers to them as 'people places ... intended to be used by people, usually through spontaneous, everyday and informal use' (Carmona et al. 2010). Uses include necessities like 'going to school or to work, shopping, waiting for a bus or a person, running errands' (Gehl 2006) and optional activities that 'take place only when exterior conditions are favourable, when weather and place invite them' – things like 'taking a walk to get a breath of fresh air, standing around enjoying life, or sitting and sunbathing' (Gehl 2006). Social activities on streets require the close proximity of people in homes, gardens or balconies, offices or other public spaces. These activities may occur spontaneously, as is often the case with children playing and people chatting – these are what Jan Gehl calls 'passive contacts' (2006).

Walkability is essential to the liveability of everyday streets and important for necessary, optional and social activities. The pedestrian scale, John Friedmann (2010) explains, 'allows people to interact in a variety of mostly unplanned ways, on the street or in business establishments among other spaces of habitual encounter'. The degree to which a street's public space facilitates pedestrian flows influences its uses and street life: 'pedestrian movement is circulation, but also permits economic, social and cultural exchange' (Carmona et al. 2010). Sigrid Kroismayr and Andreas Novy address the question of walkability in their chapter on Vienna, demonstrating that high accessibility for pedestrians facilitates the use of adjacent squares with complementary use programs.

The importance of prioritising pedestrians to boost the liveability of streets has been highlighted by researchers for decades, but the need for more walkable public spaces was amplified by the Covid-19 pandemic. Vikas Mehta (2013) identifies three factors that determine the degree to which a street is a sociable space: social (places that have special meanings for the community), behavioural (land uses and their mix) and physical (form and space characteristics). The chapters by Matthew Carmona on London high streets and Deepti Adlakha on Chennai's Pondy Bazaar describe the effect of recent pedestrianisation efforts. Adlakha looks specifically at short-term, low-cost, citizen-led interventions, which are commonly referred to as tactical urbanism (Lydon and Garcia 2015). Carmona prioritises the improvement of the pedestrian experience through adequate space for pedestrian movement and activities in the hierarchy of interventions for street space enhancements. This section's chapters address the behavioural and physical aspects of streets as social spaces and discuss how to develop them into meaningful places for the local community.

The unique morphology of everyday streets can facilitate social and economic change. Urban environments and urban life evolve over time, and the physical elements of urban form change at varying speeds. For example, the evolution of street networks occurs over long periods of times, while individual buildings evolve at a far faster pace (Scheer 2006). Importantly, however, the aforementioned form types (Berghauser Pont et al. 2019; Hausleitner and Berghauser Pont 2017) are resistant to sudden major shifts, slowing the physical effect of incremental changes in social processes. Research on the resilience of urban form has shown that streets 'have a stabilizing effect and constrain the reconfiguration of smaller-scale morphological elements' (Romice et al. 2020). Although buildings show 'limited capacity to generate systemic change', Romice et al. (2020) explain that in 'special circumstances bottom-up processes can trigger wide-ranging transformations'. John Friedmann (2010) described such bottom-up actions as inherent to 'lived-in' spaces through which 'actual physical and social spaces [are] … transformed … through the simple fact of being lived in … as newcomers arrive, old residents depart'. In her chapter on Naples, Orfina Fatigato describes how building transformations can be seen in the appropriation of different types of spaces, with voids filled with new community functions. In other words, social changes occupy the existing fabric in new ways. Another example of such 'bottom-up' change is shown in Birgit Hausleitner and Mae-Ling Stuyt's chapter on Amsterdam, which describes the transformations inside buildings that allow businesses that require more space to fit into relatively small shops by combining two or more units.

Small-scale adaptation between uses and spatial form mainly occurs in what Philippe Panerai (2005) calls the 'urban leeway' – the zone between the building and the street where either the public or the private can expand. This zone often shows differences in use at different times of the day or on different days of the week. Such informal shifts in use are facilitated by the permeability of the boundaries between spaces, which are 'simultaneously means of separation and communication' (Madanipour 2003). Orfina Fatigato, in her chapter on Naples, refers to this as the 'porosity' of spaces, related to the definitions of Paola Viganò (2006) and Sophie Wolfrum (2018). John Habraken (2016) 'territorialises' this zone, embedding it in the logic of Anne Vernez Moudon's concept of nestedness: 'A territory resides in a larger one and may contain smaller ones … the control of access that comes with a territory means that what reaches the boarder's room must first cross boundaries of larger fields.' The sequence of spaces between public and private areas produces what John Habraken (1998) calls 'territorial depth', Machiel van Dorst (2006) calls 'privacy zoning' and Jane Clossick (2017) calls 'urban depth' – a relational spatial concept that differentiates spaces by their degree of accessibility. These zones of varying degrees of depth facilitate different uses, not only in buildings and transition zones but also in nested public spaces. Hausleitner and Stuyt note that, in Amsterdam, these territories operate at building, block and neighbourhood scale levels, offering many places with a variety of uses on everyday streets and their hinterland. For Carmona, the everyday street functions best in London when uses cross the street threshold, flowing between inside and outside.

Finally, site matters. Kahn and Burns (2021) elaborate on three bounded domains that frame every site: a distinct climatic region, the material expression embedded in local building traditions (influenced by climate and geomorphology) and a sphere of cultural practices. The coherent spatial design of sites, which comprises these three domains, contributes to the identity of a place. Maria Luna Nobile's chapter on Kiruna is the most interesting in this respect, as it describes the relocation of an entire Arctic city and reflects on what this relocation means for the city's everyday streets. Birgit Hausleitner and Mae-Ling Stuyt's chapter on Amsterdam elaborates on landscape and water engineering as a prerequisite for a settlement and, in turn, for everyday streets.

The chapters in this section also focus on the overarching theme of this book: inclusiveness. Each chapter describes an everyday street with a morphology and range of uses that include broad sections of society. For Fatigato, the *vicoli* of Naples constitute a place for both traditional residents and new tourists, though spatial conflict may emerge between them as ground-floor residential units transform into Airbnbs. For Hausleitner and Stuyt, the diversity of Amsterdam streets accommodates everyday uses that the city needs, including those of large-scale industry. For Adlahka and Carmona, prioritising pedestrians allows their needs to be included in streets' primary functions. Nobile assesses the translation of identity and the inclusion of the Sámi people and new residents in the relocated streets of Kiruna. Finally, for Kroismayr and Novy, the provision of a walkable foundational economy facilitates the inclusion of a wide range of socioeconomic groups in Vienna.

Bibliography

Berghauser Pont, Meta and Per Haupt. 2010. *Spacematrix: Space, density and urban form*. Rotterdam: NAI.

Berghauser Pont, Meta, Gianna Stavroulaki, Jorge Gil, Lars Marcus, Miguel Serra, Birgit Hausleitner, Jesper Olsson, Eshan Abshirini and Ashley Dhanani. 2017. 'Quantitative Comparison of Cities: Distribution of street and building types based on density and centrality measures'. *Proceedings, 11th International Space Syntax Symposium*.

Berghauser Pont, Meta, Gianna Stavroulaki and Lars Marcus. 2019. 'Development of Urban Types Based on Network Centrality, Built Density and their Impact on Pedestrian Movement', *Environment and Planning B: Urban Analytics and City Science* 46(8): 1549–64. https://doi.org/10.1177/2399808319852632.

Carmona, Matthew, Steve Tiesdell, Tim Heath and Tanner Oc. 2010. *Public Places Urban Spaces: The dimensions of urban design.* 2nd ed. Abingdon: Routledge.

Chiaradia, Alain, Bill Hillier, Christian Schwander and Martin Wedderburn. 2009. 'Spatial Centrality, Economic Vitality/Viability. Compositional and spatial effects in Greater London'. *Proceedings, 7th International Space Syntax Symposium*.

Clossick, Jane. 2017. 'The Depth Structure of a London High Street: A study in urban order'. PhD thesis, London Metropolitan University.

Corboz, Andre. 1983. 'The Land as Palimpsest', *Diogenes* 31(121): 12–34. https://doi.org/10.1177/039219218303112102.

Fleischmann, Martin, Alessandra Feliciotti, Ombretta Romice and Sergio Porta. 2021. 'Methodological Foundation of a Numerical Taxonomy of Urban Form', *Environment and Planning B: Urban analytics and city science*. https://doi.org/10.1177/23998083211059835.

Friedmann, John. 2010. 'Place and Place-Making in Cities: A global perspective', *Planning Theory and Practice* 11(2): 149–65. https://doi.org/10.1080/14649351003759573.

Gehl, Jan. 2006. *Life Between Buildings.* 6th ed. København: Danish Architectural Press.

Gil, Jorge, José Beirão, Nuno Montenegro and Jose Duarte. 2012. 'On the Discovery of Urban Typologies: Data mining the many dimensions of urban form', *Urban Morphology* 16(1): 27–40. Accessed 1 November 2022. https://www.researchgate.net/publication/256895610.

Habraken, John. 1998. *The Structure of the Ordinary: Form and control in the built environment*, edited by J. Teicher. Cambridge, MA: MIT Press.

Habraken, John. 2016. 'Cultivating Complexity: The need for a shift in cognition'. In *Complexity, Cognition, Urban Planning and Design*, edited by J. Portugali and E. Stolk, 55–74. Berlin: Springer. https://doi.org/10.1007/978-3-319-32653-5_4.

Hausleitner, Birgit and Meta Berghauser Pont. 2017. 'Development of a Configurational Typology for Micro-Businesses Integrating Geometric and Configurational Variables'. *Proceedings, 11th International Space Syntax Symposium*.

Kahn, Andrea and Carol Burns. 2021. *Site Matters: Strategies for uncertainty through planning and design.* 2nd ed. Abingdon: Routledge.

Lydon, Mike and Anthony Garcia. 2015. *Tactical Urbanism: Short-term action for long-term change.* Washington, DC: Island Press.

Madanipour, Ali. 2003. *Public and Private Spaces of the City.* Washington, DC: Taylor & Francis. https://doi.org/10.4324/9780203402856.

Marcus, Lars. 2005. Plot Syntax: A configurational approach to urban diversity. *Proccedings, 5th International Space Syntax Symposium*.

Mehta, Vikas. 2013. *The Street: A quintessential social public space.* Abingdon: Routledge.

Moudon Vernez, Anne. 2019. 'Introducing Supergrids, Superblocks, Areas, Networks, and Levels to Urban Morphological Analyses', *International Journal of Architecture & Planning* 7: 1–14.

Panerai, Philippe. 2005. 'The Scale of the Urban Block'. In *Atlas of the Dutch Urban Block*, edited by S. Komossa, H. Meyer, N. Jutten and S. Thomaes, 10–14. Bussum: Toth.

Scheer, Brenda. 2016. 'The Epistemology of Urban Morphology', *Urban Morphology* 20(1): 5–17.

van Dorst, Machiel. 2006. 'Sustainable Liveability: Privacy zoning as a physical condition for social sustainability'. In *Environment, Health and Sustainable Development*, edited by A. Abdel-Hadi, M.K. Tolba and S. Soliman, 1–10. Göttingen: Hogrefe.

Viganò, Paola. 2006. 'The Porous City: Prototypes of idiorrhythmical conglomerates'. In *Comment vivre ensemble: Prototypes of idiorrhythmical conglomerates and shared spaces*, edited by Pellegrini Viganò. Rome: Officina Edizioni.

Wolfrum, Sophie (ed.), Heiner Stengel, Florian Kurbasik, Norbert Kling, Sofia Dona, Imke Mumm and Christian Zöhrer. 2018. *Porous City. From metaphor to urban agenda.* Basel: Birkhäuser.

8

Vicoli as forms of proximity: Naples' Spanish Quarter

Orfina Fatigato

The narrow streets of the historic centre of Naples are called 'vicoli'. This term refers to the physical size of the streets as well as the ways in which they are lived. The spaces of the vicoli host a diverse body of occupants, and they often shift from linear, continuous spaces to sequences of 'rooms', where public and private meet. This chapter focuses on the concept of 'porosity' as the basis for the unique relationship between public space and private space in the streets of the Spanish Quarter. Porosity facilitates the nuanced occupation of space in these streets, changing seamlessly over time.

The *vicoli* of Naples: porous urban interiors

City streets, according to Benjamin, constitute the home of the collective:

> The collective is a being in constant motion, constantly agitated, which lives, experiences, knows and invents as many things between the facades of buildings as individuals within their four walls … The walls with 'Prohibition of Posting' signs act as desks; the newsstands are libraries, the letterboxes are the room's trophies, the benches are bedroom furniture and the café terrace is a cantilevered window from which you can look at your home … The street space, more than in any other place, appears here as the familiar and furnished interior of the masses. (1934, 440)

SPANISH QUARTER

NAPLES, ITALY ├────────┤ 2km ⊕

Figure 8.0: Map of Naples © Anna Skoura

This account of streets as large urban interiors is particularly pertinent in a city like Naples, the streets of which host infinite situations – oftentimes unpredictable, ironic and even alienating events. Benjamin directly references the city of Naples in his letters to Asja Lacis, describing the city's historic centre as a space where architecture is porous, like the rock upon which and with which it was built:

> Structure and life continually interfere in courtyards, archways and stairways. The living space capable of hosting new, unexpected constellations is preserved everywhere. The definitive, the characteristics are rejected. Balconies, windows, stairs, roofs are both loggia and stage-set scenery. Private life is fragmented, porous and discontinuous. The street enters the buildings and apartments. Intersections are continuous between night and day, noise and silence, external light and internal darkness, between the public space of the street and the private space of the apartment. (2020, 60)

This porosity, a characteristic feature of the space in the ancient city of Naples (Velardi 1992), manifests itself in the osmotic relationship between outside and inside – between the space of the street and the space of the buildings' interiors. From the street, a place of movement, meetings and integration, one can move through the hallways and courtyards of buildings. The thresholds between such spaces – open and continuous during the day, closed and filtered in the evening – mark the boundaries between different degrees of internality, creating intermediate spaces that allow for the gradual passage from the public realm to a collective and/or private one. Applied to the physical and metaphysical sense of the city, according to Ian Chambers, the idea of porosity can be broadened to include its historical and cultural formation:

> The porous substance absorbs whatever it encounters, and assimilates external elements while retaining its original form. It embodies and incorporates extraneous elements and external pressures. The History of Naples is also, and perhaps more significantly, the history of these processes. (2008, 87)

Such physical and material conditions have always influenced ways of living and accessing the spaces in the streets of Naples' historic centre. In a sense, Naples' condition of fragility and many indefinite thresholds – between inside and outside, between public and private spaces, between streets and homes – has historically contributed to the strengthening of its entire system of intangible relationships, meaning the ways in which inhabitants live in and experience the city and its spaces. Dines (2018) also comments on the specificity and complexity of Italian streets, citing *vicoli* as a street type that invokes a relationship between morphology and a way of life.

Therefore, the *vicoli* have emerged with various informal and creative appropriative practices, through which street spaces are 'domestically converted' for private use: extensions of domestic spaces in ground-level homes (*bassi*) along the street, commercial vendor stands with makeshift counters, and an ever-increasing number (especially following increases in mass tourism throughout Naples) of outdoor tables and dining apparatus set up by restaurants. The *vicoli* in the Spanish Quarter are where such forms of conquest are most evident. There is a perceptible aim to transform city spaces, and, given the scarcity of proper public squares, street spaces are often used as playground areas for the city's youth and sitting areas for its elderly, who often leave their chairs in the street. Examples of this urban dynamic are effectively depicted in a documentary called *Homo Urbanus* by Bêka and Lemoine (2019), who travel to 10 cities around the world, including Naples, and describe how their histories are based on continuous and reciprocated adaptations between humanity and the urban structure in an uninterrupted process of transformation.

The Spanish Quarter, from the street to the sky: historic stratification and social mix

The Spanish Quarter is a key part of Naples' historic centre. It spreads along a slope between the hill dominated by the Certosa di San Martino and the Via Toledo roadway further down. The construction of the Spanish Quarter's first cluster dates back to the sixteenth century, when it was decreed by viceroy Don Pedro de Toledo that living quarters for military garrisons and soldiers passing through Naples should be provided. This initial purpose explains the limited size of the building blocks and the narrow streets (five metres wide on average), as the area was essentially conceived as a space for the march of small militias. The orthogonal mesh grid – originally fifteen by six streets – was adapted to steeply sloping terrain, with several expansions made later.

The fabric of the Spanish Quarter maintains its distinct features today: the compact, high-density buildings characterised by alternating city blocks and narrow streets and stairways that follow the slope of the terrain. Along Via Toledo, which marks the neighbourhood's 'downhill' border, lies a part of the city that can be viewed as a porous system, with views through the alleys that rise up the hill. It gives the impression of a system of canyons carved into a constructed mass of buildings through which one might climb and get lost. Looking from above – from Corso Vittorio Emanuele to the slope of the hill, following its contour line – the neighbourhood can be viewed as a system of rooftops and terraces, overlapping one another at varying heights and levels. While the alleys traversing the orthogonal mesh are the channel lines that visually connect the hill to the sea, the longitudinal alleyways are located at the various orographic slope levels, producing a series of 'terrace-style' systems that run parallel to Via Toledo.

While the Spanish Quarter has changed over time, it retains its most distinct characteristics – both material and immaterial. In fact, it is difficult to speak of the Spanish Quarter without referencing the strong connection between its material aspects and its vibrant social life, which unravels in its narrow *vicoli* and dense network of buildings. The neighbourhood comprises 170 city blocks consisting of four- and five-storey above-ground buildings that, while designated as single-apartment blocks, are frequently divided into several different building spaces, with narrow staircases and floors with one or two rooms each.

Overall, in the approximately 600 condominiums, there are nearly 3,000 units housing about 15,000 inhabitants. Many of the people live in ground-floor units with a single window looking out onto the street. The variety and vitality of this area are signalled by the presence of artisan workshops, vendors and many other facilities, including garages and storage units (Laino 2001).

Despite the strong identity often associated with Naples' Spanish Quarter, the area suffers from economic weakness, building decay stemming from lack of care, and a persistent risk of social marginalisation. The social composition of its inhabitants has changed over time but remains diverse, including long-time residents, broken-up families, urban underclass, new upper-middle-class groups (who moved in recently, drawn in by the vitality of the centre), university students, and both new and deeply rooted migrant communities. In his socio-logical commentary – with a degree of literary humour – Giovanni Laino, a well-known scholar of the area, writes:

The families of the Spanish Quarters can be divided into three fundamental social groups, which in recent years have joined two new tribes:

The Eduardians, referring to the theatrical works of Edoardo De Filippo, or substantially 'healthy' families, with average schooling, who work (although often in very precarious conditions), mostly live in rented houses, participate in popular culture, and are affected in only limited cases by deviant experiences.

The Vivianians, referring to the works of Raffaele Viviani, are families in which school is rarely attended, and whose mostly male members are involved in the activities of Camorra mob organisations, while the women and children give life to the neighbourhoods' streets, made up of informal and oftentimes illicit networks.

The lower-middle classes of workers, generally made up of public employees who only partially live in the neighbourhood, more as residents than as inhabitants, since their social life takes place for the most part outside of the Quarters.

The Indian and Filipino migrants who mostly live in the lower ground floor *bassi* street-level apartments, which are oftentimes the former storage deposits for the area's craft businesses.

The new bourgeois, a newly introduced upper-middle-class group that began to move into the neighbourhood during the late 90s, was attracted by affordable real estate prices and managed to purchase and renovate rather degraded properties in this very central part of the city. (Laino 2001)

Laino goes on to demonstrate how these listed categories were joined in recent years by a rising population of university students who came to the Spanish Quarter in search of off-campus housing. They could not afford to rent apartments in the *Centro Antico*, as that area was largely transformed into short-term rentals. In addition, there are tourists who enjoy temporary residence in this part of the city, often by finding deals for short-term stays in the various properties offered on digital rental platforms such as Airbnb.

This unique social blend at the heart of a central historic district in a great European city makes Naples' Spanish Quarter a continental treasure that, even today, remains a true expression of rare urban vitality.

Despite its changes over time, the Spanish Quarter's *vicoli* continue to constitute a microcosm whose small spaces have always played host to a strong and stratified coexistence of activities, including artisan production, various illicit and unregulated operations, systems of social housing, and informal public gathering spaces. The 'spatial constriction' of its streets has engendered an economy of proximity – often referred to in Italian as the 'economy of the *vicolo*'. As uniquely exhaustive as it is self-sufficient, the *vicoli* are becoming increasingly impoverished in the modern era.

Transformation of the Spanish Quarter's *vicoli*

The bassi

The most important transformations of the *vicoli* spaces and their unique 'economy' date back to the 1980s. That decade witnessed radical changes in the market economy's production systems, which resulted in the gradual extinction of the craft activities that were typical of the area, as well as the 1980 earthquake, which exacerbated the area's environmental degradation. The street-level *bassi* – the ground-floor street-facing structures initially used as storage areas for craft workshops – began to be used as housing units in blatantly unsanitary conditions.

After the emergency response to the earthquake of 1980, several important public initiatives were established (namely URBAN 1996–2001 and the S.I.Re.Na Project). However, despite the plethora of proposals made, no real action was ever taken to mitigate the depletion of artisan activities that were so characteristic of the area and its *vicolo* economy, or to limit the seemingly uncontrollable spread of other commercial operations such as restaurants. This inaction dealt a serious blow to the Spanish Quarter's *vicoli*. Towards the end of the 1990s, an important opportunity was missed with proposals to update the historical economic system of *vicoli* in the Spanish Quarter and recondition the ground floors of the area's buildings, restoring the relationship of extensive permeability and porosity between the street space and the ground-floor levels of the various residential buildings devoted to craft and manufacturing.

Until about 15 years ago, Naples could still boast a historic centre that was largely spared from gentrification. This is not the case today, as the urban condition has changed. This is due in large part to the spread of the tertiary sector and the resultant expulsion of artisan workers. Additionally, gentrification has stemmed from the significant pressures of tourism, which, prior to the Covid-19 pandemic, was growing at an annual rate of 10 per cent. This growth resulted in the widespread emergence of economic circuits linked to global tourism platforms. Evidence of such growth is clear from the large increase in rental units listed on peer-to-peer platforms such as Airbnb. Many street-level *bassi* units have been transformed into short-term rental apartments, turning places with undignified living conditions into highly attractive destinations for tourists looking for an 'authentic' Neapolitan experience (Pollice 2019). This trend has added a new layer to the centuries-old stratification of living spaces in Naples' historic centre. It represents a substantial modification of the city's real estate – one that has largely occurred in a highly unregulated manner.

The old buildings of the Spanish Quarter are characterised by strong social stratification – from the street-level *bassi* to the upper-level apartments overlooking the narrow streets. Even the highest apartments, the terraces of which provide incredible views of the city and the sea, have all witnessed a rise in local properties intended for tourist rentals. Thus, the varied makeup of inhabitants in these 'vital' condominium complexes has shifted in recent years to include many tourists who, as transient inhabitants, enjoy 'identity' and 'authenticity' – immersion in the unique lifestyle of the neighbourhood. After the first transfer of inhabitants to the periphery of Naples following the 1980 earthquake, Naples is now witnessing the transition of *bassi* into accommodation for tourists. This process is ongoing, and the risk of gentrification is strong. The impact of these new short-term housing facilities is not limited to the internal spaces of historic buildings; it is well known that the intensification of tourism can result in a series of 'chain-reaction' transformations involving public space.

In the Spanish Quarter's *vicoli*, one can observe a substantial modification of commercial establishments over the last five years, with the progressive disappearance of proximity trade and bartering and just a few remaining historical craft trades that resisted the great emptying of the 1990s. This modification paved the way for an exponential increase in commercial, mainly cuisine-oriented activities that appeal to tourists.

Figure 8.1: Cultural, social and economic possible network. Image: researchers at SQUIN Laboratory, DiARC. © Orfina Fatigato

This transformation is most clear in the first band of the neighbourhood flanking Via Toledo; its role as a major roadway, which for centuries has always been intended for walking and trading, was strengthened following its pedestrianisation in the late 1990s. This substantial modification resulted in another transformation regarding the use of ground-floor areas in the *vicoli* parallel to Via Toledo, decreasing in intensity the further one moves from the main road. These changes, in line with the topographical conditions of the various roads relative to Via Toledo, persisted and strengthened over the years, as shown by recent transformations stemming from the rise in tourism.

For the most striking examples, consider the three longitudinal streets of Vico Lungo del Mulso, Via Speranzella and Vico Lungo Teatro Nuovo. These *vicoli* have begun to be characterised by a series of informal practices, including the placing of tables, seats and benches for outdoor dining of the area's restaurants and bars. The 'popular' aspect of these informal businesses can be deceiving in their attempt to pass as long-standing cultural traditions in the neighbourhood. On the contrary, the extent of these deceptions is beginning to homogenise certain aspects of the *vicoli*; they are contributing to the development of a false image of these places that closely resembles the folkloric imagery of the local neighbourhoods conveyed by tourism marketing.

This seemingly unstoppable trend, strongly fuelled by neighbourhood merchants adapting their activities to meet tourists' expectations, suffered a major setback in 2020 due to the Covid-19 pandemic. This hurdle has revealed the fragility of an economy based solely on satisfying tourists' expectations, and has shed light on the need to consider urban redevelopment proposals for integrated and inclusive projects capable of engendering cultural innovation as a key element of the local economy.

Amid the ongoing pandemic, the Spanish Quarter's *vicoli* have been places of vitality and solidarity in which traditional forms of sociality and economies of proximity have been activated. Naples can be viewed as a site of persistent deviation towards unconventional paths with regard to the organisation of urban space, culture, production, work, profit and politics (Chambers 2008). With its unique forms of adaptation, there may be a way for the Spanish Quarter to combine twenty-first-century mass tourism with its historical culture of living enabled by its urban character.

Voids and the SQUIN project

Another form of porosity that provides viable opportunities for everyday life in the Spanish Quarter is residual spaces. These small, abandoned voids can be important resources in the dense fabric of Naples' historic centre (Figure 8.2). They are currently listed in the city's municipality plans as 'ruins and sediments resulting from demolition', representing 'voids in waiting'. Such residual spaces constitute a significant resource in a city like Naples – especially in the Spanish Quarter – given the high density of the built environment and the widespread lack of open spaces, public squares, gardens and other public gathering spaces. The SQUIN project[1] was concerned with the 'void spaces' located in the heart of the Spanish Quarter, aiming to investigate the re-qualification of small, empty city fragments and their transformation into new spaces for local communities. This work sought to stimulate development and bring life to these gaps in the city of Naples.

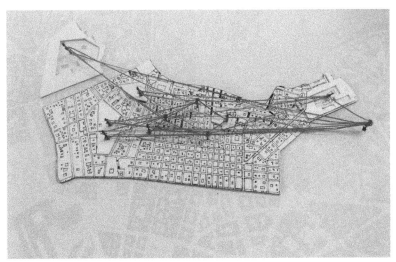

Figure 8.2: Voids as nodes in the *vicoli* network. Image: students at SQUIN Laboratory, DiARC. © Orfina Fatigato

Investigating the potential

Four urban 'voids' of different sizes were selected for project design proposals. This project focuses on two of the four – those located along Vico Tofa, taking up the space of an entire city block, and those along Via Emanuele De Deo (which corresponds to an incomplete residential block that was rebuilt after WWII). Today, the void along Vico Tofa is completely abandoned and bordered by an impenetrable wall, while that along Emanuele via De Deo is used informally as a space for meeting and watching SSC Napoli matches (this practice has been considered in the project).

This study interprets these voids as nodes in the network of the *vicoli*, serving to facilitate encounters among residents, exchanges of skills and knowledge, and collective learning. It imagines various strategic scenarios to create this urban network and fill the void fragments with buildings or open spaces, and rethink them as the different sites of a new cultural infrastructure. Temporary residences proposed for welcoming tourists, considered as the area's new and transitory inhabitants, small living quarters for students and young workers, neighbourhood kitchens to facilitate the exchange of culinary experiences between migrant communities and Neapolitan families, collaborative work-study spaces for nearby universities, co-working

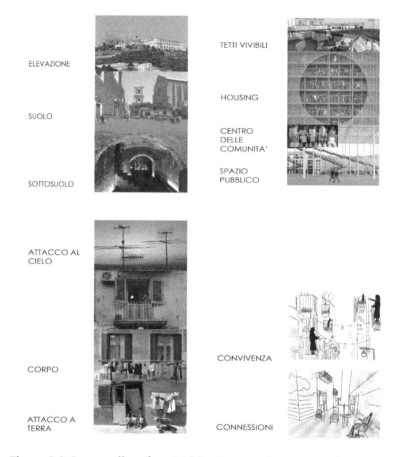

Figure 8.3: Image collage from Melting Pot: an urban strategy for the voids. Image: students and researchers at SQUIN Laboratory, DiARC. © Orfina Fatigato

spaces and play areas divided into interior spaces and outdoor playgrounds, designed to be on the terraces of the new buildings.

All of the proposed interventions were designed to align with the street space. However, they entail the widening of the narrow streets of the *vicoli* to expand ground-floor space and elaborate spatial components, such as stairways, terraces, small squares and gardens, and vegetable gardens that enhance the porosity of the neighbourhood (Figure 8.4).

The proposed infrastructural elements are conceived of as 'inhabited sections' in which the street can gain new spaces for neighbourhood life at different levels. These new buildings include roof

Figure 8.4: New infrastructural elements as an extension of the *vicoli* space. Image: students at SQUIN Laboratory, DiARC. © Orfina Fatigato

structures – upper-level public squares accessible by urban stairways from the *vicoli* below. In this way, the *vicolo* can benefit from new vantage points, encompassing the neighbourhoods and overlooking the city, so that the places of life along it gain new space, light and air going upwards towards the sky.

Conclusion

The research on the Spanish Quarter entailed broad reflection on the theme of urban regeneration and means of activating synergistic and virtuous processes by working with authentic spaces, their inhabitants and their system of uses, and the relationships that characterise them. The historical reading of the Spanish Quarter and its *vicoli* visualises a space of sociality, commerce, exchange and movement made possible by extending interior spaces to the exterior. The elaboration of scenarios for reinhabiting and revitalising small, empty residual spaces allows for an interpretation of their role as important resources in the Spanish Quarter's dense fabric.

This project on small-scale urban voids with a focus on new volumes as an extension of the street space reinterpreted the porosity of the Spanish Quarter – a specific character of the historic urban fabric and of the specific way of hybrid dwelling between interior and exterior, between public and private. The new volumes reinterpret the value of the *bassi* through high permeability and porosity, allowing for the reinterpretation and appropriation of such spaces as dynamics change over time. Volumes that act as potential 'condensers' of social values – as hybrid, inclusive and open as possible – should be prioritised. The new volumes have been imagined as activators establishing new relationships with the historical activities of the district but also as places of cultural and economic experimentation and innovation. Together with the newly established network of places, a definition of possible functional programs could support a wider economic network in the city and facilitate increased social mixité.

The project proposals, driven by careful reflection on the connections between places, actors and relationships, are configured as possible intervention strategies and supported by strongly contextualised, adaptive decision-making processes that are capable of regenerating social, economic and cultural values over time. This methodological approach aims to trigger a change in the historic city, beginning by interpreting tangible and intangible values and experimenting with how they might be used as resources for cultural and economic innovation.

Notes

1   As part of the research and teaching activities at DiARC, UNINA has developed an experimental project called the 'Spanish Quarters Inhabiting Network' (SQUIN) project. This project entailed local residents, students and researchers working together to elaborate proposals and scenarios for the transformation of some of these 'void spaces' at the heart of the Spanish Quarter.

Bibliography

Bêka, Ila and Louise Lemoine. 2019. *Homo Urbanus: A citymatographic odyssey.* Accessed 1 November 2022. http://www.bekalemoine.com/homo_urbanus.php.

Benjamin, Walter. 1934. *'Le flaneur', Paris Capitale du XIXe siècle: Le livre des passages.* Paris: Cerf.

Benjamin, Walter. 2020. *Lacis, Napoli porosa.* Naples: Libreria Dante & Descartes.

Chambers, Ian. 2008. *Mediterranean Crossings: The politics of an interrupted modernity.* Durham, NC: Duke University Press. Italian: 2007. *Le molte voci del Mediterraneo.* Milan: Raffaello Cortina Editore.

Dines, Nick. 2018. 'What's In A Word? Contextual diversity, urban ethnography and the linguistic limits of the street', *Sociological Review* 66(5): 952–67.

Laino, Giovanni. 2012. *Il fuoco nel cuore e il diavolo in corpo: La partecipazione come attivazione sociale.* Milan: Franco Angeli.

Laino, Giovanni (ed.). 2018. *Quartieri Spagnoli: Note da quarant'anni di lavoro dell'associazione.* Naples: Cavalcavia.

Pollice, Adriana. 2019. 'Questa città non è un albergo', *Il Manifesto*, 2 April.

Velardi, Claudio (ed.). 1992. *La città porosa: Conversazioni su Napoli.* Naples: Cronopio.

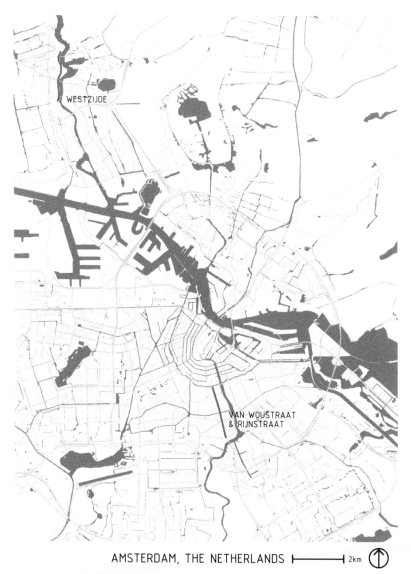

WESTZIJDE

VAN WOUSTRAAT
& RIJNSTRAAT

AMSTERDAM, THE NETHERLANDS ├──────┤ 2km ⊕

Figure 9.0: Map of Amsterdam © Anna Skoura

9

Spatial-structural qualities of mixed-use main streets: two case studies from the Amsterdam metropolitan region

Birgit Hausleitner and Mae-Ling Stuyt

Streets are where the needs and values of different users and activities come together. Main streets in the Netherlands were either planned in major urban expansions or developed over time in the shape of ribbons upon dykes – 'long lines' of continuously active streets. This chapter presents two cases from the Amsterdam metropolitan region: vanWoustraat-Rijnstraat, a main street planned as part of an urban expansion, and Westzijde, a main street that developed over time as part of a long line. While vanWoustraat-Rijnstraat is tightly organised and coherent in both appearance and function, Westzijde is characterised by a multitude of different buildings and functions. This study visualises the spatial-structural qualities that facilitate the evolving economic activities of these two streets. It explores the variation between them by morphological differentiation and determines several spatial characteristics that enable the mix: modularity of the urban plan, complementary 'front' and 'back' sides, structural coherence and territorial depth – the sequence of spaces between the urban 'front' and 'back' sides of buildings, blocks and neighbourhoods.

Introduction

Amsterdam, in line with many other major cities, has recently begun to promote a 'mixed-use' environment (Gemeente Amsterdam 2011; Gemeente Amsterdam 2021; Hoppenbrouwer and Louw 2005) for two primary reasons: first, mixed-use development promises health (Stevenson et al. 2016), a reduced need for travel (Hoppenbrouwer and Louw 2005), urban vitality (Jacobs 1961; Kang et al. 2020) and safety (Bellair and Browning 2010; Coupland 1997); second, mixed-use development is compact, meaning that it aligns with the aim of limiting urban growth to the pre-existing boundaries of an urban fabric (Gemeente Amsterdam 2021). Compactness and mixed-use are increasingly prioritised in urban development as land becomes more scarce (European Commission and UN Habitat 2016). In this context, the question regarding mixing industrial and other uses on everyday streets is no longer 'do we want it?' but 'how can we make it work?' – what spatial qualities support the integration of various functions? Everyday streets in Amsterdam constitute a reliable site for such an investigation, as they include both 'the ordinary and extraordinary' (Highmore 2002, 16).

One consequence of the push for compact, mixed-use development is the increasing multi-functionality of urban environments. Diverse activities increasingly occur in close proximity to one another, often with conflicting needs. Grant (2002) considers that there are three categories of mixed-use environments depending on their potential for conflict. The first is a mix of dwelling types. The second is a mix of residential and commercial facilities. The third is the integration of typically segregated uses, such as industry and housing. However, the presence of multiple functions in one area does not necessarily make a mixed-use neighbourhood. Montgomery (1998) names three pre-conditions for a truly mixed-use environment: 'users must use the same streets and spaces, users must use at least some of the same facilities, and activity must not be concentrated into a particular time of the day.' In other words, the spatial scale of the mix of functions and the proximity of different activities and users are central; Montgomery's pre-conditions focus on the street as a key space in which to integrate users and activities through design.

Each of the two main streets presented in this chapter belongs to a neighbourhood with historically and contemporarily diverse functions. The first, vanWoustraat-Rijnstraat, is more common. It features a

mix of residential, commercial, retail and service functions; industrial activities are usually excluded by functional zoning. The second,
Westzijde, comprises fragments of industrial typologies and uses that
are integrated with residential and commercial facilities. The historical
evolution of the two streets is significant, as it is indicative of the type
of mix that residents expect on their everyday street, which influences

Figure 9.1a: Location of the main streets parallel to the main waterways,
including main commercial and industrial activities
Figure 9.1b: Streetlife on vanWoustraat (bottom left) and Westzijde
(bottom right). © Hausleitner and Stuyt 2022

what they appreciate or object to. Both streets are parts of neighbour-hoods considered to be 'liveable' (Leefbarometer 2020). Main streets in the Netherlands were either planned in major urban expansions or developed over time in the shape of ribbons upon dykes – 'long lines' of continuously active streets. vanWoustraat-Rijnstraat is one of the former; Westzijde one of the latter.

Spatial form is an important factor with regard to economic activities; the two are intimately intertwined. Jacobs (1961) was the first to suggest that spatial and functional diversity are related. The impact of the street network and its differentiation on economic activities have since been extensively explored (Chiaradia et al. 2009; Froy 2021; Hillier and Hanson 1984; Marcus 2000; Narvaez et al. 2014; van Nes 2005). In addition, places that accommodate urban economic processes (e.g. shops, factories) can be identified by how the main elements of urban form are combined and differentiated (Hausleitner and Berghauser Pont 2017): the street network (centrality of a place), the built density (building types), the grain of parcellation, and terri-torial depth (the sequence of spaces between the urban 'front' and 'back' sides of buildings, blocks and neighbourhoods) (Hausleitner 2012; Hausleitner 2019). This chapter explores streets in two types of areas with regard to how a functional mix occupies street space and what spatial qualities facilitate the mix.

Two mixed-use main streets: one planned, one developed over time

The two streets evolved in different ways. These differing histories resulted in different patterns of spatial form. vanWoustraat-Rijnstraat was planned with aesthetic and functional considerations, while Westzijde was shaped by landscape engineering and functional require-ments. vanWoustraat-Rijnstraat (see Figure 9.1a) is centrally located in modern Amsterdam South, crossing two neighbourhoods: Pijp and Rivierenbuurt. The street runs parallel to the city's namesake, the river Amstel. It lies 300–450 metres (the equivalent of two to four city blocks) away from the western riverbank, the old main dyke along the Amstel. Similarly situated by a waterway, Westzijde (see Figure 9.1a) runs along the Zaan (a canal) northwest of Amsterdam and through the neighbourhoods of Oud Koog and Oud Zaandijk. Along its length, its official name varies – Zuideinde, Lagedijk, Hoogstraat and Lagendijk. The street is separated from the canal by a strip of plots ranging in depth from 50 to 200 metres. While the development of Pijp and Rivier-enbuurt was driven by large-scale development plans executed over a relatively short period of time, the development of Oud Koog and Oud Zaandijk occurred slowly, plot-based, over a far longer period.

The urban plan for Pijp, which included vanWoustraat, was part of the nineteenth-century Plan vanNieftrik-Kalff, initiated in 1877 (Figure 9.2, top left), while Rivierenbuurt, which included Rijnstraat, was part of Berlage's plan for Amsterdam's southern expansion in 1915 (Figure 9.2, top right). Plan van Niftrik-Kalff aimed for the area 'by means of form continuity to be experienced as a total' (Van der Hoeven and Louwe 1985). It based the area's street network on agricultural land divisions (Jobse 1980), resulting in narrow, stretched urban blocks that have been rationally subdivided into plots with maximised street-front and relatively little depth. Van der Hoeven and Louwe (1985) describe the resulting urban plan as a system that could deal well with exceptions and maximise the number of houses. The plan behind the development of Rivier-enbuurt, south of Pijp, follows a different rationale: Berlage did not consider previous agricultural parcellation. Instead, he emphasised two main aspects: a monumental system of main streets and intro-verted residential sub-areas. Berlage emphasised coherently designed streets and pleaded for at least whole blocks to be designed by a single architect to achieve cohesion (Hoekstra 2018).

vanWoustraat-Rijnstraat links Pijp and Rivierenburt. In Pijp, the street was planned as a 20-metre-wide main radial connection to the old part of Amsterdam, featuring shops and a tram line. Two special streets cross Pijp's section of Woustraat-Rijnstraat. First, Albert Cuypstraat was built along the former sawmill waterway. At an average of 15 metres wide, Albert Cuypstraat is wider than most side streets and has accommodated a market since 1905. Second, Centuurbaan is part of a continuous street that encircles the seventeenth-century city; at 30 metres wide, it leads to a bridge across the Amstel at the eastern edge of Pijp. Both Centuurbaan and Albert Cuypstraat accentuate vanWoustraat and host more commercial activities than most other side streets (see Figure 9.1a). Extending vanWoustraat, Rijnstraat was initially conceptualised in the Berlage plan as a main traffic connection only. In its realisation, Rijnstraat became a main street with social and economic activities. The orientation of the long sides of the urban blocks along Rijnstraat results in fewer side streets connecting Rijnstraat and its hinterland. This spatial setting led to a differentiation of a mixed-use main street with a predominantly residential hinterland.

In contrast to the planned nature of vanWoustraat-Rijnstraat, Westzijde, which runs through Oud Koog and Oud Zaandijk, was developed piecemeal alongside local developments in water engineering. The dyke constituted the main connection between settlements; as those settlements grew, they eventually merged into a long line parallel to the Zaan (Figure 9.2, left). Westzijde is an exemplary ribbon-shaped settlement that runs along the top of dykes on the high ground of the 'lowlands'. Its hinterland is characterised by land divisions that followed drainage ditch patterns dug during the reclamation process (Palmboom 1990). After the dykes were built in the thirteenth century, settlers developed an intricate system of ditches and both high and low dykes. Farmers built their houses on the high dyke along the Zaan. To cultivate the land, they dug ditches perpendicular to the dykes. This practice led to land subsidence. To keep the land dry, they extended the system of ditches plot by plot along the dyke. Around 1580, industrial activities began to occupy land previously used for agriculture. Serving the markets of Amsterdam and Haarlem, the area around the Zaan did not receive city rights, which would have come along with strict regulations, so more polluting industries settled. At the beginning of the seventeenth century, larger homes and warehouses were built on the riverside of the dyke, overlooking the agricultural land and the mills, oriented away from the river. Ditches perpendicular to the dyke led to the industrial mills on the land side, with small workers' homes established along these paths.

During the second industrialisation in the late nineteenth century, large steam-engine-powered factories replaced the mills. These factories were mainly located between Westzijde and the Zaan – outside of the dykes, as these plots were accessible by ships. These buildings and plots were larger than those built during earlier periods. Many homes, offices and shops were established along the dykes to serve the factories and their workers. On the land side of the dyke – the western side of Westzijde – small wooden workers' homes were replaced by warehouses and larger villas for factory directors with a direct view of their factories and the Zaan. The rail network was developed in the area around 1860, attracting many settlers. The village paths and dykes were hardened, and ditches were reclaimed to serve traffic instead of boats. During the twentieth century, the number of factories increased, resulting in increased housing demand. New workers' neighbourhoods were built between the dyke and path structures (Figure 9.2, bottom-right). After World War II, new neighbourhoods were developed in line with modernist principles, no longer viewing the water system as

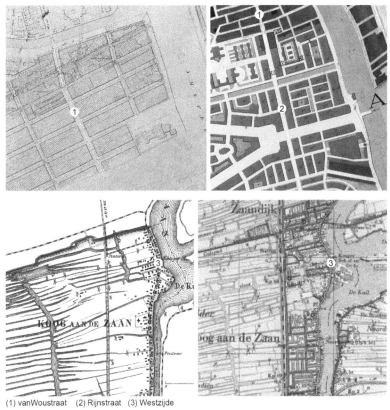

(1) vanWoustraat   (2) Rijnstraat   (3) Westzijde

Figure 9.2: Historic plans of the case study areas. Top: plan Kalff (left) and plan Berlage (right). Bottom: Koog aan de Zaan in 1868 (left) and 1950 (right). Sources (websites accessed 1 November 2022): Top left: plan by Jan Kalff 1875.

a structuring element. The piecemeal development of Westzijde over more than 500 years resulted in an urban grain that is very different from that of the planned districts around vanWoustraat-Rijnstraat.

Today's variation in the mix of economic activities

The historical maps (Figure 9.2) and narratives of the two streets indicate two different development paths that have impacted today's uses and are the underlying conditions for their different economic and urban lives. On vanWoustraat-Rijnstraat in Pijp and Rivierenbuurt, shops are dominant. On Westzijde in Oud Koog and Oud Zaandijk, industry is dominant. However, there is a diverse mix of uses on both streets. Their varying economic activities reveal a distinct pattern in both areas. Figure 9.1a shows these patterns, including commercial (red) and industrial (dark grey). As a result of their divergent histories, Pijp and Rivierenbuurt are about three times more densely populated than Oud Koog and Oud Zaandijk, and the residential densities are mirrored by different dwelling types prevailing in each neighbourhood.[1] The planned Pijp and Rivierenbuurt areas feature almost exclusively multi-family housing with closed urban blocks, while most homes in Oud Koog and Oud Zaandijk are terraced, single-family homes.

The types of uses on the two streets (and in the neighbourhoods through which they pass) are similar overall but distributed differently as a result of their morphology and available building typologies. Additionally, business density is more than five times higher in Pijp and Rivierenbuurt than in Oud Koog and Oud Zaandijk. In Pijp and Rivierenbuurt (see Figure 9.1a, left), there is significant variation in the density of economic activities. In Pijp, small-scale manufacturing, construction and logistics companies are relatively spread out across the area, which hosts a lively community of small-scale furniture makers, printing houses, shoemakers, metal and woodworkers, bakeries, fashion and textile designers, and creative businesses. The main sectors represented here are commercial shops and service providers, both of which align well with small plot sizes. Further south, Rivierenbuurt hosts a few bakeries and some home-based craft workshops in metalworking, clothing design and furniture making. Overall, Pijp is more commercial with higher business density, while Rivierenbuurt hosts more small-scale amenity providers spread throughout the area in relatively smaller numbers. On average, there are twice as many manufacturers and service providers in Pijp than in Rivierenbuurt.

Westzijde, in contrast, has a distinctly industrial character. It features larger factories producing at scale with smaller crafts businesses serving local areas. Manufacturing industries are the dominant sector in the area, followed by business services and shops. The factories produce cocoa, chocolate-making equipment, oils and starch; the smaller businesses include metalworkers, woodworkers, bakeries and breweries as well as producers of furniture, musical instruments and electronics. Unlike vanWoustraat-Rijnstraat, which is relatively homogenous in terms of scale and functional mix, despite the spatial differences between Pijp and Rivierenbuurt, Westzijde hosts industrial clusters alternating with residential clusters featuring some commercial activities. Overall, Westzijde does not have a continuous line of commercial activities; rather, it boasts clusters with various functions (see Figure 9.1a, right). The intersection of Westzijde and Guisweg, a street linking Westzijde to the provincial road, features a cluster of shops, restaurants and hotels, a fire department, a furniture store, a construction business and a stone supplier, serving a larger area than just the local neighbourhood. Due to the larger plots available in Oud Koog and Oud Zaandijk, business density is more than five times lower there than in Pijp and Rivierenbuurt.

In all of the discussed neighbourhoods, commercial activities and amenities are concentrated along the main street. However, the reach of these activities differs. Most shops and services on vanWoustraat-Rijnstraat, such as clothing stores and hairdressers, perform typical functions of a main street, serving their local community. One exception is the market in Albert Cuypstraat, which attracts people from across the city and constitutes a tourist destination. Thus, it features a disproportionate number of cafes. Like Albert Cuypstraat, supported by its high connectivity, Westzijde and around its intersection with Guisweg is a similar exception, hosting functions serving tourists going from the train station to the Zaanse Schans, a popular tourist attraction.

Mapping the mixes shows that the mixed-use environments in both areas manifest at different scales with differing distributions. The mix of uses shown in Figure 9.3 was calculated using four simple categories: housing, retail and services, productive industry and business services.[2] Figure 9.3b shows the degree of mixed-use in buildings (the darker the grey, the more businesses) and the mix in each street segment (the darker the red, the more mixed), as measured by Simpson's diversity index (Simpson 1949). Many buildings in Pijp are mixed-use, particularly on vanWoustraat-Rijnstraat and its cross streets adjacent to the main street. In Rivierenbuurt, the street is predominantly mixed, with a lower diversity of economic activities in the buildings than in Pijp. Behind the main street, Rivierenbuurt has only a few mixed-use buildings. In contrast, most of the buildings in Oud Koog and Oud Zaandijk are mono-functional, while mixed-use buildings are primarily located on Westzijde, where use diversity is present in adjacent buildings.

Importantly, in both of the case studies, the main street seems to constitute the main structural element organising a mix of functions. In Pijp and Rivierenbuurt, the mix changes in a gradient away from the main street. In Oud Koog and Oud Zaandijk, the mix changes sequentially along the street.

number of functions within building		diversity of business types along a street segment
▨	1	━━━ high diversity
▨	2 - 3	══
▨	4 - 8	══
▨	8 - 20	⋯⋯ low diversity
▨	> 20	

Figure 9.3: Degree of mixed-use buildings and mixing in street segments in vanWoustraat-Rijnstraat (left) and Westzijde (right). © Hausleitner 2022

Differentiation of spaces of economic activities

Economic activities appear in different ways on the two streets. Here, we turn to the question of how spatial form facilitates mixed-use differences.

vanWoustraat-Rijnstraat and Westzijde (see Figure 9.4) are in their neighbourhoods the main central street, the 'front' side, which is generally associated with high footfall and in both cases contain the highest number of shops and services (see Figure 9.1a). The clear urban front sides of the blocks that line vanWoustraat-Rijnstraat (see Figure 9.5) make these buildings particularly suitable for public-facing

economic activities, such as shops. The entirety of both Pijp and Rivierenbuurt is designed with closed urban blocks that clearly define the
border between public and private on the block scale, creating clear
urban front sides facing the street. Westzijde, in contrast, does not have
a clearly defined front side. Instead, the alignment of the buildings
with the street and facades with entrances oriented toward the main
street form the front side. The places at the river and the canal form
the 'back' sides on the neighbourhood scale (see Figure 9.4); these are
less accessible from the main street and are complementary to the main
street. Such 'back' sides are not as clear in their shape as the 'front'
side in both places but appear to cluster building types, and plot sizes
differ from those of the front sides (see Figure 9.4). The large grain
plots along the river – originally factory sites – constitute an exception
in Pijp and Rivierenbuurt, providing space for activities with a larger
footprint. The 'back' side location takes further advantage of the lower

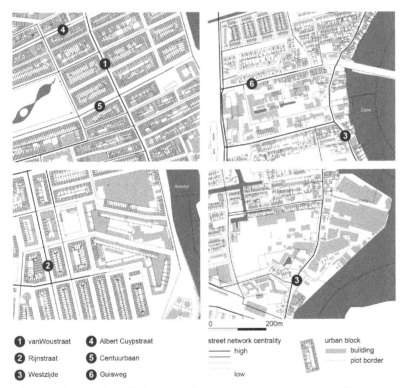

❶ vanWoustraat	❹ Albert Cuypstraat	street network centrality		urban block	
❷ Rijnstraat	❺ Centuurbaan	───── high		building	
❸ Westzijde	❻ Guisweg	low		plot border	

Figure 9.4: Mapping of plots, buildings and betweenness centrality
in two zooms in vanWoustraat-Rijnstraat (left) and Westzijde (right).
© Hausleitner 2022

connectivity to the main street. Vehicular traffic attracted to the back side comes from the road along the waterfront without impacting life on the main street.

On a smaller scale, variation within blocks forms complementary 'back' sides, offering space for extraordinary activities. Some of the western side streets of vanWoustraat feature craft workshops and car-repair workshops with a larger footprint in mostly low-rise industrial buildings in the courtyard of the block (see Fig. 9.5). Similarly, on Westzijde, medium-grain areas along the main street facilitate buildings with a larger footprint behind the street-front buildings. These courtyard activities are facilitated by deeper plots in both places, providing space for a second building in the blocks' interior (see Figures 9.4 and 9.5). A pre-condition for active back sides is their accessibility (see Figure 9.5). The back sides in Pijp and Rivierenbuurt are accessible via doors on the main street's front buildings. The back side buildings on Westzijde have access roads and are often accessible from multiple sides of the plot. This means less industrial traffic and, in turn, fewer nuisances on the main street. These accessible courtyards along Westzijde also provide loading space, which Woustraat-Rijnstraat lacks. Thus, on the latter main street, delivery trucks have to unload on the 'front' side. Evidently, this distinction between 'front' and 'back' sides is relevant on plot, block and neighbourhood scale for ordering activities with similar needs.

Territorial depth creates distance between the front and back sides on multiple scales. In both cases, the streets between the main street (the urban front side) and the river (here interpreted as the urban back side) increase the territorial depth on the neighbourhood scale. A differentiation of the street network is visible in both cases, though this is much more explicit along Westzijde, where the main street is considerably wider than its side streets. Proximity to the river means that the side streets east of vanWoustraat-Rijnstraat are less accessible, resulting in less economic activity than on the side streets west of vanWoustraat-Rijnstraat. The urban blocks on the northern part of vanWoustraat-Rijnstraat are oriented with their short side along the main street. Consequently, fewer turns are necessary to access the main street from every part of the neighbourhood. In contrast, more turns are necessary on the southern part of vanWoustraat-Rijnstraat, as long blocks build a barrier between the main street and its hinterland. Thus, the predominantly residential area behind this part of the main street is more 'private' than the main street. On both vanWoustraat-Rijnstraat and Westzijde (see Figure 9.4) deeper urban plots foster

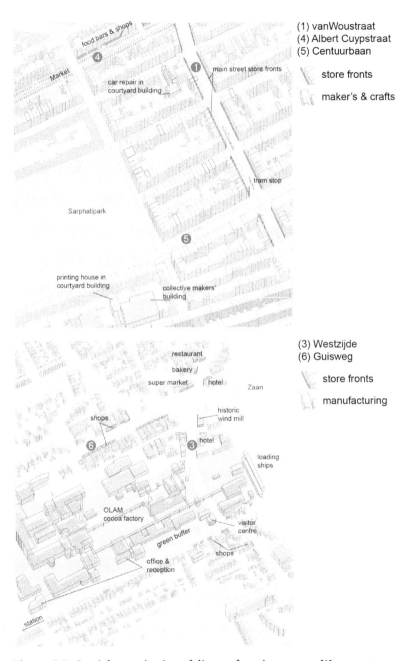

(1) vanWoustraat
(4) Albert Cuypstraat
(5) Centuurbaan

store fronts

maker's & crafts

food bars & shops

Market

car repair in
courtyard building

main street store fronts

tram stop

Sarphatipark

printing house in
courtyard building

collective makers'
building

(3) Westzijde
(6) Guisweg

store fronts

manufacturing

restaurant

bakery

super market   hotel

Zaan

historic
wind mill

shops

hotel

hotel

loading
ships

OLAM
cocoa factory

visitor
centre

green buffer

office &
reception

shops

station

Figure 9.5: Spatial organisation of diverse functions on vanWoustraat
(top) and Westzijde (bottom). © Hausleitner and Stuyt 2022

a gradual decrease in publicness inside the block. In the more fine-grain, higher-density areas around both streets, public storefronts have more hidden storage and office space behind publicly accessible rooms. Residential units are located on the upper floors of mixed-use buildings – a vertical step from the main street. While the findings in this chapter concern the differentiation of places by territorial depth for business activities, Clossick and Smink (this volume) have found that depth is of similar importance for social conditions. Evidently, distance can be created by different types of morphological elements or spaces.

In terms of buildings and plots, the scale of the urban grain on vanWoustraat-Rijnstraat is largely homogeneous. Westzijde, however, boasts high variation in plot and building sizes on account of its fragmented development. Still, variation in the density of the street mesh leads to some variation in block sizes on vanWoustraat-Rijnstraat. Especially on its southeastern part, a less dense street network near the river results in relatively large urban blocks, contrasting with the rest of the neighbourhood. These large blocks host a tram shed and large commercial buildings on the site of a former car factory.

Minor variations in footprint and storefront size of the buildings on vanWoustraat-Rijnstraat enable a variety of public-facing businesses to occupy these buildings. The urban blocks along the northern part of vanWoustraat-Rijnstraat tend to have slightly deeper plots in their middle sections (see Figure 9.5), providing open space in the blocks' interior. Here, the ground floor is typically divided into two- or three-deep units. Each has a short storefront along the main street, both providing businesses with sufficient floorspace to operate and taking advantage of their place on the main street. The corner shops, while operating in smaller buildings, have more metres of storefront. In some cases where businesses require more space, ground floors have been internally connected.

Westzijde, in contrast, depicts alternating sequences along the street with fine-grain and large-grain urban blocks. Plot sizes vary greatly, accommodating many different use types, including large-scale industry. Blocks with fine-grain plots and buildings for shops and housing facilitate functional diversity by integrating medium-size plots into the block. These medium-sized plots facilitate buildings with larger footprints behind the main street.

The main spatial and morphological diversity along vanWou-straat-Rijnstraat is evident in the differentiation of its hinterland. There, one can find a wide range of businesses that do not require a public frontage but may still benefit from their proximity to the main street. vanWoustraat-Rijnstraat entails a typological and functional transition – gradients of combinations of plots, building types and accessibility: from highly accessible, small-grain and similarl sized mixed-use buildings along the main street (the 'front' side) to less accessible, relatively lower-rise buildings with larger footprints on the 'back' sides of the blocks. Pijp and Rivierenbuurt have gradients on the block and street-network scales. Additionally, they demonstrate typological contrast with large-scale industrial inserts behind Rijnstraat.

Along Westzijde, street sections of small-grain plots and buildings with small local shops, service providers and housing alternate with street sections of large-grain industrial plots and buildings. Surrounding the clusters of large-scale industry along Westzijde is a gradual typological and functional transition between industry and housing. Surrounding the industrial plots, medium-sized and small-grain plots feature construction companies and multi-business centres. Finally, surrounding these are housing units. On the plot level, the large industrial plots of Westzijde comprise office and storage buildings along the public sides of the block, offering a buffer from the production and logistics activities occurring in the centre of the plot. The industrial plot of the cocoa factory is such an example. Notably, it occupies an entire block on both sides of the main street. Although the factory has a public frontage facing the main street, the continuous line of facades on the main street is interrupted due to the factory's need to access the waterfront. The production process is conducted on both sides of the street, enabled by pipes crossing above the main street. The factory here is just one example of the interesting functional alternations on Westzijde.

Accommodating mixed use in main streets

Vital mixed-use streets are not merely containers for a random mix of functions; rather, they afford function combinations based on specific functional-spatial relations. In both of the discussed localities, the type and scale of the uses found on the main streets and in their hinterlands are dependent on available building types, which are, in turn, dependent on plot sizes, connectivity and centrality, which are, once again, dependent on local topography, geography and history – whether the place was planned or developed organically. While shops and services can generally fit in smaller spaces, most manufacturing industries require space beyond that offered by standard mixed-use city plots and buildings. Manufacturing at scale requires proper consideration in the planning of the urban layout, by providing larger business units and considering routing to prevent overlaps in road traffic by trucks and slow traffic. From the observations made in the two case studies, we can draw four main conclusions regarding the urban structural conditions that afford a mixed-use environment on main streets and their hinterlands:

Modularity of the urban plan on the building, plot and block scale levels helps to maintain coherence along the street while still allowing for differences and adaptability. Modular organisation in the urban plan enables the upscaling and downscaling of business space based on a smaller unit within the units of the next higher scale (building combinations up to the plot, plots combined up to the block). The large-scale aggregation of multiple blocks can be successful if the main street and street network remain permeable for all users. Within a modular frame, variation in building types, plots and streets forms the basis for their future occupation, businesses of various sizes, and needs.

Providing complementary 'front' and 'back' sides in proximity and across several scales is a pre-condition for providing places with different environmental conditions. On the neighbourhood scale, main streets are the most public place – the 'front' side. The presence of territorial borders near the main street in the form of rivers or infrastructure elements enables the integration of spaces for producing and selling in proximity. Larger plots and main traffic routes form urban 'back' sides. These are good sites for industrial facilities and large-scale amenities. They foster a mixed-use environment by clustering similar spatial needs and providing separate routes for industrial and slow traffic. Without territorial borders, physical design on other scales becomes relevant to the creation of distance between spaces, allowing the co-existence of disparate activities. The topology of the street network differentiates place accessibility. Public front sides and interior back sides on urban blocks afford differentiation in visibility, allowing for less capital-strong economic activities to have a place next to 'A-locations' along the main street.

Structural coherence that still allows for exceptions creates a clear character for the street space. While neither of the case studies showed solid structural coherence, they indicate two different ways to achieve it: spatial sequences that show transition gradients and spatial sequences that show typological contrast. The front-to-back transition gradient has two purposes: first, it organises affordability of place; second, it organises the alignment of environmental qualities, which supports functional diversity in proximity and thus mixed-use.

Territorial depth with steps between front and back sides provide for transitions between environmental qualities (e.g. from more noisy to less noisy, from more footfall to less footfall). Such transitions can be organised at different scales and supported by elements of the urban plan, such as varying grades of accessibility, or varying plot sizes and building types (the latter two being aspects of modularity). Various spatial elements can facilitate transitions from one to the other zone: fences or hedges, stairs, new building types, plot sizes or street turns. Thus, spatial transitions can appear as horizontal or vertical. Both case studies showed places where the 'extraordinary' function appears with typological contrast of built form. In both cases the processes that could result in nuisances for the main street had little spatial overlap with the main street, meaning that such business can use the main street, but only when minimising their operation along the main street. Integrating factory shops along the main street – that part of factory activity most similar to common main street activities – can facilitate mediation in places of functional-spatial typological contrast. In this way, coherence is not necessarily provided by spatial characteristics; it is provided by activities that align with the common functions of the main street.

vanWoustraat-Rijnstraat was planned as a part of a major urban expansion. It appears, in its functional mix, to be more closely in line with what is commonly thought of as a main street, being embedded in a residential, mixed-use neighbourhood. Westzijde boasts activities in the mix that are more commonly thought of as incompatible, shifting from an industrial street to one with more commercial and residential places. The spatial-functional description of the two streets presented here has shown how spatial-structural characteristics are related to the functionality of everyday street spaces and the appropriate location for production and selling – from craft and manufacturing at one end of the spectrum to retail on the other. It has offered guidelines for urban designers who wish to facilitate a mixed-use environment.

Notes

1   Data on the sub-neighbourhood areas have been aggregated, including CBS 2022 for inhabitants and BAG 2018 and fieldwork for businesses.
2   The business categorisation employed SBI codes (G, I and parts of S covered retail and services; F covered production industries; J, K, L, M and N covered business services). Source: ARRA business database provided by DRD Amsterdam.

Bibliography

Bellair, Paul and Christopher Browning. 2010. 'Contemporary Disorganization Research: An assessment and further test of the systemic model of neighbourhood crime', *Journal of Research in Crime and Delinquency* 47(4): 496–521.

Chiaradia, Alain, Bill Hillier, Christian Schwander and Martin Wedderburn. 2009. 'Spatial Centrality, Economic Vitality/Viability: Compositional and spatial effects in Greater London'. *Proceedings of the 7th International Space Syntax Symposium*, Stockholm.

Coupland, Andy. 1997. *Reclaiming the City: Mixed-use development*. Oxford: Alden Press.

European Commission and UN Habitat. 2016. *The State of European Cities 2016. Cities leading the way to a better future*.

Froy, Francesca. 2021. 'A Marvellous Order: How spatial and economic configurations interact to produce agglomeration economies in Greater Manchester'. PhD thesis, University College London.

Gemeente Amsterdam. DRO. 2011. *Structuurvisie Amsterdam 2040. Economisch sterk en duurzaam*. Accessed 1 November 2022. https://www.amsterdam.nl/publish/.../structuur-visie_def_maart2011_web.pdf.

Gemeente Amsterdam. Ruimte en Duurzaamheid. 2021. *Omgevingsvisie Amsterdam 2050. Een Menselijke Metropool*. Accessed 1 November 2022. https://amsterdam2050.nl.

Grant, Jill. 2002. 'Mixed-Use in Theory and Practice', *Journal of the American Planning Association* 68(1): 71–85.

Hausleitner, Birgit and Meta Berghauser Pont. 2017. 'Development of a Configurational Typology for Micro-Businesses Integrating Geometric and Configurational Variables'. *11th International Space Syntax Symposium*, Lisbon.

Hausleitner, Birgit. 2012. 'Redefining the Border between Public and Private in Ambiguous Modernist Areas: The case of Amsterdam Nieuw West'. In *Ambivalent Landscapes: Sorting out the present by designing the future. Public spaces, urban cultures conference proceedings*, Lisbon.

Hausleitner, Birgit. 2019. 'Mixed-Use City: Configurational conditions from urban street network to plot'. In *Delft Architectural Studies on Housing*, DASH Home Work City, 56–67. Rotterdam: nai010 Publishers.

Highmore, Ben. 2002. *Everyday Life and Cultural Theory*. Abingdon
: Taylor & Francis.

Hillier, Bill and Julienne Hanson. 1984. *The Social Logic of Space*. Cambridge: Cambridge University Press.

Hoekstra, Maarten Jan. 2018. *Stedebouwkundig(e) ontwerpen in woorden: Honderd jaar stedebouwkundige begrippen*. Delft: TU Open Publishers.

Hoppenbrouwer, Eric and Erik Louw. 2005. 'Mixed-Use Development: Theory and practice in Amsterdam's Eastern Docklands', *European Planning Studies* 13(7): 967–83.

Jacobs, Jane. 1961. *The Death and Life of Great American Cities*. New York: Random House.

Jobse, Rein. 1980. 'Van kelderwoning tot hoogbouwflat: Honderd jaar bouwen en wonen in Amsterdam'. In *Wonen, werken en verkeer in Amsterdam, 1880–1980*, 19–102. Amsterdam: Vrije Universiteit. Geografisch en Planologisch Instituut.

Kang, Chaogui, Dongwan Fan and Hongzan Jiao. 2020. 'Validating Activity, Time, and Space Diversity as Essential Components of Urban Vitality', *Environment and Planning B: Urban analytics and city science* 48(5): 1,180–97.

Leefbarometer. 2020 'Ministerie van Binnenlandse Zaken en Koninkrijksrelaties'. Accessed 1 November 2022. https://www.leefbaarometer.nl/home.php.

Marcus, Lars. 2000. 'Architectural Knowledge and Urban Form: The functional performance of architectural urbanity'. PhD thesis, KTH Royal Institute of Technology School of Architecture.

Montgomery, John. 1998. 'Making a City: Urbanity, vitality and urban design', *Journal of Urban Design* 3(1): 93–116.

Narvaez, Laura, Alan Penn and Sam Griffiths. 2014. 'The Spatial Dimensions of Trade: From the geography of uses to the architecture of local economies', *A/Z ITU Journal of the Faculty of Architecture* 11(2): 209–30.

Palmboom, Frits. 1990. *Rotterdam, verstedelijkt landschap*. Rotterdam: Uitgeverij 010.

Simpson, Edward. 1949. 'Measurement of Diversity', *Nature* 163: 688.

Stevenson, Mark, Jason Thompson, Thiago Herick de Sa, Reid Ewing, Dinesh Mohan and Rod McClure. 2016. 'Land Use, Transport, and Population Health', *The Lancet* 388: 2,925–35.

Van der Hoeven, Casper and Jos Louwe. 1985. *Amsterdam als stedelijk bouwwerk: Een morfologische analyse*. Nijmegen: SUN.

Van Nes, Akkelies. 2005. 'Typology of Shopping Areas in Amsterdam'. In *5th International Space Syntax Symposium Proceedings*. Amsterdam: Techne Press.

LARS JANSSONSGATAN

KIRUNA, SWEDEN ├────────┤ 2km ⊕

Figure 10.0: Map of Kiruna © Anna Skoura

10

Kiruna, lost and found: identity and memory in the streetspace of an Arctic town

Maria Luna Nobile

Kiruna is a Swedish mining town that is currently on the move; the new town is being constructed, while the centre of its initial settlement is being demolished. Its mesh of streets is an expression of the town's unique culture, way of life and Arctic climate. The town's relocation presents an intriguing question: Is it possible to retain the relationships developed between the town's inhabitants and streets over the course of a century while moving the town? This chapter reflects on the relocation of Kiruna by exploring the spatial and temporal conditions of the existing town and considering the plans for its new form. It offers some reflections for the designers behind the new Kiruna.

Kiruna is one of the northernmost Swedish towns, located 145 kilometres north of the Arctic Circle. It is known for being one of the largest iron-mining settlements in the world, supplying 90 per cent of Europe's iron. Recently, it has come to be known as a city on the move (Lindstedt and Walldin 2014), as extensive mining activities and related subsidence below the old town centre have made Kiruna no longer safe to inhabit. At one point, a choice emerged between saving the mine and saving the town – and the mine won. The town's extreme conditions and industrial nature are embedded in its very identity, yet the town itself is now on the move, presenting a unique town-level displacement.

Despite its current mobile status, Kiruna's population is growing. While climate change has recently begun to force architects and urban planners across the world to rethink development values, several cities in Sweden – especially in Norrland, where Kiruna is located – are confronting massive development as a result of small towns' populations being displaced. Over the last 10 years, northern Sweden has hosted a significant increase in construction as a result of population displacement; this trend is expected to continue in the coming years (Boverket 2021). This trend has been elevated by a regulatory shift: since 2009, people have been permitted to hold ownership rights in housing blocks rather than just single-family homes. This change has encouraged people to purchase flats in housing blocks, boosting population growth in towns like Kiruna.

The history of Kiruna

Kiruna is a modern, twentieth-century settlement borne of industrial necessity. Founded in 1900, the town is located in an environment characterised by forests, natural streams and rivers. Kiruna was planned by architects Per Olof Hallman and Gustaf Wickman, who were commissioned to design a town by the state-owned Swedish mining company, LKAB. The settlement is a mesh of streets and housing blocks adapted to the site's geographical conditions; it is endowed with social and cultural amenities inspired by Camillo Sitte's model town plan (Nilsson 2010). Its streets were adapted to the southwestern slope and designed to shelter residents from the northern winds. In the early 1960s, LKAB began to excavate the first tunnels beneath Kiruna alongside the development of the town's new civic centre.

> I went out for a walk around the town, admiring the plants in the glow of LUX lights. What do I see? An electric tramway, modern cottage houses, vast stores. One person with a kindly smile pointed me to a 'men's outfitter' while I was in a linen shop looking to get ends for my braces. They thought I was from the countryside. So I felt [like that], too. The hundreds of lights of Kirunavaara glimmered in rows, steam whistled and hissed, cars roared. I felt at home. (Hallström 1907)

The settlement in and around Kiruna changed the lives of the nomadic Sámi people, who had lived in the area for centuries. The first non-Sámi inhabitants were largely male miners, but the population grew rapidly. By 1910, industrial development in the area had led to the population reaching 8,000 (also in 1910, the first of 15 hydropower plants was

Figure 10.1: Kiruna imaginary. © Maria Luna Nobile

built along the Lule River) (Shapiro 2020). As observed by Hallström in 1907, the town was vibrant and busy early in its history. The area's industrial development and new status as a tourist destination (Eklund 1946) made the native Sámi people realise that there was a conflict brewing between their peaceful, nomadic way of living and the new modern reality. There was an inherent contradiction between the Sámi people's nature-driven life and the mining industry's prioritisation of economic growth; many Sámi people began to settle in the area and work for local industries (Granås 2012). This oppressive overlap between industrial development and natural origin defines Kiruna's modern identity (Maudsley 2020).

> We shall never forget that the mine, at its beginning, forced two Sámi villages off their grazing land. Now it's the turn of the Kiruna people to leave their homes. (Shapiro 2020)

Kiruna faces radical seasonal changes in terms of both light and temperature, with particularly harsh conditions during the winter. This dynamic climate aligns well with the town's inherent instability.

Moving the town centre

> Shifting the city two miles east presents an unparalleled opportunity to transform Kiruna into a vibrant, low impact and economically diverse urban hub for current and future generations. (White Arkitekter 2014)

In 2004, LKAB announced that worsening ground conditions alongside new mining plans meant that the town of Kiruna would need to gradually relocate (Shapiro 2020). Kiruna's town centre was built upon rich seams of iron; to take advantage of this resource, the ground below the town would continue to be undermined, causing dangerous subsidence. While the resultant definition of a new plan involved both public and private actors, it was largely driven by LKAB in consultation with public agencies. The town's inhabitants were not consulted; those responsible took for granted the idea that their extreme response was appropriate in this state of emergency. In truth, the town's subsidence was made inevitable years prior, when industry transformed the local landscape.

LKAB, which owns most of Kiruna's land and buildings, began to plan the transfer and demolition of a large part of the historic city in 2012. It planned to move the town centre three kilometres to the east. Kiruna landmarks and symbols, including its first wooden houses, wooden church and clock tower, were to be dismantled and rebuilt, while other elements of the town would simply be demolished, such as the Kvarteret Ortdrivaren, a brutalist modern housing estate designed by Ralph Erskine (Laestadius 2020; Figure 10.2). In June 2012, the Kiruna Municipality, in partnership with the Swedish Association of Architects, invited 10 architectural offices to take part in a competition pertaining to the vision, strategy and design of a new Kiruna. This competition was won by White + Ghilardi Architects, making them responsible for gradually remaking the town's urban core – physically, socially and politically.

> The whole development process is a paradox. At the same time as new attractiveness is created, other parts will decay; and meanwhile, the entire city has to be kept alluring and attractive. Very great importance thus attaches to communicating that the new Kiruna is a place radiating sustainability, attractiveness and character.[1]

These words from the chairperson of the competition's jury demonstrate the way in which the Kiruna Municipality sought to communicate the project as a necessity. It wanted the town's inhabitants to view the development of the new Kiruna as a unique opportunity for modernity rather than a destruction of their place of dwelling, memories and identity. Of course, regardless of how they interpreted the change, the demolition of the town's symbols, places and streets inevitably has a strong impact on the lives of its inhabitants (Figure 10.3).

Figure 10.2: Kvartet Ortdrivaren, designed by Ralph Erskine, and its position in relation to Kirunavaara. © Maria Luna Nobile

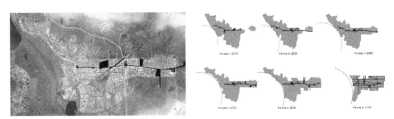

Figure 10.3: 'Kiruna 4 Ever', plan for the Kiruna of tomorrow. © Maria Luna Nobile

The meaning of streets in Kiruna

Lars Janssonsgatan is the main street that connected the core of Kiruna's former city centre to the town's train station and town hall, both of which were demolished in 2018; the street passed by the Ortdrivaren housing estate and continued to the Folket Hus square. It served as a link between private spaces of domestic life (Ortdrivaren) – and as a link to places of everyday life of at least three different generations of Kiruna inhabitants: the square, the school, the swimming pool. These places formed the heart of Kiruna's social and civic life, meaning their loss will inevitably be felt deeply by its inhabitants. Lars Janssonsgatan will gradually disappear over the coming years; by 2033, it will be just a faint trace of the town's history. It will become a park that will replace the historical centre of Kiruna.

Streets like Lars Janssonsgatan reflect the relationships that define a city. Streets reflect the identity and image of a city: by closely examining its streets, we can decipher the social, cultural, and political life of a city. Streets are arenas for individual and group expression, sites for [the] exchange of information and ideas, forums for dialogue, debate and contestation, spaces for conviviality, leisure, performance and display, places for economic survival and refuge, a system of access and connectivity, and settings for nature in the city. Fulfilling these roles, the street works with its own logic and has its own ecology. (Mehta 2014)

With regard to how long-term relationships relate to notions of identity, there are two dimensions of 'identity': *spatial*, identified by specific parameters measurable by architectural and urban planning tools; and *temporal*, identified by parameters embedded in historical, political and social dynamics that represent interactions between a place and its inhabitants (Taylor 1955).

Spatial parameters describe the relationship between elements of urban form and their uses. In a new town, forms and uses are often driven by architects and planners. In Kiruna, in terms of spatial identity, there is a geographic relationship with the mountain of Kirunavaara, which has been drastically modified by the mining industry. It serves as a landmark, establishing a connection with the towers and the Ortdrivaren housing complex. The main streets in Kiruna host wooden houses, churches, housing blocks, municipal buildings, cultural spaces, sports facilities, bars, shops and libraries, all of which influence its spatial identity.

The aspects of *temporal* identity in Kiruna are elements determined by four processes: first, cultural, political and social interactions between inhabitants and the streets; second, the landscape and climatic conditions of the extreme north that have historically defined the Sámi people's routes and nomadic settlements; third, the recent phenomenon of touristification; and fourth, the turning point of the industrial development. Affection held for the streets is influenced by the rituals and habits of the miners; these streets constitute a place for huge demonstrations that play an important role in the memory of generations of workers.

Spatial and *temporal* elements of Lars Janssonsgatan can be identified along the path that currently connects the Kvarteret Ortdrivaren to Kiruna's centre. The street assumes a particular meaning in the Arctic context, where weather and light conditions strongly impact the way public spaces are experienced throughout the year. This concept has been explored by Ralph Erskine (1960), and

Mínguez Carrasco focused on the ongoing relocation of the town in their *Kiruna Forever* project (2020). Arriving in Kiruna, walking toward the Kvarteret Ortdrivaren with its orange and yellow buildings, one's path is illuminated by blended light; the *Kaamos* (a word in Finnish meaning 'polar night') is the intense blue tone of an early November afternoon following 'the hundreds of lights of Kirunavaara glimmering in rows'. It refers to a readiness to understand the exceptional value of this on-the-move town.

> There are several different proposals as to how the memory of the city now disappearing is to be treated. Archives of different kinds obviously have their part to play. The older wooden buildings are movable, but the modern heritage, which includes, for example, Erskine's buildings and the Town Hall, cannot be relocated and given a context in the same way. The memory of these buildings and of the structure of the old city is [far] more evanescent. (Kiruna Kommun 2013)

At the southern end of Lars Janssonsgatan is the Ortdrivaren housing complex, designed and built in 1960–2 by Ralph Erskine as part of an urban development plan for Kiruna (Maudsley 2020). The demolition of the town's southern end is currently planned for 2023. The spatial identity of this area is unique. The position of its buildings on a slope represents the inhabitants' relationship with their local landscape. Additionally, their aerodynamic shape was defined in response to the Arctic climate; this makes it possible for them to maintain internal temperatures during even the harshest winters. Their pitched roofs prevent snow from falling on sidewalks. Their balconies constitute natural refrigerators while allowing for the permeation of sunlight during summer months. The internal paths between buildings in the housing complex connect to the lower part of the town, where the main road currently links the relocated station with the urban centre.

In terms of temporal identity, the social, political and cultural life that has existed in Ortdrivaren will also disappear when it is demolished. This warrants reflection on the relocation of Kiruna with regard to the town's physical fabric and the memories that it wields – memories of multiple generations that could be erased from existence. How might it be possible to keep track of these memories when demolishing and rebuilding an entire housing complex? This is the biggest challenge identified by the brief of the aforementioned competition.

The challenges of master-planning Kiruna

In relocating a town, the everyday practices that define the space must be accommodated in a new place. The notion of space as a place of everyday practice was introduced by De Certeau (1984), who conceived that space comes into being when performed and activated by users – 'when it is caught in the ambiguity of an actualization, transformed into a term dependent upon many different conventions' (91). Spaces are determined by inhabitants as well as local political, cultural and historical dynamics. 'Thus, the street geometrically defined by urban planning is transformed into space by walkers' (De Certeau 1984, 91).

According to the competition brief, the project proposal must show a vision for the Kiruna of tomorrow that boasts sustainability, attractiveness and identity. The vision must affirm growth and new, robust patterns of living. It must also outline a strategy: a basic sustainable structure for accomplishing the urban transformation through a dynamic, quality-creating process in which new and pre-existing elements form a holistic entity and will function throughout the transformation process. Finally, it must detail means of shaping a sustainable, distinct and pleasant urban centre in the east, within a holistic structure encompassing the entire city (Kiruna Kommun 2013). This study has demonstrated that *identity*, both spatial and temporal, is a core value that must be considered during the relocation process.

In the brief of the aforementioned competition, the street is one of the main elements regarded as fundamental to urban transformation:

> Five types of public spaces are presented as structuring elements for the new city: streets, squares, neighbourhood parks, city parks and nature parks. These are tailored to meet the challenges of the suburban climate and new urban life of Kiruna. (Ghilardi 2014)

One of the most important challenges in establishing the guidelines for urban transformation is defining a clear strategy that considers social, cultural, practical and experiential aspects as well as the views of Kiruna's inhabitants. The competition constituted an opportunity to identify and decode new means of defining the notion of street while considering unique Arctic conditions. The streets of the former urban centre (e.g. Lars Janssonsgatan), with which its users identified, will be erased by their demolition. The meaning of these streets will be translated into new spaces – or at least there will be an attempt to do so. It is possible, if the everyday practices of the old Kiruna can be adequately accommodated in the new Kiruna, for the spatial and temporal identities and memories of Lars Janssonsgatan and Kvarteret Ortdrivaren to be replicated and retained in a new place.

Conclusion

The unexpected relocation of a town represents an opportunity to assess how social, cultural and spatial conditions are reflected in the transformation of spaces in which everyday life occurs and how relationships are rooted in urban fabric (Overud 2019). Displacement facilitates reflection by architects and planners responsible for building a new space on the following questions: Is it possible to translate the meaning of relationships established over long periods of time between inhabitants and streets while moving a city? How and in what ways is it possible to translate relationships between urban form and uses in connection to the experience and atmosphere of a place? What are the limits of architecture in defining the traces of life?

The notion of reinventing a city presents the possibility (or risk) of encouraging harmful environmental modifications, such as those that forced Kiruna to relocate. In the plan for the new Kiruna, the streets are connections between a new sequence of spaces: a square; a New Town Hall, which is already in place; houses, hotels and shops. The 'hundreds of lights of Kirunavaara' will be four kilometres away; they'll be substituted by the artificial light of a commercial street – by a symbol of globalisation.

> Kiruna will continue changing, and perhaps one day it will move to mend its pathological relationship with nature. For now, its relocation serves as proof not of the omnipotence of design and technology, but rather of the contingency that lurks behind the surest plans. Kiruna's displaced residents have something in common with groups around the world who must leave their homes, a situation that is occurring with increasing frequency. Kiruna – and the culturally resurgent Sámi – may ultimately offer lessons for other communities on the move. (Shapiro 2020)

One sentiment that frequently emerges from dialogue with Kiruna inhabitants is a contradiction: the mine is both an expression of the town's identity and the reason for the town's demise. 'A community reinventing its city' (White Arkitekter 2019) is the slogan employed by the architects who won the design competition. The word 'community' here links together the Sámi people, mine workers from across the country, refugees, scientists and other specialised workers; it attempts to reflect the town's social diversity. As Shapiro (2020) points out, this type of transition is not unique to the people of Kiruna; lessons should be learned to ease future transitions among other peoples.

One key lesson is to recognise the spatial and temporal identity of major streets – to acknowledge that such places host cultural heritage and memories. The *Kiruna Forever* project, recently also the object of an extensive exhibition at the Swedish Centre for Architecture and Design, attempts to gather these cultural elements before the town is destroyed. It serves to recognise the instrumental value of the nature of Kiruna – to encourage us to reflect on the architectural, cultural, historical and political machinery that has always influenced the image of the city. For architects and urban planners, the relocation of Kiruna points to the need to consider spatial and temporal relationships in the definition of a town. The complex ecosystem of social, political, material and immaterial values represented by connections between inhabitants and places should constitute the basis for any future development initiatives.

Nevertheless, the natural conditions and resources that led Kiruna to become a town, due to its position and relationship with the Kirunavaara mountain, are paradoxically the reason behind this recurring change in its definition as a town, as a place, as a community.

The current uncertainty of our position as architects invites us to re-consider the *spatial* and *temporal* parameters in a way that considers the notion of alignment with evolving dynamics. The Kiruna of tomorrow will likely represent another temporary step in the process – one that is open to the challenge of post-industrial society but exposed to the challenges of the future.

Notes

1   Christer Larsson, Malmö City Planning Director, Jury Chairperson of the KIRUNA Competition, 2014.

Bibliography

De Certeau, Michel. 1984. 'Part III: Spatial practices'. In *The Practice of Everyday Life*, 91–130. Berkeley, CA: University of California Press.

Eklund, Johannes Emanuel. 1946. 'Kiruna: Drag ur samhällets, socknens och gruvbrytningens historia med ledning av namnen på Kirunas gator, Samlade på uppdrag av Kiruna lokala turistorganisation'. Wallerströms bokhandel.

Erskine, Ralph. 1960. 'Building in the Arctic', *Architectural Design* 5: 194–7.

Granås, Brynhild. 2012. 'Ambiguous Place Meanings: Living with the industrially marked town in Kiruna, Sweden', *Geografiska Annaler: Series B, Human Geography* 94(2): 125–36.

Hallström, Gustaf. 1907. 'Diary' (manuscript no. 7). Archeologist Gustaf Hallström Archives 1880–1962, Umeå University Library.

Kiruna Kommun. 2013. 'A New City Centre for Kiruna. Jury Pronouncement, March 2013. Accessed 1 November 2022. https://www.arkitekt.se/app/uploads/2014/06/Tävlingar-2013-Ny-stadskärna-i-Kiruna-Jury-Pronouncement.pdf.

Laestadius, Ann-Helén. 2020. 'The Place where I Became Me'. In *Kiruna Forever*, edited by C. Mínguez Carrasco, 184. Stockholm: ArkDes.

Lindstedt, Krister and Victoria Walldin. 2014. 'Moving Kiruna: A community reinventing its city'. LSE Cities public lecture series hosted by the London School of Economics. Accessed 1 November 2022. https://lsecities.net/media/objects/events/moving-kiruna-a-community-reinventing-its-city.

Maudsley, Ann. 2020. 'The Architect who Claimed the Arctic: Ralph Erskine's ideal towns in Kiruna, Svappavaara and Resolute Bay'. In *Kiruna Forever*, edited by C. Mínguez Carrasco, 132–3. Stockholm: ArkDes.

Mehta, Vikas. 2014. 'The Street as Ecology'. In *Incomplete Streets: Processes, practices, and possibilities*, edited by S. Zavestoski and J. Agyeman, 94–115. Abingdon: Routledge.

Mínguez Carrasco, Carlos. 2020. 'Kiruna Forever: Relocating a city in territories of extraction'. In *Kiruna Forever*, edited by C. Mínguez Carrasco, 36. Stockholm: ArkDes.

Nilsson, Bo. 2010. 'Ideology, Environment and Forced Relocation: Kiruna – a town on the move', *European Urban and Regional Studies* 17(4): 433–42.

Overud, Johanna. 2019. 'Memory-Making in Kiruna: Representations of colonial pioneerism in the transformation of a Scandinavian mining town', *Culture Unbound* 11(1): 104–23.

Shapiro, Gideon Fink. 2020. 'Kiruna, Forever Changing', *Places Journal* August. https://doi.org/10.22269/200804.

Taylor, Richard. 1955. 'Spatial and Temporal Analogies and the Concept of Identity', *Journal of Philosophy* 52(22): 599–612.

White Arkitekter. 2022. Kiruna Masterplan project description. Accessed 1 November 2022. https://whitearkitekter.com/project/kiruna-masterplan/

VIENNA, AUSTRIA ├─────────┤ 2km

Figure 11.0: Map of Vienna © Anna Skoura

11

Foundational economy and polycentricity in the five squares of the pedestrian zone of Favoritenstrasse, Vienna

Sigrid Kroismayr and Andreas Novy

The Viennese pedestrian zone Favoritenstrasse is located in a densely populated, low-income area with a high share of migrants. The section of the street discussed here comprises five squares, all within walking distance of one another. In our description of them we focus on various sectors of the foundational economy, including food retail, mobility, and cultural initiatives. The five squares form a line of sub-centres that provide foundational goods and services essential to everyday life. Shops, market stalls, social amenities including a public swimming hall, public administrative offices, public benches, public playgrounds and green spaces provide a beneficial mixture of commercial and non-commercial uses for low-income residents who depend on local provisions. The urban form explored in this study facilitates access to basic goods, services and infrastructure within walking distance of one another.

Introduction

The desire to create lively public spaces as well as an aspiration to provide 'a good life for all within planetary boundaries' (O'Neill et al. 2018) have guided Viennese policy ambitions in recent years (Stadt Wien 2019). In 2019, the municipal council passed a document entitled 'Technical Concept: Centres of urban life – Polycentric Vienna (MA 18

2020a), which emphasised the importance of mixing commercial and non-commercial uses. This urban planning strategy aligns with the 'foundational economy' approach's focus on vital everyday activities, which have often been overlooked by policymakers.

The foundational economy approach (Bärnthaler et al. 2021; Foundational Economy Collective 2018) stems from a comprehensive understanding of economic activities and the actors involved in working and consuming. It concerns the local provision of essential basic goods via the interrelationships among individual consumption, public services and infrastructure, both material (e.g. energy, transport, water) and social (e.g. education, healthcare). The Covid-19 crisis revealed that both types of infrastructure are crucial to daily living; they are so essential to everyday life, in fact, that they were excluded from closure during lockdowns. The foundational economy – as well as what is called the 'overlooked economy' of non-essential local provisions, such as restaurants, hairdressers, culture and the arts – not only forms the everyday economy but is also an integral part of civilised life (Krisch et al. 2020). Therefore, this paper aims to understand its structure and components.

To achieve this aim, we present a case study of Favoritenstrasse, a Viennese pedestrian zone, and explore how the provision of foundational goods, services and infrastructure shapes everyday life. As the foundational economy includes various socioeconomic activities, we selected one sector from each of the following three categories: food provision via supermarkets and a local market, mobility in and around the pedestrian zone as an example of public infrastructure, and cultural initiatives as a (only apparently) non-essential service. The research is based on statistical data, the analysis of policy documents, and qualitative interviews with 25 local stakeholders across various fields, including administration, politics, economics, social services and civic initiatives. The interviewees were asked about recent trends at Favoritenstrasse and possible measures to improve its potential.

First, we provide an overview of the general characteristics of the research area and the people living around Favoritenstrasse. Second, we describe the use of its five squares with a focus on food retail, mobility and cultural initiatives. Based on our empirical findings, we discuss how the foundational economy can be fostered more effectively in Favoritenstrasse to improve polycentric city life.

Research area: Favoritenstrasse

The research area is a 1.3-kilometre-long section of the Favoriten-strasse and its neighbourhoods, located in Favoriten, Vienna's 10th and most populous district (207,193 residents in 2020). The research area has repeatedly been referred to as the 'Centre of Favoriten' (WKO Wien 1999) or the 'Favoriten Central Area' (WKO Wien 2015), located between Sonnwendplatz and Reumannplatz on one side and Laxen-burgerstrasse, Sonnwendgasse and Herndlgasse on the other.

Over the last 20 years, the composition of Favoritenstrasse's inhabitants has changed considerably, as many migrants have come to Favoriten. However, the most prominent ethnic groups have remained those originating from Turkey and the former Yugoslavia. Since the admission of Eastern European countries to the European Union in 2004, there has been a significant increase in migrant populations, particularly those from Romania, Poland and Bulgaria. Most recently, refugees from Syria have begun to settle in Favoriten, which is now home to many different nationalities. Between 2001 and 2019, the proportion of people with Austrian citizenship in the research area dropped from 70 per cent to 46 per cent.[1] As this figure includes immigrants who have gained Austrian citizenship, the actual share of autochthonous Austrians is even lower. The conditions for settling in Favoriten are favourable for new arrivals. Due to its history as a working-class district, the cost of accom-modation is significantly lower than in other areas (WKO 2011; WKO 2020). Furthermore, since different migrant groups already live there, it is easier for newcomers to find their way around (Knierbein 2016). Importantly, however, not having Austrian citizenship excludes migrants from municipal and national elections, reducing the bargaining power of significant parts of the local population vis-à-vis public authorities.

The research area is an old neighbourhood built between the second half of the nineteenth century and the beginning of World War I. Its population density (330 residents per hectare) is five times higher than the average of its district (60 residents per hectare) (Gruber and Jauschneg 2016, 13). Recent population growth started only in 2011, increasing the population by 15 per cent in the last 10 years. This can, according to interviewees (1, 9), be attributed to families moving into the homes of elderly people following their death or those of people who had moved to newly constructed buildings in Sonnwendviertel, one of Vienna's nearby urban development areas. There are no private gardens and only a few green and small public spaces in the vicinity. Per local policy, 4 m² of public space per resident should be available within 500 metres of walking distance. At Reumannplatz, the biggest square in the research area, this value is only 0.54 m² (Gruber and Jauschneg 2016, 20). As the rest of the area has even less green and open space, residents rely heavily on the public space of the pedestrian zone and its squares.

Inhabitants in this area have limited financial resources; net income is the third lowest in Vienna, and the unemployment rate is above average. Recent years have seen substantial gentrification, induced by the opening of the new main railway station in 2014 – and, in turn, new hotels – reducing living space. Two adjacent urban development areas, one already largely completed (Sonnwendviertel) and the other in its final planning phase (Neues Landgut), attract financially stronger residents, potentially exacerbating displacement according to some interviewees (7, 17, 18).

The pedestrian zone

The pedestrian zone in Favoritenstrasse is one of Vienna's longest shopping streets and the district's social and commercial centre (Figure 11.1). Within a short distance there are five squares: Reumannplatz, Viktor-Adler-Markt, Keplerplatz, Columbusplatz and Sonnwendplatz. Each has unique functions in everyday life. While the upper part of Favoritenstrasse is highly frequented, the lower part is less so. In the most recent pedestrian count carried out by the Vienna Economic Chamber, four times as many pedestrians were counted in the upper section than in the lower section (see Table 11.1).

Table 11.1: Overview of the characteristic features of the squares

	Reuman-nplatz	Viktor-Adler-Platz	Keplerplatz	Columbus-platz	Sonnwend-platz
Size	27,000m²	6,600m²	5,000m²	5,500m²	3,400m²
Section	Upper section			Lower section	
Pedestrian zone	Since 1975			Since 2005	
Number of pedestrians[2]	64,799	47,716		15,039	
Main building	Amalienbad	Domenig House	Church, district office	Shopping centre	Bahnorama (demolished)

1 Sonnwendplatz

2 Columbusplatz

3 Keplerplatz

4 Viktor-Adler-Platz

5 Reumannplatz

Figure 11.1: The pedestrian zone of Favoritenstrasse and its squares.
© Birgit Hausleitner

Reumannplatz

Reumannplatz is a public transport hub and the largest square in the district – 27,000 m² larger than the other four squares combined. Its shape resembles a slice of cake, with an extensive arched boundary in the south that narrows in the north into the centre of Favoritenstrasse. Due to its size, it is hardly perceptible that it is a central public transport hub with an underground station, two tramway lines, several regional coach-line termini, and an underground parking facility. Instead, its dominant feature is its design as a park with lots of trees and benches (Figure 11.2). The eastern side of the square features *Amalienbad*, a large public bathing establishment. When it was built in the 1920s, it was the most modern public bath in Europe. On the western edge of the square, there are several established shops, including *Tichy*, an ice cream shop known throughout Vienna and one of the few remaining longstanding local businesses. Alongside it are a pharmacy, a hairdresser's shop and a jewellery store, all of which have a longstanding presence.

Conflicting interests meet at Reumannplatz, as demonstrated by its recent remodelling. On the one hand, local business together with the Vienna Economic Chamber presented a plan for establishing an 'upscale gastronomy', including a prosecco bar, with the desired side effect of keeping 'dubious audiences' away from the square. On the other hand, a citizens' initiative mobilised against these plans,

Figure 11.2: Benches alongside trees at Reumannplatz. © David Pujadas Bosch

referring to a socio-spatial analysis and a proper citizen participation process whose findings were published in another report, acknowledging that Reumannplatz is already a very intensively used square. Therefore, the square must maintain its non-commercial functions (Gruber and Jauschneg 2016).

The square has a diverse user base. In particular, it is a popular meeting place for young men with a migrant background, regardless of the lack of public sports facilities and adequate shelter from the elements. Since 2014, the girls' group 'Girls for Favoriten' has been active at the square with support from Local Agenda 21, a publicly funded organisation supporting civic engagement, organising events at the square and in its vicinity.

The remodelling of the square concluded in 2020 and featured a 'girls' stage', the first public stage in Vienna exclusively reserved for girls. Notably, the remodelling did not entail a gastronomic zone. This planning conflict illustrates emerging gentrification dynamics and efforts to displace less influential, partly marginalised groups from public space, as well as successful resistance and the capacity of weaker social groups to articulate their interests.

Viktor-Adler-Markt

Only 250 metres into the city, Viktor-Adler-Platz is a large marketplace with fruit and vegetable traders, butchers and grocers trading in spices, fruits and foreign delicacies. There are also a few restaurants and clothing shops at its edge. It is the third most densely built-up market in Vienna, with narrow paths between the market stalls, contributing to an intimate atmosphere. The farmers' market in a Viktor-Adler-Markt side street is advertised as a unique feature of the district, with the most original and loudest sellers in Vienna (Figure 11.3) providing a unique market experience (Otto Immobilien 2020, 70).

At the corner of the square is the Domenig House, the only building of architectural significance in the pedestrian zone due to its expressive facade of curved stainless steel panels. It was built in the 1970s as a bank branch and cultural centre. On account of bank mergers and several ownership changes, the building is now being converted into a hotel. However, according to interviewee no. 12, it would be ideal for use as a district cultural centre.

Viktor-Adler-Platz is a popular meeting place for the autochthonous population and migrants alike, as the market is well known for its low prices. In recent years, the average number of customers has

Figure 11.3: Farmers' market in Leibnizgasse. © Peter Gugerell

dropped by at least a third[3] despite other Viennese markets enjoying rising popularity. One explanation for this trend may be that many of the market's goods are also available at four supermarkets within walking distance. These supermarkets also offer organic fruits and vegetables – products not found at the market (Troppmann 2015, 30). At the same time, however, some stall traders stock products that are unavailable in supermarkets but in demand among migrant communities, such as pita bread. Some of the butchers at the market also enjoy great popularity, with their shops often featuring long queues.

The many nations represented at this market have inspired cultural initiatives. For example, the association 'Mitten-in-Favoriten' organises food tours, on which one can get to know ethnic cuisine and dishes. Caritas Vienna, a non-profit organisation run by the Catholic Church, is in charge of a market stall – Stand 129 – that doubles as a cultural and art space. This space features films, exhibitions, cooking rounds, choir rehearsals, and workshops for children during school holidays. Subsidies from various public bodies help both organisations offer their events free of charge, bringing people together and promoting (cross-cultural) exchange.

Keplerplatz

A stone's throw away from Viktor-Adler-Platz is Keplerplatz, featuring a church at its centre. The primary symbol of the square is the Kepler church surrounded by a park. There are plenty of benches around

Figure 11.4: Church (foreground) and district office (background) at Keplerplatz. © David Pujadas Bosch

the church and a walkway to a pedestrian zone (Figure 11.4). On one side of the square runs Gudrunstrasse, a very busy street with two bus stops, and a pedestrian crossing. (Until the 2000s, people could not cross the street, needing to use the pedestrian subway. As more and more people started to jaywalk across the street, a safe crossing was provided with traffic lights.) Behind the church is the district's administrative centre – the district office – which hosts a school and a kindergarten. Children and youth groups use the playground and the football cage at the square. A group of alcoholics who linger at the edge of the pedestrian zone in front of the church have repeatedly given rise to complaints. Measures such as an alcohol ban or a lack of seating have not been implemented so far, as this would also mean implementing restrictions on other, less problematic groups.

Columbusplatz

Nearby is Columbusplatz, in which restaurants and cafes take up a considerable share of public space. In the early 2000s, a shopping centre was constructed with a glass front and parking lot beneath the square (Figure 11.5). As a consequence, large, shady chestnut trees gave way to newly planted trees, which can no longer take deep roots and will never reach the size of the old trees, making Columbusplatz appear empty. As a result, this area constitutes one of the city's heat islands (ORF 2019). The former tram stop was also relocated to the

Figure 11.5: Parking entrance beneath Columbusplatz, behind the glass front of the shopping centre with glass front. © David Pujadas Bosch

adjacent Laxenburgerstrasse. The square is busy and frequented by locals due to the area's high population density and the lack of alternative open spaces. There are some public benches, but they are less comfortable than those at Keplerplatz; additionally, they are too far apart to facilitate conversation between more than two people. Since 2000, the square has hosted the annual two-day 'Stumm & Laut' in memory of the silent film tradition in the 10th District at Laaer-Berg. This event is organised by Kulturraum 10, a local initiative that promotes cultural activities in the district. The square has repeatedly attracted the interest of artists seeking to beautify it, but no project has yet been implemented.

Sonnwendplatz

Sonnwendplatz, a square-shaped extension of the Favoritenstrasse in the north, marks the other end of the pedestrian zone, though it is generally devoid of the varied civic life of the other squares. During the construction of the main railway station, an observation tower called the Bahnorama was established, though it was demolished following the conclusion of the construction work. Its site now hosts a car park. Several interviewees (1, 3, 9, 11, 12) considered this to be an improper decision. Although it would not have saved the local economy, as one interviewee (11) said, it was an initiative pointing in the right direction because the tower was a landmark, and people liked to

Figure 11.6: Free space alongside a car park at Sonnwendplatz. © David Pujadas Bosch

go there. It would have been possible to preserve the Bahnorama, as Wiener Wohnen, a municipal housing company, owned the plot. One cafe on the corner of the pedestrian zone has been vacant for over a year, and other pubs at the square seem to be only moderately attended. Thus, the square is perceived as 'dead space' (Figure 11.6). Interviewees expressed a desire for the revitalisation of this square to offer services to the neighbourhood, Viennese residents and tourists. In 2020, an artist group submitted a proposal to Shift – a Viennese programme to improve local cultural assets outside the city centre – for the construction of a wooden stage. The project was approved and ran between May and October 2021 with various performances (e.g. music, dance, readings) organised by Stand 129. Eventually, the wooden stage was removed from the square and deployed somewhere else.

Discussion

The squares in the pedestrian zone in Vienna's 10th district form a line of sub-centres within walking distance that are unique in their physical space, social infrastructure, and provision of goods and services.

One key purpose of a pedestrian zone is shopping. In two of the squares, located at either end of the street, commercial uses are particularly pronounced although in different ways. At Columbusplatz, a shopping centre and gastronomic businesses dominate the scenery, while Viktor-Alder-Platz features the biggest marketplace in the district. The Viennese population traditionally identifies strongly with markets and squares in the living area (Häberlin 2021, 47). To this day, Viktor-Adler-Platz is important to the people of Favoriten, both for shopping and for socialising. It is so popular that political campaigns often hold events there.

Squares with non-commercial primary usage are found in the middle of the pedestrian street with a church and a small surrounding park at the two ends of the central pedestrian zone. These two sites differ fundamentally from one another. While Reumannplatz is a big, highly frequented square divided into different sections of green and open space, the smaller Sonnwendplatz provides hardly any green space or seating on which to linger, failing to offer civic amenities.

Each square in the pedestrian zone has its own unique character-istics. Aside from Sonnwendplatz, they all address the basic daily needs of the local population in various ways. Each features a specific combi-nation of the foundational economy's economic sectors or, in contrast, a single sector dominates. This dynamic has resulted in various types of centres with different primary functions along the pedestrian zone (Table 11.2).

Accessibility within walking distance or by public transport is crucial for establishing a centre (Häberlin 2021, 47); this prerequisite is well established in the literature. Many customers at Viktor-Adler-Platz, for example, live within walking distance of the square (44 per cent), and a considerable share of its visitors (37 per cent) use public transport (Wührer 2014, 69), available in nearby Reumannplatz.

Furthermore, public buildings contribute significantly to converting squares or streets into urban centres (MA 18 2020a, 52). Prominent examples in the area include the Amalienbad at Reuman-nplatz, the district office, a kindergarten, and a school at Keplerplatz. In general, public facilities in education, healthcare and leisure – to mention a few – provide the foundational services of daily needs and boost the diversity of services provided at the site. People can visit these facilities to run errands or visit cafes and pubs. In doing so, they foster the ongoing vitality of local urban centres. Similarly, publicly supported cultural initiatives, such as 'Stumm & Laut' in Columbus-platz, make an important contribution to vivid public spaces.

Local markets and surrounding supermarkets do an excellent job of providing foundational goods in the area. Stall traders at the marketplace offer their goods at very low prices, providing low-income residents with a cheap supply of food. In recent years, Syrians have

Table 11.2: Overview of selected features of the foundational economy

	Reumannplatz	Viktor-Adler-Platz	Keplerplatz	Columbusplatz	Sonnwendplatz
Main usage					
Commercial		X		X	-
Non-commercial	X		X		-
Public transport					
U-Station	X	X	X		
Tramway	X			X	
Bus stops	X		X		
Private parking	X			X	X
Space for recreation					
Park	X		X		
Benches	X		X	X	X
Cultural initiatives					
Continuous	X	X			
Occasional		X		X	
Type of centre	Traffic hub / recre-ation centre	Market-place	District centre	Consu mption centre	No centre function

become stall traders in droves, showing that the market serves as a helpful starting point to settle in and secure a livelihood. It is a place where migrant groups can find relatively easy access to work and communicate in their own language (or through basic facial expressions and gestures), facilitating low-threshold steps in language acquisition (Knierbein 2016, 54–55).

Local residents also appreciate open-air shopping settings. This aligns with general trends in consumer behaviour, with businesses merging shopping and leisure experiences (MA 18 2020a, 26). Food tours of the market conducted by a local cultural association help to expand personal culinary habits and may increase interest in the products and dishes offered there. In recent years, the market has profited from the arrival of Syrian refugees. Nevertheless, market stall traders struggle to compete with supermarkets, as shown by the declining numbers of customers. The dense network of supermarkets within walking distance in the shopping street seems to increase competition rather than reinforce synergies. Compared to other federal states, Vienna ranks second in Austria in the number of organic farmers (APA 2020). As the municipality oversees the renting of market stalls, it would have room to manoeuvre to promote new arrangements that bring producers and consumers together by making market stalls available to food co-ops or organic farmers.

Open space is scarce and, in turn, extremely precious in densely populated, historically working-class quarters. The pedestrian zone and (green) squares allow users to walk around safely. However, a glimpse into the side streets of the pedestrian zone reveals a different image. Parked cars dominate public space, making streets narrow and dark with few lively ground-floor zones. Private parking still enjoys high priority in the district, hindering walkability and conviviality. Moreover, the pedestrian zone's side streets constitute a heat island (MA 18 2020b). Further improving polycentric life would require a reduction in the number of parking spaces on side streets to boost accessibility for both commercial and non-commercial uses.

Conclusion

The pedestrian street at Favoritenstrasse is a great example of a polycentric urban form that effectively hosts multiple sectors of the foundational economy. It shows that none of the squares needs to simultaneously accommodate all commercial and non-commercial uses. What is lacking in one can be offered by others nearby. Each square hosts a unique blend of commercial and non-commercial uses. This aligns with the recommendations of the municipal technical concept of polycentricity, which was elaborated in a broad consulting process with professionals from business and the public and private sectors, and stresses the importance of a mix of uses to attract various groups of people, (MA 18 2020a, 18).

Public space design is a key policy area through which city planners can directly improve quality of life (Häberlin 2021, 51). Publicly funded community work currently supports citizens in elaborating ideas for the design of public spaces. This approach widens public and green spaces for non-commercial use (Bork et al. 2015, 31), such as *Grätzeloasen* or parklets[4] used by inhabitants. This type of small-scale innovation in neighbourhood revitalisation is rarely employed by native residents or immigrant communities.

The Covid-19 health crisis and the climate crisis continue to pose new challenges for urban policy. Densely populated areas are hit particularly hard by both. During the Covid-19 pandemic, many citizens enjoyed having foundational goods and services nearby, as the share of walking increased in 2020 from 28 to 37 per cent in Vienna (DerStandard 2021). Lower-income residents depend even more on local provisions, ensuring access to basic goods, services and infrastructure within walking distance. In fact, the strengthening of the foundational economy alongside a polycentric urban approach demonstrated by Favoritenstrasse empowers underprivileged inhabitants and provides conditions that facilitate a good life for all.

Notes

1   The statistical figures in this section are based on data from MA 23 (Municipal Department for Business, Labour and Statistics) and the authors' own calculations.
2   In Favoriten, there are three counting sites: Favoritenstrasse 107/126 (between Reumannplatz and Viktor-Adler-Markt), Favoritenstrasse 93/108 (at the corner of Keplerplatz) and Favoritenstrasse 63/78 (between Columbusplatz and Sonnwendplatz). Figures for the number of pedestrians are from 2018.
3   Data from the relevant authority (Wiener Marktamt) provided by Alexander Hengl on 12 January 2021.
4   The city of Vienna supports civic initiatives in parking lots to improve the liveability of streets and extend the function of urban public spaces beyond parking.

Bibliography

APA. 2020. 'Bio Austria: Pro Tag 114 Fußballfelder zusätzliche Biofläche in Österreich'. Accessed 1 November 2022. https://www.ots.at/presseaussendung/OTS_20200214_OTS0100/bio-austria-pro-tag-115-fussballfelder-zusaetzliche-bio-flaeche-in-oesterreich-bild.
Bärnthaler, Richard, Andreas Novy and Leonhard Plank. 2021. 'The Foundational Economy as a Cornerstone for a Social-Ecological Transformation', *Sustainability* 13(18): 1–19.
Bork, Herbert, Stefan Klinger and Sybilla Zech. 2015. *Kommerzielle und nicht-kommerzielle Nutzung im öffentlichen Raum* (nr. 16). Vienna: Arbeiterkammer Wien.
DerStandard. 2021. *Zahl der Öffi-jahreskarten in Wien nahm um 33.000 ab.* Accessed 1 November 2022. https://www.derstandard.at/story/2000124279168/zahl-der-oeffi-jahreskarten-in-wien-sinkt-auf-819-000.
Foundational Economy Collective. 2018. *Foundational Economy: The infrastructure of everyday life*. Manchester: Manchester University Press.
Gruber, Sonja and Martina Jauschneg. 2016. *Reumannplatz. Funktions- und Sozialraumanalyse*. Vienna: Stadt Wien.

Häberlin, Udo. 2021. 'Öffentliche Räume als Plattform einer solidarischen Stadt und Baustein der Gemeinwohlorientierung', *Dérive* 92: 46–53.

Knierbein, Sabine. 2016. 'Öffentliche Räume als Handlungssphären des städtischen Struktur-wandels in Europa'. In *Wien wächst – Öffentlicher Raum. Die Stadt als Verteilungsfrage*, edited by P. Prenner, 40–60. Vienna: Arbeiterkammer Wien.

Krisch, Astrid, Andreas Novy, Leonhard Plank, Andrea Schmidt and Wolfgang Blaas. 2020. *Die Leistungsträgerinnen des Alltagslebens. Covid-19 als Brennglas für die notwendige Neubewertung von Wirtschaft, Arbeit und Leistung*. Accessed 1 November 2022. https://foundationaleconomycom.files.wordpress.com/2020/11/die-leistungstragerinnen-des-alltagslebens_fe_layout-final.pdf.

MA 18 – Stadtentwicklung und Stadtplanung. 2020a. *Fachkonzept: Mittelpunkte des städtischen Lebens. Polyzentrales Wien*. STEP 2025. Vienna: Stadt Wien.

MA 18 – Stadtentwicklung und Stadtplanung. 2020b. *Stadtklimaanalyse Stadt Wien 2020*. Accessed 1 November 2022. https://www.wien.gv.at/stadtentwicklung/grundlagen/stadtforschung/stadtklimaanalyse.html.

O'Neill, Daniel, Andrew Fanning, William Lamb and Julia Steinberger. 2018. 'A Good Life for All Within Planetary Boundaries', *Nature Sustainability* 1: 88–95.

ORF. 2019. Hitzekarte zeigt heißeste Stadtviertel. Accessed 1 November 2022. https://wien.orf.at/stories/3007245/.

Otto Immobilien. 2020. #Wien. Vienna: Otto Immobilien GmbH.

Stadt Wien. 2019. *Smart City Wien Rahmenstrategie 2019–2050: Die Wiener Strategie für eine nachhaltige Entwicklung*. Vienna: Stadt Wien.

Troppmann, Christina. 2015. *Marktraum – Eine Transformation des Viktor-Adler-Marktes*. Vienna: Diplomarbeit Technische Universität Wien.

WKO Wien. 1999. *Kaufkraftstromanalyse. Wien 1998*. Vienna: Unveröffentlichter Bericht.

WKO Wien. 2011. *Immobilienpreisspiegel*. Vienna.

WKO Wien. 2015. *Kaufkraftstromanalyse. Wien 2014*. Vienna: Unveröffentlichter Bericht.

WKO Wien. 2020. *Immobilienpreisspiegel*. Vienna.

Wührer, Simone. (2014) *Sozialraum Markt: Eine Analyse der sozialräumlichen Bedeutung des Wiener Viktor-Adler-Marktes*. Vienna: Masterarbeit FH Campus Wien.

12

Reclaiming streets for people in urban India

Deepti Adlakha

One key target of the Sustainable Development Goals (SDG 11.7) is to provide universal access to safe and inclusive public spaces – particularly for women, children, older adults and persons with disabilities – by 2030. In Mumbai, India, there are just 1.28 sq. metres of public space per person, far below London's 31.68 sq. metres and New York's 26.4 sq. metres. India's chaotic, cacophonous and colourful streets host a diverse array of sociocultural exchanges – informal marketplaces, spontaneous gatherings, festivals, and everyday interactions – while battling a sharp rise in traffic congestion, road injuries and carbon emissions. This chapter documents the transformation of a car-centric shopping district into a people-friendly promenade in Chennai, India.

Pondy Bazaar

The Sustainable Development Goals (SDGs) were adopted by the United Nations in 2015 as a universal call to action to achieve global sustainability amid multiple international crises, including to make cities inclusive, safe, resilient and sustainable by 2030 (United Nations 2020). One key target (SDG 11.7) is to provide universal access to safe public spaces – particularly for women, children, older adults and persons with disabilities – by 2030. In Mumbai, India, there are just 1.28 sq. metres of public space per person, far below London's 31.68 sq. metres and New York's 26.4 sq. metres (Kirtane et al. 2017; Udas-Mankikar 2020). In India, streets constitute a matrix within which everyday life occurs. They bring people together

PONDY BAZAAR

CHENNAI, INDIA ⊢————⊣ 2km ⬆

Figure 11.0: Map of Chennai © Anna Skoura

socially and serve multiple functions, providing a physical setting for various socioeconomic activities (Edensor 2021). Scholars have asserted that 'With the possible exception of the railroad, streets capture more about India than any other setting. On its streets, India eats, sleeps, works, moves, celebrates and worships' (Appadurai 1987; Tandon and Sehgal 2017). They host informal marketplaces, spaces for spontaneous social gatherings, festivals, celebrations and interactions (Tandon and Sehgal 2017).

This chapter examines the transformation of Pondy Bazaar, a prime shopping district in the metropolitan city of Chennai (previously Madras), the capital of India's southern state of Tamil Nadu. Just a few years ago, Pondy Bazaar was synonymous with congestion, chaos and pollution (Chennai Metropolitan Development Authority 2010). Pedestrians competed with motorised traffic, rickshaw-pullers, auto-rickshaws, hawkers and mobile vendors selling local specialities. In 2019, the local governing civic body – the Greater Chennai Corporation – initiated a bold plan to pedestrianise the shopping area. The redesign transformed the street from a motor-centric mobility corridor to a public space where people have priority over vehicles. Today, Pondy Bazaar boasts a new, vibrant look, attracting people of all ages, abilities and socioeconomic groups. It welcomes people from all walks of life – families, children and older adults – with supportive child-friendly features such as outdoor play areas, age-friendly facilities such as seating and shade, and social spaces for music, dance, commerce, art and cultural events.

First, this study documents the transformation of a busy, car-clogged shopping hub into a place where people take priority over vehicles. Second, it illustrates the competing forces in urban development in a low- and middle-income country setting. Third, it examines the city's radical shift towards public participation and collaborative decision-making to design inclusive, accessible and equitable public spaces. Finally, the study concludes by reflecting on the Covid-19 pandemic, its catalytic role in mobilising pedestrian-friendly initiatives, and the urgent need to convert them into permanent solutions alongside long-term urban policy changes in India.

Making places for people

For most residents of Chennai, the 1.5-kilometre-long stretch of Pondy Bazaar brings back fond childhood memories (Adlakha 2016; Greater

Figure 12.1a: Detail. Map of Madras 1893. Maps of Constable Hand Atlas
Figure 12.1b: Current map of T. Nagar neighbourhood. Pondy Bazaar.
Google Maps

Chennai Corporation 2019). Located in Thyagaraya Nagar, commonly known as T. Nagar, Pondy Bazaar is one of Chennai's busiest shopping streets. It serves as a commercial satellite hub, with shops selling everything from fresh flowers to designer clothing (Sharma 2018). At the western end of Pondy Bazaar is a historical landmark called Panagal Park – an eight-acre (3.2 hectares) public green space – frequented by residents of adjoining neighbourhoods (Keerthana 2012).

T. Nagar, created in 1920, was Chennai's first planned urban neighbourhood. Its original design was guided by Parisian principles of spatial planning, with Panagal Park resembling the Arc de Triomphe and Pondy Bazaar resembling the Champs-Elysées (*The Hindu* 2019). Initially planned as a residential neighbourhood, it is now the largest shopping district in India by revenue and one of Chennai's major central business districts (Malviya and Kandavel 2013). Today, T. Nagar is a commercial and residential neighbourhood featuring a mix of middle-income and affluent districts with some of the costliest real estate in Chennai. Pondy Bazaar offers a host of affordable products appealing to a diverse array of socioeconomic and ethnic groups. From big-brand retail stores to street shopping, people from all walks of life look for a bargain at Pondy Bazaar (Varghese 2006). In addition, some of the city's iconic shops, cafes and restaurants line the shopping street.

Until a few years ago, Pondy Bazaar was one of the most congested shopping destinations (Srinivasan 2010). Pedestrians jostled for space on narrow footpaths, packed with street-food hawkers and peddlers selling daily utility goods and general merchandise (Adlakha 2016). Streets were choked with motor vehicles, causing traffic jams, travel delays, pedestrian collisions and road traffic crashes (Shankar and Datta 2010). Inadequate and poorly managed parking facilities resulted in illegal, haphazard parking on nearby streets and footpaths. High-end retail stores surrounding Panagal Park attracted a large number of shoppers and traffic. As a result, access to the park was obstructed by parked cars, motorbikes and auto-rickshaws (Chennai Metropolitan Development Authority 2010). Due to inadequate surveillance and enforcement, the narrow footpaths intended for pedestrians became illegal parking spots for taxis and other vehicles. These conditions hampered the normal flow of traffic and inconvenienced pedestrians.

Over the last decade, Chennai has also witnessed a 300 per cent rise in private vehicle ownership, leading to traffic congestion worsening across the city (Bansal and Kockelman 2017; Census of India 2011). This can largely be attributed to rising incomes and purchasing power among India's burgeoning middle class (Bansal and Kockelman

Figure 12.2: The Pondy Bazaar retail area, one of the central shopping districts of Chennai, with shops selling a wide variety of clothing, accessories and footwear. © Deepti Adlakha

Figure 12.3: The newly redesigned Pondy Bazaar pedestrian promenade featuring wide footpaths (sans hawkers) and brightly painted benches to provide space for families to gather. © Deepti Adlakha

2017). The high availability of loans and automobile-financing schemes with low interest rates has also led to a sharp rise in sales of motorcycles and scooters. Indian motorcycle sales reached an all-time high in 2019 at 21 million units – almost double the 2011 figure of 11.77 million (Statista Research Department 2021).

Today, the Pondy Bazaar boasts a new, vibrant look that was unimaginable just a few years ago (Figures 12.2 and 12.3). In 2011, the Greater Chennai Corporation initiated the Pondy Bazaar Pedestrian Plaza project under India's Smart City Mission, funded by the World Bank in partnership with the Institute for Transportation and Development Policy and Chennai City Connect (Soni 2019). The design was inspired by the transformation of public spaces in progressive cities like Paris, Barcelona, Copenhagen and Bogotá, which have moved away from the dominance of cars and towards pedestrianisation and human-scaled urban development.

The original design concept for this iconic street included the strategic reallocation of road space for a large public plaza and pedestrian promenade with wide footpaths, dedicated cycle tracks and new bus lanes alongside a slew of pedestrian facilities, such as public conveniences, benches, food courts and vendor areas (Adlakha 2014). The project introduced a 'road diet', removing on-street parking and several lanes of traffic, redirecting vehicles and banning certain through-traffic (Soni 2019). Street vendors from the footpaths were relocated to a newly built multi-storey shopping complex. Widened footpaths were created to facilitate shoppers, play areas for children, and street space for concerts, plays and public awareness campaigns. Camera-equipped streetlights were installed to gather traffic data and improve public safety (Srikanth 2020).

Rather than viewing the street exclusively as a mobility corridor for motorised transport, the Pondy Bazaar Pedestrian Plaza was redesigned as a social, people-friendly space for all road users (Prabhakar 2020). The plaza was envisioned as a place for walkers and shoppers and a cultural hub with space for music, dance, art and cultural programmes. It was publicised as an 'open-air mall' in the heart of Chennai. However, this transformation was not without strong opposition from the community.

Behind the scenes

The pedestrianisation of Pondy Bazaar was vehemently opposed by local businesses and traders, who claimed that reducing traffic lanes and removing parking would decrease footfall and harm their businesses. This is unsurprising, as pedestrianisation efforts in Europe have triggered similar backlashes (Bruntlett and Bruntlett 2018; McPartland 2016; O'Sullivan 2016; Trentini 2017).

Outreach and community engagement

The Pondy Bazaar Merchants Association was not convinced by the design proposal. Their primary concern was the removal of traffic lanes and parking from the main road, both of which they claimed would affect business (Staff Correspondent 2016). Between 2012 and 2018, the Pondy Bazaar pedestrianisation project underwent an iterative design process with systematic community engagement and public participation (Soni 2019). The Greater Chennai Corporation organised regular meetings and consultations with local stakeholders, business owners, vendors, shopkeepers and residents on proposed measures such as repurposing parking spaces, road closures and new pedestrian infrastructure. A review of evidence related to the design of accessible, people-friendly places was critical to the public participation process. City officials illustrated the benefits of pedestrian-friendly streets using global case studies to persuade residents, community stakeholders and local businesses to develop, implement and support pedestrian safety measures. The design phase deliberated over the values, needs and expectations of citizens and stakeholders (Greater Chennai Corporation 2019). Potential changes to the streets and public spaces were modelled and discussed with citizens in a workshop alongside narrative descriptions of the real-world situation.

Community support was sought via outreach activities and engaging the public by distributing surveys, hosting focus groups and conducting an environmental audit. A 2017 survey and pilot test of the pedestrianisation efforts indicated that only 50 per cent of shoppers used private vehicles to reach Pondy Bazaar and welcomed the move to pedestrian-friendly streets (Adlakha 2016). In addition, widened footpaths, new street infrastructure and play areas attracted greater footfall and, in turn, increased retail sales (Figure 12.4). These pilot

Figure 12.4: Pedestrian infrastructure improvements have increased footfall in the shopping area, leading to increased retail sales. © Deepti Adlakha

results helped to appease the shopkeepers, who subsequently engaged in multiple discussions with the engineers, architects and city corporation officials.

The Pondy Bazaar Pedestrian Plaza opened a few weeks before Diwali (a major Indian festival celebrated every year in early autumn) in 2019. To capitalise on the festive fervour, the city corporation planned a series of celebrations, including music shows, street plays and other outdoor activities (Greater Chennai Corporation 2019). After the first few weeks, the pedestrian streets were handed over to the key stakeholders – shopkeepers and local business owners – for continued civic engagement and feedback. A separate operation and maintenance contract was executed to maintain the street furniture and keep the plaza clean. The pedestrian plaza successfully transformed one of Chennai's busiest car-centric streets into a pedestrian promenade by prioritising people over vehicles. It enhanced the unique shopping experience for which Pondy Bazaar was once renowned (Soni 2019). This project is an example of the power that public space wields in transforming how people experience their city and interact with one another. Getting local businesses and shopkeepers on board constituted a significant challenge, but it has evolved into a great success story of public participation.

In its current state, newly widened footpaths and pedestrian-only zones flanked by bollards allow visitors to experience Pondy Bazaar in new ways (Soni 2019). Children's play equipment and street furniture, including benches, sculptures, landscaping and painted murals, create an urban space in which people can gather and celebrate the city. In addition, a bike-sharing docking station was established near Panagal Park. The new pedestrian plaza serves a broad range of users, attracting people of all ages and abilities. Families now gather, sit on benches and chat as their children play on brightly coloured slides. The new design has reclaimed public space to create attractive, lively streets on which to walk, run, play, socialise, sit, linger and observe.

Traffic overflow

While the Pondy Bazaar pedestrian plaza has successfully reclaimed space for pedestrians, residents of neighbouring streets have expressed concerns over a rise in motorised traffic since the plaza opened. Streets adjacent to the plaza that were once peaceful and unaffected by vehicular congestion have witnessed a sharp rise in traffic and parked cars (Srikanth 2020). Residents in the vicinity of Pondy Bazaar have voiced concerns about visitors using residential streets as overflow parking and the frequent plying of auto-rickshaws and two-wheelers resulting in increased traffic congestion as well as air and noise pollution (*The Hindu* 2021).

Initial studies indicate that this rise in traffic in adjacent neighbourhoods may be redistributive (i.e. diverted from parallel routes), stemming from the 'road diet' in Pondy Bazaar (Cervero and Hansen 2002). However, research on induced demand and traffic management indicates that these traffic gains and spillovers are likely to 'evaporate' over time. Several cities worldwide have shown that closing some roads to motorised traffic can reduce traffic congestion in the long term (Cairns et al. 2002). Although counter-intuitive, this effect of 'traffic evaporation' was revealed in a seminal study of 100 locations in the UK (Goodwin et al. 1998). After an initial settling period following road capacity being reduced, cities witnessed a reduction of 25 per cent in overall traffic after controlling for potential increases on parallel routes (Cervero 2002).

Covid-19 street transformations

The global Covid-19 pandemic accelerated the speed at which people-friendly initiatives were implemented; many cities began to reallocate road space for pedestrians, cyclists and non-motorised transport (Combs 2020). City authorities closed roads to vehicles, widened pavements, added cycling lanes and reappropriated parking spaces for outdoor dining. Local communities and grassroots citizen-led groups implemented short-term and low-cost minimal interventions to enhance public spaces – commonly known as tactical urbanism, guerrilla urbanism or pop-up urbanism (Lydon and Garcia 2015).

In India, heightened anxiety and fear of infection on public transportation resulted in more people walking and cycling (Mehta and Dhindaw 2020). India's cycling community known as 'Relief Riders' helped to deliver essential goods to vulnerable groups during the pandemic (Sudevan 2021). Residents sought to implement temporary solutions to reduce crowding and facilitate proper distancing in public spaces and outdoor markets. Citizen-led initiatives aided street transformations by rebuilding pavements, reallocating pedestrian road space with bollards and litter bins, and reclaiming public spaces for emergency relief efforts. Car-free roads channelised the movement of emergency vehicles and essential services. 'Maidans' (open grounds) and local public spaces served as hubs of pandemic relief operations, including food distribution, medical centres and temporary makeshift markets (Malagi and Mehta 2020).

These efforts highlight the central role of people in cities and the urgent need to reduce the dominance of vehicles on our streets. Despite this new momentum, challenges remain for the pedestrianisation of Indian cities. The car symbolises socioeconomic status, touted as the fastest, easiest and most comfortable way to travel (Venkatesh 2018). India is one of the world's fastest-growing car markets, with about a million sold each year (Statista Research Department 2021). This same sentiment has permeated India's countryside, where young men drive motorbikes – an advancement from bicycles, which were the primary mode of transportation in rural towns and villages (Waldman 2005). This trend aligns with the developed world, where car ownership has risen significantly since automobiles were pioneered in the nineteenth century (Dargay et al. 2007). Mistaken beliefs about traffic flows and the strength of the car lobby constitute two significant obstacles. Pondy Bazaar's transformation is a work in progress, as the city continues to face a rising number of private vehicles and an insatiable demand for parking spaces.

Pathways to healthy, liveable and sustainable cities in India

Inevitably, making driving less convenient comes as a shock to some motorists. Still, the end result – a healthy, liveable and sustainable city in which streets are designed and operated to safely accommodate all users regardless of age and ability – is a lucrative option for ecological, economic and social sustainability in low- and middle-income countries like India. Six Indian cities – Delhi, Mumbai, Bengaluru, Chennai, Jaipur and Kolkata – are part of the C40 Cities Climate Leadership Group, a global network of 97 cities defining and amplifying their call to national governments for greater support and autonomy in creating a sustainable future. India's Ministry of Housing and Urban Affairs recommended the pedestrianisation of up to three markets and the addition of more bicycle lanes in every city.

In 2015, India launched an urban renewal programme – The National Smart Cities Mission – with the goal of making 100 urban centres in India more liveable and sustainable (Government of India 2015). The project aims to drive economic growth and improve the lives of citizens across the country by harnessing digital infrastructure and smart technology for urban development. Smart city technologies use various types of electronic methods, automation techniques and sensors to collect data from citizens, devices, buildings and assets, all of which is then processed and analysed to monitor and manage traffic and transportation networks, utilities, and community services. This aspiration to build and plan 'smarter' has ignored users of non-motorised transport and removed citizens from local planning processes. A smart city is not just about implementing high-tech digital solutions; it is also about creating people-oriented, community-first initiatives. Pedestrian-friendly principles of street design should be at the forefront of Indian cities' efforts to rethink road space, both in response to Covid-19 and in the long term. Current research also points to a crucial need to incorporate public participation and civic engagement into planning processes to preserve the intangible social and cultural heritage evident in streets and public spaces in India (Mehta 2013). India's cultural ecosystem of shopping streets merits safeguarding. Implementing participatory planning approaches that place residents at the centre of decision-making in their community can foster socially inclusive and multicultural streets and public spaces (Zukin et al. 2021).

In order to serve citizens well, Indian cities cannot afford to return to the pre-pandemic status quo. Instead, they must bounce back as more resilient, liveable, sustainable and equitable places. Bold steps to prioritise people over cars may take time to percolate into India's urban-planning ethos – reclaiming city streets from the domination of cars is not easy – but the pandemic has provided India with a timely opportunity to remake cities. It will never be easier than it is right now. Necessary measures introduced during the pandemic can rewire Indian mobility trends. To make these changes permanent, pedestrian accessibility must be prioritised in urban planning policy.

Policymakers must develop appropriate legal, administrative and technical frameworks appropriate for local contexts while constructing pedestrian-, cycling- and transit-friendly environments that reduce private motor-vehicle dependency. Financial incentives, including taxes and subsidies, can be used to encourage population-wide behavioural changes and promote more active modes of mobility, such as walking and cycling (Martin et al. 2012). The long-term longitudinal evaluation of the Pondy Bazaar's pedestrianisation can serve as a model for other metropolitan cities in India, aiding policymakers in understanding the needs of stakeholders. Indian cities must explore opportunities to more efficiently use space previously designated for cars, such as parking lots and garages.

It is essential to contextualise global best practices and learn from low- and middle-income countries that share similar mobility patterns. For example, Bogotá continues to provide its residents with a weekly opportunity to enjoy the city without cars through its Ciclovía (car-free streets) programme, which sees around one million people take to the streets on bikes or on foot every Sunday from 7 am to 2 pm, when traffic is banned on 70 miles of the city's busiest thoroughfares (Cervero et al. 2009). Over the last decade, the Bogotá model has been replicated at least twice a year in 496 cities across 27 countries (Hurd 2015). As cities emerge from lockdowns, the pedestrianisation of public spaces and the provision of safe and equitable modes of transportation are of the utmost importance in urban India.

Conclusion

Walking and cycling are essential transportation modes for the people in Indian cities, providing low-cost, affordable means of travel. Yet only 1 per cent of all streets in India have walkable footpaths or cycling infrastructure, leaving pedestrians and cyclists vulnerable to road traffic collisions (Government of India 2019). Radical new plans to reduce traffic and limit dependence on cars have sparked bitter conflict in cities across the world. Ironically, many city officials still believe that the solution to traffic congestion is road expansion, adding lanes to accommodate more vehicles. However, global increases in pedestrian fatalities, traffic congestion, air pollution and carbon emissions underscore the fact that the future of sustainable transportation lies in discouraging our dependence on cars.

Over the last five years, Chennai has carved out more than 100 kilometres (62 miles) of pedestrian-friendly streets and introduced car-free Sundays in various neighbourhoods (Government of India 2015). Transforming these successful pilot projects into larger, city-wide networks of complete streets requires cities to embrace a progressive, long-term vision. Cities must rationalise how streets and public spaces are designed and implemented, as they are vital to the public health, sociability, environmental sustainability and economic vitality of our cities. Changing the way cities are planned, built and managed requires political leadership, bipartisan agreements, community engagement and evidence-based implementation. There is an urgent need to rebalance, reprioritise and provide better, safer and more equitable infrastructure and policies in India.

Bibliography

Adlakha, Nidhi. 2014. 'Pondy Bazaar Gets a Revamp'. *The Hindu – Property Plus*.
Adlakha, Nidhi. 2016. 'Pondy Bazaar gets a "Smart" Makeover with a Pedestrian Plaza'. *The Hindu*.
Appadurai, Arjun. 1987. 'Street Culture', *The India Magazine* 8: 12–22.
Bansal, Prateek and Kara Kockelman. 2017. 'Indian Vehicle Ownership: Insights from literature review, expert interviews, and state-level model', *Journal of the Transportation Research Forum* 56(2).
Bruntlett, Melissa and Chris Bruntlett. 2018. *Building the Cycling City: The Dutch blueprint for urban vitality*. Washington, DC: Island Press.
Cairns, Sally, Stephen Atkins and Phil Goodwin. 2002. 'Disappearing Traffic? The story so far'. Proceedings of the Institution of Civil Engineers, *Municipal Engineer* 151(1): 13–22.
Census of India. 2011. Mode of Transportation 2001–2011.
Cervero, Robert. 2002. 'Induced Travel Demand: Research design, empirical evidence, and normative policies', *Journal of Planning Literature* 17(1): 3–20.
Cervero, Robert and Mark Hansen. 2002. 'Induced Travel Demand and Induced Road Investment: A simultaneous equation analysis', *Journal of Transport Economics and Policy* 36(3): 469–90.
Cervero, Robert, Olga L. Sarmiento, Enrique Jacoby, Louis Fernando Gomez and Andrea Neiman. 2009. 'Influences of Built Environments on Walking and Cycling: Lessons from Bogotá', *International Journal of Sustainable Transportation* 3(4): 203–26.
Chennai Metropolitan Development Authority. 2010. Chennai Comprehensive Transportation Study.

Combs, Tabitha. 2020. 'Local Actions to Support Walking and Cycling During Social Distancing Dataset'.

Dargay, Joyce, Dermot Gately and Martin Sommer. 2007. 'Vehicle Ownership and Income Growth, Worldwide: 1960– 2030', *The Energy Journal* 28(4): 143–70.

Edensor, Tim. 2021. 'The Culture of the Indian Street'. *Public Space Reader*. Abingdon: Routledge.

Goodwin, Phil, Carmen Hass-Klau and Sally Cairns. 1998. 'Evidence on the Effects of Road Capacity Reduction on Traffic Levels', *Journal of Transportation Engineering + Control* 39(39): 348–54.

Government of India. 2015. 'Smart Cities Mission'. Accessed 1 November 2022. http://mohua.gov.in/cms/smart-cities.php#:~:text=The%20Government%20of%20India%20has,Mission%20on%2025%20June%202015.&text=The%20objective%20is%20to%20promote,application%20of%20'Smart'%20Solutions.

Government of India. Ministry of Housing and Urban Affairs. 2017. 'Smart Cities Mission: The Complete Streets Framework Toolkit'. Accessed 1 November 2022. https://www.itdp.in/resource/complete-streets-framework-toolkit/

Greater Chennai Corporation. 2019. 'At Pondy Bazaar Plaza, Chennai to Turn a Corner'. Accessed 1 November 2022. https://cscl.co.in/node/204.

Hurd, Duncan. 2015. 'Ciclovias are Opening Up Cities to People Around the Globe'. Accessed 1 November 2022. https://momentummag.com/six-ciclovias-opening-cities-people-around-globe/.

Keerthana, R. 2012. Once Upon a Time in Thyagaraya Nagar ...', *The Hindu*, 1 May.

Kirtane, Gautam, Sayli Mankikar and Dwip Racchh. 2017. 'Endangered Future of Mumbai's Open Spaces: MCGM's open space journey'. Observer Research Foundation. 26.

Lydon, Mike and Anthony Garcia. 2015. *Tactical Urbanism: Short-term action for long-term change*. Washington, DC: Island Press.

McPartland, Ben. 2016. 'Paris Makes "History" by Banning Cars on River Bank'. *The Local*, 26 September.

Malagi, Rajeev and Prerna Vijaykumar Mehta. 2020. 'Tactical Urbanism: An adaptive tool for safe distancing'. Accessed 1 November 2022. https://wri-india.org/blog/tactical-urbanism-adaptive-tool-safe-distancing.

Malviya, Sagar and Sangeetha Kandavel. 2013. 'India's Biggest Shopping District Theagaraya Nagar in Chennai to Get a Retail Makeover', *The Economic Times*, 7 February.

Martin, Adam, Marc Suhrcke and David Ogilvie. 2012. 'Financial Incentives to Promote Active Travel: An evidence review and economic framework', *American Journal of Preventive Medicine* 43(6): e45–e57.

Mehta, Vikas. 2013. *The Street: A quintessential social public space*. New York: Routledge.

Mehta, Prerna Vijaykumar and Jaya Dhindaw. 2020. 'Reconfiguring Public Spaces within the New Normal'. *WRI India*, 19 May.

O'Sullivan, Feargus. 2016. 'Paris's Groundbreaking Car Bans Face a Backlash'. *CityLab, Bloomberg*, 30 November.

Prabhakar, Bhavani. 2020. 'Creating Streets for Walking: Can Chennai create more Pondy Bazaars?' *Citizen Matters*, 10 December.

Shankar, R. and D. Datta. 2010. 'Jam Session'. *India Today*, 6 September.

Sharma, Shweta. 2018. 'Cultural Theory of Poverty and Informal Sector: A case study of street vendors of Pondy Bazaar, Chennai', *Research Journal of Humanities and Social Sciences* 9(3): 557–66.

Soni, Aishwarya. 2019. 'Making Places for People: The launch of the Pondy Bazaar pedestrian plaza'. Accessed 1 November 2022. https://www.itdp.in/making-places-for-people-the-launch-of-the-pondy-bazaar-pedestrian-plaza/.

Srikanth, R. 2020. 'Pedestrian Plaza in Chennai's Pondy Bazaar Shifts Vehicular Congestion to Nearby Localities', *The Hindu*, 21 January.

Srinivasan, N.S. 2010. 'Calming Traffic in Shopping Areas, like Pondy Bazaar'. *Madras Musings* XIX(18).

Staff Correspondent. 2016. 'Residents in, Traders Out on T Nagar Pedestrian Plaza'. *The Times of India*, 21 November.

Statista Research Department. 2021. Two-Wheeler Domestic Sales in India FY 2011–2021. S.R. Department of India.

Sudevan, Praveen. 2021. 'How Cycling Communities are Helping Indian Cities Deal with the Second Wave of COVID-19', *The Hindu*, 6 May.

Tandon, Meeta and Vandana Sehgal. 2017. 'Traditional Indian Religious Streets: A spatial study of the streets of Mathura', *Frontiers of Architectural Research* 6(4): 469–79.

The Hindu. 2019. 'As T. Nagar Nears 100, A Look at its History'.

The Hindu. 2021. 'Nothing has Changed Since 2016, Say T. Nagar Residents'.

Trentini, Sergio. 2017. 'The "Superblocks" of Barcelona: Despite protests, city follows with sustainable strategy'. *The City Fix, World Resources Institute*.

Udas-Mankikar, Sayli. 2020. 'Formulating Open-Space Policies for India's Cities: The case of Mumbai'. Observer Research Foundation.

United Nations. 2020. *Sustainable Development Goals Report 2020*. Department of Economic and Social Affairs.

Varghese, Nina. 2006. 'T. Nagar: Shop till you drop, and then shop some more. *Business Line, The Hindu*.

Venkatesh, Mahua. 2018. '"Mera sapna, meri Maruti" – How a car became the status symbol of a young, working India'. *The Print*, 2 December.

Waldman, Amy. 2005. 'In Today's India, Status Comes with Four Wheels', *New York Times*, 5 December.

Zukin, Sharon, Philip Kasinitz and Xiangming Chen. 2021. 'Spaces of Everyday Diversity: The patchwork ecosystem of local shopping streets. In *Public Space Reader*, edited by V.M. Miodrag Mitrašinović. New York: Routledge.

13
Investing in (post-Covid) street appeal

Matthew Carmona

Whether we are walking to school, waiting at a bus stop, cycling to work, shopping, or even driving through a city, how streets handle and balance the varied, complex and often conflicting needs of users has a profound impact on our daily lives and wellbeing. Streets are often highly constrained physically – and were even more so in the Covid-19 dominated world of 2020 and 2021 – and we need to make hard choices about which functions to prioritise and where. Drawing on (pre-Covid) research which examined the multiple benefits of investing in London's local high streets (its mixed traditional shopping streets) and on UK-wide research conducted during the pandemic, in this chapter the case is made for investing in the social, visual and economic appeal of streets as places for people, not cars.

Introduction

Cities around the world are having to make choices about how to prioritise space in urban streets. Prior to the Covid-19 pandemic, increasingly such choices were prioritising streets as more than just movement corridors to facilitate the passing of traffic. From well-known exemplar cities such as Copenhagen with many decades of experience reclaiming the public realm (Gehl 1996), to the Complete Streets movement in the USA which has helped to mainstream these practices in North America over the last 15 years (McCann 2013), the balance between pedestrians and cyclists on the one hand and private cars on the other has been on the move. In the UK, this has been characterised as a re-balancing of

WOOLWICH ROAD
NELSON ROAD

VENN STREET
THE PAVEMENT

MARKET SQUARE

HOMELAND RISE

LONDON, UK ├──────────┤ 5km ⬆

Figure 13.0: Map of London © Anna Skoura

the 'movement' and 'place' functions of streets (DCLG & DfT 2007), the latter reflecting their role as environments within which we meet and (in normal circumstances) socialise, where businesses are located, where we walk and cycle, and where the public life of the city carries on – Covid or not.

Some have argued that as we move to a post-Covid world, we may be tempted to move back into our cars in order to avoid mixing with others. Despite huge drops in carbon emissions in 2020 (Le Quéré et al. 2020), evidence already suggests this is happening with significant dips in public transport ridership (Bird et al. 2020), housing markets suggesting a favouring of suburban over urban forms (Hammond 2020) and the car industry reporting steady growth in sales (Paul 2020). All too easily we could find ourselves retrenching from practices that have sought to move us away from vehicle dominance in our cities.

This would be a mistake. Not only would it exacerbate another longer-standing health crisis – the obesity one (Booth et al. 2005; Ewing et al. 2003) – but it would put a further nail in the coffin of many traditional shopping streets which are struggling to recover from the months of lockdown seen in different parts of the world during 2020 and 2021. International evidence suggests that the more appealing streets are physically for walking and cycling, the more conducive they are likely to be as locations where the social, economic and even cultural life of the city will flourish and where populations will be healthier and perhaps even happier and more engaged with their local communities (Dumbaugh and Gattis 2005; Engwicht 1999; Frank et al. 2019; Hart and Parkhurst 2011).

My own (pre-Covid) research – *Street Appeal* – examined the multiple benefits of investing in the local street environment of London's high streets (Carmona et al. 2018a; 2018b) – its traditional and often highly mixed local shopping streets. If anything, the findings are even more relevant now in the very different world in which we find ourselves.

'Network efficiency' to 'movement & place'

The funder of the *Street Appeal* research, Transport for London (TfL), has itself been on a journey in this regard, with recent innovations in street design reflecting a significant move from a 'network efficiency' model of street management to a 'movement and place-based' one (Mayor of London and Transport for London 2019). In this, streets are seen as places of complex social and economic exchange as well as channels for movement. This is a fundamental change in our understanding of the planning, design and use of streets, but the benefits and/or problems that flow from it still need to be better understood, and it is these that the *Street Appeal* research attempted to understand.

Unfortunately, as a research problem, investigations of this type are fraught with practical and conceptual challenges. The re-design of streets is likely to bring with it concerns from businesses or residents along the route who may be worried that parking, servicing and other amenities will be compromised, or that street improvements may lead to unintended impacts on the price of local housing or to gentrification. This was certainly the case in London – pre-Covid – where TfL's 'mini-Holland' (cycle priority streets) have suffered from a very negative response as drivers and some businesses discovered that giving priority to pedestrians and cyclists necessitated reducing it for them (Hill 2015). The danger is that these very real and tangible concerns can drown out consideration of intangible and hard-to-measure benefits such as more space to socialise and enjoy the environment, greater encouragement of walking and cycling with associated health benefits, or the knock-on impacts on private investment in an area.

There are also challenges associated with how to ascribe value to intangible qualities, such as the well-being benefits of a more convivial walk to the shops, or the social benefits provided by a local cafe with external seating in a sunny spot. Whilst it is difficult to overcome these sorts of difficulties entirely, the aim must be to overcome them sufficiently in order to deliver reliable and testable results. This requires a robust research methodology.

How did we do it?

In an attempt to address head-on the multiple conceptual and practical challenges associated with this sort of research, a mixed comparative research methodology was adopted. The key features of the approach were:

1. *Pairwise comparisons* – the use of five paired high-street environments (Figure 13.1), chosen as a means to track the impact of design interventions in comparable locations against value outcomes whilst controlling, as far as possible, for extraneous factors. In each case five improved cases

Figure 13.1a: Pairwise comparisons Bromley (improved). © Matthew Carmona

Figure 13.1b: Pairwise comparisons Orpington (unimproved). © Matthew Carmona

(subject to significant new public realm interventions – widened pavements, street trees, cycle lanes, new street furniture, simplified signage, etc.) were compared against five unimproved comparators that were nevertheless broadly comparable in terms of their socio-economic context, physical structure and position within the retail hierarchy. These local mixed high streets represent particular challenges in

London: not only are they complex social spaces, but typically they follow busy arterial routes in and out of the city and are therefore heavily trafficked.

2. *A holistic analytical framework* – once selected, comparative analysis demanded the collection of suitable available data to represent both the quality and value aspects of street interventions. A holistic framework representing the key dimensions of street functionality was adopted: as pieces of physical built fabric, as places for social/economic exchange, as movement corridors, and as complex bits of real estate (Figure 13.2).

3. *Data selection, gathering and analysis* – data was selected and analysed for each dimension both case by case and across the pairs, with the intention of understanding the consequence of investing (or not) in the street environment. This included on-site physical analysis against a place quality checklist modified from TfL's 'Healthy Streets' work (Mayor of London and TfL 2017) (Figure 13.3), analysis of office rental values, residential sales values and retail rental and vacancy rates (using CoStar, land registry and GOAD/Experian datasets), static traffic counts (using Department for Transport National Road Traffic Census and TfL ad-hoc traffic count data), street life analysis using on-site observations, and on-site interviews with street users and occupiers/managers of local businesses.

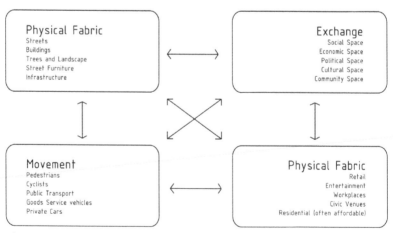

Figure 13.2: A holistic framework for analysis. © Matthew Carmona

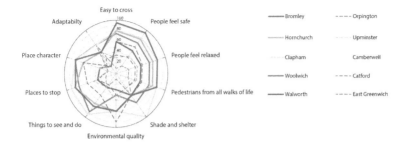

Figure 13.3: Physical qualities of the streets compared. © Matthew Carmona

Street Appeal – the headlines

The research found that improvements to the quality of the publicly owned and managed street fabric in London's mixed high streets return substantial benefits to the everyday users of streets, and to the occupiers of space and investors in surrounding property in multiple ways. Across the cases these included:

o   A one-third uplift in the physical quality of the street as a whole from interventions in the publicly owned street space.

o   An uplift in office rental values equivalent to an 'additional' 4% per annum, helping to support investment in business space in these locations in the face of pressures to convert to more profitable residential uses.

o   A larger uplift in retail rental values equivalent to an 'additional' 7.5% per annum, reflecting the more attractive retail environment that has been created and the encouragement this is giving to investment in these locations in the face of online and out-of-town competition.

o   A strongly related decline in retail vacancy, leading to a sizable 17% per annum divergence in vacancy rates between improved and unimproved street environments, alongside a greater resilience (against trend) of traditional and comparison retail, and a growth in leisure uses.

o   An almost negligible impact on residential values, helping to counter concerns that street improvements, by themselves, will further inflate house prices and drive up pressures for gentrification.

o   Inconsequential impacts, from the street improvements alone, on traffic flows or the modal choices made by individuals when travelling (unless road capacity is deliberately removed as part of a scheme).

o   A large 96% boost in static (e.g. standing, waiting, sitting) and 93% boost in active (e.g. walking) street behaviours in improved over unimproved areas, with strong potential health benefits in the resulting more active lifestyles.

o   A particularly large 216% hike in the sorts of leisure-based static activities (e.g. stopping at a cafe or sitting at a bench) that only happen when the quality of the environment is sufficiently conducive to make people wish to stay.

o   Very strong perceptions amongst both everyday street users and local property occupiers that street improvement schemes significantly enhance street character, walkability, ease of crossing, opportunities for siting, and general street vibrancy.

A hierarchy of interventions

Collectively the findings suggested that to have the most impact (meaning the delivery of the greatest social and economic benefits against the four street functions), we should view potential projects in terms of a hierarchy of interventions (Figure 13.4). The most important level of intervention, and the foundation for everything else, should involve improving the pedestrian experience by making adequate space for pedestrian movement and activity. This, of course, was even more of a priority during the Covid-19 pandemic, when streets were being managed to allow social distancing to be maintained. Whilst the study did not explicitly single out cycling for analysis, we can confidently add other active modes of travel here as well.

Next comes the *enhancement of social space, notably the creation of attractive and comfortable space for sitting, people-watching,*

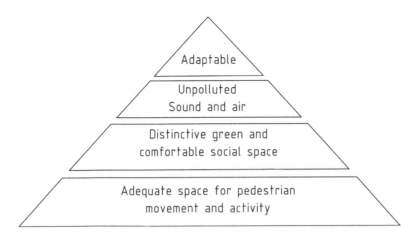

Figure 13.4: A hierarchy of interventions. © Matthew Carmona

socialising and so forth. If we are to stand any chance of saving our traditional shopping streets against the onslaught of online retail (on which we all became so reliant during lockdown), this is a critical priority over the short to medium term. Making these streets distinctive and pleasant places where people want to be is critical. In the UK, for example, a new wave of retail business failures following the coronavirus pandemic has acted to demonstrate how vulnerable the industry is for brands that fail to offer something special that people can't get online (Centre for Retail Research 2020). The same applies to the streets where shops are located.

Finally come interventions relating to the ***creation of environmentally unpolluted (sound and air) and more adaptable spaces that can be used in multiple ways with a good interplay between the street and ground-floor frontages***. At the time of the research it was felt that these would be the most difficult and challenging to achieve, although – as we found out during the height of the pandemic – if people drive less, then these factors to a large degree take care of themselves (Neill 2020). Certainly, having street space that can flex and which we can re-allocate as and when required has become vitally important and is behind many of the most interesting and successful tactical urbanism interventions in cities around the world. The challenge is to continue flexing such streets away from the car.

Let us take the Clapham case as an example (Figure 13.5). The first intervention around the area of Clapham Old Town focused on the repaving of Venn Street into a level shared surface, with increased

Figure 13.5a: Clapham Venn Street. © Matthew Carmona
Figure 13.5b: The Pavement. © Matthew Carmona

footway space while retaining limited car access and parking spaces. The scheme included a shared maintenance agreement with businesses on the street who contribute largely through the renting of outdoor space. The works on Venn Street were completed in 2011 and received positive feedback from locals, prompting the launch of a wider plan for Clapham Old Town which was directed at improving the connectivity and overall quality of the public realm.

The core of a second phase of improvements centred on The Pavement, where a cluster of bus stands used to occupy the majority of the space and vehicles generally dominated the public realm. The scheme limited the bus stands and removed the pre-existing gyratory, opening up a new small square. This space was designed with a range of greening and seating elements and was linked to the surrounding pedestrian network via improved crossings. The paths connecting the area to Clapham Common and the High Street were also improved, with widened pavements, new cycling provisions and renewed paving. Together the range of interventions traversed the hierarchy by i) carving out more space for pedestrians, ii) establishing new characterful and comfortable social streets where previously vehicle movement and car parking had dominated, iii) largely removing vehicles from Venn Street and idling busses from The Pavement, and iv) establishing two new adaptable public spaces that are used for a range of commercial and social activities throughout the year, with Venn Street, in particular, filling with life at lunchtime and during the evening, and at weekends when it hosts a local community food market.

A Covid silver lining

As summarised in the research headlines already set out, the *Street Appeal* work strongly confirmed that improvements to the quality of the publicly owned and managed fabric of our mixed urban streets brings substantial benefits to the everyday users of streets, to the occupiers of space and to businesses in surrounding properties in multiple ways. Later work – *Home Comforts* – conducted during the first Covid-19 lockdown in the UK confirmed that the sorts of benefits seen in the *Street Appeal* research were, in fact, an increasing aspiration and expectation amongst citizens.

Home Comforts aimed to stress-test the homes and neighbourhoods of people from across the UK during a period when much of the population was forced to remain at home and within their home neighbourhoods (Carmona et al. 2020). The research took the form of a national survey consisting of a series of 25 open and closed questions that sought to understand how comfortable people were in their homes, and how their neighbourhoods and local communities supported them during that time. The survey was completed by 2,500 participants who – as far as their housing choices were concerned (house and neighbourhood mix and type, tenure, demographic profile, space standards in the home, levels of occupancy, access to private external space) – broadly reflected the make-up of the British population.

As two contrasting quotes from participants in the survey reveal, responses showed that the availability of less trafficked streets and good walking and cycle routes from the home were particularly prized during lockdown, as were wider pavements where they existed:

> 'Front gardens have become very important as they provide a space for social activity while socially distancing. The streets have a more enjoyable and intimate level of activity, and streets are quieter.'

> 'Pavements outside are too small for social distancing. Our street is dominated by motor vehicle traffic both parked and moving and it highlights how much space is taken up by this mode of transport.'

Many who responded to the survey viewed the crisis of Covid as an opportunity to deliver better street-based environmental standards and long-term health and quality of life benefits through the potential for a permanent switch in modes of travel, a material change in the quality of streets and open spaces, and a safer and more pleasant environment. This seemed to mark a major change in public opinion in contrast with the sorts of pre-Covid responses that were typical of proposals to encourage people out of cars (Kantar 2020).

Two factors were by far the strongest predictors of satisfaction with neighbourhoods during the pandemic: proximity to a park or significant green space, and the availability of local facilities (shops and services) within easy reach of the home, with large shops not too far away. On both fronts, facilities within a five-minute walk of the home maximised satisfaction, and this dropped off markedly the further away facilities were, and significantly when over 10 minutes. There was much talk about a 15- or 20-minute city during lockdown (Whittle 2020; Stanley and Hansen 2020); *Home Comforts* suggested that a 5- or 10-minute city should be the aim, with (critically) cycling and walking facilitated by high-quality street connections within which people could interact. As one respondent commented:

> 'We are seeing neighbours more regularly and talking more when we do see each other. There are more pavement chalk drawings with children having more time to play outside more regularly.'

Figure 13.6: Re-prioritising street space in the short term. © Matthew Carmona

A time to choose

If the coronavirus pandemic has marked a one-in-one-hundred-years health emergency, then it also has the potential to mark a sea change in how streets are used and valued. Some changes have been short-term and temporary, designed primarily to deal with social distancing in traditional streets unsuited to such requirements (Figure 13.6). Others are longer term and even permanent, designed to encourage a switch in how streets are used (Figure 13.7). All emphasise the vital importance of the full range of interventions covered by the hierarchy in Figure 13.4, including, notably, the adaptability that traditional streets allow. Continuing with London as an example, in a letter to its 33 Boroughs in the summer of 2020, the national Department for Transport offered the following advice: 'We have a window of opportunity to act now to embed walking and cycling as part of new long-term commuting habits and reap the associated health, air quality and congestion benefits' (Furness 2020). Such an approach from the UK Government was unprecedented, and whilst prompted by extraordinary times, it marked a real change in direction, supported by a sea change in public opinion

Figure 13.7: New cycle lanes, re-prioritising street space permanently in East Greenwich (one of the unimproved Street Appeal case studies). © Matthew Carmona

as reflected in the responses to the *Home Comforts* survey and in more recent large-scale public opinion surveys (Kantar 2020). In turn this is leading to the investment of significant new funds in walking and cycle infrastructure for what is described as the creation of a 'new era of walking and cycling' (DfT 2020).

Of course, short-term changes and government announcements are one thing and permanent era-defining change is quite another. Nevertheless, if the aspirations in the UK are mirrored elsewhere, if the lessons of Covid are not too quickly forgotten, and if an acceptance of the long-term value of street appeal becomes part of the lexicon of city investment, then there is a real prospect of securing a long-term health dividend from the short-term health crisis and building a better and move liveable environment for all. As UN-Habitat (2013) concluded in their report *Streets as Public Spaces and Drivers of Urban Prosperity*:

> Those cities that have failed to integrate the multi-functionality of streets tend to have lesser infrastructure development, lower productivity, a poorer quality of life[,] … social exclusion and generate inequalities in various spheres of life.

We need to grab the tentative Covid-inspired changes that we have seen and build on them. The evidence seems definitive that this will be good for each of us, good for society and good for the planet. We need to invest in post-Covid street appeal – it's the very essence of a 'no-brainer'!

Bibliography

Bird, Julia, Sebastian Kriticos and Nick Tsivanidis. 2020. Impact of Covid-19 on Public Transport, 6 August. Accessed 1 November 2022. https://www.theigc.org/blog/impact-of-covic-19-on-public-transport/.

Booth, Katie, Megan Pinkston and Carlos Poston Walker. 2005. 'Obesity and the Built Environment', *Journal of the American Dietetic Association* 105(5): 110–17.

Carmona, Matthew, Tommaso Gabrieli, Robin Hickman, Terpsi Laopoulou and Nicola Living-stone. 2018a. *Street Appeal: The value of street improvements.* Summary Report. Accessed 1 November 2022. http://content.tfl.gov.uk/street-appeal.pdf.

Carmona, Matthew, Tommaso Gabrieli, Robin Hickman, Terpsi Laopoulou and Nicola Living-stone. 2018b. 'Street Appeal: The value of street improvements', *Progress in Planning* 126: 1–51.

Carmona, Matthew, Valentina Giordano, Garima Nayyar, Jessica Kurland and Clare Buddle. 2020. *Home Comforts: How the design of our homes and neighbourhoods affected our experience of lockdown and what we can learn for the future.* London: Place Alliance.

Centre for Retail Research. 2020. *The Crisis in Retailing: Closures and job losses.* Accessed 1 November 2022. https://www.retailresearch.org/retail-crisis.html.

Department for Communities & Local Government and Department for Transport (DCLG and DfT). 2007. *Manual for Streets*. London: Thomas Telford.

Department for Transport (DfT). 2020. '£2 Billion Package to Create a New Era for Walking and Cycling', 9 May. Accessed 1 November 2022. https://www.gov.uk/government/news/2-billion-package-to-create-new-era-for-cycling-and-walking.

Dumbaugh, Eric and John Lewis Gattis. 2005. 'Safe Streets, Liveable Streets', *Journal of the American Planning Association* 71(3): 283–300.

Engwicht, David. 1999. *Street Reclaiming: Creating liveable streets and vibrant communities.* British Columbia: New Society Publishers.

Ewing, Reid, Tom Schmid, Richard Killingsworth, Amy Zlot and Stephen Raudenbush. 2003. 'Relationship between Urban Sprawl and Physical Activity, Obesity, and Morbidity', *American Journal of Health Promotion* 18(1): 47–57. http://doi.org/10.4278/0890-1171-18.1.47. PMID: 13677962.

Frank, Laurence, Jared Ulmer, Bruce Appleyard and Alexander Bigazzi. 2019. 'Complete Healthy Streets'. In *The New Companion to Urban Design*, edited by T. Banerjee and A. Loukaitou-Sideris. Abingdon: Routledge.

Furness, Rupert. 2020. 'Emergency Active Travel Funding Indicative Allocations', unpublished letter to Chief Executives and London Borough Transport Officers and Transport for London, 28 May, Department for Transport.

Gehl, Jan. 1996. *Life Between Buildings: Using public space.* 3rd ed. Skive: Arkitektens Forlag.

Hammond, George. 2020. 'UK House Buyers Look to Swap Cities for Suburbs', 11 July. Accessed 1 November 2022. https://www.ft.com/content/72e12347-89f1-4ccc-9b58-92a99f5dcf7f.

Hart, Joshua and Graham Parkhurst. 2011. 'Driven to Excess: Impacts of motor vehicles on the quality of life of residents of three streets in Bristol UK', *World Transport Policy & Practice* 17(2): 12–30.

Hill, Dave. 2015. 'Waltham Forest "Mini-Holland" Row: Politics, protests and house prices', *The Guardian*, 7 November. Accessed 1 November 2022. https://www.theguardian.com/uk-news/davehillblog/2015/nov/07/waltham-forest-mini-holland-row-politics-protests-and-house-prices.

Kantar. 2020. *Public Opinion Survey on Traffic and Road Use*, Department for Transport. Accessed 1 November 2022. https://assets.publishing.service.gov.uk/government/uploads/system/uploads/attachment_data/file/934617/DfT-Public-Opinion-Survey-on-Traffic-and-Road-Use-Phase-1-Report.pdf.

Le Quéré, Corinne, Robert B. Jackson and Matthew Jones. 2020. 'Temporary Reduction in Daily Global CO2 Emissions during the Covid-19 Forced Confinement', *Nature Climate Change* 10: 647–53.

McCann, Barbara. 2013. *Completing Our Streets: The transition to safe and inclusive transportation networks*. Washington, DC: Island Press.

Mayor of London and Transport for London. 2017. *Guide to the Health Streets Indicators: Delivering the Healthy Streets Approach*. Accessed 1 November 2022. http://content.tfl.gov.uk/guide-to-the-healthy-streets-indicators.pdf.

Mayor of London and Transport for London. 2019. *Streetscape Guidance*. 4th ed. Accessed 1 November 2022. http://content.tfl.gov.uk/streetscape-guidance-.pdf.

Neill, P. 2020. 'Brits are Driving 550 Million Miles Less than Before Lockdown', 26 November. Accessed 1 November 2022. https://airqualitynews.com/2020/11/26/brits-are-driving-550-million-miles-less-than-before-lockdown/.

Paul, Kari. 2020. 'Car Sales Rise and Car-Share Companies Boom as Pandemic Upends Transportation', *The Guardian*, 12 August. Accessed 1 November 2022. https://www.theguardian.com/technology/2020/aug/12/car-sales-covic-19-coronavirus-uber-zipcar.

Stanley, John and Roz Hansen. 2020. 'People Love the Idea of 20-Minute-Neighbourhoods. So why isn't it top of the agenda?', 19 February. Accessed 1 November 2022. https://theconversation.com/people-love-the-idea-of-20-minute-neighbourhoods-so-why-isnt-it-top-of-the-agenda-131193.

UN-Habitat. 2013. *Streets as Public Spaces and Drivers of Urban Prosperity*. Nairobi: UN-Habitat.

Whittle, Natalie. 2020. 'Welcome to the 15-Minute City', *Financial Times*, 17 July. Accessed 1 November 2022. https://www.ft.com/content/c1a53744-90d5-4560-9e3f-17ce06aba69a.

Part III
Localography
Jane Clossick, Birgit Hausleitner and
Agustina Martire

There are many ways to absorb knowledge from an everyday street
– some overt, some tacit – but it's important to understand that some
street knowledge is specific to particular people and groups. The third
section of this book addresses the issue of how to conduct research into
everyday streets, asking the following question: *What methodologies
are best suited to unravelling the multiplicity and complexity of everyday
streets?* In this introduction, we discuss drawings, on-site engagement
and action research, the various temporalities that our authors have
encountered, and the value of participant observation. The approaches
in this section offer an alternative to the simplistic definition of people
on everyday streets as 'users', which deprives groups and individuals of
their distinct identities in an attempt to quantify that which is inherently unquantifiable. In contrast, the authors here – in the streets of the
US, Canada, UK, Ireland and Germany – dive deep into the relationships between people and the streetspace they occupy using a range of
approaches that can collectively be referred to as 'localography'.

'Localography' is an anthropological and ethnographic approach
to understanding local environments that acknowledges that these
environments comprise people, cultures, material things, the ways in
which these material things are used and the researcher herself. The
term 'localography' captures the variety and richness of the many layers
of knowledge embedded in the physical, economic, historical, civic
and social life of everyday streets. Manuel Ramos coined the term to
capture the relationship between ethnography and anthropology while
challenging the uncritical survival of the 'ethno-' prefix by replacing
it with 'local' to emphasise the importance of being and studying in
a local context (Ramos 2016). Localness is a core characteristic of

the everyday street, meaning that studies on this matter must be site- and context-specific. Localographies are inherently unable to capture anything beyond fragments of the whole scene; however, through the interpretation of these fragments, we can achieve deep knowledge of the everyday street.

With localography as methodology, the methods employed in this section serve to uncover the multi-layered and multifaceted nature of everyday streets. Localography requires the collection of data spanning several senses – sound, sight, smell and touch – as the sense of a place is driven by the sensory experiences of built environments (Degen and Rose 2012). The authors in this section aim to capture the full spectrum of human experience using both standard and non-standard research tools: interviews, observations, drawings, diagrams, installations, participatory action research, listening and walking.

These attempts to capture the human experience of everyday streets are part of a nascent field centred around schools of architecture, in which practitioners and academics aim to achieve fuller psychosocial and sociospatial accounts of urban phenomena (Clossick and Colburn 2021; Kuschnir 2011; Pink 2008). Graphic anthropology, explored by Tim Ingold (2011), Ray Lucas (2019) and others, is a method of recording data and observations as drawings, and analysis carried out and communicated through drawings. An early example of graphic anthropology, Jan Gehl's (1989) examination of life 'between' buildings was groundbreaking in the sheer level of detail included in his observations of everyday life in the public realm. His later work with Birgitte Svarre (2013) paired their methodologies to comprehensively measure public life. These approaches stem from the philosophical field of phenomenology (Berger 1971; Merleau Ponty 1945; Norberg-Schulz 1979; Seamon 2018), which prioritises embodied and perceptual experiences over objectively measurable 'truth'. Streets and places have been investigated in depth by Suzanne Hall (2012), Sergio Porta and Ombretta Romice (2010), Laura Vaughan (2015) and Phil Hubbard (2017), whose works use ethnographic, morphological, space-syntax and socio-political approaches. What is unique about this section is the authors' use of localography with a focus on drawings, action research and participant observation to uncover the multiple layers and overlapping temporalities of everyday streets.

Assessing a setting via drawing provides researchers with access to embodied and encoded information that is otherwise inaccessible; it enables them to encounter both social and physical structures – what Maurice Mitchell and Bo Tang (2017) collectively refer to as 'constraints' and 'affordances'. Assessing a setting while being in it requires bodily, social and spatial engagement with the objects of study. This is demonstrated by Jane Clossick and Rebecca Smink's chapter on London streets, which employs participant observation and drawing experiments that reveal generally invisible socio-spatial structures. One can draw both seen and unseen elements; drawings can capture non-material phenomena and lend them weight equal to that of material elements, such as social boundaries. This is explored by Anna Skoura, who maps the everyday practices of a Belfast barbershop. Finally, Carole Levesque and Thomas-Bernard Kenniff demonstrate, using 'inventories' of the streets of Montréal, that one cannot draw everything; however, they show that the process of selecting what elements of the sociospatial field to draw provides clarity about what elements are important. Curiously, none of the authors in this section uses photography to any great extent, preferring instead to draw. Photography may be viewed as part of the modern 'mediascape' (Appadurai 1996, 35) rather than an objective means of depiction. In a sense, a graphic notetaker's selection process for objects, motifs and materials constitutes a more 'live' process than taking a photograph (see Taussig 2011).

Some of the authors in this section offer projects engaging with drawings in place – a merger of drawing and installation. Following the tradition of participatory and 'action research' (Till et al. 2005), nearly every author in this section has a personal involvement with the place being studied and either sought for their research to have a material real-world impact or turned personal activism or pedagogy into a research methodology. *Architecture and Participation* (Till et al. 2005) and *Future Practice* (Hyde 2012) both discuss new approaches to architecture that engage with policy and the public in different ways, occupying public space with installations or events to interact with places and access information that remain hidden to standard methods.

Of course, drawing is a slow process, especially when done on-site. and when made on site the embodied and articulated engagement that they entail goes on for a long while, drawing people into conversation, while simultaneously giving the author time to watch and be part of the social life of the place. These dynamics were considered by Antje Steinmuller and Chris Falliers when they employed on-site 'co-drawing', their 'methodology for collective action', in Berlin and California. Similarly, Miriam Delaney and Orla Murphy incorporated their drawings into an installation – the 'Free Market' – which toured Irish Towns and acted as a locus for conversation, influencing Irish policy at the national level.

Participatory actions like these bring stakeholders together, especially in public spaces with both private stakeholders and common stakeholders or where there is control over a place by one agency, while the primary users are voiceless. Installation is a way to extract local knowledge, engage with the public and reveal local experts: resident-experts, citizen-experts or student-experts (covered in Lévesque and Kenniff's chapter about student inventories in Montréal). Hierarchical and grassroots types of power are spatially interlinked. These links are embodied in specific places, meaning that spatial, social and civic engagement in such places can be particularly fruitful for political inclusiveness.

In terms of the varying temporalities that our authors have encountered, what brings methods together is the representation of a juxtaposition of stillness and movement and of a constant state of flux. The everyday street consists of elements that change rapidly and those that change slowly as well as the ever-evolving collective and individual cultural memories of those who reside on it. The varying temporalities of everyday streets and neighbourhoods are most prominently explored by Elen Flugge and Timothy Waddell in Belfast through their 'soundwalking' technique, which pairs audio recordings with architectural drawings. Similarly, Degen and Rose (2012) used street observations, walk-alongs and participant-led photography to uncover how experience is mediated not only by the present moment but also by perceptual memories – memories of previous personal experiences. Moreover, encounters with everyday streets are mediated by people's cultural and historical context and knowledge. This fact aligns with Halbwach's (1992) notion of 'collective memory', which asserts that sensorial and experiential knowledge is built over time, both within individuals and among the collective. Skoura engages deeply with these notions, arguing that, to achieve true inclusiveness, we must recognise that the cultural heritage embodied in an ordinary high street shop is equally as important as more widely recognised types of heritage, such as statues and civic architecture; thus, such forms of collective memory should be carefully preserved.

The act of drawing and the act of being a place are both linked to a traditional research method in the social sciences: participant observation. This method is related to 'deep mapping' (Bodenhamer et al. 2015) and thick description (Geertz 1973), which entail detailed observational descriptions. Previously, observational, mobile and visual studies have been conducted on mundane street life to ascertain how people navigate 'routeways' in cities and, in turn, to examine the role of complex temporalities and materialities in daily journeys (Jiron 2010). This type of study also captures the fleeting aspects of environmental perceptions, such as sensory experiences and emotions, as they unfold in real time and space (Kusenbach 2003). Some of the authors in this section occupied everyday streets for an extended period of time, interviewing people they encountered in casual or formal formats. Paired with drawings done through a reciprocal process, these techniques revealed new knowledge about the potential for social integration in London (Clossick and Smink), the importance of everyday cultural heritage in Belfast (Skoura), and means of influencing urban power structures in Ireland (Delaney and Murphy).

Each chapter in this section focuses on one aspect of inclusiveness. The authors consider the social life of everyday streets while acknowledging the influence of their own presence, which is instrumental in the process of interpretation. The practices in this section may appear to be 'undisciplined' in the sense that they fall outside the scope of any standard academic discipline, with the researchers following their nose to see what they find. However, one could also view this approach as explicitly inclusive, refusing to prioritise any particular method as more 'true' than others. Thus, the discipline of these studies lies in their 'undiscipline', mirroring Levesque and Kenniff's *Bureau d'étude de pratiques indiscipinées*. Debord (1958) defines the dérive as 'a mode of experimental behaviour linked to the conditions of urban society: a technique of rapid passage through varied ambiances'. Like architecture itself, these papers inclusively bring together multiple disciplines, languages, senses and human experiences.

Bibliography

Appadurai, Arjun. 1996. *Modernity at Large: Cultural dimensions of globalization*. Minnesota, MN: University of Minnesota Press.

Berger, John. 1971. *Ways of Seeing*. London: Penguin Classics.

Bodenhamer, David J., John Corrigan and Trevor M. Harris (eds). 2015. *Deep Maps and Spatial Narratives*. Bloomington, IN: Indiana University Press.

Clossick, Jane and Ben Colburn. 2021. 'Design Precepts for Autonomy: A case study of Kelvin Hall, Glasgow'. In *Architecture and Collective Life*, edited by Penny Lewis, Lorens Holm and Sandra Costa Santos. Abingdon: Routledge.

Debord, Guy. 1958. 'Definitions'. Internationale Situationniste. Paris (1). In *Situationist International Anthology*, edited and translated by Ken Knabb (2007). Berkeley, CA: Bureau of Public Secrets.

Degen, Monica Montserrat and Gillian Rose. 2012. 'The Sensory Experiencing of Urban Design: The role of walking and perceptual memory', *Urban Studies* 49(15): 3,271–87.

Geertz, Clifford. 1973. *The Interpretation of Cultures*. 3rd ed. New York: Basic Books.

Gehl, Jan. 1989. *Life Between Buildings*. 6th ed 2011. Washington, DC: Island Press.

Gehl, Jan and Birgitte Svarre. 2013. *How to Study Public Life*. Washington, DC: Island Press.

Halbwachs, Maurice. 1992. *On Collective Memory*. Chicago, IL: University of Chicago Press.

Hall, Suzanne. 2012. *City, Street and Citizen: The measure of the ordinary*. Abingdon: Routledge.

Hubbard, Phil. 2017. *The Battle for the High Street: Retail gentrification, class and disgust*. London: Palgrave Macmillan.

Hyde, Rory. 2012. *Future Practice*. Abingdon: Routledge.

Ingold, Tim. 2011. *Redrawing Anthropology: Materials, movements, lines*. Abingdon: Routledge.

Kuschnir, Karina. 2011. 'Drawing the City: A proposal for an ethnographic study in Rio de Janeiro', *Vibrant, Virtual Brazilian Anthropology* 8(2). https://doi.org/10.1590/S1809-43412011000200029.

Lucas, Ray. 2019. *Drawing Parallels: Knowledge production in axonometric, isometric and oblique drawings*. Abingdon: Routledge.

Merleau Ponty, Maurice. 1945. *The Phenomenology of Perception*. Abingdon: Routledge.

Mitchell, Maurice and Bo Tang. 2017. *Loose Fit City: The contribution of bottom-up architecture to urban design and planning*. Abingdon: Routledge.

Norberg-Schulz. 1979. *Genius Loci: Towards a phenomenology of architecture*. New York: Rizzoli.

Pink, Sarah. 2008. 'An Urban Tour: The sensory sociality of ethnographic place-making', *Ethnography* 9(2): 175–96.

Porta, Sergio and Ombretta Romice. 2010. 'Plot-Based Urbanism: Towards time-consciousness in place-making'. Working paper, University of Strathclyde.

Ramos, Manuel. 2016. 'Collaborators'. StreetSpace. Accessed 1 November 2022. https://www.streetspaceresearch.com/general-5.

Seamon, David. 2018. *LIFE TAKES PLACE: Phenomenology, lifeworlds, and place making*. Abingdon: Routledge.

Taussig, Michael. 2011. *I Swear I Saw This: Drawings in fieldwork notebooks, namely my own*. Chicago, IL: University of Chicago Press.

Till, Jeremy, Peter Blundell Jones and Doina Petrescu. 2005. *Architecture and Participation*. Abingdon: Taylor & Francis.

Vaughan, Laura. 2015. *Suburban Urbanities: Suburbs and the life of the high street*. London: UCL Press.

14

Learning from Castleblayney: conversation and action in a small Irish town

Miriam Delaney and Orla Murphy

The purpose of this chapter is to describe the evolution of a travelling installation by a travelling installation named Free Market *and its subsequent political role as a catalyst for rural town and street regeneration in Ireland. It outlines the aims, design and outcomes of* Free Market,[1] *a touring architectural exhibition and public engagement programme, atypical in its ambition to align political action with close listening and public engagement. The chapter focuses on the installation of* Free Market *in the small market town of Castleblayney, tracking the impact of the project. There were several lessons learnt in combining horizontal engagement on the street with vertical action in political advocacy and policy making. These include the importance of a physical presence in towns, around which political action can coalesce; the significance of deep listening to both grassroots and the vertical institutions of power; and the fact that socially engaged practice needs to work simultaneously at multiple levels to have significant long-term impact.*

The state of the street in the contemporary Irish town

The streets of towns in Ireland resonate to an awkward rhythm. You could drop a needle on their groove, and it would jump between late nineteenth-century traditional music, post-World War II jazz and 1980s disco. A tour along the main street of a typical Irish town today presents a quirky, somewhat decaying assortment of predominantly two- and three-storey simple single-plot buildings, with retail or service on the ground floor. Undertakers, butchers, pharmacies, pubs, charity

GATE OF
HOPE CASTLE

CASTLEBLANEY, IRELAND ┣━━━━━┫500m ⊕

Figure 14.0: Map of Castleblaney © Anna Skoura

shops, hairdressers, insurance brokers, cafes, two-euro shops, fast-food takeaways, betting shops, hardware shops, Polish and Halal grocers and everything shops, in a mixed material bag, that ranges from timber-framed signs written simply, to mosaic-clad, deep-threshold explosions of colour, to plastic back-lit tackiness. They often carry family surnames – O'Brien's, Fallon's, Mulroy's, Walshes, Golden's, McCormack's; locals know the shop by the name, not the function. The apostrophe may or may not be there and you will not find the typeface on your computer. These shops, and the streets and public spaces that they address, form the backdrop to the daily exchange in the life of one third of the population of Ireland (Murphy 2012, 17). The rich character of rural towns' streetscapes is so ubiquitous as to be often taken for granted. Anngret Simms observed in her introduction to *Irish Country Towns* that 'Ireland is a country of small towns'. She points out that 'They are a significant aspect of our identity and a real force in shaping Irish men and women' (Simms and Andrews 1994, 7).

The historical geography and morphology of Irish towns have been researched by notable geographers including Kevin Whelan, Anngret Simms and R.A. Butlin, and urbanists such as Valerie Mulvin and Patrick Shaffrey. Historians H.B. Clarke, Jacinta Prunty, Raymond Gillespie and others have contributed to the long-term historical mapping of Irish towns as editors of the Royal Irish Academy's *Irish Historic Towns Atlas* project. The contemporary rural Irish town forms the backdrop to much of the recent literary fiction of authors including Kevin Barry, Donal Ryan and Colin Barrett, often capturing the state of limbo between past and future in which many towns now find themselves:

> The village was an unimpressive tangle of a dozen streets. There was a main street and a square, one as drab as the other, and a woeful few streets subsidiary to these. There was an insignificant river, brown and slow, and granite hills beyond – these, it was said, gave the place a scenic charm but in truth, it was forlorn. The people were terraced in neat rows and roofed in with grey slates and were themselves forlorn, but they wouldn't easily have said why. (Barry 2007, 62)

The physical manifestation of this limbo is still visible today in the widespread decay and dereliction of streets and spaces in many rural towns. Vacancy in Irish towns is above European averages, and in many towns at a critical level.[2] Yet, spatial policy and discourse in Ireland has largely neglected the changing shape and systemic problems of rural towns over recent decades – a problem compounded in the wake of the 2008 recession. Rob Kitchin points to a lack of coordination of the role of towns within national spatial strategy, claiming that 'there was no strategic planning beyond the local, and no sense in which rural towns fitted into the urban and economic hierarchy, or of how they might best be nurtured' (2018, 17). More recently, there is a growing realisation that the complex challenges of towns need to be addressed holistically and collaboratively, as seen for example in the Collaborative Town Centre Health Check process, coordinated by the Heritage Council, and in the establishment of University College Dublin's transdisciplinary Centre for Irish Towns. However, a general lack of a strategic and coordinated approach to towns persists. Architect Rosie Webb has described the critical fault-lines in current attempts at rural town regeneration: siloed political thinking at local and national level, and lack of designer involvement in decision making. According to Webb, the absence of structures and support for public engagement on urban issues, and the flaws in public funding schemes, lack holistic strategic coordination:

> Top down, it is increasingly difficult to find a place for urban design professionals within local Government structures. Simultaneously, local, amateur and professional input (bottom-up contributions) are being disabled, due to increasingly onerous statutory and regulatory systems. An approach to solving complex urban problems centred on facilitating, enabling and supporting local communities involves primarily an investment in time and human resources over monetary investment. (Webb 2018, 18)

Free Market: modes of operation

Within this context of political stasis and rural town decline, *Free Market* was an architectural exhibition curated and designed by the authors in collaboration with Jeffrey Bolhuis, Jo Anne Butler, Tara Kennedy and Laurence Lord, which toured from *La Biennale Venezia* in 2018 to the public spaces of four towns in Ireland in 2019. The exhibition aimed to tell the story of deterioration in public space in Irish towns, to highlight vacancy and loss of town centre living, but also to present the nuance of culture, potential and possibility latent in towns as a fundamentally optimistic call to reconsider the future of Irish rural

Figure 14.1: *Free Market News.* © Matthew Thompson

towns as places to live sustainably. The content of the pavilion included our own research into 10 case-study rural towns (with propositional design projects in four of these), comparative morphological mapping of 77 market towns, a narrative map of government policies, agencies and funding that impact on towns, and a newspaper entitled *Free Market News* (Figure 14.1).

Work by the curators was supplemented with that of photographers, writers, journalists and urbanists, so that visitors could choose multiple ways of interacting with a broad range of media and content. In designing and planning the *Free Market* pavilion, exchange – social, cultural and commercial – became a significant theme, in the design of the installation and in the means through which visitors encountered and experienced the work.

The theme of exchange, and the role that dialogue and conversation play in that exchange, continued to evolve as the exhibition moved from Venice to Ireland, building on a shared curatorial interest in an expanded field of architectural practice that encompasses design, teaching, research, curation, and public engagement with architecture. Participatory spatial planning and design has yet to be broadly valued or adopted in Ireland; the culture of space-making is still dominated by a rigid, top-down, consultation-based planning system.[3]

Our work has been informed by an interest in alternative modes of architectural practice, in particular in the understanding of the production of space as a 'shared enterprise'; that 'social space is intractably political space' and that making of public space is an evolving negotiated process and therefore not subject to a finite start and finish (Awan et al. 2011, 29). As such, the role of architects as actors within this system of production can be seen as one of bridge-building between spatial design, community activism and political engagement. Harriss, Hyde and Marcaccio (2021, 9) posit that the role of the architect needs to be recast as 'a creative mediator, bridging between different forms of knowledge, seeking clarity amongst complexity, bringing together disparate communities, building and combining emotional power with pragmatic potential'.

The challenges of socially engaged practice are not ignored here. The risk of 'placing excessive demands on the time, energy and goodwill of laypeople' is highlighted by Suzanne Hofmann in setting out Die Baupiloten's methodology for participatory design (2014, 17). And Tatjana Schneider finds participatory design and socially engaged modes of operation at times naive and easily co-opted by existing power structures without having lasting impact (2018, 11). Her critique of the long-term effectiveness of socially engaged architectural practice supports the necessity of direct political engagement to make the systemic changes needed to address the scale of difficulties facing towns, aligning with Tahl Kaminer's call to action in *The Efficacy of Architecture* for architects to take their role in political realms to affect societal change (2016, 11). Within the methodological framework of socially engaged practice, our aim in developing the *Free Market* installation was to build coalitions across multiple constituencies, drawing on Kossack's understanding of the critical role of exhibition:

> ... the challenge for any progressive and critical praxis engaged in architectural installation working in today's context is therefore to develop the installation as a continuous laboratory in which to experiment with new forms of architecture and the way it is produced. (Kossak 2009, 126)

Free Market resisted the urge to draft a manifesto for towns. Instead, as we prepared for our initial exhibition in Venice, we wrote a *Charter for Everyday Practice: Learning from small towns*. The lessons of the tour subsequently confirmed our initial claim that 'when we relax our need to be the driver of solutions we create a *freespace* for deep curiosity. We ask what is missing in the stories we tell about rural communities? We learn from their commitment to working together and their acceptance of imperfections' (Bolhuis et al. 2018).

Moving in: *Free Market* in Castleblayney

A blended and open approach – working both horizontally with community groups, in open-ended dialogue, and vertically with decision makers and politicians – became important in the planning and production of the National Tour of *Free Market*. Working with partners in the Local Authorities, we selected four towns which the pavilion would visit over the course of summer 2019: Castleblayney in County Monaghan, Macroom in County Cork, Mountmellick in County Laois and Killmallock in County Limerick.

As an illustration of some of the key challenges and findings, here we look at the installation in Castleblayney: the immediate impact of that installation on the ground in the town, the subsequent outcomes, and the modes of operation which led to long-term political outcomes and important regeneration projects. Typical of many market towns, Castleblayney (Figure 14. 2) boasts a distinctive Market House and square, a direct connection to classical landscape in Hope Castle and Lough Muckno and strong built fabric of streets lined with terraced buildings, mainly dating from the eighteenth and nineteenth centuries. The same town fabric has suffered from years of neglect: the Market House and Hope Castle are both derelict, and a high proportion of buildings in the town centre are vacant.

Advance planning for the exhibition began months ahead of the opening, negotiating the location, licences and installation logistics of the exhibition supported by representatives from Monaghan County Council. The initial plan was to locate the pavilion beside the Market House as a means to highlight the need to address the ongoing dereliction of this notable town-centre building. However, during the winter of 2018 the roof of the Market House collapsed, putting the future of the building in doubt. Temporary works stabilised the building, but a question mark over its long-term future, including the option of demolition, now arose. The location of the *Free Market* installation was moved to the gates of Hope Castle, still within view of the derelict Market House. Meanwhile, we continued to plan the arrangement of the pavilion and exhibition content, tailored for the town. In curating the national tour, we also commissioned a new graphic identity for the

Figure 14.2: Aerial photograph of Castleblayney showing the Market House and its relationship to the town and Hope Castle estate, 2018. © Magnaparte

engagement elements and designed a bespoke programme of events for each stop, overlapping with local festivals or events to maximise engagement potential. In the months preceding the installation in Castleblayney, and assisted by Monaghan County Council, we met with local activists, historians, and the festival committee of the annual *Mucknomania* festival, with which *Free Market* deliberately overlapped. Aware that we were guests, and not the experts in each town we visited, we invited local community leaders and historians to lead walking tours, and in Castleblayney this invitation was enthusiastically taken up as an opportunity to share deep knowledge and close insight into the character of the town. The Local Authority also reacted to the *Free Market* project positively from the outset, and key personnel generously provided guidance and logistical support before, during and – importantly – after the exhibition. This relationship building in advance of the installation was key to establishing trust in the local community.

In our travels with the *Free Market* pavilion, the use and value of the pavilion, a physical market stall with attendant architects/curators wearing orange aprons, was evident. The installation of the pavilion and exhibition, as it gradually took shape in public space in the week before the launch, generated public curiosity and interest. During its four-day stay it provided a meeting place, a punctuation mark on the street for people to congregate around, and a base for tours and talks as well as informal conversations (Figure 14.3).

Figure 14.3: The *Free Market* pavilion in Castleblayney. © Orla Murphy

The pavilion worked as a physical, tangible demonstration of how public space could be actively used by people. In Castleblayney, we temporarily removed car-parking spaces and activated the public realm of streetscapes through a programme of events and an exhibition. Public life folded around the pavilion. At various times it operated as a site of exchange, casual performance, exhibition, a supportive framework – we hosted tea and sandwiches, a poet gave an impromptu performance and the cycling stage of a triathlon funnelled through it. These events animated the more formal content of the pavilion (photography, drawings, models and books) in unique ways in each site. The appropriation of the pavilion by townspeople allowed it to become part of the life of the street, and through its temporary difference prompted reconsideration of spaces that are sometimes overlooked through familiarity.

The question mark over the future of the Market House, and the fact that Castleblayney had recently been selected as one of six pilot towns to be part of a government programme focused on residential town centre vacancy, generated significant media attention for the launch of the exhibition. Reacting to the spotlight of attention on the Market House, the Chief Executive of the Local Authority made a public commitment to restore the Market House at the launch of the *Free Market* exhibition.

Figure 14.4: Conversations at the *Free Market* pavilion. © Paul Tierney

Our initial focus on the installation and design of the pavilion was on formal and perhaps traditional content – drawings, models, photographs, books. As the project became situated in rural towns, the content receded in significance as conversation and dialogue became our primary modes of operation, and means of continuing to learn from towns, rather than to project our thoughts on to them.

Formal and informal conversations were an integral part of the public engagement programme of the Irish tour. *Stories for Oranges* consisted of recorded vox-pop interviews with visitors to the outdoor pavilion, voice recorded with permission, by the curatorial team. The same questions were used as prompts, to tease out stories about the value of towns, their past and future purpose, and the degree of belonging and attachment felt. It was clear that people know and love their towns, but in some cases felt alienated from decisions about how they worked:

> I have magic memories, of a childhood growing up, of walking to school with other children. We met each other as we walked, by the time we got to the top of the street there would be nine or ten of us. All of that relationship building is lost, and much more isolated now. That simple activity of walking to school with other kids, being able to chat with other kids is gone. (Michael, Castleblayney)

Challenges around mobility, the practical day-to-day complexity of doing business in a changed retail landscape, the perception that towns were not compatible with a good quality of life due to noise and air pollution, and a fear of being left behind in the bigger political decisions that impact upon towns contrasted with the clear love of being at the heart of things, of being part of a tight-knit community, and an appreciation of the easy scale of towns, their shared history and heritage.

> It will take creative thinking. Cars are the problem. If you could create the Market Building to be reanimated as a centre, it would be a catalyst for other things to happen around it. You can start with creative thinking about the future of the street. What can it be? To reanimate it. What happens in that building is important in terms of how it regenerates other things that can happen around it. Not just preserved but as a catalyst. (Michael, Castleblayney)

In almost all cases, there was a sense of appreciation for the chance to air grievances – 'Muckno Street has died a death' (Niall, Castleblayney); to be heard, to have an opinion valued and listened to. A small token of thanks was offered in exchange for these stories: a postcard, a badge, an orange, a promise that their story was valued. Despite the proscribed list of questions, conversation often veered away from the formula and interviewees talked to us about their memories, concerns and hopes for their towns.

> My father and grandfather are from the town, it's always been a part of my life. I've moved to Dublin but I did feel homesick. I missed the talking and the people. I'm fairly confident I would come back and live here. (Oisín, Castleblayney)

The impact of *Free Market*

At the conclusion of the tour we presented feedback to the Local Authority. The comments made by those who engaged with the exhibition were instrumental in the decision by Monaghan County Council to instigate a community-led project to develop a brief and spatial strategy for regenerating Market House. Members of the *Free Market* team remained involved in the redevelopment of the Castle-blayney Market House, and undertook an extensive public engagement project to identify and design appropriate community functions for the building. Their report formed the basis of a tender call to continue the project to detailed design, with the expectation that the Market House redevelopment will begin in 2023.

By engaging with the vertical hierarchical power structures of governance, and by simultaneously installing the project in situ, the *Free Market* project had direct political impact. As a result of conversations on the ground in Castleblayney, we were invited by a local Teachta Dála (member of parliament) to present our findings the Department of Housing, Planning and Local Government, to the Department of Rural and Community Development and to the Joint Oireachtas Committee on Rural and Community Development, which is focused on coordination of grant aid to support rural towns and villages. We presented six recommendations for political action, including the need for a multi-level town partnership model similar to Scotland's Towns Partnership; for support for a transdisciplinary academic centre focused on towns; to establish exemplar demonstrator projects; to strengthen mechanisms for participatory planning and decision making; to appoint town architects within local authorities with responsibility for towns; and to design long-term co-created vision plans for towns. Our recommendations were accompanied by first-hand accounts from representative groups from several towns, including Castleblayney Town Team. In 2020 the newly formed coalition government promised to draft a Town Centre First Policy as part of its Programme for Government. An Interdepartmental Group was convened to draft this policy and as part of the now established UCD Centre for Irish Towns, we had a seat on the Advisory Group to this process. The first Town Centre First Policy for Ireland was published in February 2022. This policy includes many of the recommendations we had presented to senior politicians and civil servants over the previous three years, illustrating a direct impact at national policy level of the conversations and presentations we have made. Working with community groups, Local Authorities and funders, members of the team have been developing a new model for 'Town Action Plans', prioritising broad community engagement as a first step towards developing design and implementation strategies, and have been engaged in further studies particularly related to vacancy and dereliction in towns. While *Free Market* in itself is of course not responsible for the full extent of local or national momentum that has built around action on rural towns, it can be said that a combination of the on-the-ground listening, gathering and feedback has actively informed and helped to sustain the momentum for change related to rural towns in Ireland.

Conclusion

In the lineage of socially engaged architectural practice, and working directly in the context of rural towns in Ireland, the *Free Market* exhibition and subsequent political actions point to ways of working to tackle the seemingly intractable issues of vacancy and dereliction that dominate the streetscapes of so many small Irish towns. Weak attempts by the state to incentivise town centre renewal through grant schemes have been largely unsuccessful, placing the risk and cost back on the private individual. Volunteers in towns face burn-out and frustration as they invest time and energy in unwieldy bureaucratic processes in an effort to find support and funding, and Local Authorities remain under-resourced and under constant pressure to squeeze projects into restrictive cycles of annual funding. Our experience of working directly with community groups, Local Authorities and politicians in Castle-blayney, as well as in the other three towns on the tour, has taught us that socially engaged practice needs to work simultaneously at multiple levels to have significant long-term impact. Some criticism of community-led, bottom-up projects points to the limited wider impact or ripple effect of tactical urbanism – successes, when they occur, remain discrete and have effectively failed to challenge underlying structural inequalities (Schneider 2018). In addition, operating outside more precise and defined scientific enquiry can mean that projects like this are not subject to in-depth human research ethics review, and may thus be at risk of capturing insufficiently diverse or divisive views. Conclusions drawn from these stories therefore need to be contextu-alised within the time and limitations of the enquiry and not claimed to be representative of all views.

Despite these limitations, *Free Market* demonstrates the value in working simultaneously with community groups, on the street, in open-ended dialogue, and with decision makers and politicians to achieve systemic change. These axes of action suggest ways to increase community engagement for long-term impact; listening carefully to specific issues at a local scale can both inform and shape broader decisions on policy and funding. This work continues to evolve and deepen as we work with community groups and Local Authorities in the regeneration of a number of rural Irish towns.

Our work in rural towns evolves as we continue to directly assist communities in Town Action Plan projects, which combine listening carefully to townspeople's self-identified needs and developing spatial strategies and designs – providing enabling mechanisms for communities to enact change. We continue to assist politicians and civil servants too in designing effective policies to achieve active streetscapes. There are no 'quick-fix' solutions, but aligning deep listening, learning and open knowledge sharing with political action can provide the basis for an informed and reciprocal approach that seeks to value and admit diverse voices in the reimagining of towns as resilient, nimble places of exchange. We happily continue to declare our love of these streets and squares, perch on their cills, hop between their grooves, and imagine and advocate for their future.

Notes

1   *Free Market* are Jeffrey Bolhuis, Jo Anne Butler, Miriam Delaney, Tara Kennedy, Laurence Lord and Orla Murphy.
2   Although no data exists on longitudinal vacancy in Irish towns, baseline data is now being measured for ground-floor retail space in rural towns through the Heritage Council's Collaborative Health Check (CTCHC) programme and further data collection is promised through the Town Centre First Policy. Initial CTCHC baseline reporting for the following towns has been recorded: Ballyshannon 17.5%; Bundoran 10%; Carrick-on-Shannon 30.5%; Donegal 13.5%; Dundalk 24%; Ennis 17%; Letterkenny 18%; Sligo 18.4%; Tralee 19%. See https://www.heritagecouncil.ie/projects/town-centre-health-check-programme (accessed 1 November 2022). Vacancy at upper-floor levels is understood to be considerably higher in most towns.
3   Notable exceptions include the work of Callan Workhouse Union, Co. Killkenny, the Irish Architecture Foundation's ReImagine programme, and local authority projects and public realm upgrade works in Cork county towns, led by Giulia Vallone.

Bibliography

Awan, Nishat, Tatjana Schneider and Jeremy Till. 2011. *Spatial Agency: Other ways of doing Architecture*. Abingdon: Routledge.
Barry, Kevin. 2007. *There are Little Kingdoms*. Dublin: Stinging Fly Press.
Bolhuis, Jeffrey, Jo Anne Butler, Miriam Delaney, Tara Kennedy, Laurence Lord and Orla Murphy. 2018. *Free Market Charter for Everyday Practice*. Dublin.
Harriss, Hariett, Rory Hyde and Roberta Marcaccio (eds). 2021. *Architects After Architecture: Alternative pathways for practice*. Abingdon: Routledge.
Hofmann, Susanne. 2014. *Architecture is Participation: Die Baupiloten – methods and projects*. Berlin: Jovis Verlag.
Kaminer, Tahl. 2016. *The Efficacy of Architecture: Political contestation and agency*. Abingdon: Routledge.
Kitchin, Rob. 2018. 'The Future of Rural Towns in Ireland'. In *Free Market News*, edited by Jeffrey Bolhuis, Jo Anne Butler, Miriam Delaney, Tara Kennedy, Laurence Lord and Orla Murphy. Dublin.
Kossak, Florian. 2009. 'Exhibiting Architecture: The installation as laboratory for emerging architecture'. In *Curating Architecture and the City*, edited by Sarah Chaplin and Alexandra Stara, 117–28. New York: Routledge.
Murphy, Orla. 2012. *Town: Origins, morphology and future*. Connecticut: Westport.

Schneider, Tatjana. 2018a. 'Problematizing Social Engagement: The Canadian Centre for Architecture (CCA)', 10 September. Accessed 1 November 2022. https://www.youtube.com/watch?v=-Ym9wUxi7KU.

Schneider, Tatjana. 2018b. 'What if … or Toward a Progressive Understanding of Socially Engaged Architecture'. In *The Routledge Companion to Architecture and Social Engagement*, edited by Farhan Karim, 3–13. New York: Routledge.

Simms, Anngret and J.H. Andrews (eds). 1994. *Irish Country Towns*. Dublin: Mercier Press.

Webb, Rosie. 2018. 'Back to the Future for Town Squares'. In *Free Market News*, edited by Jeffrey Bolhuis, Jo Anne Butler, Miriam Delaney, Tara Kennedy and Orla Murphy, 18. Dublin.

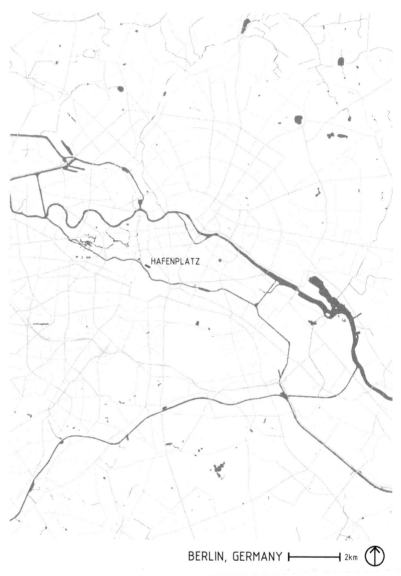

HAFENPLATZ

BERLIN, GERMANY |⎯⎯⎯⎯| 2km ⬆

Figure 15.0: Map of Berlin © Anna Skoura

15

Co-drawing: a design methodology for collective action

Antje Steinmuller and Christopher Falliers

In the design of public spaces, collaboration with multiple stake-holders can promote the rethinking of architectural protocols and production processes. This study proposes 'co-drawing' – a design methodology that establishes frameworks for collective action, evolving development strategies and multivalent designs – as an alternative to conventional instruments, urban masterplans, community meetings and design guidelines. By producing collaborative drawings through carefully designed events in urban street spaces, architects and urban practitioners can engage citizens in participatory planning processes that blend professional expertise with the lived experience and local expertise of a community.

Public spaces as an interface

There are multiple stakeholders in any public space – people for whom the space has use or meaning. Co-drawing as a forum for public dialogue holds promise for urban streets and other public environments in which developers or city planners build in opportunities for citizen groups to self-determine, co-design and co-manage their environment. Collaboration with stakeholders could lead to the rethinking of architectural protocols, with the traditional masterplan giving way to architectural frameworks for collective action, evolving development strategies and multivalent designs. Public spaces can turn from 'object' to 'interface' (Baudrillard 1988) and can be used to engage and harness the lived experiences and expertise of urban communities. This chapter describes collaborative drawings produced at 'co-drawing events' (Steinmuller and Falliers 2018) in two urban street spaces in Berlin, Germany and Palo Alto, California. Free from the control of a single agent, co-drawing promotes both utopian endeavours and the development of realistic democratic visions for today's and tomorrow's streets. Applicable to various contexts and locations, co-drawings – and the events that catalyse them – are co-authored, cooperative instruments. They position the architect as a designer of public communication and the developer of tools that stimulate multi-stakeholder involvement in visualising, advocating and recapturing streets as truly collective spaces in the city.

Street space as commons

The character of streets and sidewalks has changed considerably across many Western cities in recent decades. In Berlin, one of the two test sites for the co-drawing methodology presented here, these spaces accommodate encounters between increasingly diverse populations and present important places for community events and rituals that make immigrants feel at home. The pathways on American campus environments like the second test site in Palo Alto, California similarly serve as meeting places for ever more diverse student populations. Here, circulation spaces are further charged by the traditional siloisation between academic disciplines that is manifest in the layout of separate buildings that these pathways connect. In both locations, recent restrictions related to the Covid-19 pandemic have brought additional focus onto streets and other outdoor spaces for gatherings. For a design process that adapts the street spaces of Berlin, larger campus environments like the one in Palo Alto, or other urban circulation spaces elsewhere into an 'urban commons' for everyone, planning for a common use is not enough – what is needed are tools to transform streets into spaces of collective production and stewardship.

In order to successfully produce a local commons, it is key to gather and leverage the expertise of those who use them. Residents hold deep knowledge on the evolving needs of neighbourhood communities, their make-up, movement and use patterns and culturally rooted markers of identity and orientation. Processes that gather and translate this knowledge help to build a sense of community and wield great promise to initiate long-term citizen stewardship. The lack of clear tools and spaces for citizen collaboration on such public-commons projects for neighbourhood streets presents opportunities for designers, architects and urbanists. Traditional methods include community meetings, in which verbal contributions are recorded in reports; however, what is truly needed are collaborative tools with which community members can share their experiences and desires with one another. The expertise of trained designers and architects can contribute event frameworks, protocols and artefacts that facilitate citizen interaction. With the aim of supporting productive, inclusive and equitable collaboration, such processes can reach beyond traditional community meetings at city hall, and benefit from being situated in the public spaces being discussed. They entail the modelling and anticipation of a collectively formed and inhabited future street space as a commons. Using drawing to visually record knowledge serves as a catalyst for further dialogue during, and within the space of, a co-drawing event.

While the term 'commons' stems from the sharing of natural resources (such as pastures or fisheries), it has recently come to be used to describe the collective appropriation and regulation of shared everyday concerns in contemporary cities (Kip et al. 2015). In the urban context, commons are still understood as a system by which community members equally share and steward spatial resources with minimal reliance on the state or market. In *Common Space: The city as commons* (2016), Stavros Stavrides describes 'a set of spatial relations produced by commoning practices' that govern everyday use, regulate access, distribute labour and, ultimately, constitute a relational social framework associated with a physical space. Commoning practices allow for a sense of ownership and control in dialogue with others who share the same interests. Ultimately, such practices have the potential to create alternative forms of community within urban life – a community that collectively creates, uses and stewards urban space.

Collectively managed neighbourhood gardens constitute a familiar type of urban commons, but there are many other forms. Economic austerity and reduced government resources for the creation of public recreational infrastructure have resulted in the emergence of participatory forms of the production of such spaces including a reexamination of streets as a collaboratively revitalised common space. Building on the now prominent public-private partnerships (PPPs) that have produced often highly controlled and privately stewarded open spaces in town centres, we now see alternative public-private – or public-commons – partnerships. Public-commons partnerships have been described as indicative of the 'commonification' of public space, 'where the role of state is realigned, from its current support and subsi-dising of private for-profit companies, towards supporting commoning and the creation of common value' (Fattori et al. 2013). The Living Alleys Program in San Francisco is an example of a street-revitalisation effort that converts street and sidewalk spaces into 'commons' through design improvements initiated and stewarded by local citizen groups (Steinmuller 2018). The program operates at the scale of street improvements for a block-length narrow street. Funds are made available to citizens via impact fees from nearby housing developments and, once completed, citizens are expected to manage and maintain the improvements. However, little guidance on how to bring together local citizens' knowledge and needs exists for such collective development processes. Illustrating this complexity, the Living Alleys Program has only fully realised two alleyway improvements in San Francisco's Hayes Valley since the program was pioneered with the launch of its 'toolkit' in 2015.

Collaborations: design activism meets relational art

The co-drawing events discussed in this study frame questions, direct conversations and record local knowledge while enabling professional assessments of problems and potential. A collaborative drawing process situates the architect as a designer of spatial and social frameworks that encourage citizen interaction. The drawing as an interface acts as a tool of active envisioning and the archiving of consensus and productive dissent. Designed as a combination of catalytic artefact, protocol and event in the street space, co-drawing is both site and document, recording both idealistic visions and realistic projections. Its development was driven by three spheres of influence: design activism, relational art, and multi-authored and multi-centred drawing compositions (a type of drawing with multiple foci across the surface).

The first sphere extends practices that merge design advocacy and activism with short-term catalytic interventions. In Archigram's sequential drawings for *Instant City*, a catalytic event is depicted in six steps in which a blimp represents the initiation of a new form of limited-duration urbanism. A catalyst for long-term change, the processes initiated by the blimp seed a new sense of self-reliance among citizens and construct a network for future connections. Similarly, Raumlabor's *Pioneer Fields*, relating to Berlin's Tempelhof Airport (Raumlaborberlin 2010), described open spaces where citizens could initiate, build and host a range of activities and events over a three-year period. A site for testing and acknowledging local residents as 'experts', these temporary uses served to offer lessons for potentially suitable longer-term programmes. In such projects, tactics for the production of public space extend beyond the design of physical interventions. They involve architects embedding themselves within a community, the design of processes that facilitate local involvement, and the initiation of dynamic and evolving transformation processes (Steinmuller and Falliers 2019).

The second sphere, 'relational art', positions a designed artefact and/or action in public to be acted out with and by the public, as a catalyst for social exchange. In his book *Relational Aesthetics*, Nicolas Bourriaud (2002) identifies art practices that position the artist as the 'catalyst of exchange', with outcomes that often take the form of lived social situations or environments. Similarly, Futurefarmers' *Ethnobotanical Station* (2012) employs a combination of artefacts (a mobile cart, map and information-gathering equipment) and workshops (information-gathering and discussion workshops) as a platform to assess the interactions between people and their environment, catalysing collective knowledge building. With a focus on social encounters in the street space, these works present strategies for designing a physical-spatial interface with protocols that facilitate a collaborative knowledge-building process.

The third sphere, 'multi-centred and multi-authored compositions', has a history in utopian speculation and critical depictions of public life. Atelier Bow-Wow explores collaborative representations of the city and representations of the collective through drawings of public behaviours. In drawings like *Temple of Heaven* (Kooperatives Labor Studierender and Atelier Bow-Wow 2016), architect-designed artefacts, people and ad hoc spatial configurations are rendered with graphical equivalence and architectural precision in multi-centred drawing panels. Raumlabor's *Stick-On City* (Venice Biennale 2008; Raumlaborberlin 2008) situates a co-drawing of an imagined, partially completed city within a gallery in which a workshop-like table prompts the public to add drawing patches to the line-drawing base. As frameworks for dialogue, activation and interpretation, approachability and participation are key to activation in multi-authored drawings. For co-drawing as a community tool, limited duration, continued engagement with those who draw and dialogue curation are key to maintaining sufficient control over the design and enhancing community-architect dialogue.

Framing a collaborative canvas: components of a forum for public dialogue

Co-drawing events are interactive, situated within street space or other public spaces. These events entail three core design tasks: the platform for public engagement (the artefact), the planned structure of dialogue with the public (the protocol) and the choreography of gatherings to catalyse interaction and conversation (the event). The artefact takes centre stage, as it frames the act of drawing collaboratively. It includes a designed object, or spatial environment, that facilitates interaction and discussion (as in Futurefarmers' *Ethnobotanical Station*) as well as a drawing surface. Built on prior analysis and curation, the artefact includes a base drawing that constitutes a carefully calibrated framework, capturing familiar references and using projections and techniques that are legible and recognisable to the audience. Next, the protocol may draw on local social conventions to encourage interactions. Protocols provide instructions for engagement, offer straightforward starting points and prompt dialogue between participants. Finally, the choreography necessitates thinking through a temporal sequence. It includes the production of a framework within which others may produce events in the future (as in Raumlabor's *Pioneer Fields*) as well as means of documenting the gathered knowledge (Raumlabor's *Stick-On City*). The events aim to be transformative, ideally leaving behind altered environments or instigating future action (Archigram's *Instant City*).

Drawing table: Berlin

Two versions of co-drawing have been tested in street space and other public spaces in two very different locations – Hafenplatz in Berlin, Germany and Stanford University's campus in Palo Alto, California. In the first experiment, a forward-thinking developer of a large site in a diverse neighbourhood at Hafenplatz in central Berlin engaged a design team comprising Raumlabor, the authors and students from California College of the Arts with the goal of engaging local citizens in a participatory visioning process. The site currently hosts a large housing complex that has attracted a diverse mix of recent immigrants, elderly lower-income Berlin residents, young families and students, each with a different perspective on living near the centre of a gentrifying

Berlin. Rather than displacing the local community, the developer sought to engage residents in the transformation of their environment. They used co-drawing to gather knowledge about locations and local housing types that signify 'home' and are meaningful to local inhabitants. Everyone in the housing complex and the adjacent buildings was invited to participate. The co-drawing event served to kick off a series of in-depth collaborative conversations about the future of the site.

The event took place in a mostly pedestrianised but high-traffic access road into the housing complex, flanked by an abandoned supermarket storefront and a small green. It was designed as an eight-hour neighbourhood event aimed at casually engaging as many people as possible. Referred to as *zeichentisch* (drawing table), the artefact was a 30-foot-long table with a base drawing showing the necessary background information via axonometric and perspectival drawings of the context. There was also a corresponding base drawing showing slightly different angles of the same locations placed inside the adjacent storefront windows, transforming the glass into a secondary drawing surface. Intended as a site of conversation, drawing and dining, the table invited residents to pause, catalysed conversation (Figure 15.1), and acted as a canvas for knowledge gathering and record keeping. Food and drinks were provided at the drawing table to create a relaxed atmosphere and encourage 'napkin drawings' (Figure 15.2). To direct the conversation and encourage citizens to draw, the design team presented questions about spaces with relevance to local identity and community in the form of 'menus' on the table. Simple prompts acted as icebreakers, inviting residents to share local places that they feel strengthen their bond with the community. These loose protocols solicited axonometric drawings of personal, temporal and communal focal points to be placed into the axonometric drawings on the 'table cloth'. The secondary drawing surface on the storefront's windows, by contrast, became the curated record of collected knowledge translated into more formal drawings by the professional design team. The design team conversed with as many residents as possible, encouraging hesitant participants and probing verbal narratives for key elements that could be drawn by citizens at the table.

While multi-centred and multi-authored, the resulting table-surface drawing remained individual and fragmented. Individual participants added drawings of how they had personalised outdoor spaces, focusing on private spaces that they would like to see for themselves rather than on meaningful community spaces in the neighbourhood. The information collected through this co-drawing event

Figure 15.1: Zeichentisch. 2018. Berlin. Collage of table and drawing artefacts at Berlin Hafenplatz with a supermarket storefront in the background. © Antje Steinmuller

Figure 15.2: Zeichentisch. 2018. Berlin. Base drawing detail; co-drawing in progress. © Antje Steinmuller

was intended to provide insight into spaces that are meaningful to residents and, in turn, ideas for programmes and places that might strengthen their sense of community – but this aim did not come to fruition. opportunities for them to feel at home together in the neighbourhood, but it did not quite work out that way. The citizens' focus on individual desires rather than the collective may have been due to the fact that most of the drawings emerged through dialogue with members of the design team rather than dialogue among citizen participants. While the event's length allowed for the gathering of many different types of users who engage with the space at different times of day, it did not connect them to one another. Instead, they engaged with the table in separate groups over the course of the day. The catalysing prompts and questions also proved to be too open-ended, resulting in a range of topics and elements in the drawings so wide that it prevented a thematically focused collection of ideas about 'commons' with direct implications for design.

Drawing the continuous campus: Palo Alto

With lessons learned from the *Zeichentisch* event, the second iteration used the context of an academic conference and a hypothetical project to test a more game-like approach to drawing prompts. These altered protocols – alongside a far shorter duration of 60 minutes – were leveraged to achieve more focused engagement *among* participants rather than between participants and the design team. This experiment took place in a shaded arcade on the Stanford University campus in

Figure 15.3: Drawing table. 2019. Stanford. Deployable co-drawing tables with base drawing as the tabletop. © Antje Steinmuller

Palo Alto, California. Here, the site and subject were both the campus: as an environment of knowledge production and exchange. The authors developed a re-deployable drawing table from commercially available folding tables (Figure 15.3), whose surface featured plan drawings of Stanford University and other iconic American educational institutions, from nineteenth-century schoolhouses to the University of Virginia (founded by Thomas Jefferson), tailoring the drawing type to an audience of academics, architects and urbanists. While this was not the audience of non-architect citizens which the co-drawing method ultimately aims to engage with, this iteration of the work allowed a focus on how drawing type, content and prompts can and must adapt to each specific audience.

Critiquing the spatial hierarchies and frequent siloisation of knowledge fields embedded within typical educational building types, the event asked participants to rethink the streets, pathways and other open spaces on traditional campuses as potential sites for knowledge exchange and collective knowledge production. Framed as a workshop session at the conference, this event presented 14 volunteer conference participants (architects, urban designers and theorists) with protocols in the form of a set of large 'Yardzee' dice. One set of dice contained precedents for space activation from relational art and activist projects – strategies for producing more public, interactive and non-siloed sites of conversation and exchange. These strategies were presented on the dice through labelled drawings and descriptions of well-known works by artists and design activists, such as Futurefarmers, Raumlabor Berlin and Santiago Cirugeda (Figure 15.4). The other set of dice contained suggestions for specific spatial conditions that could serve as alternative knowledge-exchange sites, such as stairs, halls, niches and other less conventional sites on the campus (Figure 15.4). The event was organised as a design collaboration in which participants could engage in cross-disciplinary dialogue framed within the rules of the shared dice and act on the base drawing to project future shared knowledge-exchange spaces (Figure 15.5). While the project was hypothetical, the participating academics had an interest and a stake in the campus environment, prompting them to quickly engage in dialogue. The addition of the dice as both a playful artefact and a protocol lowered the threshold for engagement and sparked interaction between participants.

Of the three subgroups that shared a dice set, two engaged in extended conversations – one while drawing together, the other prior to drawing together. The third group spoke only briefly before drawing

Figure 15.4: Drawing table. 2019. Stanford. Dice as protocols, displaying references in both written and drawn form. © Antje Steinmuller

Figure 15.5: Drawing table. 2019. Stanford. Co-drawing event and participant dialogue in progress. © Antje Steinmuller

individually. The resulting drawings, made easily legible through a more prescribed use of colour, presented inventive strategies for breaking down spatial boundaries and for re-reading and re-imagining campus pathways. The groups who worked together were introduced to one another in a playful yet productive setting, enabled by the dice and a focused timeframe.

Co-drawing street space

Through the occupation of sites in Berlin and Palo Alto, the questions asked and the audiences engaged, the two experiments to date offer lessons on the possibilities and limitations of co-drawing as a tool for citizen engagement in the transformation of neighbourhood streets. The design of an artefact, protocol and event necessitates that traditional design methods – as well as the roles and actions of architects and urban designers – are both essential and modified. Design expertise is balanced with concessions of design control to participants at a level calibrated to the relative expertise offered by participants. Based on these experiments, 'co-drawing' presents opportunities for the co-authored documentation of street space and local knowledge, offering cooperative frameworks that stimulate criticisms, expressions and aspirations among citizens. For architects and urban designers, it offers a less hierarchical platform for exchange between professional expertise and lived experience. It can establish frameworks for collective action as an essential component of producing new and shared public spaces in the context of public-commons partnerships. Expertise in architecture and urban design is brought to bear on less familiar processes: the design of a base drawing to capture and curate citizen input (artefact), the framing and moderation of dialogue (protocol) and the definition of the setting and timeline for dialogue (event).

While the co-drawing process did not have a direct translation into built reality in either Berlin or Palo Alto, it modelled both participatory methodology and a temporary collective production of a social space – one of discussion and joint visioning. The street space at Hafenplatz was not going to outlast the redesign of the block, yet the typology of pedestrianised access roads in combination with green space is common to many new developments nearby. The co-drawing event brought to the foreground the catalytic role that collective micro-gardens and spaces for joint meals might have for this immigrant neighbourhood in the future. The conversations of experts in Palo Alto exposed threshold conditions as sites ripe for redesign in a campus context.

Two keys to unlocking co-drawing seem to be to gamify the process, and prevent it becoming too loaded with expectations on the participants. The experiments reveal that, with a lay audience such as that in Berlin, ongoing engagement by the designers during the event is critical to overcoming people's fear of drawing. Engaging with participants, in these cases, includes encouragement through conversation, joint sketching and, significantly, the use of dice. During the Berlin event, members of the design team translated notes and rudimentary sketches into interpretive drawings, adopting a role akin to that of a sketch artist when participants seemed hesitant. When drawing *for* someone, however, it is important for designers to be careful – they must be sensitive to the power hierarchy in place between designer and participant. Efforts should be made to create a playful and light-hearted environment for conversation to minimise the pressure to perform; this can be achieved through the base drawing, protocol prompts and verbal interaction. Once participants are comfortable with drawing and/or hold design expertise, reluctance to start drawing is less prominent. Still, the design of initial prompts (or protocols) is critical, and an introduction (such as instructions to a game) seems to be necessary to catalyse the event. This study, in prioritising a playful multiplicity of ideas, offered the dice as a catalyst for norm-breaking, forward-pointing conversations grounded in familiar references. As game-like props, the dice worked well to trigger curiosity and conversation; while not yet tested, they would likely work well with a non-expert audience so long as the content and prompts on the dice are adjusted accordingly.

Offering meaningful prompts is another way to ensure the success of a co-drawing. Responding to prompts about locations that were significant to the community, the Berlin participants revealed citizen expertise regarding their relationship to the local environment, indicating places of significance in which inhabitants found a sense of community and reminders of their countries of origin through regular activities. Spaces of collective food production and consumption featured prominently in the drawings. Correspondingly, the Stanford audience offered spatial expertise on rethinking and transforming known typologies in ways that questioned rigid thresholds in favour of circulation spaces that doubled as spaces for collective seating and discussion. In the Berlin experiment, the design team asked questions related to participants' direct, subjective experience past and present.

In the Palo Alto experiment, the design team asked the participants to speculate on the future. This difference makes the results difficult to compare. However, the team in the Berlin case deliberately avoided asking non-expert participants to 'design'; instead, it used co-drawing to reveal and record the local, experience-driven expertise that these participants brought to the table. The degree of conversation among participants differed between the two events (limited exchange in Berlin; lively discussions in Palo Alto). However, having results presented in drawing form sparked conversation and new drawings in both locations, supporting the idea that drawing is more important than verbal exchange. Prompts must be specific and concise to facilitate focused conversations and productive drawing sessions. Thus, the prompts and protocols used in these experiments demonstrate how co-drawing can spark dialogue, frame conversation using references and record knowledge.

It is also important to tailor a co-drawing event to a specific audience's capacities. To meet each audience's ability to read drawings, the base drawings for the Berlin drawing table were more pictorial, providing easy relatability, while the Stanford base drawings capitalised on the abstraction of reduced-plan drawings to provide a canvas for spatial ideas. Forms of abstraction – where possible across both drawing types – were helpful in keeping the drawings open-ended but recognisable.

Given its ability to adapt to different audiences and contexts, co-drawing constitutes a design tool as well as part of a process to co-produce public space. Realisable in any street space that is temporarily closed to vehicular traffic, the table setting produces a familiar and quasi-familial atmosphere in which spontaneous and informal dialogue between the design team and citizens – as well as among the citizens themselves – can emerge. As with any other engagement between design teams and citizen stakeholders, the relationship between parties must be established in advance with care.

Co-drawing is a framework for stimulating and absorbing public contributions, for facilitating engagement between stakeholders, including local government and developers, and for setting in place further action and consensus. The drawing as both an interface (multi-centred) and a process (multi-authored) leverages design expertise towards frameworks for collective dialogue. If incorporated early and periodically into a multi-stakeholder partnership and design process – as with the emerging public-commons collaborations – co-drawing represents a method for facilitating informal and playful engagement among all stakeholders and encouraging interactions and collaborations that develop relationships among participating groups. In the context of revitalised street space, co-drawing – as methodology, action and artefact – offers a canvas for diverse inputs in shaping new typologies of a truly common, shared street space.

Bibliography

Baudrillard, Jean. 1988. *The Ecstasy of Communication*. Cambridge: Semiotext(e) / Foreign Agents.

Bourriaud, Nicolas. 2002. *Relational Aesthetics*. Dijon: Les Presses de Réel.

Fattori, Tomaso et al. 2013. *Living in Dignity in the 21st Century: Poverty and inequality in societies of human rights. The paradox of democracies*. Council of Europe.

Futurefarmers. 2012. 'Ethnobotanical Station'. Accessed 1 November 2022. http://www.futurefarmers.com/projects/ethnobotanical.

Kip, Markus et al. 2015. 'Seizing the (Every)day: Welcome to the urban commons!' In *Urban Commons: Moving beyond state and market*, edited by Mary Dellenbaugh, 9–10. Basel: Birkhaeuser.

Kooperatives Labor Studierender and Atelier Bow-Wow. 2016. *Urban Forest*. Berlin: Haus der Kulturen der Welt and Spector Book, p. 106.

Raumlaborberlin. 2010. 'Pioneerfelder'. Accessed 1 November 2022. https://www.raumlabor.net/wp-content/uploads/2009/02/pplan_pionierfelder.pdf.

Stavrides, S. 2016. *Common Space: The city as commons*. London: Zed Books..

Steinmuller, Antje 2018. 'The (Un)Natural Proprietors of San Francisco's Alleyways: A study of a city-initiated urban commons'. In *Jane Jacobs is Still Here – Jane Jacobs 100: her legacy and relevance in the 21st Century*, edited by R. Rocco. Delft: Delft University of Technology.

Steinmuller, Antje and Christopher Falliers. 2018. 'Co-Drawing: Forms of spatial communication as formats for collective dialogue'. Proceedings of the 2018 ACSA International Conference, Spain.

Steinmuller, Antje and Christopher Falliers. 2019. 'Shaping Public Space, in Public, with the Public: Co-drawing the continuous campus'. Proceedings of the 2019 ACSA Fall Conference, California.

von Schönfeld, Kim Carlotta and Luca Bertolini. 2017. 'Urban Streets: Epitomes of planning challenges and opportunities at the interface of public space and mobility', *Cities* 68: 48–55.

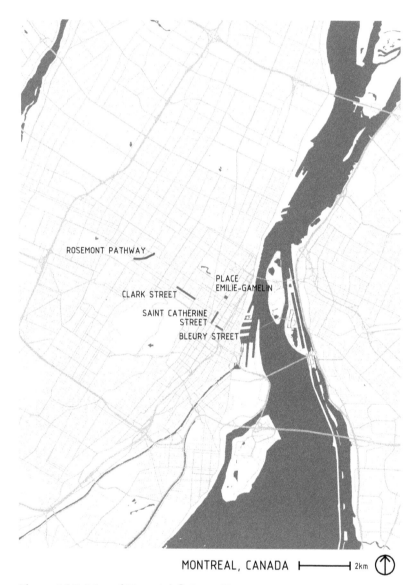

ROSEMONT PATHWAY

PLACE
EMILIE-GAMELIN

CLARK STREET

SAINT CATHERINE
STREET

BLEURY STREET

MONTREAL, CANADA ⊢———⊣ 2km

Figure 16.0: Map of Montréal © Anna Skoura

16

An inventory of the street: case studies from Montréal

Carole Lévesque and Thomas-Bernard Kenniff

In this chapter, the inventory is presented as a pedagogical, research-by-design process that engages with the street as both a multitude and a public space. An inventory is a situated exploratory practice of documentation and representation consisting of the exhaustive observation and recording of urban phenomena in ways that resonate with the subject. An inventory is also a practice of design that serves to register that which is and project that which could be. Through a series of student projects, this chapter discusses street inventories in Montréal, Québec. Through direct and indirect observations as well as methodological inquiries, these street inventories produce new ways of looking at and understanding cities and their streets. The novel methodology of the inventory emphasises the agency of documentation and representation with respect to streets, going beyond preconceived notions of design and disciplinary boundaries.

The street as a multitude

What do we see when we study the street? Physical things – people, animals, curbs, signs, lights, buildings – and immaterial things – movement, occupation, atmosphere, bylaws, land divisions. Generally contemplated in a state of distraction, the street is a whole, buzzing with sounds and elements that leave our sensory field as fast as they appear. This messy picture seems less like a meeting of individual things and more like a sort of impression: a rapidly constructed landscape. However, a large part of our blindness to the street stems from the way in which we *consume* it at a superficial level, reading it at a glance without ever taking its inventory. The street rewards extended observation. In an attempt to 'exhaust' a Parisian place, Georges Perec (2008) sought to document 'what happens when nothing happens'. Sitting at the same café terrace for several days, he took note of everything that he would have missed had he merely been observing the street distractedly (e.g. numbers on buses, signs, food items, number of cars). Through accumulation and repetition, he developed a picture of the street that was both truthful and entirely new. The prolonged observation of urban space is the aesthetic equivalent of film's fixed single-sequence shot, the secret of which, according to director Michael Haneke (2006), is the fact that it lasts longer than that which the typical audience deems acceptable. In terms of observation, we shift from 'move on quick' and 'I get it' to boredom and impatience; after some time, however, we finally arrive at the act of truly looking.[1]

Streets are some of the most complex urban spaces; in most cases, they can stand as spatial, temporal and cultural markers for a city of which they are a microcosm. In Canada, where we are writing this paper, streets are arguably the most important and diverse type of public space. Identified by Jane Jacobs as the main public places of North American cities (Jacobs 1962, 29), streets are where social and political matters are performed and take shape. They are – in contrast to squares, places or parks – the quintessential example of exterior public space taking shape through negotiated boundaries (Massey 2005), social interaction and political action (Arendt 1958) whose meaning resides more in contradictions and paradoxes than in consensus (Kenniff 2018). The street is a wonderful mix of social times (Gwiazdzinski 2013; Lefebvre 1992), hard and soft edges (Franck and Stevens 2007; Gehl 1986; Sim 2019), overlapping jurisdictions and territorial claims – a grotesque mix of bodies and things, competing languages and sounds. When we take time to observe this multitude and take its inventory, the street takes on a different meaning. Rather than an undifferentiated fleeting mess, the street constitutes a microcosm of objects, people and systems. Inventories engage with parts, so the close observation of only a small fraction of that which makes up the street can provide insight into the street as a whole.[2] In Michelangelo Antonioni's *Close Up*, the meaning of what was thought to have been witnessed and photographed (a landscape) and what was actually there (a body hidden behind a bush) is brought to a head in the aggrandisement of the photograph's details. The inventory reverses this order by starting with constitutive parts, repetitive elements, aberrations and recurrence – by starting with the small – and returning to 'the street' as something entirely new. In doing so, the inventory avoids rushed interpretation and classification (e.g. commercial, residential), quick qualifiers and presupposed problems (e.g. public, private); instead, it engages with the street as a multitude.

Inventory

This study suggests that the inventory, as a critical approach to the street for both pedagogy and research-by-design, not only reveals but also changes, creates, draws forward and projects. In other words, it manages the dissolution and transgression of the boundary between inquiry and design, establishing a dialogue between research (observation and documentation) and practice (anticipation and invention). The means through which documents are gathered, categorised and represented is a process that extends beyond what would otherwise be a simple collection of observations. Even if the inventory falls outside of the conventions of a developed design scheme, the representation that it puts forward renders it both propositional (in the ways that streets can be assessed) and transformative (in the ways that these novel considerations call for action) (Kenniff and Lévesque 2021). While the hierarchy of inventory operations and the subjects of inventories may vary, all inventories share the common ground of the built environment – somewhere between the scale of the everyday and that of the territory.

Three methodological principles link all inventories: situated practice, documentation and representation. Through inventories, these investigative principles lead to projection. Situated practice places the researcher-designer in direct dialogue with the field of research to integrate knowledge within action. In the case of the inventory, the field of research is defined by its objects, materiality and sites. As described by Jane Rendell (2006), the material physicality of both data and place are implied in situated practice, as is the on-site performance of the researcher-designer. Situated practice demands obsessive observation: a disposition to notice and record, perhaps at first doing so intuitively but eventually doing so with urgency through intent and diligent note taking, with observation giving way to documentation. Whether recorded through text, images or found artefacts, the observed conditions are made tangible to others through documentation (Latour 2011), an enterprise that accumulates proof and renders visible a reality that is otherwise difficult to grasp, incomplete or unsuspected. Documentation must have clear organising principles and methods if it is to have any meaning. Indeed, the act of documenting as part of the inventory emphasises the obligation to organise, categorise and make sense of the documentation. Thus, knowledge produced by the inventory resides both within the collection of objects, images or drawn observations and within the tangible commitment necessary to collect the information. This physical engagement with what is observed and the site on which it occurs emphasises the inseparable tie between knowledge and process, as the subject of the inventory is revealed incrementally.

The meaning of documentation emerges from the representation of observed conditions. In its effort to organise and elucidate the subject, representation plays with that which exists. By examining the scales, relations or variations of a given condition based on its geographical location, for instance, representation demands that the subject is looked at repeatedly, allowing for the juxtaposition of otherwise disconnected physical elements in order to achieve a new understanding. Representation, undertaken through various forms (e.g. cartography, drawing, model, photography, multimedia), holds meaning beyond a mere demonstration or explanation of collected data; it is a process with its own agency and the capacity to transform observed and catalogued phenomena into autonomous and potential realities (Corner 2011, 89).[3]

In fluidly moving between situated practice, documentation and representation, the researcher-designer develops new knowledge and considers questions that require them to return to further on-site observation and documentation – each time in a different manner – to better represent, understand and raise new questions. Thus, an inventory constitutes an investigation, one that is interrogative and exploratory rather than explicative or demonstrative. It is essential to consider the inventory as the construction and exceeding of the subject rather than its resolution. Through this long, obsessive and laborious endeavour, the inventory brings about questions rather than reaching finalities and investigates methods rather than developing formal proposals. Lacking clear and definitive finality, the inventory renews the possible readings of a subject through continuous progression until it is reinvented. Therefore, the inventory is a situated exploratory practice of documentation and representation that manifests itself as a practice of design.

The urban inventory project

We have been developing the inventory as a framework and method in our own research-by-design projects (at the research lab Bureau d'Étude de Pratiques Indiscipinées[4]) and our teaching since 2017. Our projects have largely been concerned with public spaces, *terrains vagues*, municipal architecture and urban landscapes; each time, we practised documentation and representation as independent design projects (Kenniff 2019; Kenniff 2021; Lévesque 2019; Lévesque 2021; Lévesque 2019). This chapter goes over a pedagogical exercise, the *urban inventory*, that we implement in the context of an undergraduate course that we teach at l'École de Design at Université du Québec à Montréal. The course, offered to third-year students, aims to interrogate broad issues of design – context, ethics, sustainability, project scale, time and site, among others – and the ways in which they overlap in theory and practice. Inquiry is our core pedagogical and reflexive approach; we divert our students from their accustomed view of design as problem-solving to a view of design as problem-setting. Thus, they find themselves in uncertain territory, encouraged to find their way through open questions and hypotheses, to re-evaluate their standard means of operation and to find validity in doubt.

The tools that students use and the act of representation come into sharp focus during the inventory project. We ask the students to select a single mode of representation and use it to record an urban condition of their choosing. Modes of representation include drawing, photography, video, photogrammetry, collage and narrative, while subjects include social interaction, thresholds negotiating uses on the street, urban artefacts made to exclude certain uses or users, suburban housing, desire paths (where a street ought to be), street smells, streets at night, play and illegal occupations. The restriction to just one mode of representation does not limit the students' possibilities; rather, it encourages careful observation, accumulation and reflection, prompting them to understand the aesthetic and ethical dimensions of their representational approaches.

While we do not specifically task the students with studying the street, many of the projects gravitate toward street-related contexts and exemplify the methods and results of the inventory approach. The projects vary widely, as students are free to choose their subjects. Each inventory adds to the next, so the heterogeneity of the street comes across as a microcosm of a larger urban ecosystem. Within the range of inventories, three main categories of street-related studies speak to the different inventory dimensions described above: those that look at streets directly, those that look at urban conditions that can be traced back to the street, and those that exemplify documentation, representation or invention.

Looking straight at the street

The 240 drawings of front yards by Marie-Ève Martin and Antoine Quimper-Giroux document the liminal spaces between duplexes and the street on a five-block stretch on Clark Street. They show both the repetitive aspect of front yards in Montréal (i.e. wrought iron fences encircling small areas on either side of the main entrance) and the unique elements of each front yard, used, decorated or transformed to best suit its occupants. Annotated and sketched by hand on site, their inventory shows the paradox of front yards caught between a private, occupiable threshold and a simple left-over public space (Figure 16.1).

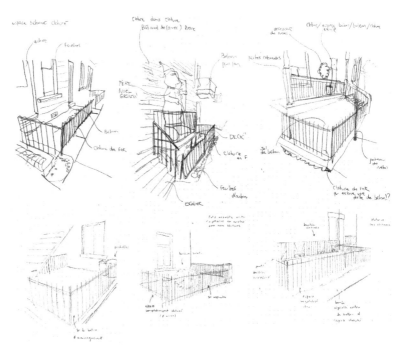

Figure 16.1: L'inventaire comme projet: le croquis (Inventory as project: sketches). © Marie-Ève Martin and Antoine Quimper-Giroux. 2019

Figure 16.2: L'inventaire comme objet: le chez-soi (Inventory as object: home). © Sema Camkiran and Frédérique Desjardins. 2019

Assessing what differentiates home from homelessness, Sema Camkiran and Frédérique Desjardins' inventory documents traces of occupation surrounding an emergency shelter in downtown Montréal. They find that the nearby streets and adjacent public squares have become a new home for the homeless. They use collage as their mode of representation because their subject is not fixed in space or time. Building on Superstudio's collages of the infinite grid, they examine the concept of home beyond mere spatial definitions where homelessness is at its most critical urban condition (Figure 16.2).

Noting that sounds and smells are often overlooked when describing urban experiences, Marie-Hélène Chagnon-St-Jean and Charles-Antoine Beaulieu's inventory traces an olfactive and acoustic landscape of streets in downtown Montréal. Using a phenomenological approach to documentation, their collages constitute both diagrams

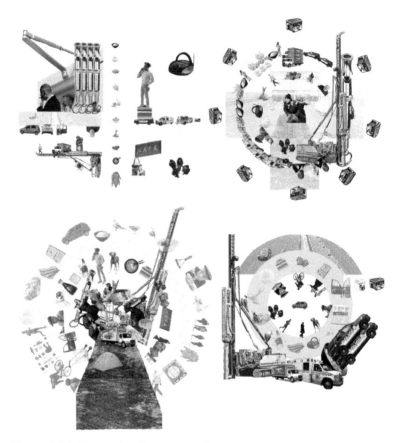

Figure 16.3: Inventaire (Inventory). © Marie-Hélène Chagnon-St-Jean and Charles-Antoine Beaulieu. 2019

and experiential cartographies. The documented smells and sounds of a street are compressed and organised to offer correspondence between experience and invention. Their efforts to navigate between objectivity, subjectivity, documentation and invention lead them to show silence as the true absence in our experience of the street (Figure 16.3).

These three examples, by looking directly at the street, identify subjects that are usually registered as part of a cursory and fleeting experience of the street. Here, the repetitions and differences among residential front yards, acts of dwelling, and the smell- and sound-scapes of urban territories take form through sustained observation. The careful representations produced through considerable documentation necessitate that these observations be thought of as a puzzle to be solved – a design project – that can now be turned back towards the street and our practice as designers to inform how we might think about and engage the street.

Urban conditions traced back to the street

Axonometric drawing is used in Juliette Mondoux-Fournier's inventory as a means of comparison. The documentation of benches at a subway station, drawn at the same scale and using a single projection, reveals variations across the network with a focus on aspects that deter loitering and sleeping. This technique is particularly adept at expressing non-identical sameness across large fields of repetitive urban artefacts, employing the strategic nature of axonometric projection to highlight the connections between the social acceptance of 'undesirable' public behaviour and strategies of urban design (Figure 16.4).

Taking photographs of house fronts across four neighbourhoods, Claudelle Larose-Roger and Frédéryke Lallier study suburban residential streets. Assembled in grids, in line with Berndt Becher and Hilda Becher, their images capture the repetitive nature of their subject through simple juxtaposition. Their inventory highlights the importance of extended observations, as small variations between seemingly identical constructions only become apparent over time (Figure 16.5).

The contradiction between pedestrian movement and prescribed passages in the city is revealed by Julia Arvelo-Pelchat's inventory. As informal streets, desire paths are a backstage to the city that transgress

Figure 16.4: Inventaire des bancs du métro de Montréal: discrimination de la population itinérante par le design d'un objet urbain (Inventory of Montréal's subway benches: discrimination against the homeless population through the design of urban objects). © Juliette Mondoux-Fournier. 2019

Figure 16.5: Learning from the suburbs: inventaire typologique de la banlieue montréalaise (typological inventory of Montréal's suburbs). © Claudelle Larose-Roger and Frédéryke Lallier. 2019

established conventions. Stemming from a photographic documentation that reveals the characteristics and changing conditions of these paths, her collage proposes a hypothetical urban space through which alternative and more intuitive means of navigating through the city could run (Figure 16.6).

Dispersed and disconnected in the city, the representation of these examples is necessary to gather them in a coherent form and have them make sense as subjects. Each depicts urban conditions that seem

Figure 16.6: Trajectoires alternatives (Alternative trajectories). © Julia Arvelo-Pelchat. 2019

to be matters of fact: a bench whose arm rests or dividers act as structural elements; houses from the same development that look similar to one another; a path created across a train track as a fast and convenient way to move between two areas of a city. However, what these examples really show is that designed urban conditions and, in turn, streets, can be unwelcoming by deterring certain people or practices (inability to rest), driven by abstract financial calculations detached from the ground (profit over experience), or shown to be either poorly planned or based on outdated premises, meaning that they no longer serve the city or ensure the safety of pedestrians. Only through an inventory can these concerns be understood and clearly demonstrated.

Exemplify documentation, representation, invention

The reconstruction of urban sites is explored by Joël Videaud-Maillette's inventory through photogrammetry. The technical process demands the rigorous photographing of existing conditions to enable the combination of individual images into a three-dimensional model. By shifting his gaze towards abandoned sites, his inventory represents a subject in a state of construction rather than one that is decrepit. Photogrammetry entails the use of a camera to record a site in great detail, investigating

Figure 16.7: La photogrammétrie (Photogrammetry). © Joël Videaud-Maillette. 2019

literally every nook and cranny. The resulting model is a representation of both the site as it appears to be built as well as the invention of a new site manifested through the researcher's movement (Figure 16.7).

In the inventory of Mégan Morrissette and Sharlène Dupont-Morin, photography is both the recording tool and the invention tool. From a series of conventional images of a cultural centre lining Rue Ste-Catherine in Montréal's entertainment district (Quartier des spectacles), Morrissette and Dupont-Morin distil the aesthetic experience of the street into long-exposure shots in which the masses of concrete give way to ephemeral traces of light and colour (Figure 16.8).

Instead of taking specific urban conditions as their subjects, these last two examples focus on the processes and methods of the inventory. By shifting their methods of representation – photogrammetry and photography – towards a single architectural object, the situated experience and presence of the researchers, rather than the

Figure 16.8: L'inventaire comme projet: la photographie (Inventory as project: photography). © Mégan Morrissette and Sharlène Dupont-Morin. 2019

repetition of their actions across different sites, inform their under-standing. Observer performance, here, gives form and meaning to the inventory, from which it is indissociable. Process becomes a project in and of itself through situated practice, from which an alternative physi-cality may be invented.

These eight student projects are just a few examples of the inventory's potential as a pedagogical exercise and research-by-design approach. By closely investigating a subject at length rather than performing a cursory representation – by asking questions rather than finding solutions – students develop new ways of understanding and looking at the city and its streets that, ultimately, lead them to question their preconceived notions and positions. By encouraging them to reconsider their environment and their place in it, their expected appreciation of urban conditions is transformed.

Undisciplined inventories

We began this chapter by stating that streets cannot be fully repre-sented from a specific viewpoint. As they are constructed with overlapping details and conditions, a complete and finite inventory of the street is impossible. Still, we can aim for an accumulation of inventories from various distinct viewpoints to achieve a fairly compre-hensive understanding of the street. Inventories allow for sharp focus on specific elements and conditions; the larger the pool of gathered inventories, the better we can understand the street's often-conflicting realities. Importantly, however, as urban environments – and streets in particular – are fluid and dynamic, new conditions consistently appear, requiring additional inventories. This inability to achieve a permanent comprehensive understanding must be acknowledged if we are to recognise the depth of streets' social, economic and political values and protect them as genuinely public spaces. In introducing students to this interrogative engagement with their urban environment and the in-depth investigation of one of its components, the complexities of the urban condition unfold before them. Some students have told us that they are now seeing potential inventories everywhere, suggesting that the investigation of one detail opens the door to that of many more. In their future work as designers, they now understand that design can emerge from careful and exhaustive documentation – that the former not only follows from but is implied in the latter. This critical stance highlights the agency of documentation and representation in bringing about change to the built environment, bringing them well beyond a pedagogical exercise and the false imperative that design must lead to building. Indeed, the interrogative stance of the inventory opens all dimensions of the built environment – be they physical or abstract – to inquiry and engages reflection-in-design with all disciplinary interests and knowledge of the city. In this sense, inventory, as a practice, is *undisciplined*. Far from lacking discipline or rigour, it resists the confines of a single discipline, a single method or a single set of questions; it gazes both in and out – expanding, meandering, assembled, unpredictable. Inventory is a practice that aligns with the experience of the street.

Notes

1   Paraphrased by the authors from the original French.
2   Here, the authors build upon a long tradition of the focused gaze and the significance of moments, from ethnographic fieldwork (Whyte 1955; Whyte 2011) and theories of social organicism (Barnett 2012; Jacobs 1962) to recent crossovers between anthropology and design, in which the social event takes precedence over planning (Gehl 2012).
3   The notion of representation put forward alongside the concept of inventory is also indebted to the aesthetics of the repertoire through which one is able to generate new understandings. See, as a telling example, Susan Buck-Morss' (1989) analysis of Walter Benjamin's *Passegenwerk*.
4   Translates as 'Investigative Bureau of Undisciplined Practices'. The work can be viewed at www.be-pi.ca.

Bibliography

Arendt, Hannah. 1958. *The Human Condition*. Chicago, IL: University of Chicago Press.
Barnett, Jonathan. 2012. 'Jane Jacobs and Designing Cities as Organised Complexity'. In *The Urban Wisdom of Jane Jacobs*, edited by S. Hirt and D. Zahm. Abingdon: Routledge.
Buck-Morss, Susan. 1989. *The Dialectics of Seeing: Walter Benjamin and the Arcades Project*. Cambridge, MA: MIT Press.
Corner, James. 2011. 'The Agency of Mapping'. In *The Map Reader*, edited by M. Dodge, R. Kitchin and C. Perkins, 89–101. Chichester: John Wiley & Sons.
Franck, Karen A. and Quentin Stevens (eds). 2007. *Loose Space*. Abingdon: Routledge.
Gehl, Jan. 1986. '"Soft Edges" in Residential Streets', *Scandinavian Housing and Planning Research* 3(2): 89–102.
Gehl, Jan. 2012. *Pour des villes à échelle humaine*. Montréal: Les Éditions Écosociété.
Gwiazdzinski, Laurent. 2013. 'Urbanisme des temps. Premières chorégraphies de la métropole hypermoderne', *L'Observatoire* (43): 3–8.
Haneke, Michael. 2006. '71 fragments d'une chronologie du hasard'. Interview by Serge Toubiana in *71 Fragmente einer Chronologie des Zufalls*. Directed by Michael Haneke. New York: Kino International Corp.
Jacobs, Jane. 1962. *The Death and Life of Great American Cities*. London: Jonathan Cape.
Kenniff, Thomas Bernard. 2018. 'Dialogue, Ambivalence, Public Space', *Journal of Public Space* 3(1): 13–30.

Kenniff, Thomas Bernard. 2019. 'Altering Research: Making room for difference in architectural studies'. In *Speaking of Building: Oral history in architectural research*, edited by J. Gosseye, N. Stead and D.V. Plaat. New York: Princeton Architectural Press.

Kenniff, Thomas Bernard. 2021. 'Public Inventories as Political Inventions'. In *Inventory: Documentation as design project*, edited by T.B. Kenniff and C. Lévesque, 82–89. Montréal: BéPI.

Kenniff, Thomas-Bernard and Carole Lévesque (eds). 2021. *Inventory: Documentation as design project*. Montréal: BéPI.

Latour, Bruno. 2011. 'Drawing Things Together'. In *The Map Reader* by Martin Dodge, Rob Kitchin and Chris Perkins, 65–72. Chichester: John Wiley & Sons.

Lefebvre, Henri. 1992. *Éléments de la rythmanalyse: Introduction à la connaissance des rythmes*. Paris: Syllepse.

Lévesque, Carole. 2019. *Finding Room in Beirut: Places of the everyday*. California: Punctum Books.

Lévesque, Carole. 2021. 'Entre réel et invention: L'inventaire comme projet'. In *Inventory. Documentation as Design Project*, edited by Thomas-Bernard Kenniff and Carole Lévesque, 116–21. Montréal: BéPI.

Massey, Doreen. 2005. *For Space*. London: SAGE.

Perec, Georges. 2008. *Tentative d'épuisement d'un lieu Parisien*. Paris: Christian Bourgois.

Rendell, Jane. 2006. *Art and Architecture: A place between*. London: I.B. Tauris.

Sim, David. 2019. *Soft City: Building density for everyday life*. Washington, DC: Island Press.

Whyte, William F. 1955. *Street Corner Society: The social structure of an Italian slum*. Chicago, IL: University of Chicago Press.

Whyte, William H. 2011. *The Social Life of Small Urban Spaces*. New York: Project for Public Spaces.

ORMEAU ROAD

BELFAST, UK ├──────┤ 2km

Figure 17.0: Map of Belfast © Anna Skoura

17

A walk between disciplines: listening to the composition of Ormeau Road

Elen Flügge (text and recordings) and Timothy Waddell (drawings)

This chapter employs a methodological approach that pairs techniques from the fields of architecture and sound studies to investigate an arterial route in Belfast: Ormeau Road. Reflecting on this high street from divergent disciplinary perspectives brings attention to its varied physical and sensorial aspects. This study juxtaposes an architectural depiction of Ormeau Road via plans and sections with a sensorial depiction based on 'soundwalking'. Ultimately, this multidisciplinary approach to Ormeau Road results in a nuanced understanding of the local street that articulates its unique characteristics while reflecting on the challenges in aligning the methodologies of two fields that reference different temporalities. This study concludes that it is possible to produce valuable insights by incorporating personal reflection into the study and combining approaches that capture different manifestations of qualities (e.g. repetition, thresholds, masking) that exist in urban environments.

Street listening and drawing on Ormeau Road

A main artery in Belfast, Ormeau Road bears many of the desirable elements of the city as a whole – an active art and music scene and neighbourliness – as well as some of its less desirable elements, namely high vehicle density. It stretches southeast from Belfast City Centre across the River Lagan. It serves as a high street for a residential area with diverse inhabitants, including long-time inhabitants, recent expats, academics, artists, entrepreneurs and pockets of unionists and nationalists – communities with opposing political leanings.

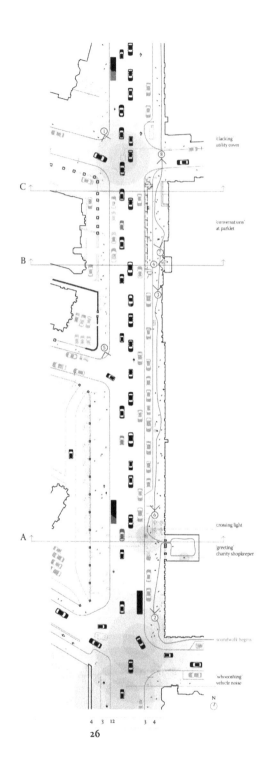

'clacking'
utility cover

'conversations'
at parklet

crossing light

'greeting'
charity shopkeeper

soundwalk begins

'whooshing'
vehicle noise

N

4 3 12   3 4

26

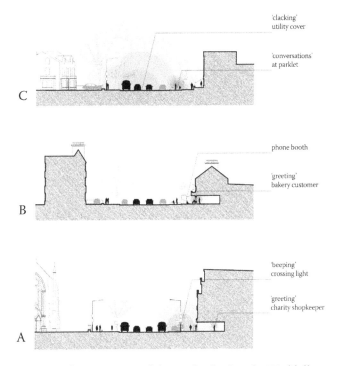

Figure 17.1a: A plan of the segment of the study. © Timothy Waddell
Figure 17.1b: Sections of the segment of the study. © Timothy Waddell

Nearby dwellings include an array of red-brick terraces, low-rise flats, semi-detached houses, newly constructed tenement blocks and historic Victorian buildings (e.g. the former city gasworks building) (Maguire 2009, 141). The street offers access to the green space of Ormeau Park as well as independent pubs and coffee shops alongside contentious development sites. Ormeau Road's uniqueness lies largely in personal attachment – long-term inhabitation facilitating the development of social bonds – in place-making (Cresswell 2004; Tuan 1977). Locally driven interventions (e.g. parklets) support rich sociality and a distinct character, enabling residents to shape the street through incremental placemaking. As lockdowns limited access to urban spaces in 2020, Ormeau Road constituted an ideal location – as it lies just a few steps from the authors' homes – in which to experiment with a mixed approach that employs techniques from the fields of both architecture and sound studies. One key question emerges: what might a walk down this high street say about the two disciplines?

Streets are socio-spatial compositions; they comprise interplays of material, social and sensorial elements. Architectural form can be described through drawing, and urban experience can be retold through written language via personal accounts; however, there is an apparent separation between these understandings. Richard Sennett (2018) described a tension between *ville*, material-built structures, and *cité*, a mentality related to collective living. A nuanced understanding of the tension between these disparate epistemologies and their associated methodologies is necessary to capture and understand a street's 'depth' in a way that, as framed by Jane Clossick (2017), simultaneously considers architectural, social and temporal elements.

This study employs an architectural eye and an artistic ear to spark interdisciplinary understandings of Ormeau Road, with spatial and sonic methods informing each other. It illustrates Ormeau Road's structure in architectural terms in line with Allan B. Jacobs (1995) and considers several 'soundwalks' along the street – walks with a focus on listening – in line with sound scholar Hildegard Westerkamp (1974). Drawing is a foundational tool in architectural practice. A common method for understanding urban spaces is drawing out their structure to form a tactile grasp of the site's visual information. Such drawings are often done without occupation, considering purely dimensional aspects (e.g. doorway positions, landscaping, parking zones, massing), which can make the social use of streets seem of secondary importance. In contrast, listening to a street places the primary focus on activities and the people engaging in them. This study details visual and sonic stimuli through written accounts, walking you through our footsteps and weaving a personal narrative through sensorial experiences.

Interactions between sonic and visual approaches

Walks happen over time, while a drawing freezes a single moment; this contrast is fertile ground for methodological exploration. These two approaches link different senses of time in a place (Jacobs 1995; Wunderlich 2008). According to architect Jeremy Till, 'Architectural space, in the purity of its formal and conceptual genesis, is emptied of all considerations of time and is seen as a formal and aesthetic object. Time is frozen' (2000, 157). Drawing *can* capture time – an imagined future, a fleeting present or a forgotten past. In contrast, sonic experience is continually shifting. Over the course of a soundwalk, countless momentary impressions rise and fall. Ormeau Road's aural repetitions are never exact, however; Jane Jacobs notes, 'The ballet of the good city sidewalk never repeats itself from place to place, and in any one place is always replete with new improvisations' (1961, 65–66). This inevitable fluctuation can be difficult to grasp, while a drawing allows the dynamic dance to pause briefly – allows for a momentary stasis – offering an orientation point on which to pin evanescent sensory impressions. A drawn section serves to focus on a structural moment – a brief melody in the symphony of a street – enabling onlookers to consider various elements that change slowly over time (e.g. buildings). Architecture as a discipline relies heavily on static means of representation, rarely employing media that could indicate the temporal flow of a dynamic streetspace; this reality clashes with the words of urbanist Antonella Radicchi: 'to experience the work of architecture and of the city necessarily implies a spatial and temporal dimension as well as a perception involving all the senses' (2017). A street is made up of such varied elements – structures and activities that can be understood at different levels and speeds and through multiple sensory modes – that developing a deeper understanding of a streetspace nearly requires an interdisciplinary approach that brings together an array of skills native to various fields.

In stark contrast to the stillness of drawings, walking, listening and recording are common in urban sound studies and sonic arts. Composer Westerkamp (1974) has described 'soundwalks' as 'any excursion whose main purpose is listening to the environment', but soundwalking can refer to numerous practices, including those entailing performance and recorded compositions (McCartney 2014). The goal of listening does not mean that other senses are ignored; it simply means that attention is focused on that which is heard. In the field of urbanism, soundwalking is used to research sonic experience and atmospheres in cities (Adams et al. 2008; Paquette and McCartney 2012; Radicchi 2017; Semidor 2006) and to conduct case studies on the sound quality of sites aimed at improving city sound planning (Claus 2015; Maag and Bosshard 2012). We contend that a formal drawing of a street structure remains largely inert without an indication of the activities that enliven a street's physical composition. Similarly, an aural recording of the flow of street life can be disorienting without a visual representation of where it was taken. Merging these approaches offers a more comprehensive sense of the street.

To document sonic experiences on Ormeau Road, this study used *narrative* and *conversational* walks,[1] though soundwalks can also be done as silent observation, akin to an awareness exercise (Drever 2013). The narrative approach involved one researcher recording audio while walking along Ormeau Road and pausing at numerous points to orally describe their immediate experience, position, or personal observations. Conversational soundwalks, done in tandem, entailed short phases of silent listening and pause points to discuss shared experiences and observations. Conversational soundwalks can indicate whether it is easy to hold a conversation at various points on the street. For these recordings, we employed binaural audio recording, which entails the use of two microphones – one placed at each ear – to record spatial audio information. When heard back through headphones, the recorded streetspace unfolds as sounds placed appropriately in aural space. To effectively track and compare our positions on walks, we counted paces along the street to trace the shifting atmospheres and demarcate points of interest. Of course, various other forms of active and situated listening could be used by urban planners and architects to achieve a greater understanding of cities' sonic aspects (Ouzounian and Lappin 2014).

Tracing daily exercise

Clunk. The latch of the door shuts behind me. I walk from our calm residential street towards Ormeau Road. Footsteps are audibly repetitive on the grainy asphalt.

Vshhhhhssss. Shhhvvvvvvvvvvvsh. Vvvvvssssshhhhh. The high street starts before my feet arrive, its rumble of traffic rising to greet me. I reach the corner, where a former bakery was converted to apartments. The ground floor holds a furniture shop; its windows give a fleeting sense of looking into someone's bedroom.

'1, 2, 3, 4, 5.' From this corner, I begin counting steps under my breath, though I no longer hear my footfalls alongside passing vehicles. Pacing by a familiar sequence of shops and cafes, their physical presence promises a return to active street life, even while many remained closed this year.

Ding ding ding ding ding. My ears are arrested by the hasty beeping of a crossing light near the corner, its noise a rare rhythmic tone punctuating the surrounding atmosphere. The crossing also changes the traffic rhythm, bringing a pause – idling and acceleration – to its wash of vehicular sound. The bell is a call to attention, signalling that it is safe to cross. Instead of the street, I turn away from the traffic, crossing a threshold into the hush of a charity shop.

'Hullo Elen how'r you?' The cheery owner greets me, recognising me even behind a mask. The shop is a point of public contact: brief, friendly and reliable. I know from time spent there that it serves as a place of encounter for others – especially older customers – who return regularly for society as much as for stuff. I enjoy perusing varied objects, fabrics, porcelain cups, rusted lamps and lost buttons while overhearing conversations. Inside, sensory attention can focus on tactile minutiae. Exiting, my sensory field opens up and widens, in line with architectural space.

I continue down Ormeau Road, my left ear aware of cars, past the grocery and hairdresser. Soon, I spy people ahead sitting at a new little parklet or waiting for orders at the corner cafe, whose coffee has reached my nostrils. I am excited at this sight of life and sociality, curious about the humans interacting with other humans.

'That's you there, thank you very much.' The woman at the bakery thanked a customer. Counting 145 steps, I see what is offered: giant almond cookies obscured by powdered sugar. 'Hiiii,' said the man sitting against the telephone booth. Sometimes, he seems as much a fixture as the booth. Usually, I nod hello; other times, I avoid interacting, feeling uncomfortable. I hear other people now too, chatting around the parklet. Its tables are back, having disappeared during the latest lockdown. The parklet ends at the corner, a threshold after which Ormeau Road seems to socially lull. Its atmosphere surrenders to traffic drones again, making the interruptive metallic *caclackcaclack* of a utility cover whenever cars drive over it all the more present.

Sonic-spatial effects: repetition, masking and thresholds

Over the course of this study, the two knowledge-gathering methods were in constant discourse. In response to our soundwalk observations, we added elements to the architectural illustrations. For example, we extended their reach to include the experience of approaching cross streets. Additionally, we highlighted noticeable sounds using shaded points. *In situ* experiences – both sonic and social – also informed the places chosen for the three drawn sections (shown in Figure 17.1b). A narrative account describes the sonic elements alongside the spatial and social elements of the soundwalk, as these were interrelated and intertwined in the authors' experiences. The path that the narrative describes is traced in the drawing with a red line (Figure 17.1a).

Listening is key for observing 'sonic effects', or what we are here describing as sonic-spatial effects: aural events shaped by material structures (e.g. buildings, sidewalks) and individual experiential perspectives (Augoyard and Torgue 2005). This study focused primarily on three sonic-spatial effects on Ormeau Road: repetition, masking and thresholds. These three effects are all evident in the narrative account, the recordings and the drawings.

Repetition

> *Ding ding ding ding ding.* My ears are arrested by the hasty beeping of a crossing light near the corner, its noise a rare rhythmic tone punctuating the surrounding atmosphere.

There are numerous types of repetition, one prominent type being personal repetition in daily returns to the same places along Ormeau Road. On repeated walks, certain sounds, smells and sights may become predictable (e.g. the smell of a bakery's bread, how traffic noise crescendos after a crossing light). Recurring routines, habits and cycles of urban life can be framed as urban rhythms (Adhitya 2013; Lefebvre 1991; Wunderlich 2013). Architect Felipe Matos Wunderlich describes 'place-temporality' as 'defined by four sensuous attributes and meaningful experiences: a vivid sense of time; an experience of flow; a distinct soundscape; and rhythmicity' (2013, 385). Sound-walks bring one's focus to streets' temporal dynamics – towards events that occur repeatedly within a short span of time. The crossing bell (Figure 17.2) is a repetitive tone that interrupts car traffic, punctu-ating its flow at Section A. This rhythmic sonic interjection of the crossing is repeated, like a motif, at many crossings along the street, building rhythms within rhythms. However, as the drawing empha-sises, Ormeau Road does not have significant architectural repetition along this particular stretch. Facades change in three marked ways along one side, and there are multiple different facades on the opposite side: an area with a church and open grounds, a cross street, a small set

Figure 17.2: View from the initial corner: approaching the crossing light and charity shop; a sonic repetition of beeping, and rhythmic brickwork. © Elen Flügge

of buildings, another cross street, and a set of buildings set at an angle. Reflecting on repetition, rhythm may refer to wholly separate elements of the environment – spatial and physical, sonic and social – and their complex interplay on Ormeau Road.

Thresholds

> I turn away from the traffic, crossing a threshold into the hush of a charity shop … Inside, sensory attention can focus on tactile minutiae. Exiting, my sensory field opens up and widens, just like the architectural space.

Material and lived thresholds are everywhere in cities, and the soundwalk-drawing methodology offers unique insight into their significance. Going in and out of shops produces a sonic effect – a 'cut-out', an attenuation of sound – created by the movement of either the listener or the sound source (Augoyard and Torgue 2005). The drawing in Figure 17.1b outlines street depth by illustrating the interiors of the buildings that line Ormeau Road and showing the side streets from which people approach and leave the road; it details the material structures that influence experiences of sonic thresholds (Clossick 2017; Whyte 1980).

Figure 17.3: View, from across the street, of the corner building that partially blocks sound from reaching the residential street (left side). Thresholds can be visual, as in street markings, or designate particular social spaces. © Elen Flügge

We experienced several sonic thresholds on our soundwalks. First, we experienced the audible transition between a residential street and Ormeau Road, which was characterised by an intense experience of vehicle sounds. However, Ormeau Road's layout muffles the sounds for those on the residential street. Section A in Figure 17.1b shows the corner building that partially blocks traffic sound (seen in Figure 17.3). Second, we experienced the sonic threshold at the door of the charity shop, which attenuated the outside noise but allowed us to hear sounds from the shop's interior (Section B in Figure 17.1b). Third, we experienced a sudden shift at the end of the block at 180 paces, with a concentration of social activity stemming from a popular eatery, a bakery and a parklet (Figures 17.4 and 17.5), which lie just before a stretch of more subtle shops, including a pharmacy and a bank after Section C (Figure 17.1b). This is visible in the drawing, which shows the proximity of buildings and the phone booth contributing to a sense of enclosure. Thresholds are usually described as a feature of architecture, but our study takes the sound-studies perspective that, like cut-outs, they constitute an experiential event and may even be lived

Figure 17.4: View of the parklet; tables removed during lockdown.
© Elen Flügge

Figure 17.5: Scones visible; smell of coffee in the air. © Elen Flügge

Figures 17.6 and 17.7: Views of the path down Ormeau Road, obstructed by signs, posts and booths. Sounds, such as those made by traffic, are masked by buildings. © Elen Flügge

by city-dwellers as a primarily sonic-spatial experience. A key aspect of this concept is that some element of movement is necessary for a threshold to be actualised (e.g. walking from a trafficked area into a park). Thresholds contribute to the rhythm and repetition of Ormeau Road; soundwalkers – as well as ordinary walkers – cross material divides and are exposed to the rise and fall of sounds as they pass buildings that block traffic noise and encounter different social groups (Figures 17.6 and 17.7).

Masking

'1, 2, 3, 4, 5'. From this corner, I begin counting steps under my breath, though I no longer hear my footfalls alongside passing vehicles ... *Vshhhhhssss. Shhhvvvvvvvvvvvsh. Vvvvvsssshhhhh.* The high street starts before my feet arrive, its rumble of traffic rising to greet me.

Masking is the phenomenon of one sound or object blocking another. Ormeau Road, as part of Belfast's A24, hosts significant traffic that often dominates the atmosphere. A drawing can neither depict the experience of droning noise, which is immediately present when walking on site, nor demonstrate how voices become inaudible as buses pass or planes fly overhead. However, such effects are evident in recordings of conversational soundwalks, in which we were forced to raise our voices at certain points in response to masking by traffic noise. Upon reviewing recordings, the strain in our voices stemming from the necessary volume increase suggests that noise levels are unsociably high. Meanwhile, drawings can depict street furniture that visually masks views along the street (Gehl 2013). A final relevant sense of masking is the informational masking driven by selective attention. Audio recordings show that we miss a significant amount of sonic input when walking through urban spaces. It is surprising, when reviewing recordings, to realise how much sound occurs from moment to moment, demonstrating the true aural intensity of many everyday urban places.

Masking is linked to both repetition and thresholds, as thresholds can mask sounds, and the ways in which sounds are masked by one another are repetitive, contributing to the rhythm of a street. Like thresholds, masking may be considered to be a physical phenomenon, with one object in front of another; our study, however, considers that sounds also behave in this manner and, as a result, impact social life and the activities and conversations that can occur in certain places. When traffic is too loud, people cannot easily speak to one another. Finally, we revealed the pivotal role of focused human attention on the experience of a city street, showing that it is necessary to record and re-listen to sounds to fully grasp their richness and complexity. Similarly, drawing through prolonged visual observation at a particular spot can facilitate the articulation of visual details that may go unnoticed while walking past. Comparatively, sonic and spatial tools – drawing, recording and listening – can highlight various instances of masking, but they are all significant in the design and understanding of streets.

Methodological reflections

Bringing together drawing and audio recording through soundwalks offers unique insights into Ormeau Road. Both drawings and audio recordings serve to verify, repeat, examine and interpret personal sensory experiences. During a walk, one may recall experiencing numerous sound qualities at different sites. Recordings serve as audio references that allow for a more precise determination of the elements that contribute to a site's aural qualities. For example, our recordings at Section A demonstrated that this corner was more spatially open than the others, while those at Section C showed that this part of the street hosts faster-moving vehicles. Drawing, meanwhile, depicts enclosure and scale, both of which are crucial when assessing that which shapes a street's atmosphere. Our findings suggest that physical compression and slower traffic can contribute to a calmer and more conversation-friendly atmosphere. Thus, these tools, when employed in tandem, can provide insights into the elements that shape street character.

Sonic experiences at a particular place and time can be profoundly influenced by minor spatial interventions. The Ormeau Parklet is a recent addition, designed by OGU and MMAS architects as a test place-making project.[2] This change replaced a few parking spaces with tables, chairs and a plant-laden material barrier between the parklet and the street. This parklet hosts increased pedestrian interaction (Figure 17.4 and Figure 17.8). During the soundwalks, it was clear that this parklet significantly influenced the street atmosphere. While some aspects of Ormeau Road are determined on a large scale (e.g. traffic pattern), small-scale interventions with a social focus can have a remarkable impact on sonic experience. Notably, however, these impacts would have gone unnoticed without merging techniques from the fields of architecture and sound studies.

Figure 17.8: A social corner, with a cafe and an open parklet.
© Elen Flügge

This study's methodological combination facilitates engagement with street elements that shift across varying time spans and speeds. A route may exist for centuries, its buildings and activities may evolve over years, and people may traverse it within a few minutes. A drawing can be useful for visually compiling the layers (or assessing the depth) of spatial and social information linked to a static moment in time. Such moments can be used to capture significant changes in the architectural environment, as buildings are constructed or demolished over decades. Comparatively, audio recordings can easily capture temporal activity flows, such as passing conversations and routine activities. On-site recordings made at multiple points in time can be used to compare sonic flows at these points in time. It is difficult to represent the minutiae of sonic flow – the myriad fleeting sounds – using words, as more dynamic input exists than can be accurately articulated. Thus, narrative texts can be used to jump between different moments of time, refer to routine and cyclical events – such as rhythmicity and a vivid sense of time (as cited by Wunderlich) – and present a sense of events experienced on site over longer periods of time that can be socially or spatially contextualised and assessed. Thus, audio recordings may be characterised as useful for capturing temporal flow across short- to medium-term periods of time. In contrast, drawings may be characterised as useful for capturing a paused moment that can be compared to distinct historical instances. Finally, narrative text can serve to connect references to various moments and time frames.

A soundwalk incorporating intermittent verbal reports – a solo or conversational narration – adds to an inter-sensory and multi-temporal depiction of Ormeau Road. Including personal impressions in a recorded soundwalk can capture the recordist's personal experience of a site, in line with field notes. Conversational walks, including exchanges with interlocutors, can increase the complexity of observations by increasing the number of relevant perspectives. Recorded discussions about shared sites and sensory events incorporate a social element into research. Alongside visual observations and recordings, these soundwalks form multiple perspectives that can be juxtaposed. Conversational walks can underscore site conditions such as conversality, evidence how distinctly one can record speech and other sounds at that place and time, and demonstrate ways in which individuals filter their impressions of their surroundings. This study was primarily interested in individual sonic experience. Individuals listen and observe subjectively, influenced by personal background, biases, and the given situation. Such self-reflection, which can reveal how the recording-listener's attention may be directed, was often traditionally considered to be peripheral in conventional field recording; however, it is now increasingly utilised in sound studies and sonic arts (Anderson and Rennie 2016). Researchers are never truly absent from observations and recordings, especially in studies on everyday situations (Pink 2015). Both soundwalking and narrative text highlight the personal nature of studying streetspace.

Conclusion

We approached this study considering the significance of personal experience in soundwalks along a familiar route, which extends beyond built structures and social dynamics. Our cross-disciplinary approach served to provide insight into streetspace by capturing various fragments of the countless spatial, temporal and social elements that comprise a street. We contend that a formal drawing of a street's structure is inert without a description of the occupations and activities that the street hosts. Similarly, an aural recording of the flow of street life can be disorienting without a visual representation of where it was taken. Merging these approaches offered a more comprehensive sense of the street.

One challenge encountered in this study was the terminological and conceptual disconnects between the fields of architecture and sound studies. These two fields often interpret the same concept (e.g. rhythm) in different ways, presenting methodological issues. Additionally, it was difficult to present sonic elements of research, as the field of architecture – and, more generally, academia – is invested in visual and textual means of communicating findings. This challenge is inevitable for research aiming to represent sonic concerns to spatial fields, such as the publication *The Sound-Considered City* (Lappin et al. 2018) which uses drawing to highlight dominant sounds at various Belfast sites. As it was unfeasible for us to include audio in this paper, we sought to convey information from the recordings through the descriptive text of the walk, drawings and our analysis. Still, integrating multiple sensory forms constitutes a great advantage in urban research by bringing attention to less obvious street elements. We hope that this short study demonstrates one way of merging spatial, personal and sonic perspectives to allow for comprehensive understandings of streets.

Notes

1   Soundwalks and recordings completed in December 2020. The terms 'narrative' and 'conversational soundwalk' used here stem from Flügge's doctoral research at Queen's University Belfast (2022).
2   See, for example, https://www.oguarchitects.com and https://www.sustainableni.org/case-study/ormeau-parklet-test-model-expand-public-space (accessed 1 November 2022).

Bibliography

Adams, Mags D., Neil S. Bruce, William J. Davies, Rebecca Cain, Paul Jennings, Angus Carlyle, Peter Cusack, Ken Hume and C. Plack. 2008. 'Soundwalking as a Methodology for Understanding Soundscapes'. Institute of Acoustics Spring Conference 2008, 10–11 April, Reading, UK.

Adhitya, Sara 2013. 'Sonifying Urban Rhythms: Towards the spatio-temporal composition of the urban environment', PhD diss., Università Iuav di Venezia & École des Hautes Études en Sciences Sociales.

Anderson, Isobel and Tullis Rennie. 2016. 'Thoughts in the Field: Self-reflexive narrative in field recording', *Organised Sound* 21(3): 222–32.

Augoyard, Jean François and Henry Torgue. 2005. *Sonic Experience: A guide to everyday sounds*. Montreal: McGill-Queen's University Press.

Claus, Caroline. 2015. *Urban Sound Design Process*. Warsaw: A-I-R Laboratory CCA Ujazdowski Castle.

Clossick, Jane. 2017. 'The Depth Structure of a London High Street: A study in urban order', PhD diss., London Metropolitan University.

Drever, John L. 2013. 'Silent Soundwalking: An urban pedestrian soundscape methodology'. AIA-DAGA 2013, the joint Conference on Acoustics, European Acoustics Association Euroregio, 39th annual congress of the Deutsche Gesellschaft für Akustik and the 40th annual congress of the Associazione Italiana di Acustica, March.

Flügge, Elen. 2022. 'Listening Practices for Urban Sound Space in Belfast', PhD diss., Queen's University Belfast.

Jacobs, Allan. 1995. *Great Streets*. Cambridge, MA: MIT Press.

Jacobs, Jane. 1961. *The Death and Life of Great American Cities*. 1994 ed. New York: Vintage.

Lappin, S., G. Ouzounian and R. O'Grady. 2018. *The Sound-Considered City: A guide for decision-makers*. Accessed 1 November 2022. https://static1.squarespace.com/static/520167f1e4b0b5e68d9b07cd/t/5a8be8699140b7effc636c3e/1519118498252/The+Sound-Considered+City+Low+Resolution+Web+Copy.pdf.

Lefebvre, Henri. 1991. *The Production of Space*. Oxford: Blackwell.

McCartney, Andra. 2014. 'Soundwalking: Creating moving environmental sound narratives'. In *The Oxford Handbook of Mobile Music Studies*. Oxford: Oxford University Press.

Maguire, William A. 2009. *Belfast: A history*. Lancaster: Carnegie.

Maag, T. and Klangraumgestaltung Bosshard. 2012. 'Fünf fallbeispiele im urbanen raum des kantons Zürich'. In *Zürich: Im Auftrag Der Fachstelle Lärmschutz Des Kantons* Zürich. BIBLIO DETAILS?

Ouzounian, Gascia and Sarah A. Lappin. 2014. 'Soundspace: A manifesto', *Architecture and Culture* 2(3): 305–16. https://doi.org/10.2752/205078214x14107818390559.

Paquette, David and Andra McCartney. 2012. 'Soundwalking and the Bodily Exploration of Places', *Canadian Journal of Communication* 37(1): 135.

Pink, Sarah. 2015. *Doing Sensory Ethnography*. London: SAGE.

Radicchi, Antonella. 2017. 'A Pocket Guide to Soundwalking. Some introductory notes on its origin, established methods and four experimental variations'. In *Perspectives on Urban Economics. A general merchandise store: a brief overview of the accounts for the shopkeeper Dietrich Henckel*, edited by Anja Besecke, Josiane Meier, Ricarda Pätzold and Susanne Thomaier, 70–73. Berlin: Universitätsverlag der TU Berlin.

Semidor, Catherine. 2006. 'Listening to a City with the Soundwalk Method', *Acta Acustica United with Acustica* 92(6): 959–64.

Sennett, Richard. 2018. *Building and Dwelling: Ethics for the city*. Harmondsworth: Penguin.

Till, Jeremy. 2000. 'Thick Time'. In *Intersections: Architectural histories and critical theories*, edited by Iain Borden and Jane Rendell, 156–83. Abingdon. Routledge.

Tuan, Y.F. 1977. *Space and Place: The perspective of experience*. Minnesota, MN: University of Minnesota Press.

Westerkamp, Hildegard. 1974. 'Soundwalking', *Sound Heritage* 3(4): 18–27.

Wunderlich, Filipa Matos. 2013. 'Place-Temporality and Urban Place-Rhythms in Urban Analysis and Design: An aesthetic akin to music', *Journal of Urban Design* 18(3): 383–408. https://doi.org/10.1080/13574809.2013.772882.

18

Mapping everyday heritage practices: Tivoli Barber Shop on North Street

Anna Skoura

While research on everyday streets has highlighted the complex relationship between their fabric and their economic and social life, it has yet to properly assess the role of cultural heritage in this relationship. Drawing on the performative nature of place as well as the concepts of everyday heritage and the taskscape, this chapter argues that mapping heritage practices develops our temporal and spatial understanding of everyday streets. This mapping is achieved by assessing the people, places and practices on everyday streets using interdisciplinary methodologies. Focusing on the case of Tivoli Barber Shop on Belfast's North Street, this chapter demonstrates the contribution of local, independent shops to everyday streets' continuity, social memory and dynamic production of cultural heritage.

The cultural heritage of everyday streets

Over the last 50 years, everyday streets around the world – and particularly in the UK – have been subject to large-scale development cycles, growing increasingly homogenous (Bandarin and Van Oers 2012; Carmona 2015; Griffiths 2015). This process has greatly influenced streets' built fabrics as well as the activities that take place on them, challenging their resilience and adaptability (Swyngedouw et al. 2002; Purcell 2009; Sassen 2019). Research on high streets has highlighted the complex relationship between their fabric and their economic and social life (Hall 2012; Vaughan 2015; Zukin et al. 2016; Hubbard 2017). However, it has yet to properly assess how the relationships among streets' fabric, activities and users influence their cultural heritage

NORTH STREET

BELFAST, UK ├────────┤ 2km

Figure 18.0: Map of Belfast © Anna Skoura

(Erlewein 2015; Moore-Cherry and Bonnin 2018; Sholihah 2016; Taylor 2016). This lack of knowledge is growing more troublesome as comprehensive redevelopment transforms everyday streets, disrupting the historic and cultural continuities of their urban landscape.

In the context of the UK, an everyday street would fall under the category of 'high street'. However, in a continental context, they resemble a 'mixed-use street' or a 'shopping street', but with less residential use. Despite this terminological variety, I employ the term 'everyday street' in this study to highlight the streets' ordinary qualities – the role of everyday practices in shaping them and their connection to 'everyday heritage'.

Everyday heritage comprises places and practices that are meaningful to the life and routine of 'ordinary' people (Dicks 2000; Mosler 2019; Samuel 1994; Schofield 2014), in contrast to the idea that heritage is a cultural construct designed to serve the interests of the elite (Lowenthal 1985; Smith 2006). Everyday heritage is the heritage that addresses the ordinary to 'offer 'ordinary people now' the chance to encounter 'ordinary people then' (Dicks 2000). This type of heritage values places and practices that play an important role in people's everyday life and routine, while contributing to their sense of place (Silva and Mota Santos 2012) and sense of past (Robertson 2012). The term *heritage* is used in this chapter very broadly to include everyday rituals, practices and traditions that inform the character of places. Often, everyday heritage includes places and practices that appear commonplace.

Drawing from the concept of dynamic authenticity, where continuity and change are interlinked (Jivén and Larkham 2003; Araoz 2008; Silverman 2015), the everyday street is understood as a site of living heritage (Poulios 2014), where the ordinary interactions between the fabric, use and users form a dynamic and essential layer to the street's heritage (Martire and Skoura 2022). Drawing on the performative and embodied nature of place (Crouch 2003; Edensor 2010; Thrift 2008), everyday heritage can be understood as the heritage produced by those who actively engage with it (Robertson 2012; Schofield 2014): in the context of everyday streets, the people that use them.

The 'taskscape', coined by Tim Ingold, conceptualises the relationships among a street's fabric, use and user. A task is conceived as 'any practical operation, carried by a skilled agent in an environment, as part of his or her normal business of life' (Ingold 1993, 158), and the taskscape is an aggregation of tasks. Taskscape and landscape are interlinked, with the landscape being the embodied form of the taskscape

(Ingold 1993). Translating these concepts into heritage-related terms, the landscape can be perceived as the tangible, while the taskscape can be viewed as the intangible aspect of a street's cultural heritage. In the context of everyday streets, the landscape is their urban fabric, while the taskscape is the uses and activities taking place on them.

Landscape and taskscape continuity are essential to the retention of everyday streets' cultural heritage. Spatial and social continuity reinforce collective memory (Connerton 1989; Halbwachs 1992; Hayden 1994; Rossi 1982). The collective memory of each everyday street relies on both its historical fabric and its shared everyday experiences (Hebbert 2005; Low 2017); thus, activities occurring on them constitute an important layer of their heritage (Robertson 2012). Of course, these activities are largely dependent on that which the street can accommodate. Continuity of uses – especially among local, independent stores – is an overlooked but vital aspect of everyday streets (Clarke and Banga 2010; Hall 2011; Zukin 2012). This chapter argues that local shops with a long-term presence constitute a meaningful part of their street's taskscape and a source of everyday heritage (Skoura 2019).

Case study: Tivoli Barber Shop, North Street, Belfast

The city of Belfast presents an extreme example of high street homogenisation. Even in conservation areas, demolitions and large-scale developments have replaced much of the existing built fabric – its uses and users – without considering the adverse effects on the city's cultural heritage. North Street is one of the oldest streets in Belfast's city centre, dating back to the first official map of Belfast from 1685. Throughout the centuries and until well into the 1960s, like many other high streets, it has proven itself to be architecturally, economically and socially adaptable, remaining relatively stable in form and hosting a diverse set of uses and activities, including shops, services and housing.

Planning decisions made between the 1970s and 1990s reduced much of North Street's activity, leading it into a steady decline through a lack of maintenance, arson attacks, apparent obsolescence and successive retail development proposals (BBC News 2015; Black 2019; Potter 2019). Such proposals have shown little appreciation of the street's landscape and taskscape; in the latest iteration, more than half of the historic fabric and its activities are to be replaced with generic 'high-street architecture' (SaveCQ 2017; O'Kane 2020). North Street exemplifies the planning system's inability to properly appreciate the character of everyday streets and adequately protect them from market forces.

One of the North Street shops that will be forced to close is Tivoli Barber Shop, an integral component of North Street's taskscape. Currently located at 15 North Street – with a continuous presence in the area since the 1920s – it is likely one of the oldest barber shops in Belfast (McRitchie 1981). Amid North Street's contemporary blight, Tivoli remains a popular barber shop for an all-male clientele: from toddlers accompanied by their mothers to people in their golden years, most of whom have been regular clients for decades.

Methodology

This study employs methods from architecture, urban design, urban history and graphic anthropology alongside ethnographic observations to conduct a nuanced assessment of the people, spaces and practices in Tivoli and, in turn, understand its heritage practices. The author visited the shop on many occasions between September 2017 and February 2018, spending several hours at a time there. Drawing was used as a method of both analysis and representation. Conceptualising drawing as a way of embodied thinking (Merleau-Ponty 1945; 2013), the selection and editing of information involved in drawing becomes a way of both analysing and synthesising the sensory information experienced by being in a place (Dutoit 2008; Lucas 2020).

Tivoli's everyday heritage is presented in this chapter through different types of drawings illustrating its taskscape and heritage narratives. The author employed approaches from graphic anthropology (Lucas 2020) and ethnographic drawing (Azevedo and Ramos 2016; Kuschnir 2016) to reflect ethnographic knowledge and used the concept of 'place ballet' (Jacobs 1961) to analyse Tivoli's taskscape through its users' place-making practices. Recording the shop's interior entailed measured survey drawings of the barber shop's inhabited space and the creation of taxonomies of objects. 'Counting people' techniques, which are widely used in urban design studies (Gehl and Svarre 2013; Whyte 1980), and mapping techniques used in human geography (Holloway and Hubbard 2001) were then employed to create a series of spatial and temporal studies and analyse movement in the barber shop.

Tivoli Barber Shop

Tivoli Barber Shop was established in 1924 at 8 Lower Garfield Street – the corner of North Street and Garfield Street. In 1936, the current owner's grandfather started working at Tivoli, followed by his sons Philip and Alfie. They bought the barber shop in the 1950s; in 2004, it was passed on to Eddie, the current owner. Although not a barber himself, Eddie has helped in Tivoli since he was a boy, initially sweeping floors and later handling the finances. In 2013, Tivoli was forced to vacate its premises after the building was deemed unsafe. It quickly relocated to 15 North Street, its current location. Since 2014, Tivoli's backroom has housed the Goose Lane Gallery, curated by a local art company. At the time of the fieldwork, Tivoli employed three barbers, two of whom were in their 50s and had been working at the barber shop for almost 20 years.

Tivoli Barber Shop has a fairly old-fashioned interior, making visitors feel like they're stepping back in time. It boasts Formica counters, traditional barber chairs fixed to a wooden floor, plain mirrors, and a leather-covered timber bench. Instead of a price list, a plain piece of paper propped up on two mirrors lists the price for the only service they offer: a haircut (see Figure 18.1).

Despite its forced relocation, Tivoli's persistent presence is something that its owner and barbers are proud of. Following the move, the owner remained the same, as did two of the three barbers. The furniture, tools and wall decorations were all moved from the previous shop too, along with the shop's taskscape, dictated by the everyday practices of barbering.

Figure 18.1: Tivoli waiting area. © Anna Skoura

Tivoli's collection of posters

The longevity of small independent stores is an overlooked but crucial asset to everyday streets. Tivoli, as a social space with a continuous presence and steady contribution to the taskscape, constitutes a place in which individual and collective memories are triggered and produced. Sharon Zukin asserts that 'the production of cultural heritage through collective memory depends on both spatial and social continuity' (2012, 286). Tivoli's continuous existence provides 'spatial continuity', while the continual visits of steady clients and their families, sometimes spanning decades, is an expression of 'social continuity'.

Eddie, Tivoli's owner, is passionate about the area's past, present and future. To him, the barber shop is an integral piece of the area – a place where memories of his family and early childhood are interwoven with the history of North Street. He has gathered anything related to the barber shop and North Street to eagerly display it in Tivoli. What started as a way to mask the physical decay of the previous premises evolved into a striking collection of images that covered every available inch of the barber shop's walls – and even parts of the ceiling. With contributions from the owner, barbers and clients, the collection consists of posters, photos and other memorabilia. Despite the apparent disorder, the pieces in Tivoli's collection are thematically organised: the history of the barber shop, the history of North Street and Belfast in general, boxing and sports, images related to barbering and Hollywood posters. During the research process every piece displayed on the walls was drawn with little detail to evoke the impression of the pieces, rather than a faithful reproduction of every item included in the collection.

These pieces connected to Tivoli's history serve as a shrine to the barber shop's past, evoking the collective memory of long-term clients. If heritage is seen as 'the existence in the present of memorials representing the lived experiences of past people' (Henson 2016, 149), Tivoli's gallery embodies heritage by emphasising the link between the barber shop and the people and places of the past.

Traditional barber shops often reproduce gender stereotypes through ideas of masculinity (Barber 2008; Philips 2007) and Hollywood's classic male role models. The displays on Tivoli's walls are no exception.

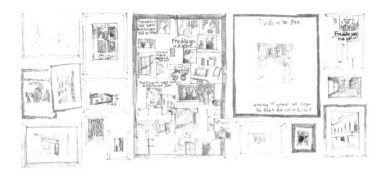

Figure 18.2: Taxonomies of Tivoli's gallery: history of the barber shop.
© Anna Skoura

Figure 18.3: Taxonomies of Tivoli's gallery: Hollywood. © Anna Skoura

Tivoli's curated collection of posters illustrates the barber shop's heritage narrative, making it a locus of personal and collective heritage narratives (Crang and Travlou 2001; Waterton et al. 2017). The survival of these narratives is essential to shaping and maintaining collective memory (Hayden 1994; Jones 2017; Low 2017).

Tivoli's place ballet

> Out of this mapping of the banal, comes something of ballet of lines of motion. (Crang 2001, 8)

Tivoli's barbers have been giving haircuts for decades, contributing to the continuity of the taskscape and giving meaning to the barber shop. Haircut practices are here analysed as spatial practices, employing the Jane Jacobs' concept of place ballet. Tivoli's place ballet can be seen as an aggregation of individual body ballets, defined by David Seamon as 'a set of integrated gestures, behaviours, and actions that sustain a particular task or aim' (Seamon 2006). In turn, North Street's place ballet can be seen as an aggregation of the dances of all of the shop spaces in terms of how they connect to the street.

The barber's body ballet during a haircut is the core sequence of Tivoli's ballet. During the 10 minutes of a typical haircut, the author observed that each barber had a precise and repetitive way of moving around the client. While his hands worked, the barber moved in a semi-circle, shuffling his feet and shifting his weight from one foot to the other. The barber was engaged in a very precise dance – a choreography devised to negotiate and appropriate Tivoli's space (see Figure 18.4).

While the barber's dance is relatively repetitive, with each haircut requiring the same general set of movements, the barber shop dance varies significantly depending on the day and the time of day. Figure 18.5 illustrates Tivoli's place ballet over the course of two days. The activity is traced as an overlay on space with differently coloured

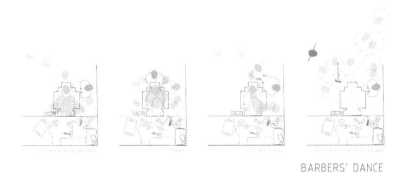

BARBERS' DANCE

Figure 18.4: Barber's dance. © Anna Skoura

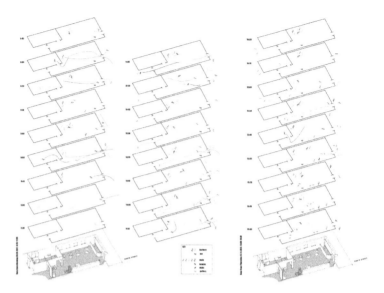

Figure 18.5: Tivoli place ballet. © Anna Skoura

footprints corresponding to different categories of people. Following these coloured footsteps, we can trace clients and barbers coming in, moving around the shop (each area corresponding to an activity) and eventually leaving.

Seamon's body ballet 'sought to describe the everyday worlds of individuals in terms of embodied phases of movement, rest and encounter' (Wylie 2007, 149). The body ballets that collectively constitute Tivoli's place ballet depict Doreen Massey's 'living place' as a 'constellation of trajectories' (2005, 149), with each trajectory spatialising one of the many everyday practices that occur in the barber shop. The barber shop as an everyday place of routine habits – expressed spatially and temporally through its place ballet – becomes a 'landmark to placemaking from below and within' (Robertson 2015, 2): a landmark of the street's everyday heritage.

Tivoli's place ballet is dynamic. It changes shape and rhythm depending on several factors, including cultural, environmental, temporal and spatial constraints. For example, its hours of operation provide a temporal envelope to the beginning and ending of the daily space ballet, while business working hours influence the flow of clients. Material and spatial constraints include everything from the barber's tools and the chairs to the posters and the building's architecture. The reciprocal relationship between space and spatial practices is governed by implicit and explicit rules, all of which can be 'read' through signs and indications in the space (Bourdieu and Wacquant 1992). Figure 18.6a shows the data from Figure 18.5 overlaid on the plan of the barber shop. It becomes clear that the place ballet revolves around specific spots; different users tend to frequent specific zones (see Figure 18.6b). Jane Clossick (2017) introduced the concept of 'depth' to explain the way in which different city spaces (ranging in scale from a single room to an urban block) host different economic and social aspects of everyday life. This depth is structured, comprising discrete zones delineated by thresholds, each with its own rules and expectations regarding user behaviour (Clossick 2021). Tivoli's main entrance connects the barber shop to North Street. Then, the main area of the

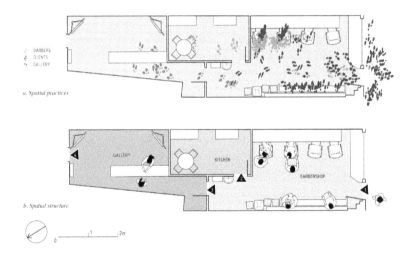

Figure 18.6: Tivoli zoning. © Anna Skoura
Spatial practices (a) and spatial structure (b) in Tivoli. Thresholds: (1) entrance, access to all; (2) door to the kitchen, access to barbers; (3) door to the gallery, access to gallery staff and visitors; (4) door to storage and WC, access to barbers and gallery staff (occasional access to clients). Zones: (1) barber shop, access to anyone entering the premises; (2) waiting area, used by those waiting for a haircut or accompanying a client; (3) kitchen, used exclusively by the barbers; (4) gallery, used by gallery staff and visitors.

shop is divided into the waiting area and the barbers' stations. The barbers stay predominantly around these stations (where the traces of the barber's dance are noticeable) and have exclusive access to the kitchen. The gallery staff exclusively use the gallery. Finally, the clients move between the entrance, the waiting area and the barbers' stations. The layout of the barber shop guides the visitor, while, at the same time, the shop layout is guided by both the architecture of the building and the anticipation of the users' needs, stressing the connection between the landscape and the taskscape.

Local shops and everyday street heritage

This chapter has highlighted two ways in which Tivoli contributes to North Street's taskscape and heritage. Its poster collection supports personal and collective heritage narratives, making Tivoli a place imbued with social memories that evokes a sense of place and a sense of belonging among its lifelong clients. Furthermore, defined by routine visits and repetitive practices linking users across time, the barber shop has contributed to the spatial and social continuity of North Street's taskscape. Understanding heritage as a dynamic process, local, independent shops with a longstanding presence constitute places where everyday heritage is produced, rendering 'a current way of life more meaningful by a sense of inheritance from the past' (Robertson 2012, 2).

While strategic placemaking practices have regularly been employed in public-realm improvements and heritage tourism on everyday streets, they have often been criticised for facilitating gentri-fication (Fincher et al. 2016; Lovell 2019; Madden 2011; Mansilla and Milano 2019; Ozdemir and Salcuk 2017). Assessing the taskscape and heritage narratives of everyday streets can inform more location-specific placemaking practices that respect each street's historical, spatial and cultural qualities (Giombini 2020; Mosler 2019; Pink 2008). Furthermore, expanding the concept of heritage to include everyday rituals, practices and traditions that are meaningful to those partici-pating in them while contributing to the character of places can help protect the historic and cultural continuities that foster inclusive and culturally rich places (Martire and Skoura 2022).

Attitudes toward new development projects are also crucial in maintaining historic continuities in the urban landscape. The proposed development looming over North Street will force Tivoli to close its doors after almost 100 years. While comprehensive redevelopment is a common influence on everyday streets' taskscape, social memory and heritage, new design initiatives that respect the scale and typology of streets' fabric and existing users and uses are possible. Such initiatives can even support the contemporary production of everyday heritage.

Tivoli Barber Shop is a place that can easily be overlooked. But as with many places that are deemed too ordinary to qualify as official heritage, it displays a continuity and adaptability supporting the street's everyday heritage. The combination of positivist approaches, traditionally favoured in planning practices, with the more interpretive ones employed in this study offers ways to map heritage practices and acknowledge everyday socially constructed spaces as equally important to the street's heritage as formally designed ones. Including such mapping of heritage practices in methodologies designed to appraise the urban fabric highlights a broader understanding of the value of places on everyday streets. It is only after close inspection that the value of the shop to the street becomes clear.

Conclusion

Using the example of Tivoli Barber Shop on Belfast's North Street, this chapter illustrated how local shops play a meaningful role in the social memory, continuity and dynamic production of everyday streets' cultural heritage. The chapter further argued that expanding our understanding of everyday street heritage to include the relationships between the street's fabric, activities and users, and noticing the way people use everyday streets, while analysing the factors that affect these both spatially and temporally, can inform more appropriate place-making that is holistic and inclusive, appreciating both tangible and intangible values of place. Considering these practices in redevelopment projects can support the social and spatial continuity that is crucial to streets' cultural heritage.

Bibliography

Azevedo, Aina and Manuel Joao Ramos. 2016. 'Drawing Close: On visual engagements in fieldwork, drawing workshops and the anthropological imagination', *Visual Ethnography* 5(1): 135–60.
Bandarin, Francesco and Ron Van Oers. 2012. *The Historic Urban Landscape: Managing heritage in an urban century*. New York: John Wiley & Sons.

Barber, Kristen. 2008. 'The Well-Coiffed Man: Class, race, and heterosexual masculinity in the hair salon', *Gender and Society* 22(4): 455–76.

BBC News. 2015. 'Belfast Royal Exchange: Uncertainty over regeneration scheme', 19 November.

Black, Rebecca. 2019. 'Fire in Belfast's Cathedral Quarter Building was Arson, Say Police', *Belfast Telegraph*, 23 September.

Bourdieu, Pierre and Loïc Wacquant. 1992. *An Invitation to Reflexive Sociology*. Chicago, IL: University of Chicago Press.

Carmona, Matthew. 2015. 'London's Local High Streets: The problems, potential and complexities of mixed street corridors', *Progress in Planning* 100: 1–84.

Clarke, Ian and Sunil Banga. 2010. 'The Economic and Social Role of Small Stores: A review of UK evidence', *International Review of Retail, Distribution and Consumer Research* 20(2): 187–215.

Clossick, Jane. 2017. *The Depth Structure of a London High Street: A study in urban order*. London Metropolitan University.

Clossick, Jane. 2021. *Uncovering Urban Depth: A market, a salon and a meetinghouse on Tottenham High Road*. London Metropolitan University. Accessed 1 November 2022. https://urbandepth.research.londonmet.ac.uk/publications/.

Connerton, Paul. 1989. *How Societies Remember*. Cambridge: Cambridge University Press.

Crang, Mike and Penny S. Travlou. 2001. 'The City and Topologies of Memory', *Environment and Planning D: Society and Space* 19: 161–77.

Crouch, David. 2003. 'Spacing, Performing, and Becoming: Tangles in the mundane', *Environment and Planning A* 35(11): 1945–60.

Dicks, Bella. 2000. *Heritage, Place and Community*. Cardiff: University of Wales Press.

Dutoit, Allison. 2008. 'Looking as Inquiry: Drawing the implied urban realm'. In *Drawing/Thinking: Confronting an electronic age*, edited by M. Treib, 148–59. Abingdon: Routledge.

Edensor, Tim. 2010. 'Walking in Rhythms: Place, regulation, style and the flow of experience', *Visual Studies* 25(1): 69–79.

Erlewein, Shina. 2015. 'Sustainable Development and Intangible Cultural Heritage: Integrating culture into development'. In *Perceptions of Sustainability in Heritage Studies*, edited by M. Albert, 71–83. Berlin: De Gruyter.

Fincher, Ruth, Maree Pardy and Kate Shaw. 2016. 'Place-Making or Place-Masking? The everyday political economy of "making place"', *Planning Theory & Practice* 17(4): 516–36.

Gehl, Jan and Birgitte Svarre. 2013. *How to Study Public Life*. Washington, DC: Island Press.

Giombini, Lisa. 2020. 'Everyday Heritage and Place-Making', *ESPES* 9(2): 50–61.

Griffiths, Sam. 2015. 'The High Street as a Morphological Event'. In *Suburban Urbanites: Suburbs and the life of the high street*, edited by Laura Vaughan, 32–50. London: UCL Press.

Halbwachs, Maurice. 1992. *On Collective Memory*. Chicago, IL: University of Chicago Press.

Hall, Suzie. M. 2011. 'High Street Adaptations: Ethnicity, independent retail practices, and localism in London's urban margins', *Environment and Planning A* 43: 2,571–88.

Hall, Suzie. M. 2012. *City, Street and Citizen: The measure of the ordinary*. Abingdon: Routledge.

Hayden, Dolores. 1994. 'The Power of Place: Claiming urban landscapes as people's history', *Journal of Urban History* 20(4): 466–85. https://doi.org/10.1177/009614429402000402.

Hebbert, Michael. 2005. 'The Street as Locus of Collective Memory', *Environment and Planning D: Society and Space* 23(4): 581–96. https://doi.org/10.1068/d55j.

Henson, Don. 2016. 'Finding People in the Heritage of Bankside, Southwark'. In *Who Needs Experts? Counter-mapping cultural heritage*, edited by J. Schofield, 147–64. Abingdon: Routledge.

Holloway, Lewis and Phil Hubbard. 2001. *People and Place: The extraordinary geographies of everyday life*. Harlow: Prentice Hall.

Hubbard, Phil. 2017. *The Battle for the High Street: Retail, gentrification, class and disgust*. London: Palgrave Macmillan.

Ingold, Tim. 1993. 'The Temporality of the Landscape', *World Archaeology* 25(2): 152–74.

Jacobs, Jane. 1961. *The Death and Life of Great American Cities*. London: Vintage

Jones, Sian. 2017. 'Wrestling with the Social Value of Heritage: Problems, dilemmas and opportunities', *Journal of Community Archaeology and Heritage* 4(1): 21–37.

Kuschnir, Karina. 2016. 'Ethnographic Drawing: Eleven benefits of using a sketchbook for fieldwork', *Visual Ethnography* 5(1): 103–34.

Lovell, Jane. 2019. 'Fairytale Authenticity: Historic city tourism, Harry Potter, medievalism and the magical gaze', *Journal of Heritage Tourism* 14(5–6): 448–65.

Low, Kelvin E.Y. 2017. 'Concrete Memories and Sensory Pasts: Everyday heritage and the politics of nationhood', *Pacific Affairs* 90(2): 275–95.

Lowenthal, David. 1985. *The Past is a Foreign Country*. Cambridge: Cambridge University Press.

Lucas, Ray. 2020. *Anthropology for Architects: Social relations and the built environment*. London: Bloomsbury.

McRitchie, Michael. 1981. 'Thousands of Close Shaves but they're Still in Trim', *Newsletter*, 12 January.

Madden, Kathy. 2011. 'Placemaking in Urban Design'. In *Companion to Urban Design*, edited by T. Banerjee and A. Loukaitou-Sideris. Abingdon: Routledge.

Mansilla, Jose A. and Claudio Milano. 2019. 'Becoming Centre: Tourism placemaking and space production in two neighbourhoods in Barcelona', *Tourism Geographies*: 1–22. http://doi.org/10.1080/14616688.2019.1571097.

Martire, Agustina and Anna Skoura. 2022. 'The Dynamic Authenticity of Local Mixed Streets. Street heritage and activism in Belfast city centre'. In *Heritage, Gentrification and Resistance in the neoliberal city*, edited by F. Hamami, D. Jewesbury and C. Valli. New York and Oxford: Berghan.

Massey, Doreen. 2005. *For Space*. Los Angeles, CA: SAGE.

Merleau-Ponty, Maurice. 1945. *Phenomenology of Perception*. 2013 ed. Abingdon: Routledge.

Moore-Cherry, Niamh and Christine Bonnin. 2018. 'Playing with Time in Moore Street, Dublin: Urban redevelopment, temporal politics and the governance of space-time', *Urban Geography* 41(9): 1–20. http://doi.org/10.1080/02723638.2018.1429767.

Mosler, Saruhan. 2019. 'Everyday Heritage Concept as an Approach to Place-Making Process in the Urban Landscape', *Journal of Urban Design* 24(5): 778–93. http://doi.org/10.1080/13574809.2019.1568187.

O'Kane, Jake. 2020. 'Tribeca Sees the Architectural Homogenisation of Belfast Continue', *Irish News*, 25 January. Accessed 1 November 2022. http://www.irishnews.com/lifestyle/2020/01/25/news/jake-o-kane-tribeca-sees-the-architectural-homogenisation-of-belfast-continue-1823049/.

Ozdemir, Dilek and Irem Salcuk. 2017. 'From Pedestrianisation to Commercial Gentrification: The case of Kadikoy in Istanbul', *Cities* 65: 10–23.

Philips, Alton. 2007. 'The Erotic Life of Electric Hair: A social history'. In *Practising Culture*, edited by C. Calhoun and R. Sennet, 193–214. Abingdon: Routledge.

Pink, Sarah. 2008. 'An Urban Tour: The sensory sociality of ethnographic place-making', *Ethnography* 9(2): 175–96.

Potter, Gary. 2019. 'Tribeca, Future Belfast'. Accessed 10 September 2019. http://www.future-belfast.com/property/royal-exchange/.

Purcell, Mark. 2009. 'Resisting Neoliberalization: Communicative planning or counter-hegemonic movements?', *Planning Theory* 8(2): 140–65.

Robertson, Iain J.M. 2012. 'Introduction: Heritage from below'. In *Heritage from Below*, edited by Iain J.M. Robertson, 1–28. London: Taylor & Francis.

Robertson, Iain J.M. 2015. 'Hardscrabble Heritage: The ruined blackhouse and crofting landscape as heritage from below', *Landscape Research* 40(8): 993–1009.

Rossi, Aldo. 1982. *The Architecture of the City*. 1984 ed. Cambridge, MA: MIT Press.

Samuel, Raphael. 1994. *Theatres of Memory: Past and present in contemporary culture*. London: Verso.

Sassen, Saskia. 2019. *Cities in a World Economy*. 5th ed. Thousand Oaks, CA: SAGE.

SaveCQ. 2017. *What's the Problem? Save the Cathedral Quarter*. Accessed 1 November 2022. https://savecq.wordpress.com/whats-the-problem/.

Schofield, John. 2014. 'Heritage Expertise and the Everyday: Citizens and authority in the twenty-first century'. In *Who Needs Experts? Counter-mapping cultural heritage*, edited by John Schofield, 1–12. Abingdon: Ashgate.

Seamon, David. 2006. 'A Geography of Lifeworld in Retrospect: A response to Shaun Moores', *Particip@tions: Journal of Audience and Reception Studies* 3(2). Accessed 1 November 2022. http:// www.participations.org/volume%203/issue%202%20-%20special/3_02_seamon.htm.

Sholihah, Arif Budi. 2016. 'The Quality of Traditional Streets in Indonesia', PhD diss., University of Nottingham.

Skoura, Anna. 2019. 'Everyday Shops', *Irish Journal of Anthropology* 22(1): 55–60.

Smith, Laurajane. 2006. *The Uses of Heritage*. Abingdon: Routledge.

Swyngedouw, Erik, Frank Moulaert and Arantxa Rodriguez. 2002. 'Neoliberal Urbanization in Europe: Large-scale urban development projects and the new urban policy', *Antipode* 34(3): 542–77.

Taylor, Ken. 2016. 'The Historic Urban Landscape Paradigm and Cities as Cultural Landscapes. Challenging orthodoxy in urban conservation', *Landscape Research* 41(4): 471–80.

Thrift, Nigel. 2008. *Non-Representational Theory: Space, politics, affect*. Abingdon: Routledge.

Vaughan, Laura. 2015. *Suburban Urbanities: Suburbs and the life of the high street*. London: UCL Press.

Waterton, Emma, Steve Watson and Helaine Silverman. 2017. 'An Introduction to Heritage in Action'. In *Heritage in Action: Making the past in the present*, edited by Emma Watson, Steve Watson and Helaine Silverman, 3–16. Berlin: Springer.

Whyte, William Hollingsworth. 1980. *The Social Life of Small Urban Spaces*. Project for Public Spaces, INC.

Wylie, John. 2007. *Landscape*. Abingdon: Routledge.

Zukin, Sharon. 2012. 'The Social Production of Urban Cultural Heritage: Identity and ecosystem on an Amsterdam shopping street', *City, Culture and Society* 3(4): 281–91.

Zukin, Sharon, Philip Kasinitz and Xianming Chen. 2016. *Global Cities, Local Streets: Everyday diversity from New York to Shanghai*. Abingdon: Routledge.

19

Urban depth and social integration on super-diverse London high streets

Jane Clossick and Rebecca Smink

Urban depth that promotes convivial interactions between different socioeconomic groups at varying city scales is crucial to facilitating optimal conditions for social integration. This chapter explores the relationship between urban depth and social integration in London at different scales (building/block, neighbourhood) in two super-diverse places in London: Tottenham and Stratford. The study is conducted using drawings, participant observation and interviews, emphasising the methodological value of reading the city closely through different types of drawings. We argue that urban depth on high streets and social integration are intimately linked. Therefore, it is necessary for planning policy to protect the type of urban depth in which diverse groups can flourish and form relationships.

Tottenham and Stratford

This study spans two places in London: Tottenham and Stratford. It examines their morphology, assessing whether they wield conditions that facilitate social integration. The high streets here represent ordinary streets on the periphery of central London. Tottenham has a high street called Tottenham High Road, which constitutes an 'ordinary' street (Hall 2012, 11). Stratford has two similar examples: Leytonstone Road and Stratford High Street. We use these as points of comparison to explore how some types of urban depth do not foster the conditions necessary for social integration. We use Tottenham and Stratford as examples of two scales: building/block and neighbourhood, respectively.

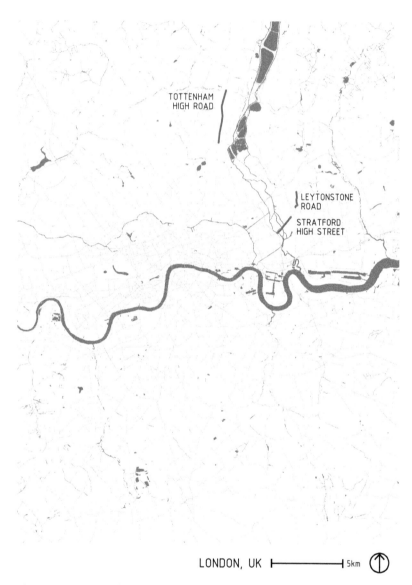

TOTTENHAM
HIGH ROAD

LEYTONSTONE
ROAD
STRATFORD
HIGH STREET

LONDON, UK ├───────┤ 5km

Figure 19.0: Map of London © Anna Skoura

Both Stratford and Tottenham are deprived places that have undergone regeneration. Stratford's economy suffered in the late twentieth century due to the closure of many London docks. However, London authorities sought to reverse this decline amid the 2012 Olympics through new development initiatives, including the huge new Stratford Westfield shopping centre. Similarly, the manufacturing hub of Tottenham declined in the late twentieth century, due in large part to globalisation. After the London riots caused extensive damage to Tottenham High Road in 2011, a number of regeneration schemes were instituted, including the designation of the Upper Lea Valley Opportunity Area. In both Stratford and Tottenham, regeneration has largely involved private-sector development, meaning it has resulted in gentrification (Dillon and Fanning 2015, 108–206; Watt 2013, 99–118); property prices have risen and local communities have been driven out. Both places remain deprived (MHCLG 2019). According to the 2019 Index of Multiple Deprivation, Tottenham's Northumberland Road, White Hart Lane and Tottenham Green are the second, fourth and thirteenth most deprived of London's 633 wards (MHCLG 2019). Newham, the borough that contains Stratford, is the 25th poorest local authority in the UK (Presser 2016).

Key concepts

Social integration

In a super-diverse city like London, social integration reflects the presence of 'social cohesion, a strong institutional foundation and a culture of acceptance' (Cruz-Saco Oyague 2008, 1). Social integration entails working towards the participation and inclusion of groups with diverse attributes. It allows such groups to experience equality of rights, opportunities and access to services. Social segregation or exclusion, on the other hand, facilitates reduced mutual understanding, conflict and unequal access to opportunities. In 2020, the Mayor of London set out a 'Vision for Social Integration' around three core themes of 'relationships', 'participation' and 'equality' (GLA 2002, 7). Of relevance to this assessment, the 'relationships' element of the vision is about finding times and places for diverse groups to interact, as 'relationships and social contact can reduce unconscious bias and discrimination' and 'facilitate access to participation opportunities' (GLA 2020, 7).

Urban depth

'Urban depth' is the depth of high streets beyond the facades: buildings, yards, alleyways, secondary streets and all contained therein. The term was coined by Peter Carl, who defines it as the capacity of the city to structure the 'fruitful coexistence of formal and informal life' (2012, 1). Social, political and economic life takes place in urban depth; it is a concept that captures cities in their multi-layered richness. 'Depth structure', coined by Jane Clossick (2021), describes the organisation of urban depth, whereby urban space at all scales is differentiated into zones characterised by different norms of decorum, privacy and access. Decorum here refers to appropriate dress, language and behaviour; required decorum is generally communicated to the users of a place through signs and signifiers. Implicit awareness of boundaries between zones coordinates where people go and what they do in cities on both individual and collective levels. Urban depth includes the many components that make up economic, social and civic life; the way this urban depth is organised and designed – its depth structure – can help or hinder our collective ethical desires for the good functioning of cities.

Well-designed depth structure has, in many studies (e.g. Carl 2011; Clossick 2017; van de Wal et al. 2016; Vesely 2006, 19), been shown to have multiple positive effects, including social and economic accessibility (Hall 2020), political participation (Clossick 2022), social integration (Clossick and Colburn 2021) and economic resilience (Clossick and Brearley 2021). The spatial configuration between rooms, for example, can influence the typical uses of those rooms (Hillier et al. 1984). At a larger scale, the integration, centrality and connectedness of routes constitute an important factor behind the vitality of districts and neighbourhoods.

Super-diversity

Super-diversity is a condition of diversity heaped upon diversity (Vertovec 2007). It refers to diversity between ethnic groups as well as within them in terms of education, class and age. The term has been expanded by Wessendorf (2014), who explored how residents of a super-diverse urban neighbourhood pragmatically negotiate difference in their everyday lives. Hall (2015) has explored the relationship between the occupation of an ordinary street and the expression of super-diverse cultural identities in its shops. Stratford and Tottenham are super-diverse places, with groups of different ethnicities, faiths and classes living in close proximity and a relative lack of conflict.

Gradation of publicness

A key mechanism that facilitates the conditions in which social integration can thrive is the 'gradation of publicness', or the tendency of places to vary in accessibility to a broader range of people, with a general pattern of places closer to the most public parts of the depth structure (e.g. the high street) being the most public (Clossick 2021). The decorum changes at each part of the depth structure, depending on its level of publicness; this varying decorum in different zones influences behaviour, language, decor, and who is welcomed or feels welcomed. Gradation of publicness is a spatial mechanism that enables vastly different cultures to coexist peacefully most of the time. In the case studies, gradation of publicness serves a mediating function between public conviviality and private cultural specificity.

Methodology

The findings presented in this chapter were gathered between 2014 and 2020 on Tottenham High Road (building/block scale) and two high streets in Stratford (neighbourhood scale). Methods employed include architectural drawing and photography, urban analysis through diagrams (Martire and Madden, this volume), and the social science methods of observation and in-depth interviews (Smink 2020). In Tottenham, we examined three case studies: an indoor Latin American market, a hair salon and a Quaker meetinghouse (Clossick 2021, 11–13). In Stratford, we examined two high streets with very different morphological conditions: Leytonstone Road and Stratford High Street. The use of drawings to investigate the gradients between public and private life enabled us to visualise the relationships between urban depth and social life and how these relationships change from the outside on a high street to their interior; this approach serves to test the value of reading cities closely through drawings (Martire 2020).

Block/building scale (Tottenham)

At a busy corner near Seven Sisters station, a large market known as Latin Village occupies an old department store (see Figures 19.1 and 19.2). It is fronted by shops facing the high street, which also have entrances from inside the market. The interior market space is divided

Figure 19.1: View of the interior of Seven Sisters Market. © Clossick 2017

into several arcades of small shops, which sell a wide range of products from specialist food to music and underwear. The majority of stall-holders are Colombian, but there are stallholders and regulars of many nationalities. The front of the building is the most widely accessible to the broadest range of people via the high street. The front of the market, facing the street, contains a luggage shop, general household goods, a grocer and a Colombian cafe. Towards the back, the shops and stalls become more culturally specific, with hair salons, food stalls and clothing shops catering specifically to Colombian customers. As one moves away from the front row of shops, the lingua franca is Spanish while at the front of the market, on the shops facing the high street, the signage is in English.

This gradation of publicness, as shown in Figure 19.2, from the front to the back and the change in decorum as one moves away from the high street gives the stallholders and regulars the possibility of convivial but casual interactions with a broad range of people at the front of the market, and simultaneously the opportunity to establish strong social bonds of loyalty and friendship at the deeper end of the market. It's important to note that the places where these bonds are formed are not off-limits to the general public; anyone can peruse the stalls and sit and eat in the tiny cafes, and they know they are welcome to do so because the front parts of the depth structure closest to the high street welcomed them in. One British regular told us that they started off coming to the butcher's shop in the market, then they began getting their hair done at a salon in the market – and now they come to the

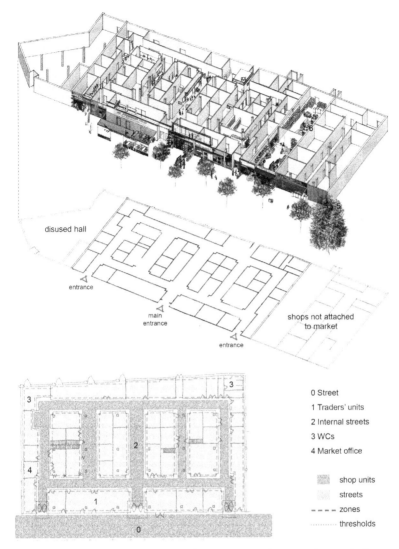

Figure 19.2: The depth structure of the interior of Seven Sisters Market, showing the gradation of publicness from the front doors to the rear of the market. © Clossick 2021

market a few times a week to chat with friends they have made at the juice bar. However, the general public has different rules of decorum than market regulars. The owner of the specialist butcher talked about being happy to let his children roam free in the market because the regulars are 'like family'; he can trust the people he knows well to keep an eye on his children. In contrast, a newcomer would not recognise his children and would not feel comfortable disciplining them or giving them instructions. At the same time, he needs new customers to find his stall and do business with him, so he does not want the market to be cut off entirely from the general public. The market is a place where both strong ties and casual, transactional relationships can be formed – all mediated through the gradation of publicness present in the market's depth structure.

An example of what can emerge as a result of social integration includes the establishment of a community group to protect the market when it comes under threat from developers. The Ward's Corner Community Coalition has been evolving for 15 years – since developer Grainger first proposed demolishing the market. A coalition of architects, academics, traders and local people, the group has successfully challenged Grainger's plans, submitting and receiving approval for their own planning initiative. This collaboration was possible because people from all walks of life, including those with architectural and planning expertise, came in and used the market, growing to enjoy it and forging links with traders. As a result, they cared about the market and were willing to campaign for its survival. This is a great example of a situation that fulfils the London mayor's desire to develop social integration through increased access to participation opportunities. The market is a spatial and social mediator that has enabled integration between disparate groups who would not otherwise have crossed paths, and this integration has led to direct political participation and empowerment. Similar everyday experiences of social integration are detailed by Suzi Hall (2012) in her exploration of a London caff through the juxtaposition of publicness and privateness enabled by the depth structure of the typical high street shop.

Hair salon

Similarly, in the Crazy Cut hair salon near Bruce Grove station, there is a gradation of publicness from the front to the back. In contrast to the market, this gradation occurs within a single business. At the front of the salon, anyone can walk in, the lingua franca is English and the decor is representative of the dominant culture of the high street. The back, however, hosts more private rooms, such as the kitchen, where religious symbols are present and people often chat in Turkish. The decorum of the different parts of the salon's depth structure is indicated by the arrangement of objects. Towards the front, shampoos

Figure 19.3: Contrasting ways in which objects are stored at the front (left) and the back (right) of the salon. © Clossick 2017

and other products are carefully and attractively arranged for sale on neat shelves; towards the back, shelves are a chaotic but homely mess of half-used products and personal items (see Figure 19.3). In the front of the salon, staff are urged by their manager to speak English, while conversations in the back are often had in Turkish.

These are fertile conditions for social integration in the context of super-diversity. The same situation, with zones of conviviality and publicness to the front and zones of culturally specific privacy towards the back, is repeated up and down Tottenham High Road. Gradation of publicness simultaneously provides space for the cultural specificity of groups within the local cultural milieu and space for the super-diverse groups of Tottenham to trade and socialise – facilitating a blend of contact and avoidance that fosters peaceful dynamics and, potentially, social integration.

Quaker meetinghouse

One useful counterexample in Tottenham is the Quaker meeting-house; rather than gradation of publicness, it has a stark public-private boundary. The meetinghouse is situated on the first floor of a small block, accessed through a side alley running between high street shops. Quakers in the Tottenham chapter are, for the most part, White British. Unlike the people in the market and the salon, they did not tell stories of integration with neighbours but rather of cooperation and integration with other groups of Quakers. Certain socio-spatial structures that house cultural diversity can potentially maintain unequal power relations and privilege, especially if they do not contain gradation of publicness.

As they are instrumental in reproducing social life, depth structures can harbour and perpetuate privilege in a number of ways. First, personal characteristics dictate both the places that an individual may enter and the decorum that they must adhere to, as in the example of the salon's kitchen. The more a person is integrated into the culture of a place, the more 'insideness' (Relph 1976) they experience and the deeper they can penetrate its most private zones. When such cultural integration is a consequence of certain personal characteristics, such as White skin, the depth structure serves as a mechanism through which institutionalised discrimination can be reproduced. Second, where zones cannot be seen and information about their decorum cannot be gleaned, an individual must possess either knowledge or blind confidence to enter them. The Quaker meetinghouse is one example of this, as one must brave a knock on the door and a conversation with the gatekeeper to be admitted. As a White, middle-class person, one of us gained entry without question, but this blind confidence is a feature of our 'privilege' (McIntosh 1988). In contrast, those inside the Seven Sisters Market can clearly see all of the zones and assess their required decorum, enabling them to make an informed decision about whether to enter. It is very important to recognise who is welcome in and excluded from places, who may perceive themselves as being excluded, and whether sufficient information is available for people to make an informed decision about whether to enter a place. These aspects are necessary if depth structure theory is to be useful in assessing entrenched power structures and institutionalised privilege, which constitute the opposite of the relationship-building underpinning social integration.

Neighbourhood scale (Stratford)

Leytonstone Road

Leytonstone Road is a high street separating the neighbourhoods of Maryland and Odessa in northern Stratford (see Figure 19.4). It is a place where conditions are ideal for building relationships. The high street can easily be reached by a broad range of local residents and visitors on foot or by car or public transport. Therefore, in terms of gradation of publicness, it can be considered the most public zone of both Maryland and Odessa; this is clear through its status as a dense retail area. Space Syntax theorists call this 'optimum centrality' (van Nes and Yamu 2018). The pairing of ease of access and functional diversity makes Leytonstone Road a place where contact between

Figure 19.4: Map showing the location of the two case-study streets in Stratford: Stratford High Street and Leytonstone Road. © Smink 2022

different social groups can spontaneously evolve on a regular basis. The melting pot of ethnic groups is evident in the range of shops offering specialist ethnic services or products. Behind the retail facades are many other functions that feed off the high street, such as nurseries, garages, primary schools, community centres and places of worship, as shown in Figure 19.5, boosting the vitality of Leytonstone Road.

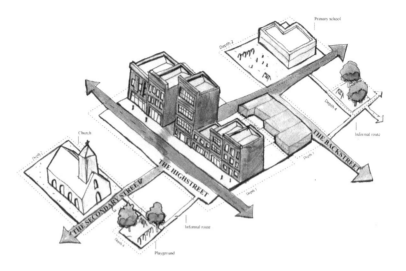

Figure 19.5: Schematic drawing of the physical depth of Leytonstone Road. © Smink 2019

Behind the frontage of Leytonstone Road, non-domestic uses are mostly one block deep, located on less public streets. Such places behind the high street form part of the local network, directly and easily accessible to fewer residents; therefore, they tend to be more culturally specific – the neighbourhood-scale equivalent of the kitchen at the back of the salon. The order of business activities is related to a coherent organisation and a more general gradient in urban form (Hausleitner, this volume). Local places like playgrounds and shared inner courtyards provide convivial engagement between people who share demographic qualities and live in close proximity; this contrasts sharply with the high street, where more disparate social groups come into contact. There is a clear hierarchical neighbourhood structure in which social and economic life takes place: a public high street and more private, residential streets and squares (Hillier et al. 2007), with gradation between (see Figure 19.6).

For an example of the kind of social relationships that form on Leytonstone Road, Janson Wines is a small convenience store located at the corner of the high street's intersection with Janson Road. During our visit, the owner mentioned that he has many regular customers from the surrounding neighbourhoods, mostly with Asian or African backgrounds. He 'loves his customers' and is delighted to chat with them on a regular basis. It is the location of Janson Wines – in the most

Figure 19.6: Schematic drawing of Leytonstone Road showing its diversity of decorum. © Smink 2019

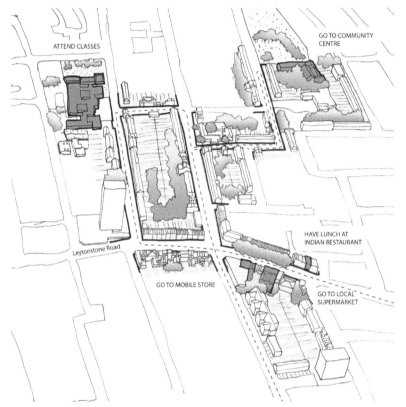

Figure 19.7: Day in the life of a local resident around Leytonstone Road. © Smink 2019

public zone of the two neighbourhoods, on Leytonstone Road between Maryland and Odessa – that enables its function as a place where relationships between very different people can grow.

Two customers of Janson Wines offered examples of engagement with others who share similar demographic qualities on or near secondary streets. An Afghan man with whom we spoke described himself as the kind of person who 'says hello to his neighbours'. He believes that people get on well together in his local area, as many residents live in shared housing and make use of the same local facilities, such as community centres. He works in a community centre located in the hinterland of Barking Road, where he helps local residents with inquiries related to tax forms and legal obligations and assists victims of domestic violence. He regards his colleagues at the community centre as some of his strongest ties, as he sees them on a daily basis (see Figure 19.7 for a mapping of this man's movement around his neighbourhood). Similarly, the shop owner described meeting his family members, who live in the area, at the park. Places such as the community centre and the local park are less readily accessible than, for example, Janson Wines, meaning that they provide opportunities for engagement between people with similar socioeconomic or cultural backgrounds. The neighbourhood structure of the more public high street and its more private hinterland with a gradation of publicness allows for both convivial interaction between diverse groups and more meaningful and deep engagement between those who share demographic or cultural characteristics.

Stratford High Street

In contrast to the gradation of publicness found on Leytonstone Road and Tottenham High Road, Stratford High Street (location shown in Figure 19.4) – like the Quaker meetinghouse – boasts a stark public-private boundary, the consequence being that its capacity to nurture social integration is limited. Stratford as a whole boasts a series of distinct socio-spatial zones with homogenous physical, economic and social qualities, as shown in Figure 19.8. Stratford High Street is designated as 'mixed-use' (LLDC 2020, 228), yet its uses are limited to large-scale businesses and global retail functions making use of the close proximity of Stratford Station, a major transit node that attracts highly skilled workers and affluent visitors. As a result, despite Stratford being super-diverse, the development of monofunctional and monocultural spatial enclaves like Stratford High Street prevents the multicultural landscape from becoming a melting pot that nurtures social integration. One dance teacher that we met on Abbey Lane noticed the lack of cohesiveness in the area, saying that she 'would like to be better connected and know who is the owner of the workshop

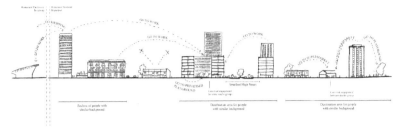

Figure 19.8: Schematic drawing of Stratford High Street showing its diversity of decorum. © Smink 2022

around the corner, or know who runs the cafe across the road, or who is the owner of the bar and restaurant'. Due to its lack of gradation of publicness and the large-scale monofunctional typology of its buildings, Stratford High Street has lost its function as a place for public conviviality at the neighbourhood scale. Hubbard (2017, 227–35) draws similar conclusions about high streets all over the UK.

Conclusion

> super-diversity + urban depth with gradation of publicness
> =
> potential for social integration

Super-diversity is a fundamental feature of London. When a street is super-diverse and wields a rich and complex urban depth with gradation of publicness, it is more likely to facilitate social integration, as this structure fosters convivial interaction between diverse groups – the basis of building relationships. The same applies to the hinterlands around high streets, where gradation of publicness allows for greater familiarity and cultural specificity in some places while offering places for convivial interactions between groups to foster peaceful coexistence in other places.

High streets like Leytonstone Road and Tottenham High Road are places where socioeconomic differences and inequalities are spatially expressed, as they are highly accessible at the city scale and, therefore, constitute a meeting place for all groups. However, social integration between groups relies on the kind of gradation of publicness found in Seven Sisters Market. In contrast, while the area around Stratford

High Street and Stratford Station is also accessible from the rest of the city, its morphology lacks the capacity to support gradation of publicness. Therefore, it does not possess the conditions that foster social integration; in fact, its conditions appear to promote social segregation.

We propose some general rules of thumb for designers and policymakers to maximise opportunities for social integration and, in turn, achieve the London Mayor's 2020 'Vision for Social Integration' (GLA 2020). First, at the building/block scale, when granting permissions for high-street accommodation, planning policy should insist on buildings that have a depth structure with the potential for gradation of publicness. The size and price of high street shops dictate the types of businesses that can occupy them, so policy should ensure that there is space available for marginal and lower-value businesses and services, which are more likely to belong to a wide range of socio-economic groups, offering opportunities for building relationships across social divides. Second, at the neighbourhood scale, it is important to understand where within the gradation of publicness a particular street sits to enable planners to decide, for example, whether residential intensification is the right choice or whether the intensification of economic and civic accommodations would be more appropriate. When engaging in master planning and urban design, streets' gradation of publicness should be considered, and different types of use should be situated in appropriate locations. Finally, as noted, some highly accessible locations tend to become monothematic enclaves of large corporations; such enclaves can encroach on the ordinary fabric of high streets and hinder their capacity to nurture social integration. Therefore, planning policy should seek to retain a wide variety of uses and users on some, though not necessarily all, high streets, though this may require updating change-of-use legislation.

London is rapidly evolving, becoming home to an increasingly diverse range of social groups. However, the city is subject to economic forces that threaten the layered richness of its high streets' urban depth. Therefore, if we are to truly value social integration in superdiverse cities, urban policy must protect rich and complex urban depth on and around high streets.

Bibliography

Carl, Peter. 2011. 'Type, Field, Culture, Praxis', *Architectural Design* 81(1): 38–45.

Carl, Peter. 2012. 'Praxis: Horizons of Involvement'. In *Common Ground: A critical reader*, edited by David Chipperfield, Kieran Long and Shumi Bose, 67–81. Venice: Marsilio Editori.

Clossick, Jane. 2017. 'The Depth Structure of a London High Street: A study in urban order'. PhD thesis, London Metropolitan University.

Clossick, Jane. 2021. 'Uncovering Urban Depth: A market, a salon and a meetinghouse on Tottenham High Road'. London Metropolitan University. Accessed 1 November 2022. https://urbandepth.research.londonmet.ac.uk/uncovering-urban-depth/.

Clossick, Jane. 2021. 'Uncovering Urban Depth: Urban depth and autonomy'. PhD thesis, London Metropolitan University. Accessed 1 November 2022. https://urbandepth.research.londonmet.ac.uk/uncovering-urban-depth/.

Clossick, Jane. 2022. 'A Place for Participation on the Old Kent Road'. In *Generosity and Architecture*, edited by Mhairi McVicar, Stephen Kite and Charles Drozynski. Abingdon: Routledge.

Clossick, J. and M. Brearley. 2021. 'A Good City has Industry: Audit, reveal and promote'. London Metropolitan University. Accessed 1 November 2022. https://issuu.com/arts_londonmet/docs/a_good_city_has_industry.

Clossick, Jane and Ben Colburn. 2021. 'Design Precepts for Autonomy: A case study of Kelvin Hall, Glasgow'. In *Architecture and Collective Life*, edited by Penny Lewis, Lorens Holm and Sandra Costa Santos. Abingdon: Routledge.

Cruz-Saco Oyague, M. 2008. 'Promoting Social Integration: Economic, social and political dimensions with a focus on Latin America'. In 'Promoting Social Integration', organised by UN-DESA.

Dillon, D. and B. Fanning. 2015. 'Tottenham After the Riots', *Critical Social Policy* 35(2): 188–206.

Greater London Authority (GLA). 2020. *Social Integration in London*.

Hall, Suzanne. 2012. *City, Street and Citizen*. Abingdon: Routledge.

Hall, Suzanne. 2015. 'Super-Diverse Street: A "trans-ethnography" across migrant localities', *Ethnic and Racial Studies* 38(1): 22–37.

Hall, Suzanne. 2020. *Why is Rye Lane Important for the Economy?* Sharing Perspectives Foundation. Accessed 1 November 2022. https://sharingperspectivesfoundation.com/video-lecture/why-is-rye-lane-important-for-the-economy-w5/.

Hillier, Bill, Alasdair Turner, Tao Yang and Hoon-Tae Park. 2007. 'Metric and Topo-Geometric Properties of Urban Street Networks'. Proceedings of the 6th International Space Syntax Symposium, Istanbul.

Hubbard, Phil. 2017. *The Battle for the High Street: Retail gentrification, class and disgust*. London: Palgrave Macmillan.

London Legacy Development Corporation (LLDC). 2020. *Local Plan 2020–2036*. Accessed 1 November 2022. https://www.queenelizabetholympicpark.co.uk/planning-authority/planning-policy/local-plan-2020-2036.

McIntosh, Peggy. 1988. 'White Privilege and Male Privilege'. Working paper, Center for Research on Women at Wellesley College.

Ministry of Housing, Communities and Local Government (MHCLG). 2019. 'Indices of deprivation' (Dataset). Accessed 1 November 2022. https://data.london.gov.uk/dataset/indices-of-deprivation.

Presser, Lizzie. 2016. 'What's Behind the Huge Fall in Deprivation in East London? And no, it's not gentrification', *The Guardian*, 12 January. Accessed 1 November 2022. https://www.theguardian.com/society/2016/jan/12/what-behind-deprivation-east-london-newham-unemployment.

Relph, Edward. 1976. *Place and Placelessness*. London: Pion.

Smink, Rebecca. 2020. 'London's Paradox. Global inclusion and local exclusion: the conflicts between social and economic space within contemporary London'. MSc thesis, Delft University of Technology. Accessed 1 November 2022. https://repository.tudelft.nl/islandora/object/uuid%3Ae4d19b75-437f-4638-8c4c-d11b6fe1ba46?collection=education.

van de Wal, H., Machiel van Dorst and T. Leuenberger. 2016. *Privacy Script: De invloed van architectuur op sociale interactie in woongebouwen*. Bussum: Thoth.

van Nes, Akkelies and Claudia Yamu. 2018. 'Space Syntax: A method to measure urban space related to social, economic and cognitive factors'. In *The Virtual and the Real in Planning and Urban Design: Perspectives, practices and applications*, edited by Claudia Yamu, Alenka Poplin, Oswald Devisch and Gert De Roo, 136–50. Abingdon: Routledge.

Vertovec, Steven. 2007. 'Super-Diversity and its Implications', *Ethnic and Racial Studies* 30(6): 1024–54.

Vaughan, Laura and Sonia Arbaci. 2011. 'The Challenges of Understanding Urban Segregation', *Built Environment* 2(37): 128–38.

Vesely, Dalibor. 2006. *Architecture in the Age of Divided Representation*. Cambridge, MA: MIT Press.

Watt, Paul. 2013. '"It's Not For Us": Regeneration, the 2012 Olympics and the gentrification of East London', *City* 17(1): 99–118.

Wessendorf, Susanne. 2014. *Commonplace Diversity*. New York: Springer.

Conclusions

Jane Clossick, Agustina Martire and Birgit Hausleitner

The streets covered in this book are embedded in places that differ in culture, social dynamics, population density, economic structure, geography, landscape and planning system. Here, we aim to provide a sharpened definition of 'everyday streets' and plead for interdisciplinary work in their reinterpretation and future design.

Defining the everyday street

As defined at the outset of this project, everyday streets are 'linear centres of civic activity, where much of everyday life takes place'. Everyday streets are intrinsically local. Their gradual transformations align with political, cultural, technological and social change. They have inherited their form, uses and social landscapes from processes that have stretched over centuries – and they continue to change in the same way. The 'physical fabric' of the everyday street is a built environment that comprises many diverse elements and features walkable streets, pavements wide enough to facilitate interior uses spilling outward, and street furniture that facilitates non-commercial social interactions. 'Uses' typically comprise economic, civic and residential purposes, while 'mixed economies' entail wholesale, retail, service and industrial business alongside the 'foundational' economy. 'Social interactions' are embedded into everyday streets' fabric and uses, defining and defined by the practices, habits and rituals of individuals and groups. Throughout this book, the authors have demonstrated how these intertwined physical and social characteristics of everyday streets manifest differently depending on local conditions of a place, their fabric, culture, and identities. The streets covered in this book share three common qualities: First, *permanence and resilience*: a fine-grain physical fabric that is adaptable, as it can sustain incremental change; Second, *identities and inclusiveness*: distributed ownership, empowering more people in the decision-making process; and third, *conflict and control* stemming from high plurality.

Permanence and resilience

Socio-spatial forces continue to evolve in the modern era, and everyday streets continue to adapt to these forces within their geographical and topographical constraints. Adaptation to change is a fundamental characteristic of everyday streets, making them highly resilient. Different elements of everyday streets change and adapt at different rates. Additionally, these streets have multiple temporalities, which may remain stable over long periods of time or be disrupted by major planning projects. Still, practices can shift rapidly in shorter periods of time; market streets that are bustling one day can be silent the next.

The existence of everyday streets as sites of culture and identity over long periods of time makes them receptacles of heritage and memory. Specific uses and associated practices occurring over centuries inevitably permeate the culture of these streets. Alternatively, uses can change while building types and the urban grain remain stable – heritage is made concrete in the street fabric. This 'everyday heritage' of urban fabric and spatial practices is not that which we usually associate with heritage – it's not a statue, a museum or a prominent building. Rather, it is intangible social heritage: physical and cultural ecosystems that merit safeguarding.

Identities and inclusiveness

Everyday streets are sites of overlapping everyday practices, habits and rituals. These spatial practices may include activities, such as shopping, working, taking children to school, socialising, and travelling from place to place on foot or using a vehicle. However, everyday streets may also host commemorations, protests, parades, demonstrations and funerals – major events, the essence of which becomes merged with the street itself. Everyday streets create and are created by the identities and culture of those who use them.

Everyday streets are places of inclusiveness as well as social, economic and political participation. They accommodate a diverse array of cultures, economic structures, and civic and social practices. Inclusion is promoted by the provision of foundational goods and services, both commercial (e.g. food, services, entertainment) and non-commercial (e.g. education, social spaces, religious sites). The streets covered in this book have presented various configurations of inclusiveness, which is a key component of social and spatial justice. Thus, everyday streets constitute an ideal location for enhancing social, political and economic participation among inhabitants. The typical fine-grain structure of everyday streets leads to inclusion and participation, as these streets are the sites of diverse cultures. Through this cultural overlap, everyday streets facilitate crossover in cultures' associated material and human practices; they provide a place where very different groups can come together.

Conflict and control

Of course, the everyday street is not always a site of joyful inclusiveness and social justice. As they often host multiple overlapping uses, cultures, identities and political ideologies, they can also be the site of serious social and spatial conflict. The distinct identities of those who inhabit streets determine those who 'belong' in the space and, in turn, those who do not. Some groups of people may feel welcome, while others feel excluded. Local identities and histories, particularly those of underprivileged and disenfranchised users, can be undermined by gentrification and touristification. When the urban fabric of a street is destroyed, the identities and place-specific cultures that were embedded in that fabric are destroyed alongside it, leaving behind only stories in the memories of the inhabitants, doomed to fade into obscurity within a few generations.

The competing needs of different groups on everyday streets can lead to the exertion of control, with one group using their power to exclude or police others. Economic power and other forms of privilege determine who wields the most control, be it physical, economic, social or legal. Control may also be highly subtle; certain groups may simply feel unwelcome in a particular place despite no *explicit* actions being taken against them. The potential types of conflict and the ways in which they are expressed are manifold; they are as varied as the range of uses and users found on the everyday street. Overall, however, everyday streets are more often places where conflicts are resolved or worked around. In no examples in this book did issues spiral into warring chaos, which is a tribute to everyday streets' resilience and adaptability.

Understanding the everyday street

Since everyday streets are a fundamental component of urban living, of the provision of foundational goods and of both inclusiveness and participation, it is important to achieve a proper understanding of them. This book has presented a wide range of examples of how to engage with the multifaceted phenomena on everyday streets and these cases have shown that different methods produce different findings. Evidently, learning about everyday streets should be a transdisciplinary endeavour – one that is approached simultaneously from the perspectives of several disciplines, including economics, social science, history, urbanism, architecture, psychology and geography.

The methods that have been successful for our authors were derived from standard practices in social science (interviews, participant observation), ethnographic (casual conversations, mapping observations), architectural (accurate drawings of architecture and public spaces) and data-driven spatial analysis. Our authors also employed more experimental methods from architectural, art and ethnographic practices, such as graphic anthropology, installations, auto-ethnography and non-standard diagrams and sketches. These methods reveal the spatial, social, economic and civic structures that comprise everyday streets. We must understand these structures if we are to design and care for everyday streets without inadvertently destroying their unique qualities.

Participatory and in-situ research processes can aid in changing places for the better, boosting inclusiveness, linking stakeholders and directly influencing streetspace. Co-drawing and participatory workshops are just two examples of engaging and giving value to those outside disciplines pertaining to the built environment of everyday streets. Overall, we can conclude that mixed-methods approaches produce the most holistic readings of everyday streets' attributes. They enable us to detect and value unquantifiable components (culture, identity, everyday practices and heritage) which do not bear an economic value.

Shaping everyday streets

It is important to protect and nurture everyday streets – to design and build them in ways that serve the evolving needs of society and promote further inclusiveness. This requires a commitment to the objective laid out in the introduction: to reclaim streetspace for people and to resist the 'optimisation' of car-led and commercial development, which strips streets of the social and spatial characteristics that make them inclusive. The streets covered in this book are all under the jurisdiction of an authority. None of them is truly informal; they were all, to some extent, planned and controlled.

The following recommendations are divided into five topics: uses on the street; movement and being on the street; urban design of the street and its hinterlands; architecture of the street; and policy.

In terms of uses, everyday streets need a mix of uses that integrates both commercial and non-commercial programmes – and complementarity is essential. It is not necessary or possible for all types of street uses to be mixed evenly everywhere; varying topographical, social and economic forces result in them being clustered in particular localities. However, it is still important to ensure that inhabitants' basic social, economic and civic needs – including those of all social groups, with their associated heritage – are provided for on their local everyday street(s). In other words, these streets must be sufficiently inclusive to enable universal social, economic and political participation.

In terms of both moving through and existing on everyday streets, these streets work best when they are equally accessible to pedestrians, bicycles and public transport rather than dominated by cars. As many of the authors in this book pointed out, walkability is particularly significant; it is important to design street spaces that are convenient to walk through to facilitate a flourishing local economic life and boost environmental sustainability. There must also be adequate space on the street to facilitate the crossover of activities and objects between inside and outside.

In terms of urban design, everyday streets need diversity in spaces, building types and unit sizes as well as variation in hinterland 'depth' to accommodate mixed-use functionality beyond the street edge. In this way, even the areas beyond the street contribute to its vitality. The built fabric of parcels, blocks and buildings that form everyday streets is shaped by the streets' physical geography and topography – by their 'topos' – and by the socio-spatial forces of planning, politics, economics and civic life. Of course, streets also influence these elements in return: differences in form affect distribution of uses and how they are clustered in streets. Not all functions and uses are found evenly distributed; they are instead differentiated between places depending on available building types and the topographical characteristics of the locality.

In terms of the architecture of everyday streets, style is less important than functionality. Everyday streets require buildings that feature adaptable spaces, are usable in multiple ways, and boast solid interplay between the street and ground-floor frontages. At the block and parcel scale, a clear distinction between 'front' and 'back' sides enables the social structuring of uses and decorum, facilitating multiple convivial overlapping uses and cultures. Finally, retaining and adapting existing street fabric when possible – rather than wholesale replacement through destruction – preserves the everyday heritage of socio-spatial practices, boosting the everyday street's resilience. To achieve this kind of retention, changes must be made to development financing that enable developers to work successfully with what already exists in terms of street fabric and uses.

Finally, in terms of public policy, policymakers should develop appropriate legal, administrative and technical frameworks that are tailored to specific local contexts and produce pedestrian-, cycling- and transit-friendly environments that reduce reliance on private motor vehicles. Financial incentives can encourage population-wide behavioural changes, promoting active modes of mobility such as walking and cycling. Similarly, such frameworks and financial incentives can promote physical changes in development that align with the principles outlined here.

Public space design is a key policy area. Urban planners are capable of directly influencing urban residents' quality of life. The evolution of everyday streets is most inclusive when it is driven by multiple stakeholders working together. We must explicitly address the needs of less privileged and minority groups to ensure that they are included in everyday streets and build cities that work better for everyone.

Index

Ingram Content Group UK Ltd.
Milton Keynes UK
UKHW020316080623
423046UK00004B/18